In the footsteps of Anne Boleyn

SARAH MORRIS & NATALIE GRUENINGER

AMBERLEY

This book is dedicated to:
My parents, to whom I will never repay my debt of gratitude. All my love.
– Sarah

My beloved husband and children, Chris, Isabel and Tristan, for their unending love and encouragement and for willingly embracing Anne and Tudor England.
– Natalie

First published 2013

Amberley Publishing
The Hill, Stroud
Gloucestershire, GL5 4EP

www.amberley-books.com

British Library Cataloguing in Publication Data.
A catalogue record for this book is available from the British Library.

ISBN 978 1 4456 0782 5

Typesetting and Origination by Amberley Publishing.
Printed in the UK.

Contents

Acknowledgements

The authors would like to thank the following people most sincerely for their contribution towards making this book possible:

Early Life

Hever Castle: Anna Spender, Castle Co-ordinator; Ashley Collins, Retail Manager; Jan Ryan, guide; Susanne Moller, guide; Heath Pye.
Pashley Manor: Kate Wilson.
Mechelen: Jessica Van Humbeeck and Nathalie Van Humbeeck. Maurits Delbaere, JS.
Château *de* Romorantin: The Tourist Information Office, Romorantin.
Château d'Amboise: Marc Metay, Director of the Château d'Amboise; Aline Colin, guide.
The Field of Cloth of Gold: Ray Irving alias 'Henry Tudor' at the Henry Tudor Company.

The Courting Years

Canterbury: Marten Rogers.
Bisham Abbey: Zoe Dixon, Head of National Centres.
Stone Place and Castle: Dr Mike Still, Curator, Dartford Borough Museum.
Shurland Hall: 'The Gentle Author'; Tim Whittaker of www.spitalfieldslife.com.
Dover Castle: Paul Pattison FSA, Senior Historian, English Heritage; Allan Brodie, Senior Investigator, English Heritage; Gordon Higgott, independent architectural historian.
Sandwich: Dr Helen Clarke, Honorary Senior Lecturer, Institute of Archaeology, University College London.
Woking Palace: The Friends of Woking Palace, particularly Jean Follett and Richard Savage.
Farnham Castle: Orian Hutton, historian and guide; Farnham Castle Operations Ltd.
Waltham Abbey: Clive Simpson and Peter Huggins of the Waltham Abbey Historical Society.
Barnet: Gillian Gear, Local Archivist.
The More: Suzanne Smith, Archivist Northwood Prep School.

Odiham: Sheila Millard, Edward Roberts and Sheila Janaway.
Carew Manor: Nicholas Hall.

Anne the Queen

The route of Anne Boleyn's coronation: Zoe Bramley.
Guildford: Mary Alexander, local historian and retired museum curator; Helen Chapman Davies, local historian and author; David Rose, local historian and writer.

The 1535 Progress

Abingdon Abbey: Judy White.
Ewelme: Carol Sawbridge, Secretary and Local History Archivist, the Ewelme Society.
Langley: Museum of Charlbury.
Thruxton: Charles Milner-Williams, Chris Rome, Ann & John McKenzie.
Sudeley: Jean Bray, Archivist.
Acton Court: Lisa Kopper and Bop Porton.
Little Sodbury Manor: Lord and Lady Killearn.
Bromham: Gerry Cullen
The Vyne: Nicola Pratt, Visitor Experience Manager.
Tewkesbury: The Reverend Canon Paul Williams and Richard Sermon, local archaeologist.
Gloucester: Abbot Francis, Prinknash Abbey; Richard Sermon, local archaeologist; Philip Moss, historian; Tim and Bridget Wiltshire.
Leonard Stanley: Jo and David Pullin.
Berkeley Castle: Eleanor Taylor.
Southampton: Dr Cheryl Butler, Tudor Revels Southampton; Tim Lambert, local historian and author.
Portchester Castle: Sam Price.
Salisbury: The Wiltshire and Swindon History Centre; the Salisbury City Guides.
Clarendon: Professor Tom Beaumont James MBE; Dr Amanda Richardson, University of Chichester.
Basing House: Margaret Scard, author of 'Tudor Survivor'; Alan Turton, retired curator of Basing House; Helen Sinnamon, curator of Basing House.
Bramshill House: Jane George, Site Performance Manager; Lindsey Kerr, Curator; Professor Helen Hills, University of York.
Easthampstead: Stewart Neil, Operations Manager, East Park Conference Centre.

I would like to take this opportunity to say thank you to my family and friends who patiently endured being dragged around a good number of the locations in this book over the last couple of years. While I enthused endlessly about bumps in the ground where noble buildings once stood, recounting tales of intrigue and romance or passion and betrayal, each and every one indulged my love of Anne and all things Tudor with elegant forbearance. Bless you! And also specifically to my parents, whose love of history and old buildings seeped into my bones as a child. Many happy hours spent touring England's country houses and castles forged a steadfast connection to the history of my forefathers, wrapped up in golden memories of a happy childhood – thank you. And finally, to my co-author Natalie Grueninger, who so warmly welcomed me into the Tudor community when I first joined Facebook with my page, *Le Temps Viendra: a Novel of Anne Boleyn*. We could not have known where this would lead, but it has been such fun and an incredible journey of adventure and friendship. Just remember one thing, my friend – keep smiling!

Sarah

First and foremost, I would like to offer a heartfelt thanks to my husband, Chris, who kept our household running smoothly while I spent a great deal of time in the sixteenth century. For my part, this book would not have been possible without his support and encouragement every step of the way. To my beloved children, Isabel and Tristan, for understanding that at times mummy couldn't play because she had to work. Thank you to my dearest mother, Silvia, for instilling in me a love of reading and writing from an early age. To my sister, Karina, I owe a huge debt of gratitude, for reading and offering insightful feedback on every word that I penned and for the weekly get-togethers and laughs! Thank you to my brother-in-law Anibal for keeping my husband entertained while my sister and I spent many an evening talking Tudor. I am also grateful to the many wonderful authors and historians that I have corresponded with over the last two years who have graciously answered my questions and offered valuable advice, too many people to name here, but I hope that you know who you are. A special thanks to my friend Mike Glaeser for the countless discussions and friendly debates, and for the many articles, photographs and resources he has sent my way. Thank you, too, to the visitors to my website (www. onthetudortrail.com) and my online Tudor community on Facebook and Twitter, for their contributions, support and enthusiasm. And last but not least, thank you to Sarah Morris, my co-author, for welcoming me into her home during our research trip, and for her friendship and dedication to this project, which has made what could have been a difficult journey, a most rewarding experience.

Natalie

The authors would also like to extend a sincere thanks to Wendy J. Dunn, Valerie Brook, Claire Ridgway and Mike Glaeser for reading and offering constructive feedback on sections of the manuscript. We are also grateful to Rebecca Gilmore; Richard Gillingwater, Chris Boey and Paul Giltrap at Accrue Communications Ltd; Debbie Berne; Chris Rew; Jo Bainbridge; Gemma Higgins at Iris Creations Photography and Kate Holeman at KHS Creative, for their contributions. And many, many thanks to the staff at Amberley Publishing: our publishers Jonathan Reeve and Nicola Gale, our publicist, Nicola Giles, Emily Brewer, editor, and publicity assistant, Alice Crick.

Introduction

On 19 May 1536, a French sword stilled the beating heart of an English queen. Her name was Anne Boleyn and she would become one of the most controversial and iconic queens in English history. In her lifetime, Anne was a force of nature; she captivated the heart and soul of a king, divided a court and ignited the Reformation on English soil, beginning a process that would transform the religious and social landscape of the country.

While after her death her enemies continued to defile her name 'full sore', her legacy lived on in her daughter, perhaps the greatest monarch that England has ever known – Elizabeth I. But more than that, in her own right Anne Boleyn was an intelligent, powerful and influential woman, who refused to be intimidated by those who sought her destruction. Her sense of destiny and purpose for religious reform carried her all the way to the scaffold with characteristic temerity, courage and grace.

Almost 500 years later, Anne's memory burns as brightly as ever. In recent times, the tireless work of historians like the late Professor Eric Ives has done much to rehabilitate the slandered reputation of Anne as the archetypal harlot, whore and home-wrecker. She is now largely recognised as being the victim of court faction, of a deadly power struggle with a man that the Boleyns had once so ardently supported – Thomas Cromwell – and of a powder keg of unfortunate circumstances that made her vulnerable to the machinations of her enemies during the first few months of 1536.

In recent years, both authors have dedicated many hours to researching and writing about Anne's life and her innocence. Dr Sarah Morris first came to Anne's story as an eleven-year-old schoolgirl. Her passion for all things Tudor remained largely as a private hobby until she set pen to paper in 2010 and began writing *Le Temps Viendra: a Novel of Anne Boleyn*; the first of two volumes was published in the autumn of 2012. The story is a fictional biography of Anne Boleyn, as seen through the eyes of a modern-day woman who finds herself drawn back in time and into the body of her historical heroine. For Australian-born Natalie Grueninger, it was a visit to the Tower of London on a wintery day in 2000 that ignited her curiosity about Anne and the world in which she lived, and set her on a path of learning that would eventually lead to the creation, in 2009, of *On the Tudor Trail*, a website dedicated to documenting historic sites associated with Anne Boleyn and sharing information about life in Tudor England. Although Natalie's interest in the Tudors was awakened in her early twenties, as a child she was fascinated with the past and the concept of time. Having been drawn together by our love of Anne Boleyn, we soon realised that we shared an insatiable curiosity for the buildings and locations associated with her, both of us intrigued by the fact that when we stand in a building or space where someone from the past once stood, it is only time, and not space, which separates us.

During the course of both of these projects, each of us amassed a veritable wealth of information about the great houses, palaces and castles that served as the stage to one of the most dramatic lives and love stories of English history. Little by little, we became beguiled by these locations, growing to appreciate that while Anne and her contemporaries had long since turned to dust, the places which she visited remained behind as stalwart witnesses linking us physically to her extraordinary past.

We found that visiting the locations brought depth, colour and texture to a life so often only accessible through words graven upon a page, the very presence of the buildings, even in ruins, often holding the energy of the ghostly footsteps that had gone before us. In some instances, such as when one stands in the Great Hall at Hampton Court Palace, Anne, Henry and the glittering, dangerous world in which they lived was so tangible that we could easily imagine catching sight of the train of a gown disappearing around a corner. In other places, where Anne's presence was more fleeting, any sense of her remained disappointingly elusive.

However, despite these differences, we soon came to realise that whether we were talking only about earthworks of a long-lost palace or an intact building that had endured the test of time, each location presented to us more than just bricks and mortar. Rather, such structures became interwoven into the very fabric of a life long-lost, revealing more about the story, influences and character of the woman who often remains so elusive.

Our aim in writing this book was primarily to provide a practical guide to places and artefacts associated with Anne Boleyn. However, over and above this, we wanted *In the Footsteps of Anne Boleyn* to be a resource, for the first time, bringing together an extensive record of these locations in one place. Finally, taking a long-term view, we wished to capture an historical snapshot in time, a record of the state of these properties and locations as we stand here at the beginning of the twenty-first century, exactly 500 years on from when Anne first left Hever Castle and set out on her incredible odyssey.

During the research process, we uncovered over twenty locations not previously known to us, despite our extensive involvement with Anne's story over the years. In many instances, pockets of local knowledge had been preserved, but the link with Anne was largely lost to a wider, global audience. In other cases, the connection of a place or property to Anne Boleyn was unknown even to the guardians or owners of the building. Re-establishing the link proved particularly satisfying, putting in place another piece of the jigsaw so that its rightful heritage could be preserved for future generations to enjoy. We hope that, whether you are learning about Anne for the first time, or are familiar with her story; whether you read about these locations from the comfort of your armchair, or choose to slip this guide book into your backpack and literally follow in the footsteps of Anne Boleyn, there will be something new here for you to discover.

In writing this book, there are several working assumptions about Anne's life that we have adopted in order to set a context for each location, or to trace her movements as part of the itinerant court. We have chosen to incorporate those facts that are held true by the majority of modern-day historians. However, as controversy often follows in Anne's wake, we appreciate that there may well be those who hold an alternative view. The following section outlines the main assumptions contained in this book.

Anne's Birth Date and the Early Years

We have taken Anne Boleyn's birth date as 1501, making Anne the second-oldest living Boleyn offspring. It is not the place or scope of this book to present an argument for and against the two most commonly cited dates for the year of Anne's birth (1501 versus 1507). Other historical sources have discussed this extensively. However, we concur with the majority that 1501 is probably the most likely date of Anne's birth, and have adopted it throughout this guidebook as a point of reference.

This means that Anne was a young girl of around twelve when she first left English shores to join the court of Margaret of Austria in the Low Countries. Because of Anne's tender age and lowly status at court, precious little is known about her movements during the seven years that she spent in modern-day Belgium and France. However, knowing that the young Anne Boleyn was a maid of honour in both courts, we are assuming (as most historians do) that Anne's movements were closely aligned with those of whichever queen she was serving at the time. This is reflected in the 'The Early Years' entries.

The Courting Years

From a letter penned by the hand of Henry himself, we know that in the summer of 1528 the English king had been 'struck by the dart of love' for over a year. Professor Eric Ives believes that the chronology of events makes it likely that Henry first declared any serious intent toward Anne around Easter 1527, when he began his pursuit of a divorce from his wife, Katharine of Aragon.

From this time until Katharine of Aragon was banished from court in June/July 1531, Anne's whereabouts have not always been explicitly recorded. We can be safely assured of Anne's presence at almost all of Henry's principal residences in London and along the Thames Valley at one point or another between the years 1528 and 1536. But what of the many other locations visited by the king and court during the annual summer progress? From our research, we can summarise the following:

1528 – Anne and Henry were separated from June through to late November/early December, and so she did not accompany the king on progress during the summer months of that year. Anne had taken refuge at Hever following an outbreak of the sweating sickness in June. She fell ill there, probably in July, but later recovered. However, with the arrival of Cardinal Campeggio in the autumn and with the Blackfriars trial imminent, it seems that for the sake of propriety, the couple remained apart for another four months, a period chronicled by a series of passionate letters from a love-sick king, which are now housed in the Vatican library.

1529 – Following the collapse of the Legatine Court on 16 July, a furious Henry and Anne left London on progress. We know that Anne was with the king, for it was at Grafton Regis in Northamptonshire that, just two months later, the famous final meeting occurred between Henry and the king's first minister, Cardinal Wolsey (see Grafton Regis). Wolsey's chronicler, George Cavendish, definitively places Anne at Henry's side, trying to influence the king to act against his first minister.

1530 – By 1530, Anne and Henry were inseparable. In May of that year, Chapuys commented that

> the King shews greater favour to the Lady every day; very recently coming from Windsor, he made her ride behind him on a pillion, a most unusual proceeding, and one that has greatly called forth people's attention here, so much so that two men have been, as I am informed, taken up and sent to prison merely for having mentioned the fact [and commented upon it].

Then, towards the end of August, we hear from the Imperial Ambassador again: 'For nearly one month the King has transacted no business at all, with the exception perhaps of that for which the above-mentioned assembly was convoked; he has given himself up entirely to hunting privately and moving from one place to another'. There is nothing to suggest that Anne was anywhere but at Henry's side. Her influence was growing daily, and we can very safely assume Anne was with Henry throughout July and August 1530, and for the rest of the hunting season.

1531 – In 1531, Katharine was left behind at Windsor, while Anne and Henry headed off on progress together for the summer. In the same year, Chapuys commented that Anne

> always accompanies the King at his hunting parties, without any female attendants of her own, while the Queen herself who used formerly to follow him on such expeditions has been ordered to remain at Vinsor [Windsor]; which circumstance, as may be imagined, is exceedingly aggravating to the Queen, not only on account of the King's studied separation, but because she fancies that his object in taking the Lady with him to such hunting parties is that he may accustom the lords and governors of the counties and districts he traverses on such occasions to see her with him, and that he may the better win them over to his party when Parliament meets again.

With Katharine banished from court, Anne now reigned supreme as the most powerful woman in the country in all but name.

1532 – By 1532 it was clear that marriage was imminent. Henry was spending more money on Anne than ever before and Chapuys reported on 29 July that the king had spoken publicly of marrying Anne: 'He [the king] was resolved to celebrate this marriage in the most solemn manner possible, and the necessary preparations must be made.' Preparations were certainly underway at the Tower of London where between June and September workers were employed to renovate the royal lodgings and other buildings in anticipation of Anne's Coronation. As Henry's official consort in waiting, we can be certain that Anne accompanied

Henry throughout the summer. Gilles de la Pommeraie, the French ambassador, was invited to join the royal progress and his correspondence attests to Anne's presence. 'Sometimes,' the ambassador informed the French minister Montmorency, 'he [the king] puts my Lady Anne and me, each with our crossbow, to wait for deer to cross our path.' He went on to report that, at other times, he and Anne are left on their own 'to watch the deer run'. Anne even presented him with a hunting frock and hat, horn and greyhound. At the conclusion of the progress, Anne was created Marquess of Pembroke, and in October 1532 she accompanied Henry to Calais as his intended wife.

And so, in summary, we have assumed that during the entire progresses of 1529–32, Anne was close to Henry's side and accompanied him to the locations included in this guidebook.

1533 – During the summer of 1533, Anne Boleyn was pregnant with the future Elizabeth I. Due to the queen's advanced state of pregnancy there was no usual summer progress. The king did however leave her behind at Windsor Castle in August, when news arrived from France that England was being sidelined during a summit meeting between King Francis I of France and the Pope. Norfolk, who had been sent to the South of France to represent the king, had dispatched George Boleyn back to England with the news and to take instructions from the king on how to proceed. In order to protect Anne from any unnecessary distress that might harm her unborn child, it appears that she was not told of the snub. Instead Henry set out to rendezvous with Lord Rochford at Sutton Place near Guildford. After a mini progress in the Thames Valley that followed, Henry returned to Windsor, shortly before travelling by barge with Anne back to Greenwich, where she was to take to her chambers.

1534 – The summer of 1534 turned out to be even more disastrous for the royal couple. Evidence suggests that Anne was at Hampton Court Palace when she endured a stillbirth of her second child at around seven–eight months' gestation. It seems that Henry left her abruptly, travelling to The More in Hertfordshire and subsequently cancelling the forthcoming trip to Calais. Although Anne's advanced state of pregnancy was given as the reason for the postponement, we find Retha Warnicke's theory on the 1534 stillbirth compelling, given the known facts. We agree that this was in fact most likely an excuse; a face-saving exercise. It seemed Henry was reluctant to admit to his royal brother (who already had three healthy sons) that God had again denied him a male child and heir.

Anne and Henry were to be apart for about one month, reuniting it seems at Guildford in Surrey at the end of July or the beginning of August. There is nothing to suggest that she did anything other than accompany the king on the rest of the summer progress from this point.

1535 – We have chosen to dedicate an entire section to the summer progress of 1535. It was the only complete progress that Anne would undertake as queen – as it turned out, it would also be her last. It has been heralded as the longest and most politically significant of Henry VIII's reign; Cromwell is often found overseeing the visitations made upon lesser monastic houses, marking the beginning of what would eventually become known as the Dissolution of the Monasteries. In addition, the royal progress through the West Country honoured men who had shown themselves as loyal to Anne and the reformist cause, culminating in the consecration of three reformist bishops in Winchester on 19 September.

The Research Process

The absence of formal references and footnotes does not mean that the book was not rigorously researched. In fact over the last two years we have, wherever possible, worked with the owners, caretakers and/or archivists at each of the locations; we have spoken with historians, local experts and archaeologists at the various historical societies, record offices, museums and universities; drawn on the latest available research and conducted our own research at the National Archives in London. We have read extensively about Anne Boleyn and sixteenth-century England, immersed ourselves in primary sources and, between us, travelled to almost all of the English locations and many of the European sites.

Our quest to follow in Anne's footsteps has not been without its challenges. On many occasions we were confronted with myths about Anne, which had become deeply ingrained over the centuries (and propagated in many popular histories, and even on television...), conflicting sources and, at times, complete silence. There have also been moments of sheer elation, moments like when we rediscovered a contemporary document about Anne and Henry's visit to Gloucester in 1535, which provided precious details about what the royal couple did during their stay, including kneeling in prayer, side by side, at the high altar in Gloucester Cathedral; who they visited; and the gifts they were given.

Gloucester is only one of more than seventy locations featured in this book, all of which were included because Anne Boleyn visited them between 1501 and 1536. Not every location that claimed an association with Anne made it into the book. An important part of the research process involved separating the authentic claims from the spurious ones; only those places where Anne's visit could be verified by a contemporary source, or where her presence could be safely taken for granted, have been included.

At the time of publication there were also a handful of additional sites that we'd recently unearthed that required further research in order to try and verify Anne's presence and pinpoint where the house originally stood. They are not, therefore, included in this edition. And indeed, given our experience to date, we believe that there may well be more locations waiting to be uncovered in the future.

How to Use This Guidebook

The locations have been separated into four categories: Early Life, The Courting Years, Anne the Queen and The 1535 Progress. Each location has a separate entry that has been arranged according to the chronology of Anne's life. This helps us follow in her physical footsteps as her story unfolds, from the cradle at Blickling Hall to her grave in the chapel of St Peter ad Vincula in the Tower. Of course there are some overlaps, such as Anne's presence at the Tower before her Coronation in 1533 and execution in 1536. Nevertheless, where possible we have tried to adhere to a physical timeline.

We have also chosen to include locations like Bridewell Palace and Durham House, where there are no visible remains extant, as well as houses that are today privately owned and not accessible to the public, like Little Sodbury Manor or Prinknash Abbey. It is our firm belief that all these locations, whether they retain much of their original fabric or have disappeared into the ground, deserve to be acknowledged and recorded for posterity. In some instances, as is the case with the 1535 progress, the locations are like the pieces of a puzzle; they connect to one another, joining up to reveal a picture of Anne's life in what was her final summer on earth. Omit one of the pieces and the image becomes fragmented and more difficult to read.

Each of the entries will provide you with information about Anne's connection to the property, including when she visited and what significant events took place there. As each entry is intended to be able to stand alone, as well as to be read as part of a continuum in time, in certain instances a fact that provides context to the visit may be repeated across several different entries.

The text is accompanied by around 130 images ranging from modern-day photographs to sixteenth-century plans and maps. Any artefacts associated with Anne that are not housed at one of the locations featured in the book are listed separately in the final section of the book, Boleyn Treasures.

For those of you less familiar with English geography, maps have been included as a visual aid to help you organise your trip, making it easier to see which locations lie within easy reach of each other. For more precise identification of each location, a postcode has been included in the visitor information section of each entry. Where they exist, website addresses, contact telephone numbers and email addresses are also provided in order that that you can uncover more information for yourself about any particular site before you visit.

Our intention is to help you retrace Anne's steps and see the sites as she would have. Your attention will be drawn to those features that were *in situ* when Anne visited, as well as to any significant Tudor artefacts housed at each of the sites. The book is not intended to be an in-depth history of each of the locations, nor a comprehensive account of every Tudor event or story associated with each of the sites. But our hope is that it will allow you to see these places with Anne's story at the forefront of your mind, and guide you on your own personal and compelling journey in the footsteps of Anne Boleyn.

We are immensely excited and proud to be cataloguing the life of such a remarkable woman, exactly 500 years from when a young Anne Boleyn first left Hever Castle for the Continent. So, let's turn around, leaving the present behind, and begin our journey into the past.

Happy time travelling!

Natalie Grueninger and Sarah Morris

2013

The Boleyn Family Tree

Courtesy of Elizabeth Griffiths and adapted by N. Grueninger & S. Morris

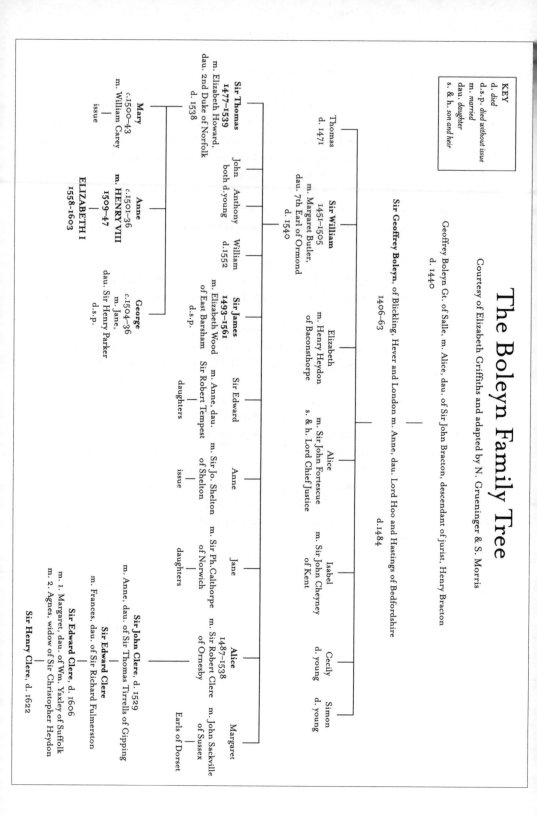

Locations
Map A

Gloucestershire
1. Acton Court *(Iron Acton)*
2. Berkeley Castle *(Berkeley)*
3. Gloucester Abbey
   (Gloucester and its Environs)
4. Little Sodbury Manor
   (Little Sodbury)
5. Sudeley Castle *(Winchcombe)*
6. Tewkesbury Abbey *(Tewkesbury)*
7. Thornbury Castle *(Thornbury)*

Berkshire
8. Byssham Abbey *(Bisham)*
9. Easthampstead Manor
   (Easthampstead)
10. Reading Abbey *(Reading)*
11. Windsor Castle *(Windsor)*

Oxfordshire
12. Abingdon Abbey *(Abingdon)*
13. Ewelme Manor *(Ewelme)*
14. The Old Palace of Langley
    (Langley)
15. The Old Palace of Woodstock
    (Woodstock)

Wiltshire
16. Bromham House *(Bromham)*
17. Church House *(Salisbury)*
18. The Old Palace of Clarendon
    Clarendon Park (nr. Salisbury)
19. Wolfhall *(near Malborough)*

Hampshire
20. Basing House *(Old Basing)*
21. Bishop's Waltham
    (Bishop's Waltham)
22. Bramshill House *(Bramshill)*
23. Hurstbourne Priors
    (Hurstbourne Priors)
24. Odiham *(Odiham)*
25. Portchester Castle *(Portchester)*
26. Southampton *(Southampton)*
27. The Vyne *(Sherbourne St John)*
28. Thruxton *(Andover)*
29. Winchester *(Winchester)*

2. Map of locations by county: Gloucestershire, Berkshire, Oxfordshire, Wiltshire and Hampshire.

Locations
Map B

Kettering

NORTHAMPTONSHIRE

Northampton

Bedford

10

1

BEDFORDSHIRE

Milton Keynes

BUCKS

Stevenage

Luton

HERTFORDSHIRE

5   **4**   Harlow

Aylesbury

3 St. Albans **6**

2

Watford

7

High Wycombe

MIDDLESEX

Twickenham

9

8

14

Woking

15 Epsom

12

11

13 **SURREY**

Guildford   Reigate

Bedfordshire
1. Ampthill (*Ampthill*)

Buckinghamshire (Bucks)
2. Notley Abbey (*Thame*)

Hertfordshire
3. College of Ashridge
   (*Berkhampstead*)
4. Hertford Castle (*Hertford*)
5. Royal Palace of Hatfield
   (Hatfield House) (*Old Hatfield*)
6. Tittenhanger House
   (*Tittenhanger / St Albans*)
7. The More (*Rickmansworth*)

Middlesex
8. Hampton Court Palace
   (*East Moseley*)
9. Hanworth (*Hanworth*)

Nothamptonshire
10. Grafton Regis Manor
    (*Grafton Regis*)

Surrey
11. Beddington Place
    (Carew Manor) (*Wallington*)
12. Farnham Castle (*Farnham*)
13. Guildford Manor and Friary
    (Guildford)
14. Richmond Palace (*Richmond*)
15. Woking Palace (*Old Woking*)

3. Map of locations by county: Northamptonshire, Bedfordshire, Buckinghamshire, Hertfordshire, Middlesex, and Surrey.

Locations
Map C

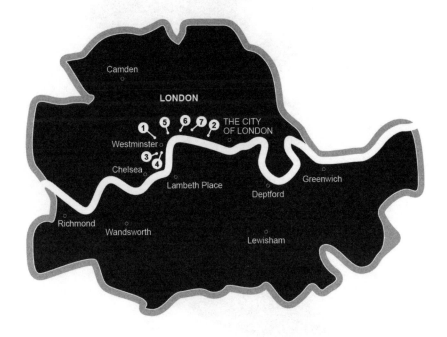

London

1. St James' Palace
   (*Pall Mall / St James's Park*)
2. Tower of London
   (*London Bridge*)
3. Westminster Abbey
   (*Westminster*)
4. Westminster Hall
   (*Westminster*)
5. York Place/Whitehall Palace
   (*Whitehall*)
6. Durham House (*The Strand*)
7. Bridewell Palace (*Fleet Street*)

4. Map of locations in London.

Locations
Map D

NORFOLK

Norwich ⑯

King's Lynn

Thetford ○

SUFFOLK

ESSEX

Colchester ○

Harlow
④　②
① ⑤ ③
Southend-on-Sea

Isle of Sheppey
⑧ ⑦ ⑬ ⑭
⑩ ⑫ ⑨ Canterbury ⑪
Maidstone ⑮
KENT Folkestone

⑥
EAST SUSSEX
Hastings ○
Brighton ○

Essex
1. Barnet *(Barnet)*
2. Palace of Beaulieu (New Hall) *(Chelmsford)*
3. Rochford Hall *(Rochford)*
4. Waltham Abbey *(Waltham Abbey)*
5. Havering Palace *(Havering-atte-Bower)*

East Sussex
6. Pashley Manor *(Ticehurst)*

Kent
7. Eltham Palace *(Eltham)*
8. Greenwich Palace *(Greenwich Park)*
9. Canterbury *(Canterbury)*
10. Hever Castle and St Peter's Church *(Hever)*
11. Whitefriars *(Sandwich)*
12. The Red Lion *(Sittingbourne)*
13. Stone Place *(Stone)*
14 Shurland Hall *(Eastchurch, Isle of Sheppey)*
15. Dover and Dover Castle *(Dover)*

Norfolk
16. Blickling Hall and Church *(Blickling)*

5. Map of locations by county: Norfolk, Suffolk, Essex, Kent and East Sussex.

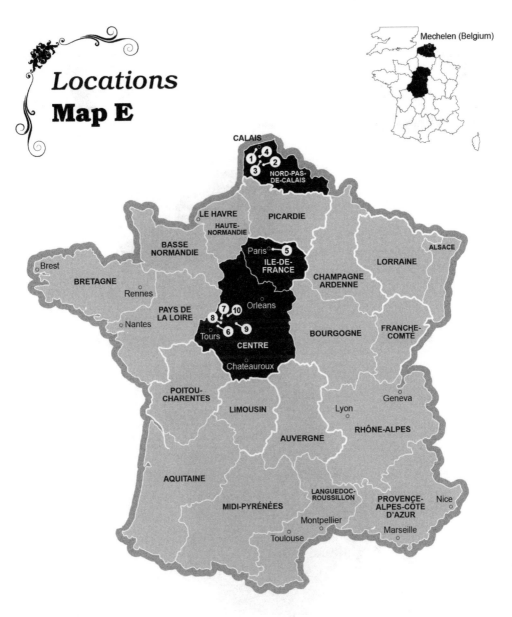

Locations
Map E

Mechelen (Belgium)

CALAIS

① ④
③ ② NORD-PAS-DE-CALAIS

LE HAVRE   PICARDIE
HAUTE-NORMANDIE

BASSE NORMANDIE   Paris ⑤
ILE-DE-FRANCE   ALSACE

Brest   LORRAINE

BRETAGNE   CHAMPAGNE ARDENNE
Rennes

PAYS DE LA LOIRE   ⑦ ⑩ Orleans
Nantes   ⑧   BOURGOGNE   FRANCHE-COMTÉ
⑥ ⑨
Tours   CENTRE

Chateauroux

POITOU-CHARENTES   Geneva

LIMOUSIN   Lyon

RHÔNE-ALPES

AUVERGNE

AQUITAINE

LANGUEDOC-ROUSSILLON   PROVENCE-ALPES-CÔTE D'AZUR   Nice

MIDI-PYRÉNÉES   Montpellier
Marseille
Toulouse

France
1. Calais *(Calais)*
2. Ardres *(Pas de Calais)*
3. Balinghem *(Pas de Calais)*
4. Guînes *(Pas de Calais)*
5. Paris *(Paris)*
6. Château d'Amboise *(Amboise)*
7. Château de Blois *(Blois)*
8. Château de Chaumont *(Chaumont-sur-Loire)*
9. Château de Romorantin *(Romorantin–Lanthenay)*
10. Château de Chambord *(Chambord)*

6. Map of locations in France and the Low Countries.

Locations
Map F

Mechelen (Belgium)

France

1. Calais *(Calais)*
2. Ardres *(Pas de Calais)*
3. Balinghem *(Pas de Calais)*
4. Guînes *(Pas de Calais)*
5. Paris *(Paris)*
6. Château d'Amboise *(Amboise)*
7. Château de Blois *(Blois)*
8. Château de Chaumont
   (Chaumont-sur-Loire)
9. Château de Romorantin
   (Romorantin–Lanthenay)
10. Château de Chambord
    (Chambord)

7. Map of locations in France (detail).

Part 1
Early Life

Blickling Hall, Norfolk

> Oh were I still a child in stature small,
> To tread the rose line paths of Blickling Hall.

Set at the end of a long drive, lined with perfectly manicured lawns and framed by 400-year-old yew hedges, Blickling Hall in Norfolk is a quintessential stately home. This grand building was constructed in the early seventeenth century on the footprint of a house that was home to the Boleyns for over a century and traditionally said to be where, in around 1501, Lady Elizabeth Boleyn gave birth to a daughter – Anne.

Here, Thomas Boleyn lived with his young family until his father's death in 1505, only then moving to Hever Castle in Kent. So Anne and Mary Boleyn spent part of their early years in a manor house built by their great-grandfather, Geoffrey, who purchased the estate from his neighbour, Sir John Fastolfe, in around 1450. According to John Leland's *Itinerary*, Geoffrey built himself a substantial brick house on the site of a rectangular, moated medieval house, erected in the 1390s by Sir Nicholas Dagworth.

Uncovering Tudor Blickling

Very little is known about Geoffrey Boleyn's brick house, where Anne spoke her first words, as it was rebuilt by Sir Henry Hobart in the 1620s and again remodelled in the 1760s. Sadly no contemporary drawing of the fifteenth-century house exists. However, an early eighteenth-century drawing of Blickling Hall's northern elevation by Edmund Prideaux shows a gable end with a Tudor window, probably a remnant of the original Boleyn home. Sir Henry Hobart's Jacobean mansion also incorporated parts of the original service wing on the western side of the house that included numerous chambers, a kitchen and a porter's lodge that survived until the 1760s. The only other clue to its appearance lies in the fact that Leland described it as a 'fair house of brike'; as Elizabeth Griffiths points out in her article about the Boleyns at Blickling, Leland often used the term 'fair' to describe decorated manor houses in the style of the surviving brick manor at East Barsham in Norfolk, and not heavily fortified castles of an earlier age. This implies that the Boleyn home was not a defensive fortress, but rather a comfortable family home, a place to raise a growing family.

After the annihilation of the noble Boleyn family, Sir James Boleyn, Thomas's younger brother and heir, inherited the family estates and tended to them until his death in 1561. As he died with no male heir, his estate was then divided between his sister's descendants, the Cleres, and Elizabeth I, eventually passing into the hands of Sir Henry Hobart.

Tudor Treasures at Blickling Hall

While the manor we see today dates mainly to the seventeenth century, its connection to this illustrious family permeates the russet Jacobean bricks and captures the imagination. Hobart acknowledged the importance of Blickling's Boleyn connection by adopting the heraldic symbol of the Boleyn family – the bull – and incorporating it into his own family crest. Bulls grace the entrance to Blickling Hall today and can be seen again on the main archway.

When visiting the house, be sure to look out for the two eighteenth-century, full-sized wooden reliefs of Elizabeth I and Anne Boleyn, housed in the Great Hall. These were inspired by figures of the Nine Worthies that once stood in the Jacobean hall. The figure of Anne is inscribed *Hic Nata* (born here), a reminder of the home's close association with this important Norfolk family.

Although Henry VIII attempted to obliterate Anne's memory, the people of Norfolk were not so quick to forget. In 1909, 1925 and 1938, Blickling Hall played host to a masque, written by Walter Nugent Monck, celebrating the life of Anne Boleyn and attended by the dowager Queen Mary, who was a patron of the pageant at Blickling – keeping the Boleyn legacy alive and strong. Photographs of the pageant are on display in the Document Room.

Blickling Hall contains a fine collection of paintings and portraits, including a handful immediately recognisable to the Tudor enthusiast. In the Great Hall, keep an eye out for a sixteenth-century portrait of Henry VIII after Holbein; the Lower Ante-Room houses two interesting nineteenth-century prints, one of an unknown lady called Mary Queen of Scots and the other of Mary Tudor after Hans Eworth. In the Dining Room you will find a sixteenth-century portrait of Elizabeth I, derived from the 'Ditchley' portrait of around 1591 and in the Long Gallery are four small imaginary portraits on copper, inscribed Edward VI, Mary Tudor, Richard III and Elizabeth I. An eighteenth-century engraving of Anne Boleyn adorns the south wall of the Document Room.

Visiting St Andrew's Church

A visit to Blickling Hall is incomplete without exploring St Andrew's Church, which sits to the south-east of the house. Here you will find an impressive collection of brasses, many to members of the Boleyn family, including: Cecilie Boleyn, Geoffrey Boleyn's sister who died in 1458; Isabella Boleyn, Geoffrey's daughter who died in 1485; and Anne Boleyn, a daughter of William Boleyn and aunt of Queen Anne Boleyn, who died aged three in 1479.

A small plate in the chancel, easy to overlook, marks the final resting place of Antony Boleyn, a son of William – and uncle to Queen Anne Boleyn – who died in 1483. Yet most moving, perhaps, is the brass of Anne Wood, wife of Thomas Asteley, who carries her two babies in her arms. Anne Wood's sister was Elizabeth, Lady Boleyn, who married Sir

James Boleyn. The story goes that in 1512 Anne Wood was visiting her sister, Elizabeth, at Blickling, when she went into labour. The babies pictured in her arms indicate that she died in or soon after childbirth; what is unclear is whether or not the twins survived.

As we know so little about the Boleyn house that once stood at Blickling, it's impossible to say whether it would have had its own private chapel. If it did not, then it's likely that the Boleyns would have worshipped at St Andrew's, as it was built in the fifteenth century, although substantially remodelled in the nineteenth century.

Perhaps the fifteenth-century baptismal font was used to baptise a newborn Anne …

In 1559, Mathew Parker, a former private chaplain of Anne's, became Archbishop of Canterbury. In his letters he was very specific that Anne came, as he did, from Norfolk. He referred to himself as her 'poor countryman', following a sixteenth-century usage where 'country', applied within England, referred to a county or district.

And so, even though time has robbed us of the house Anne called home and of all physical remnants of its Boleyn past, to visit Blickling Hall is to return to where it all began, to where Anne Boleyn took her first steps toward her place in history.

Visitor Information

Blickling Hall is managed by the National Trust. For more information on how to reach Blickling Hall and its opening hours, which are seasonal, visit the National Trust website at http://www.nationaltrust.org.uk/blickling-estate or telephone + 44 (0) 1263 73 8030.

Postcode for Blickling Hall: NR11 6NF.

Hever Castle, Kent

Remember me when you do pray, that hope doth spring from day to day.

Anne Boleyn

For anyone who loves Anne Boleyn, Hever Castle in the heart of 'England's Garden' of Kent is a natural place of pilgrimage. As the name suggests, it is located in the village of Hever and began as a country house, built in the thirteenth century. From 1462 to 1539 it was the seat of the Boleyn family.

Sir Thomas Boleyn inherited the property upon the death of his father in 1505 and subsequently set about making the rather outdated, moated medieval castle into a fine and contemporary English manor house, fit for an aspiring courtier. This he did by carrying out a number of redevelopments to the building, including the addition of the fabulous staircase gallery, which remains intact to this day.

Anne spent a good deal of her childhood at Hever, before being sent to the Low Countries in 1513 to receive an education at the court of the Archduchess Margaret of Austria. Later, during the early days of Anne's romance with Henry VIII, she would again spend periods of time at the castle, including a long sojourn there over the winter of 1527/8 when Katharine still held precedence at court over the Christmas celebrations. During this time, in February 1528, Anne received Dr Edward Foxe and Dr Stephen Gardiner on their way to visit the Pope in exile, their embassy being to obtain a decretal commission from the Holy Father allowing the divorce case to be heard in England. Then again, she returned in June of the same year. During that fateful summer, the Sweat returned to England, forcing Henry to flee to Waltham Abbey while Anne sought refuge at Hever. She was probably there with her mother and father, as both Thomas and Anne subsequently fell ill at Hever in late June/July. Fortunately, both made a full recovery and Anne returned to court sometime around early December 1528.

This quintessential fortified medieval manor house, nestled in the bottom of an idyllic, gently sloping valley, is utterly beguiling and catches your heart in an instant. The setting makes the picture-perfect English postcard: sculpted lawns with pretty, lily-covered moats; all around you, immaculately tended flower and herb gardens abound. However, do not be fooled by modern-day appearances. If you want to get a feel for how the castle looked in Anne's day, you have to think rather differently about it. So let's go back in time, to see the castle as Anne would have known it.

Touring Hever Castle: Rediscovering Its Lost Past

The first thing you would see as you approach the castle is just how different the setting is. It was much more wild and rugged than the cultivated gardens you see today. The original Norman castle had its origins in the classic motte and bailey design with a central timber-framed hall defended by a surrounding ditch and palisade. Later, in the thirteenth century, a stone gatehouse was erected, which contained its own hall; this, for a time, became the heart of the castle. To the west of the castle was the tiny village of Hever, consisting of a scattering of modest dwellings. It was the original village before it was moved by Lord Astor to its current position in the early twentieth century, thereby providing the Astor family with greater privacy.

In the sixteenth century, the area that lay in front of the building was covered in boggy marshland and was surrounded by dense forest. In Norman times, this was given the name *Andredswald*, which roughly translated means 'the woodland where no man dwells'. Even the king's map-makers of medieval England knew of its reputation as being notoriously lawless and dared not enter it.

Rather than the picturesque double moat that we see today, during the Tudor period, the front entrance to the castle was guarded only by a single moat, which was traversed by a stone bridge. The main body of the castle consisted of only two floors; the third floor was added later by William Astor. However, the gatehouse has remained unchanged since it was built in the thirteenth century.

If the setting of Hever Castle is much changed, then so is its interior, which in Anne's day would have been far less elaborate. This was last extensively renovated by the wealthy Astor family in the early twentieth century. As a result, many of its rooms are now sumptuously clad in oak panelling; the staircase and minstrels' gallery in the Great Hall are both intricately carved in the grotesque style, so popular in Henry VIII's palaces; the ceilings are ornately moulded in traditional designs and the rooms stuffed full of beautiful antiques, although not all are contemporary to the sixteenth century. Finally, its collection of Tudor portraits makes for a 'Who's Who' of the Tudor court, and has been described as second only to that of the National Portrait Gallery in London.

As you wander round this charming little home, it is not hard to imagine Sir Thomas or Lady Elizabeth, or indeed any of the Boleyn children, moving about its rooms, perhaps even receiving the King of England as he visited Hever in passionate pursuit of Anne. There is serenity about the castle and it sucks you in, leaving space for the walls to whisper their secrets to you. Let's now look at each of the rooms in turn.

The Great Hall

There would have been no fancy tapestries or fine oak panelling. Rather, the walls were covered in plain, light-coloured plaster and simple terracotta floor tiles. The fireplace had no ornate stone carving; it would have been fashioned into the simple shape of the iconic Tudor arch that we now so associate with the period. Also there was no ornate minstrels' gallery, which so dominates the modern-day room. As a result, the hall would have looked much more plain and open.

The two windows that we see today would have had no glass in them, just shutters closed at night in order to keep out the worst of the weather. The Boleyn family, like any family of the time, tended to live their life mainly outdoors; they came in only to shelter in the foulest weather, to eat, sleep or entertain guests. At the top of the hall would have stood a dais, upon which rested a grand table. Here, during the day, when he was at home, Thomas Boleyn would work on his documents and attend to family business. This place is also reserved for the lord, his family and any honoured guests to eat.

The Inner Hall

In Anne's day, this hallway did not exist. Instead this part of the castle was occupied by the kitchen, larder and buttery. In the early twentieth century, these rooms were replaced by the grand and sumptuously decorated Inner Hall that we see today.

The Library and the Parlour

On the ground floor of the west wing at Hever Castle is the elegant library created by W. W. Astor, its walls crammed with precious books in fine oak cases. However, this wing of the Boleyn family home was not always so grand. Nor is it likely that an extensive library existed; books were far too rare and precious and such libraries were probably the preserve of only the king himself. Instead, the library and the room beyond that, which is not open to the public, would have formed the main administrative, or *châtelaine*'s, office where Elizabeth Boleyn would have run the estate in her husband's absence.

The retiring room, or parlour, was the main private reception room for the family in Anne's time. Here you would be entertained in the presence of a roaring fire and offered a drink to quench your thirst. Originally, it is likely that a doorway connected the upper end of the Great Hall directly with this room, which was a withdrawing place for Thomas Boleyn and his family.

The Staircase

Another one of the major differences in the layout of the castle between the sixteenth century and now is in the position of the main staircase leading to the upper floors. The original staircase probably originated just to the right of the short gallery that separated the Great Hall from the kitchen, almost opposite the main front door. When William

Astor undertook his renovations, this staircase was flipped around so that it subsequently originated in the Inner Hall as we see it today.

Anne Boleyn's Bedroom, the 'Book of Hours' Room and the Tudor Portrait Room

This part of the castle yet again looked entirely different to how we have come to know it in our modern-day life. In the twenty-first century, it is divided into distinct and separate rooms: Anne Boleyn's bedroom in the north-west; a large, central room, which houses two of Anne's prayer books (the 'Book of Hours Room'); and finally, overlooking the moat to the south, the room containing numerous fine Tudor portraits. Nobody quite knows the arrangement of rooms on the first floor of the west wing during the sixteenth century. However, broadly speaking, it seems that these three rooms once made up the so-called *solar*, or main family room. Thus, it was a large room that extended across the entire length of the west wing. Here the family would relax and sleep. In the early sixteenth century, this room was probably open, only screens at its southern end walling off the area where Thomas and Elizabeth Boleyn might have slept in a fine, oak bed.

The Staircase Gallery

On the first floor, you will come across the magnificent Staircase Gallery, added by Thomas Boleyn in 1506 when the family first moved into the castle. It was created to connect both wings of the house on the first floor and the then newly created Long Gallery upstairs. At the time, it would have undoubtedly been the epitome of sixteenth-century fashion. Even today it is a broad, light and airy space, and during Anne's day would also have been the only place in the castle to sport expensive glass windows. Unlike the plain windows of today, it is likely that they would have been inlaid with brightly coloured heraldic emblems of the Boleyn family tree.

The Waldegrave Room and the Henry VIII Room

When the Boleyns occupied Hever, the rooms in the east wing of the castle were probably used by servants and never used by the family themselves. In truth, the magnificent Henry VIII Bedroom, which currently occupies part of this wing, is sadly only named in honour of the king; it is unlikely that he ever used this room. What is more likely, however, is that when the king visited, the Boleyn family would have decamped to Polbrooke Manor, located just a few hundred metres from the castle (today in private ownership and not open to the public) thus allowing the king to take sole occupancy of the Boleyn family home during his visits.

The Long Gallery

This particular room was created in 1506 by Thomas Boleyn, who did so by putting a ceiling over the Great Hall below and thereby reducing its height. At one point, the hall would have been open to the rafters, as was the fashion, a hole in the roof allowing smoke to escape from a central hearth. Once again, the sixteenth-century gallery appeared much simpler than the sumptuously wainscoted room that we see today, although there would have been a pretty ceiling which was highly decorative and much stuccoed with foliage. Of course, the Long Gallery served several purposes: a number of pieces of art could be displayed along its walls, while its size provided the perfect space in which to take exercise when the weather was inclement.

Authors' Favourites

We have two favourite artefacts at Hever Castle that we always enjoy seeing. The first is Anne's Book of Hours, in which Anne has rather poignantly inscribed 'Le Temps Viendra, Je [a picture of an astrolabe representing time] Anne Boleyn'. We often wonder whether Anne wrote this in a moment of quiet reflection during what must have seemed to her to be an endless courtship with Henry. Was she trying to shore up her faith that everything would turn out well in the end?

The second is the tapestry depicting the marriage of Louis XII to the eighteen-year-old Mary Tudor, Henry VIII's younger sister. It is supposed that the Boleyn sisters are depicted in the portrait, as both became part of Mary Tudor's household upon her arrival in France. If this is true, then it is certainly fun to try and guess which figure is Anne. We have our personal favourite: the top right-hand corner, fourth figure along from the right on the top row! What do you think?

St Peter's Church, Hever

> My good lord and master is dead [Thomas Boleyn]. He made the end of a good Christian man. Hever, 13 March.

St Peter's church dates back to the twelfth century and is located in the centre of Hever next to Hever Castle. Built on the site of an earlier Norman church, it has been a house of worship for the last 875 years and is a place that Anne would have known well.

Although little documentary evidence exists about the Boleyn's links with the church, they would have undoubtedly attended, especially considering the absence of a private chapel at Hever Castle. The tranquil atmosphere of the chapel is a haven from thoughts of the tumultuous – and tragic – final years of the Boleyns. Within its walls we are free to let our thoughts wander, imagining a young Anne, before her move to the court of the Archduchess Margaret of Austria in 1513, arriving at the church with her siblings, George and Mary, under the watchful eye of their parents, Elizabeth and Thomas. Perhaps they warmed themselves by the fireplace and talked with other local families before tending to their religious devotions.

Today the church is best known for being the final resting place of Anne's father, Sir Thomas Boleyn, who on 12 March 1539 passed away at Hever Castle, leaving his worldly troubles behind. On the day after Sir Thomas's death, Robert Cranewell, his auditor, wrote to Thomas Cromwell to inform him of the death of 'his good lord and master' and to assert that he had 'made the end of a good Christian man'.

His worn Purbeck marble tomb is located in the Boleyn Chapel, added to the original church in the middle of the fifteenth or early sixteenth century. On the tomb is a fine brass showing Thomas in the robes of a Knight of the Garter, the badge of the Garter on his left breast, and above his right shoulder, the falcon: the Boleyn family crest. This is said to be one of only two brasses in England depicting the full robes and insignia of the Order of the Garter.

The fireplace in the Boleyn Chapel is Tudor, as is the parish chest believed to have originally been the alms box for the church, as indicated by the slit on the top. The fine, flattened, barrel-vaulted ceiling in the nave would also have been *in situ* during Anne's visits. At some point the floor in the chapel was raised; notice how Sir Thomas's tomb stands on the original (lower) floor level.

As you look around the church, you'll no doubt be drawn to the beautiful stained glass, most of which is modern with the exception of some small pieces of old glass surviving in the Boleyn Chapel. Above the rector's seat is a replica of the Boleyn arms emblazoned in the stained-glass window. A list of past rectors dating back to 1200 is displayed on the west wall of the church. Take note of the names from the first half of the sixteenth century, as these may well have been familiar to Anne.

Thomas's brass may be the main attraction, but he is not the only Boleyn buried in the church. Henry Boleyn, son of Sir Thomas and thought to have died in infancy, is buried near his father; a simple brass cross marks his tomb. A similar cross marks the final resting place of his brother, Thomas, at Penshurst Church.

Apart from the brass of Sir Thomas and Henry Boleyn, the church is also home to another beautiful brass in memory of Margaret Cheyne who died in 1419. Margaret's husband, William, was a landowner in the area and gave his wife a fine memorial.

As you absorb the serene mood of the church and contemplate the lives of those in whose footsteps you walk, picture Anne admiring Margaret Cheyne's brass, perhaps imagining that when her time came she too would come to rest in the family chapel.

As a side note, there is an interesting legend attached to the nearby Henry VIII Inn, a name adopted in the 1830s. Originally the inn was called The Bull and local legend has it that after 'their Anne' was brutally executed the local people renamed the inn the 'Bull and Butcher' to show their anger towards the king.

This story may be apocryphal, but its true merit lies in the satisfying opportunity it provides to imagine the local people of Hever showing their indignation at the violent and unjust murder of Anne Boleyn.

Visitor Information
The King Henry VIII Inn is situated on Hever Road (postcode TN8 7NH) opposite the entrance to Hever Castle and St Peter's church. A pub has occupied the site since the late sixteenth century; however, the half-timbered pub you see today dates from 1647. To find out about opening times and menus, visit the King Henry VIII Inn website at www. shepherdneame.co.uk/pubs/edenbridge/king-henry-viii, or telephone + 44 (0) 1732 862457.

For information on prices, location and opening times of the castle, please visit the Hever Castle website at http://www.hevercastle.co.uk, or contact the castle on +44 (0) 1732 865224.

Postcode for Hever Castle: TN8 7NG.

Pashley Manor, East Sussex

> This large parish possesses many points of interest. The village is remarkably neat, and occupies a gentle eminence. It is surrounded by undulated country.
>
> Mark Antony Lower, 1870

Local legend tells that, as a little girl, Anne visited Pashley Manor in Ticehurst, on the Sussex and Kent border. It's a plausible tale given its proximity to Hever Castle, the Boleyn family home – just an hour's drive away, in modern terms – and the fact that her father owned Pashley in the early sixteenth century.

The Boleyns' Inheritance of Pashley Manor

It is believed that the first house built on the site in the thirteenth century, by the Passele family, may well have stood on the island that fills the greater part of the largest of three ponds in the garden, now called the Old Moat. In 1452, Sir John de Passhele died 'seized of Great Pashele in Tysherst', a description that has led to the idea that, after the early moated manor, there may have been a more substantial house built on higher land.

This could very well be the house that Sir Geoffrey Boleyn acquired sometime between the death of Sir John and 1455. In this year, he and one Thomas Boleyn appear as owners on a deed by which the manor is conveyed to John Lewknor and his wife Joan. Soon after, Sir Geoffrey reacquired the property, passing it on to his son Sir William and then through him to his eldest son, Sir Thomas Boleyn, who is said to have held court at Pashley Manor on 18 December 1518. This story, however, is doubtful, as the original source for this statement remains unknown and the king, by all accounts, was at Eltham Palace on this day, about 40 miles away.

Sir James Boleyn inherited the manor after his brother's death and in 1540 sold it to Thomas May of Combwell for £360, preferring instead to consolidate his holdings in Norfolk. The property then included close to 600 acres of land, a garden and a watermill with an iron furnace. It is believed that Thomas, or his son (also named Thomas), who inherited the property in 1552, was responsible for building the existing timber-framed house, subsequently altered by Anthony May, who succeeded his grandfather Thomas in 1610. It was enlarged in around 1720.

The house is not open to the public; however, the award-winning gardens are, and are certainly worth the visit. Mr and Mrs Sellick are the current owners and have worked tirelessly over the last three decades to restore and enhance the gardens and parkland.

There are a number of sculptures on display in the picturesque grounds, including a very moving sculpture of Anne by Philip Jackson, made especially to commemorate the link between the Boleyn family and Pashley Manor. She stands amid exquisite blooms on a small island in the middle of the Old Moat. Look back at her from across the lake, hands clasped, head bowed – as if in remembrance of a childhood lost.

Authors' Favourites

The authors visited in summer and enjoyed some afternoon tea against the stunning backdrop of wisteria, which completely masked the Georgian front. We wandered through the breathtaking gardens carpeted with fragrant roses and lavender, tulips and bluebells and chatted about the people that had walked there before us.

Be sure not to miss the statue of Anne Boleyn in the middle of the Old Moat.

Visitor Information

For information on how to reach Pashley Manor Gardens and its opening hours, which are seasonal, visit Pashley Manor's website at http://www.pashleymanorgardens.com, or telephone + 44 (0) 1580 200888.

Postcode for Pashley Manor: TN5 7HE.

Rochford Hall, Essex

> The mansion house is a large and stately building – but is now much decayed.
>
> Philip Morant, 1768

Rochford Hall in Essex has a long and colourful history, boasting many royal connections before coming into Boleyn ownership in 1515. In its heyday, it was a sprawling turreted manor, with a private chapel and Great Hall. It covered more than 4,000 square metres, making it one of the largest houses in the county, until a disastrous fire in 1760 reduced it by more than half its original size.

In the middle of the fifteenth century, James Butler, 5th Earl of Ormonde and 1st Earl of Wiltshire, commenced building a house on the foundations of an earlier stone manor. A staunch Lancastrian, he was executed following the Battle of Towton and the estate was confiscated and given to Edward IV's older sister, Anne, Duchess of Exeter, and then to members of the family of Elizabeth Woodville, Edward IV's queen consort: firstly to her father, Richard Woodville, 1st Earl Rivers, and then to her sons from her first marriage to John Grey of Groby – Thomas Grey, Marquess of Dorset, and Sir Richard Grey.

This succession of owners developed and extended the house commenced by James Butler, transforming it into an imposing manor. However, it is thought that the man who completed the building that the Boleyns would have known was James Butler's younger brother, Thomas Butler, 7th Earl of Ormonde – Anne's great-grandfather – who owned Rochford Hall from 1485 until 1515. Statutes passed under Edward IV declaring him and his brothers traitors were abrogated by Henry VII's first parliament.

Although an Irish peer, he was made a member of the English Parliament in 1495 under the title of Thomas Ormonde de Rochford. Upon his death in 1515, his two daughters and co-heiresses inherited his vast wealth and English estates, said to number seventy-two manors not including his Irish holdings.

His daughter, Margaret Butler, who married Sir William Boleyn, inherited Rochford Hall, eventually passing it to her eldest son, Sir Thomas Boleyn, who was elevated to the peerage as Viscount Rochford in June 1525. He held the manor until his death in 1539, during which time he is thought to have made some additions to the house and, according to tradition, visited frequently with his family. Unfortunately, no contemporary evidence survives to authenticate this. It is, though, possible that Anne visited her Butler relatives at Rochford Hall before leaving for the court of the Archduchess Margaret of Austria in 1513, or that perhaps she inspected her family home upon returning to English shores in 1521.

Rumours abound about clandestine meetings between Henry VIII and Anne Boleyn taking place at the house and even of a secret tunnel system beneath the home, which Henry is said to have used as his discreet escape route, but a lack of any reliable source casts dubious light over these tales.

Unravelling Tudor Rochford

Rochford Hall has been greatly altered over the years and part of what remains today is now privately owned and operates as a golf club; however, it is possible to make an appointment to visit.

The one surviving turret in the north-east is a reminder of the once-grand manor house that time, fire and unsympathetic alterations have stolen away. Of interest in the Rochford Hundred clubhouse is a conjectural drawing by Norman Barnes showing what the sixteenth-century house may have looked like. It gives a very good sense of its former grandeur.

The north-west part of Rochford Hall, converted into barns after the fire, was restored and converted into four Grade 1-listed residential properties completed in 1989. These were built on the foundations of the hall with some original fabric remaining.

It has been suggested that Mary Boleyn lived at the house with her second husband, William Stafford, after 1534 and that she died there in July 1543. Some historians believe that if she lived and died at Rochford, it's logical to assume that she was also buried in the local church, St Andrew's. But again, the sources are silent.

Authors' Favourites

The conjectural drawing by Norman Barnes that hangs in the clubhouse is our pick. The damage caused by the fire and alterations over the years have left Rochford Hall a shell of its former, glorious self. But after seeing the drawing in the clubhouse, Tudor Rochford Hall emerges from the layers of time and makes a tour around the site all the more meaningful.

Visitor Information

Rochford Hall is owned by Rochford Hundred Golf Club and so accessible to members of the club and their guests. Visitors not introduced by a member are also welcome to play the course on midweek afternoons. If you are not interested in playing golf but still would like to tour the hall, please contact Rochford Hundred Golf Club via their website www.rochfordhundredgolfclub.co.uk or telephone + 44 (0) 1702 544302.

Postcode for Rochford Hall: SS4 1NW.

The Low Countries

Mechelen, Belgium

> I find her so bright and pleasant for her young age that I am more beholden to you for
> sending her to me than you are to me.
>
> Margaret of Austria referring to Anne Boleyn in a letter to Sir Thomas
> Boleyn following her arrival at the Hapsburg court in 1513

In the summer of 1513, a young Anne Boleyn took leave of her parents in England, boarded a ship from Dover to Calais and in the process set out on an adventure of a lifetime. We cannot know what was in Anne's heart when she first left her homeland; of what kind of future did she dream? What were her hopes and aspirations? Whatever was the case, one can easily imagine that she never anticipated that she was taking the first steps in an apprenticeship that would set her on the road to immortality.

She was headed for the seat of power of the Hapsburg court; at the time, this was Mechelen in the Low Countries, known today as Belgium. Earlier in the year, while on embassy to the very same court, Sir Thomas Boleyn had secured a position for his youngest daughter as a *fille d'honneur* in the household of the indomitable Margaret of Austria, Regent of the Netherlands. It was a valuable prize to secure. The thirty-three-year-old, thrice-married and by then widowed Duchess of Savoy was not only a paragon of femininity, captivating *joie de vivre* and Renaissance accomplishments, but was also a powerful *femme sole*, exercising absolute power rather astutely in her role as regent for the future Charles V.

It is interesting to learn about Margaret's character, for we quickly see mirrored in it so many of the attributes that would later be ascribed to Anne herself. In Jane de Longh's biography, *Margaret of Austria*, she writes of the impression that the young duchess made upon her second husband in 1501: 'Margaret's Flemish ways, her zest for life, her inclination to luxury and show, her robust humour, her straightforward sensuality found satisfaction in this gay companion.'

Although Anne was only to stay with Margaret for around a year, one senses that the impact of the regent, known to all as 'Madame', upon the impressionable young English girl was profound. In time, when Anne reached the zenith of her power, we would see her emulate her erstwhile mistress in artistic and architectural taste, as well as in setting the same tone in the guidelines laid out for maintaining inscrutable morality within her own royal household.

Clearly, Margaret was delighted with her new charge as, having received her at court, she wrote the following to Sir Thomas:

> I have received your letter by the Esquire [Claude] Bouton who has presented your daughter
> to me, who is very welcome, and I am confident of being able to deal with her in a way which
> will give you satisfaction, so that on your return the two of us will need no intermediary other
> than she. I find her so bright and pleasant for her young age that I am more beholden to you
> for sending her to me than you are to me. [Translation from the original French]

There has been suggestion that Claude Bouton travelled to England initially on some kind of errand related to the infant Princess Mary, who had recently become betrothed to the thirteen-year-old Charles. At some point, he returned to the Low Countries with Anne as his charge. We should remember that Anne was Charles's contemporary, being just one year younger than the child who would become one of her future husband's greatest rivals.

In thinking about the city that Anne first became acquainted with upon her arrival in the Low Countries, we can once again turn to Jane de Longh; she paints an evocative picture of Mechelen at the time:

> [The people of Mechelen] lived withdrawn and peaceful behind its ramparts and canals. Across the drawbridges, through the gates, a rural traffic moved all day long of carts and wagons, pedestrians and horsemen ... in the centre of the intimate little town, along the quays of the Dijle, there was always a flapping of sails, a rattling of cranes and pulleys. Outside the walls, meadows and farmlands stretched toward the hazy Flemish horizon, the ditches which bordered them, drawing strips of light through the ever moist green land while countless windmills turned industriously in the Flemish breeze.

As we shall see shortly, whereas the streets of sixteenth-century Paris have long been swept away, Mechelen is an altogether more resilient survivor, noted even today for its abundance of Renaissance architecture in typical Flemish style. It is not so hard to see through the veneer of time in Mechelen, and recreate in your mind's eye the city that once greeted the young Anne Boleyn.

The Shaping of a Renaissance Queen

Once at court, it seems that Anne's introduction to the ducal household was a gentle one, for as Jane de Longh goes on to point out:

> In the peaceful privacy of this modest palace she [Margaret], in whose hands converged the threads of every European political intrigue, was able to create for herself a setting of feminine comfort and quiet harmony ... [in which] the spirit of courtesy and culture ... contrasted favourably with the loose and drunken manners of so many other courts.

It was the beginning of Anne's introduction to Renaissance culture, which would be matured and refined in the coming years at the French court. Although Margaret would never set aside her widow's cap, she continued to surround herself with the finest artists, poets, philosophers and musicians of the time, delighting in painting, illumination, books and, of course, music. With Anne's sharp intelligence and capacity to absorb knowledge and wisdom from those who surrounded her, she learnt quickly. After her execution, some twenty-three years later, the French poet de Carles wrote of this earlier time: 'la Boullant [Anne Boleyn], who at an early age had come to court, listened carefully to honourable ladies, setting herself to bend all her endeavour to imitate them to perfection, and made such good use of her wits that in no time at all she had command of the language.'

It seems that Anne was all too aware of her parents' high expectations for her education. In her sole surviving letter from her early years away from the English court, she wrote:

Sir,

I understand by your letter that you wish that I shall be of all virtuous repute when I come to Court and you inform me that the Queen will take the trouble to converse with me, which rejoices me greatly to think of talking with a person so wise and virtuous. This will make me have greater desire to continue to speak French well and also spell, especially because you have so recommended me to do so, and with my own hand I inform you that I will observe it the best I can. Sir, I beg of you to excuse me if my letter is badly written, for I assure you that the spelling is from my own understanding alone, whereas the others were only written by my hand, and Semmonet tells me the letter will wait unless I do it myself, for fear that it shall not be known unless I write to you, and I pray you that in the light of what you see you will not feel free to part from the will which you say you have to help me. For it seems that you are where you can, if you please, make me a declaration of your word and on my part be certain that there shall be neither nor ingratitude which might check or efface my affection, which is determined to as much unless it shall please you to order me, and I promise you that my love is based on such great firmness that it will grow less, and I will make an end to my after having commended myself right and humbly to your good grace.

Written at five o'clock by your very humble and obedient daughter,

Anna de Boullan

The Ducal Palace

The palace in which Anne was to spend her time was another reflection of Margaret's artistic tastes, rooted in the heart of Franco-Flemish style. Having arrived back in the Low Countries from Savoy, where she had been widowed, Margaret initially lodged in Margaret of York's palace, located directly opposite the regent's later palace.

Certainly, by the time Anne had arrived at Mechelen, the city had built Margaret a new palace that was to be Anne's home for the following year. It was an unpretentious place, fashioned from brick and stone, giving rise to a distinctive style that historians such as Eric Ives have linked to the palace that would be remodelled for Anne some twenty years later at Whitehall. It was structured around a central courtyard; a pretty *loggia*, with flattened arches supported by stone pillars, ran around its perimeter. And, although modest in size, the interior was resplendent, adorned with lavish fabrics, with rooms devoted to the regent's collections of art and priceless objects.

As you wander through the palace courtyard today, perhaps you might pause a while and imagine Anne's voice floating down to you from an open window as, along with other ladies of the court, she learned the art of setting prose to music, cultivating the 'sweet singing voice that would make bears and wolves attentive'.

However, before long, the wheel of fortune turned yet again. Mary Tudor, Henry VIII's youngest sister, was to be married to the King of France. Anne was required as part of the new queen's household. After gaining her release from the ducal court, Sir Thomas Boleyn ordered Anne to pack her bags and head overland to one of the most glamorous and bustling cities in Christendom. Anne was heading for Paris and her new life at the dazzling French court.

Visitor Information

Mechelen remains a relatively small city, less well known perhaps than nearby Brussels, Antwerp and Bruges. However, it more than makes up for its diminutive size with its many historical sites and superb Renaissance architecture.

The city is roughly fifteen minutes by train from Brussels. There are two train stations in Mechelen; Mechelen-Nekkerspoel will deliver you closest to the town centre, although the station is a little rundown and, according to locals, not so safe at night. If you arrive here, head toward the bell tower of St Rumbold's Cathedral; along Keizerstraat and just at the intersection on the left with Korte Maagdenstraat you will find Margaret of Austria's ducal palace.

Alternatively if you arrive at the more modern Station Mechelen, it is best is to take bus number 552 from the railway station and get off four stops later in the Keizerstraat. There is no metro or tram in Mechelen, so getting around on foot is the best way to explore the city.

The old palace now serves the courts of justice, and although you cannot go inside the building you can wander round the picturesque courtyard, allowing your imagination to indulge itself. The southern face (constructed of red brick and stone) is contemporary to Anne's time in Mechelen and would have been much as she had known it as a young girl, exactly 500 years ago. You can also visit the crown hall, which is a really beautiful building (no photos allowed).

Opening times for the palace are 9 a.m. – 5 p.m. from Monday to Friday. Note: the building is not open on Saturday.

On leaving the palace, continue in the same direction toward the Grote Markt (central marketplace). Almost immediately on your right after leaving the palace is a white stone building called the Stadsschouwburg. This was once Margaret of York's palace, and again a building Anne certainly would have known. Today, only the former entrance hall remains, and this is now the city's cultural centre and theatre.

Finally, do continue on toward the marketplace, taking time to enjoy the many boutiques and cafés and admiring the magnificent bell tower, part of St Rumbold's Cathedral, whose outline dominates this part of the city.

If you need more information on how to get to the city, opening times and places to stay, please contact the local tourist information centre via their website http://toerisme.mechelen.be/en/

France

She [Anne] became so graceful that you would never have taken her for an Englishwoman, but for a Frenchwoman born.

Lancelot de Carles

Note: Because of Anne's junior status at court while in the Low Countries and France, no specific records survive of her movements, thoughts or exchanges during this time (with the exception of one surviving letter written by Anne to her father while she was in the service of Margaret of Austria, sometime in 1513/14. See the entry on Mechelen). Therefore, we can only surmise that, unless otherwise stated, while in France wherever the king was, so was the queen. Of course, wherever the queen went, by and large, so did her ladies; we can quite safely assume that between the years 1515 and late 1521, this included Anne Boleyn.

Paris

Anne probably first arrived in the vibrant city of Paris sometime in the autumn/winter of 1514. Having been released from the Hapsburg Court, 'La petite Boulin', as she was affectionately known by Margaret of Austria, travelled to France's capital to join the entourage of Princess Mary Tudor, the younger, and by all accounts very beautiful, sister of King Henry VIII; the eighteen-year-old princess had travelled to France to marry the aged and sickly Louis XII in a ceremony that took place in Abbeville on 9 October 1514.

We do not know exactly when Anne arrived in France's capital, nor whether she had already joined with the household of her royal mistress by that time. However, arrive she did and there the court remained until April the following year, when a new king, Francis I, finally set out to establish his royal power base in the Loire region of France (see below). During this first sojourn, and in subsequent years when the court stayed in Paris, Anne would have seen, and been lodged in, several of its iconic medieval buildings. Some of these buildings still stand today, others are entirely lost or remain only in fragments.

In this section we provide the time traveller with a sense of the overall impression of the medieval city that Anne would have known. We will also take you to a number of its landmarks, which we can fairly safely assume Anne would have seen, and probably visited, in the entourage of the royal court.

Sixteenth-Century Paris

The Paris of Anne's day was essentially medieval in origin. However, as much of the ancient city was remodelled between the French Revolution and the First World War, almost the entire medieval city has since been lost and its landscape irrevocably transformed. Indeed, for the modern-day visitor, no real sense of the place that Anne once knew lingers. Wide, spacious boulevards, pleasant parks and elegant eighteenth-century buildings endow the city with light and a symmetry which is a far cry from the dark, cramped, smelly streets of the medieval citadel. However, thanks to maps made of the city from the sixteenth century, panoramas of some of Paris's most iconic buildings captured in the many illuminated manuscripts of the time, and surviving buildings and artefacts, we can still capture glimpses of the old city through the mists of time.

Perhaps Anne's first sight of Paris as she approached the city would have been its mighty medieval walls, whose construction was begun by Philippe Auguste, often referred to in French as the *Enceinte* Philippe Auguste, in 1190. These crenelated walls were built to defend his capital while the king was on crusade in the Holy Land. They encircled its entire circumference, except where it was broken by the Seine, and access to the city was via a series of *portes* or gateways situated at various points around its perimeter, including the Porte St-Antoine, which was guarded by the famous Bastille to the east of the city; more on this landmark shortly.

Rising above the crenellations, Anne would have seen the many towers, turrets, finials and the pitched, leaden roofs of some of Paris's grandest buildings outlining a majestic Gothic imprint upon the distant skyline. Then, as the city grew nearer, fields would have increasingly given way to man-made structures, clusters of timber-framed and stone buildings becoming denser as the city walls loomed ever larger. Perhaps in the distance she would have seen windmills situated on elevated ground around the citadel outwith its walls, or the old convent of Montmartre situated high upon a hill overlooking Paris to the north.

Once within those walls, Paris was a veritable rabbit warren of narrow and pestilential lanes, washed only periodically when the River Seine flooded. Having lived in Mechelen, the capital of the Low Countries, for around twelve months, Anne must have been used to the hustle and bustle of city life: a mass of humanity from all social strata going about their affairs, cries from merchants selling their wares in the markets, filth poured directly out onto the streets from windows of the houses overlooking the busy lanes below and perhaps even the rotting remains of criminals hanging from gibbets in some of the cities' open, public spaces.

However, for all the noise and dirt, French culture and civilisation were renowned in Christendom as being at the cutting edge of taste and refinement. As Europe's greatest medieval university was based in Paris, it was famed as a centre of learning, with the city drawing in the brightest minds of the age, while the most talented artists, sculptors, goldsmiths and craftsmen all flocked there to find work from wealthy patrons.

At the turn of the sixteenth century, Paris was also huge, the eighth-largest city in the world with a population of around 185,000. By contrast London had only in the region of 100,000 inhabitants at this time. The sheer scale of the citadel and its vibrancy must have been breathtaking for the young Anne Boleyn; you can easily imagine her sense of adventure and natural exuberance being stirred as she first rode through its bustling streets.

The French court's newest *demoiselle d'honneur* must have been headed for one of the city's royal palaces. In the early years of the sixteenth century, this would most likely have been either the Hôtel St-Paul or the Palais des Tournelles, both lying on today's right bank. A more remote possibility might have been the Château de Vincennes, outwith the city walls to the east, nestled in the Bois de Vincennes. Another popular residence of the French court was the Palais de St-Germain-en-Laye, again lying just outside the city walls, this time to the south-west. It is certainly safe to say that by this point the old medieval palaces of La Louvre and the Palais Royal on the Île de la Cité had long been abandoned as royal lodgings by the kings of France.

So it was in these former buildings, surrounded by the height of gothic opulence and amid one of the most revered and sophisticated courts in the world, that Anne began her apprenticeship under the guardianship of her new royal mistress, the proud and fiery Mary Tudor, the new Queen of France.

L'Hôtel St-Paul and le Palais des Tournelles

In the fourteenth century, the dauphin, Charles, moved his court to the area known as St Antoine on the east of the city. There he sequestered a 'large area of ground and several houses which were enclosed by a perimeter wall' from the Archbishop of Sens and the Abbey of Saint-Maur. When Charles became king, he levied taxes to enlarge and ennoble the Hôtel St-Paul, finding safety in the shadow of the Bastille and the nearby Château de Vincennes, which lay a few miles outside the city walls to the east. Here, on the edge of the citadel, the king and his family could enjoy the cleaner air and the pretty open spaces that surrounded the two newest royal palaces.

The Hôtel St-Paul lay to the south of the Rue St-Antoine, named today as it was in the sixteenth century, its perimeter stretching down toward the edge of the Seine. The *Curiosité de l'Histoire de Vieux Paris*, describes 'different' types of lodgings, presumably reflecting the origins of the *hôtel* as comprising a number of different houses of varying sizes and shapes, built over two floors, each separated by courtyards and gardens. The king's lodgings comprised a great bedroom, a great lower hall for dining, a council chamber, a privy chamber, a study, dressing room, oratory, chapel and two or three galleries, the smallest room being about 20 feet long. The queen occupied apartments with a similar arrangement of rooms, although a little less grandiose in their proportions. The centrepieces of many of these rooms would have been enormous fireplaces carved in stone, often fantastically decorated, as can be seen in the Louis XII wing at the Château de Blois. In terms of decor, the walls were painted with a muted shade of yellow, which was overlaid with images of devices, coats of arms or rosettes drawn in vivid colours, and hung thereabouts with tapestries or wainscoted with wooden panelling.

The same nineteenth-century book describes the very distinct ambience found within the buildings of the royal French court at the time: 'The palaces of the king ... were shrouded in the mystical character of religious buildings, and the ceremonies of the court relived the solemnities of the Christian Church.'

We will see very shortly just how much this rather sombre, dark and reverential ambience would come to contrast so starkly with that of the light, bright, airy Renaissance palaces of the Loire. Indeed, Anne had arrived in Paris right at the end of the Gothic period, the full expression of the Renaissance had yet to burst upon the French court. Thus, we can imagine her swept up in the mystique of monarchy, yet standing as a witness to the dawning of a new age.

Anne Boleyn and Events at le Palais des Tournelles

If she arrived in Paris in time, it is quite probable that Anne witnessed the great celebrations following the marriage of Mary Tudor to Louis XII, one aspect of which was a ten-day tournament held at the Palais des Tournelles, in which the English contingent, led by Charles Brandon, emerged as resounding victors. Just three months later, on 1 January 1515, she was almost certainly there when the fifty-two-year-old Louis XII died, leaving the eighteen-year-old queen a widow after only twelve weeks of marriage. While the court would have been thrown into mourning for their beloved *père du peuple* (father of the people), you can hardly imagine Mary Tudor shedding too many tears of grief, for in a matter of months she would be married to the charismatic Charles Brandon in a building just across the river, in the privacy of her chambers at the Hôtel de Cluny (see below).

Uncovering the Lost Palaces
The close-up taken from the 1550 map of Paris shows the Rue St-Pol (Paul) as the probable entrance to the eponymous Hôtel St-Paul. This street is extant today, lying just off the Rue St-Antoine.

To the north of the medieval Rue St-Antoine, opposite the Hôtel St-Paul was the Palais des Tournelles, so called because of its many turrets. This royal residence was smaller than its nearby neighbour, but nevertheless could support up to 6,000 people. The main entrance to the palace was roughly where the current Impasse Guéménée meets the Rue St-Antoine. Sadly, only a street name, the nearby Rue des Tournelles, gives us a clue to the area's place in history. If you wish to explore the area, head for the Metro station Saint-Paul which brings you up on the Rue St-Antoine. You can then walk eastwards toward La Place de la Bastille, passing the sites of the Hôtel St-Paul and the Palais des Tournelles on your right and left, respectively. You are right in the heart of the place where Anne probably had her first thrilling taste of her new life at the French court.

Visitor Information
The areas described above are open to public access at all times. Access via the Metro: Saint-Paul.

The Bastille
The Bastille was an imposing, medieval fortress, built during the fourteenth century in order to protect the Porte St-Antoine from aggressive incursions from the east. It was a dark and sinister building, whose name has become indelibly etched in the history of France on account of the storming of the Bastille during the French Revolution. Detail on the 1550 map of Paris shows its form: mighty walls forming an oblong shape, set about with eight crenelated towers enclosing a large central courtyard; a drawbridge, which is seen clearly on the right-hand side of the château, spanned the moat that surrounded it.

The Bastille sat directly to the east of both the Hôtel St-Paul and the Palais des Tournelles, and it is surely a building with which Anne would have been very familiar. What is more, we can be fairly sure that Anne also set foot inside this most austere of palaces, for when she was seventeen years old, an English delegation, including her father acting as the newly appointed English ambassador to the French court, arrived in Paris to seal the betrothal of the two-year-old Princess Mary to the dauphin, Francis. The event was accompanied by great pomp and ceremony, with the English ambassadors being warmly received and entertained by the French king.

The *Letters and Papers of Henry VIII* describes a number of these set pieces, in particular a banquet held in the Bastille on 22 December 1518. Eric Ives postulates that at such a key meeting, the services of an interpreter among the queen's ladies would have been an invaluable aide in enabling conversation between the French hosts and the English delegation. Anne, of course, would have been well placed to fulfil this role. Thus we can imagine her, close to the queen's side, enjoying a very different side to the Bastille than most people imagine. The building had been richly decorated for the event, as the following entry in *Letters and Papers* describes:

The large space in its centre was squared, and floored with timber, three galleries being raised all round, one above the other; the whole being covered in with an awning of blue canvas, well waxed, which prevented the rain from penetrating. The canvas was painted to represent the heavens, and Latin and French mottoes were suspended about the hall. White and tawny cloth was hung under the galleries, and the floor was carpeted with the same. There was an immense number of torches in sconces and in chandeliers, each torch weighing three pounds, throwing a marvellous blaze of light on the starry ceiling.

In the four corners of the hall were cupboards filled with gold and silver vases. The platform was overhung by a bower of evergreens. Tables were placed at the extremity of the platform, and down the sides, the guests being seated inside. Below the platform were two tables, extending the whole length of the place, at which gentlemen of the English embassy and Frenchmen were seated alternately with ladies. The company danced to trumpets and fifes till the third hour of the night. Then supper commenced, which lasted two hours, and consisted of nine courses: each course was announced by a flourish of trumpets. After supper several companies of maskers made their appearance, among them the King. Then came a collation of confections, served by ladies dressed in the Italian fashion, chief among whom were the daughters of Galeazzo Visconti; and by degrees the company dispersed. The Queen and Madame Louise viewed the whole of the sight from one of the galleries near the King's dais.

On the following day, 23 December, we hear that:

a fine tournament took place at the Bastille in Paris, the King and twenty-four aids being on one side, and Mons. de S. Pol and twenty-four on the other. They fought with bright swords without edges. In the evening thirty young ladies appeared, and danced with these lords; and at the second hour of the night tables were set for 250 persons. The site was approached by a long street (Rue St Antoine) covered over with evergreens and ornaments. In the courtyard of the castle a handsome building had been erected, with three tiers of balconies for the spectators. In the building was a platform, on which was a dais of cloth of gold for the King; and around it were celestial signs cut in pasteboard, and 600 torches. There were four cupboards piled with gold and silver. The Queen and Madame Louise looked on from their balcony. After dancing, tables were placed on the platform, and water presented to the King for his hands. Ladies sat between the gentlemen. The viands appeared on large dishes emitting fire and flames; they were preceded by eight trumpeters, the archers of the bodyguard, five heralds, the eight seneschals in ordinary of the household, and my Lord Steward. The King's viands were borne by twenty-four pages of honor; the rest, for those not on the platform, being borne by 200 archers. Supper ended, the music and masking commenced; after which the ladies served the gentlemen with silver dishes full of confections. Thus ended the entertainment, which, with the presents given to the ambassadors, has cost upwards of 450,000 crowns.

Visiting the Site of the Bastille

It is easy to find the site of the old fortress in modern-day Paris. At the eastern end of the Rue St-Antoine is the wide open space, still called Bastille or Place de la Bastille (Metro: Bastille). In its centre a large monument commemorates the July Revolution of 1830, while the frenzied Parisian traffic hurtles around it at frightening speed. Nothing remains to be seen of the Bastille today, which must continue to exist only in our imagination.

Hôtel de Cluny

With Louis XII dead and Paris cast into mourning, as French custom dictated, Mary Tudor was sent into isolation away from the court. Dressed in white (*La Reine Blanche*), she was to remain sealed away from the outside world at the Hôtel de Cluny for the traditional forty days, all the doors and windows to her privy apartments kept closed, her chambers cast in darkness.

Alongside the eighteen-year-old widowed queen were her ladies, some of whom had been placed there as spies by the formidable new Queen Mother, Louise of Savoy. For while Francis I had proclaimed himself to be the rightful King of France, everybody knew that if Mary proved to be pregnant with a new dauphin, he would rule only as regent until the child was old enough to take over the reins of monarchy. Perhaps unable to contain himself, Francis visited Mary to find out whether she believed herself to be carrying Louis's heir. Mary replied that she knew of no other king but himself, as she was not *enceinte*.

Somewhere in this dramatic tale, the dashing Charles Brandon was dispatched from England to negotiate the return of the widowed queen's dowry and to accompany Mary back to England. It seems that Mary was already in love with her brother's long-time boon companion, and Brandon's arrival must have been eagerly anticipated; Mary's very own knight in shining armour, ready to rescue her from her unenviable position as the unwanted, widowed queen, closeted away in the semi-darkness. One suspects that Mary was paving the way for what was to come, when she wrote to her brother in England:

> Sir, I beseech your grace that you will keep all the promises that you promised me when I took my leave of you by the waterside. Sir, your grace knoweth well that I did marry for your pleasure at this time and now I trust you will suffer me to marry as me liketh for to do … wherefore I beseech your grace for to be a good lord and brother unto me.

It seems that Francis knew of the passion that this tall, slender, grey-eyed beauty harboured in her breast for the gallant English duke and soon stepped in as improbable matchmaker to bring about their union. Of course, it suited Francis to have Mary taken off the marriage market, preventing a possible future opportunity for England to ally herself with another powerful dynasty and one of France's rivals.

In the end, Mary's tearful pleading, Francis's persuasion and the guiles of the most romantic city in the world must have worked their magic. On 3 March 1515 Brandon finally set aside his misgivings of blatant disloyalty to his king and friend and the two lovers were married in the dowager queen's privy apartments at the Hôtel de Cluny.

But where was Anne in all this? Of course, we cannot know for sure but, as one of the queen's ladies, presumably in attendance upon her mistress. It is possible, but given her tender age unlikely, that she was one of the ten witnesses to the wedding itself. However, most historians believe that she was most likely present at the Hôtel de Cluny when these events took place. As Eric Ives states in his biography of Anne, the 'pert contempt of a fourteen-year-old product of the Hapsburg nursery' over Brandon's 'undue familiarity' and the queen's decision to marry beneath herself may well have been the root of Mary's dislike of Anne in later life.

The Buildings of the Hôtel de Cluny

The current Hôtel de Cluny was built around the end of the fifteenth/beginning of the sixteenth century. Essentially, it functioned as the town house of the abbots of Cluny, whose monastery was based at Cluny in Burgundy. In order to have influence with the king, the abbots required a presence in the capital, close to the court, and thus the 'Hôtel' was constructed for such a purpose. Although it was owned by the Cluny abbots through until the French Revolution, it was common practice to let out the apartments in part or in their entirety. Thus, we can assume that this is how Mary Tudor came to be lodged there in the early part of 1515, at a discreet distance from the court.

The building is probably one of the best-preserved examples of medieval architecture of its type in the city. Laid out in a 'U' shape, the main building with two wings flanks a courtyard that once faced onto the Rue Mathurins St-Jacques, named after a large convent that stood there at the time. On the other side of the 'Hôtel' was a spacious garden, which was reconstructed in its medieval form in the year 2000; this type of garden would have been quite rare in Paris at the turn of the sixteenth century. Away from her duties, did Anne stroll there with her sister, Mary?

The courtyard was sealed off from the street by a crenelated wall, while inside the courtyard, the visitor is delighted by the sight of a whole range of mullioned windows, and ornately carved stonework abounds, nowhere more so than on the five-sided tower, which was once the main entrance to the abbot's reception rooms.

The Hôtel de Cluny today is the National Museum of the Middle Ages and houses a breathtaking array of artefacts that have the power to keep the lover of such an epoch beguiled for hours! Never has the author seen such a glittering array of medieval treasures brought together under one roof, and for this reason alone the museum is certainly worth a visit.

However, for the visitor following in Anne's trail, we can also enjoy the history of the rooms themselves, although there are no indications of this history to be found as you wander from chamber to chamber. If you wish to find yourself in the room in which

Mary Tudor was reputedly married to Charles Brandon, for a long time known thereafter as *La Chambre de la Reine Blanche,* or the Bedroom of the White Queen, make your way toward the privy chapel on the first floor. The room before you enter the chapel was once the abbot's bedchamber, and this is the room where it is believed that the clandestine marriage between a dowager queen and the English duke took place. Today, as perhaps in Mary's time, it is cast in darkness, displaying a number of fine exhibits; however, traces of an original frieze of grotesques, which were restored in the nineteenth century, are still visible around the walls.

Do also enjoy the chapel next door, which was probably the abbot's private chapel. I will leave the detailed descriptions of the architecture of this beautiful little space to the guidebooks that you can buy in the museum's shop downstairs. However, it is impossible to believe that Mary Tudor, Charles Brandon, Mary and Anne Boleyn did not enjoy its splendours, just as you are able to do today, laying their eyes upon the same carved stone, stained glass and the enchanting murals that are painted on either the side of the apse, all being original to the sixteenth century.

Authors' Favourites
Of course *La Chambre de la Reine Blanche* and the adjoining chapel are absolute must-sees for this location. The authors visited on the first Sunday of the month; at the time of writing this book, there is no entrance fee to many of Paris's museums on Sundays, thus it was busy and quite difficult to capture enough stillness to feel the imprint of history whispering from the walls. Nevertheless, it was poignant to stand where such a well-known moment of Tudor history unfurled itself and a visit is certainly highly recommended.

Visitor Information
The museum is open every day, except Tuesday. For further information, visit the website at http://www.musee-moyenage.fr/ or telephone 00 33 (0) 1 53 73 78 00.

There is also an excellent gift and book shop, with books on every conceivable subject of medieval life (although the majority of the books are in French). The authors do, though, recommend a DVD entitled *Paris de Moyen Age,* which is a fine piece of computer-animated art, reconstructing the medieval city of 1550, very much the city Anne would have recognised. The commentary is in both English and French. However, be warned, the shop can get very crowded!

La Basilique de St-Denis and Notre Dame

While we cannot be completely certain that Anne was present at the Coronation of Mary Tudor, which took place in the abbey church St-Denis on the 9 November 1514, we can be much more sure of the fact that she was there to witness that of Queen Claude, who was crowned in the same basilica on 10 May 1516. Francis had been King of France for over sixteen months by the time the crown of Charlemagne was finally placed upon Claude's head. The reason for this: Claude had been pregnant with their first child and unwell when her husband had succeeded to the throne. Clearly she had been spared the exhausting rigours of the endless ceremonies surrounding the coronation of a new monarch, and had remained in Paris while Francis had travelled to Reims for his own enthronement on 25 January 1515.

A Brief History of the Abbey Church

The origins of St-Denis go back to the fifth century; however, the cathedral we see today was largely the work of Abbot Sugar, who rebuilt portions of the church in the twelfth century in grand Gothic style, the first of its kind in France. By the sixteenth century, the basilica was part of an abbey complex of Benedictine monks, much venerated as, thanks to King Dagobert I, it had come to house the remains of St Denis himself, the martyred patron saint of Paris; he had been decapitated along with his two erstwhile missionary companions in the third century.

While the kings of France were traditionally enthroned at Reims, after Anne of Brittany was crowned in St-Denis in 1491, a precedent was set for all future queens of France to be crowned in the abbey church. Thus the stage was set for both the coronations of Mary Tudor and, two-and-a-half years later, Queen Claude.

If Anne did not catch up with the English delegation in time to witness the former, she must have been well established in the French queen's royal household by the time Claude left Paris on 9 May in anticipation of the following day's solemnities. The young Anne was around sixteen years old; perhaps even mature enough to assist Claude's other ladies in serving their mistress that day.

We are not here to present an entire history of the basilica, or to detail the architectural delights of the abbey church's interior, renowned today as a mausoleum of the French monarchy; instead make your way inside and perhaps wander down the central aisle, or take a seat in the knave to imagine the scene that unfolded there on 10 May 1517.

We can visualise Anne arriving at the basilica in a litter behind that of the queen, who was once again pregnant, this time with her second child. The litter would have been resplendent draped in cloth of silver. Was Anne among the ladies that helped arrange the queen's mantle of blue velvet lined with ermine before her diminutive figure swept into the hallowed interior of St-Denis?

The basilica must have been packed for this theatrical performance of majesty. As you walk down the central aisle of the abbey church, perhaps you are tracing Anne's very footsteps as she followed her mistress into the sacred heart of the abbey. It seems likely that Anne was close to the centre of the action, watching the ceremony unfold as Claude first prostrated herself in front of the high altar, before being anointed then crowned with the crown of Charlemagne by the king's brother-in-law, the Duke of Alençon. The queen was then led to her throne, while the Cardinal Legate of Luxembourg officiated at the Mass which followed. At the end of it all, Claude rose to signify her intention to defend the faith. As Anne looked on, she could not possibly have imagined that in sixteen years' time, she would also find herself pregnant and being crowned, this time as Queen of England, below the hallowed roof of Westminster Abbey. I wonder if she remembered that day; dusty memories of a foreign land and a happy time in the service of a long dead queen.

The Processional Entry into Paris and Notre Dame

Two days later, Claude was given a grand ceremonial entrance into Paris. Once again, Anne surely must have been in attendance in one of the many litters following the queen. Having slowly made their way the 6 miles back to Paris, the entourage would have passed through the now long-lost Porte St-Denis on route to the cathedral of Notre Dame. Interestingly, a newer construction, a triumphal archway built in the seventeenth century, now marks the spot where the old Porte St-Denis once stood.

Along the way, one of the traditional pageants that was staged in honour of the queen depicted a mechanical dove, which represented the Holy Ghost, offering Claude the crown. This symbolism was not uncommon in the coronation processions of queens, and certainly Anne would see it once more in her lifetime. During her own entry into the City of London in May 1533, the pageant held at Leadenhall would include an angel crowning Anne's falcon badge.

As was usual for great state occasions such as this, the procession terminated at Notre Dame, the magnificent gothic cathedral situated on the Île de la Cité, which had been founded on the spot where St Denis and his two companions were said to have been murdered. Once more, it is not within the scope of this guidebook to provide a comprehensive history of the cathedral or an account of its impressive architecture. There are many guidebooks that can better fulfil this role. Rather, our aim is to draw your attention to Notre Dame as a location in Anne's story of Paris. Already, at such a tender age, she was at the heart of events of huge national importance seeing, as the historian Roy Strong notes, 'traditional forms of entertainment transmuted into a vehicle for dynastic apotheoses'. It was as if, step by step, a rough slab of marble was being perfectly chiselled and sculpted into Anne's white falcon, just waiting patiently to take to the skies.

Authors' Favourites

Although we have not focused on it in this account, be sure to make enough time to fully explore the royal mausoleum at St-Denis, where all but three of France's kings have been buried from the tenth century until 1789. Of particular interest to us are the enormous renaissance tombs of Louis XII, Anne de Bretagne and Francis I and his wife, Queen Claude.

Visitor Information

The closest Metro station is Basilique de St-Denis and the building itself is within a couple of minutes' walk from the station. Do be warned though, this area is no longer frequented by kings! The Basilique de St-Denis is closed on 1 January, 1 May, 25 December and for various religious services during the year. There may be other instances in which the building is closed at relatively short notice, so it is best to check on the website for the latest opening times (these also vary throughout the year). Website: http://saint-denis. monuments-nationaux.fr/. Entrance to the body of the church is free, but if you wish to view the royal mausoleum a fee is payable.

The site of the old Porte St-Denis is at the junction between the Rue (Boulevard) St-Denis and the Rue de Faubourg, where the seventeenth-century *porte* marks the spot of its predecessor.

Finally, to reach Notre Dame on the Île de la Cité, use Saint-Michel/Notre Dame or Cité Metro stations. The cathedral is open every day of the year from 8.00 a.m. to 6.45 p.m. (7.15 p.m. on Saturdays and Sundays). Access to the cathedral is free of charge.

Le Palais de St-Germain-en-Laye

In Anne's time, the Palais de St-Germain-en-Laye was a medieval palace whose construction was commenced by Louis VI in 1124. Lying approximately 12 miles to the west of the heart of Paris, its location was much favoured on account of the good hunting to be had in the surrounding forest of Giboyeuse de Laye, and because it could be reached by water via the River Seine.

Although the early years of the reign of Francis I were based in the Loire Valley, after 1518 the court increasingly took up residence in France's capital; at this time the Palais de St-Germain became a key royal residence.

It was from the centre of Paris to this place that a very ill, and heavily pregnant, Queen Claude was moved in March 1519, prior to the birth of the future Henri II on 31st of that month. At the time, Anne's father, Sir Thomas, was the English ambassador to the French court and a series of letters penned to Cardinal Wolsey gives us glimpses into the precarious state of the queen's health, and her removal from Paris to St-Germain for her lying in. In the *Letters and Papers of Henry VIII* we learn that Sir Thomas

> wrote last on the 11th [March]. The Queen and my Lady [Louise of Savoy] left Paris the same day for St Germain, where the former was to be confined, but was taken ill by the way, and was obliged to rest at the village of La Porte de Neuilly, and that night she was in great danger. False reports were spread, first of her death, afterwards of her delivery; which kept Boleyn away from court on Saturday, when he had appointed to meet the Great Master. He was sent for, however, yesterday, and saw the lodgings of the King and Queen, my Lady the king's mother, the Duchess of Alençon, and the Great Master, at the said village. 'The Great Master hath no chimney in his chamber, but there is a great oven.' If the Queen is strong enough, she is to be conveyed by water to St Germain in 'close barges with chambers made in them;' if not, she must remain.

Sir Thomas writes that he is to lodge half a league away from the court at Poissy and subsequently we see his letters signed from there. We can conclude that Anne, in attendance upon Queen Claude, must have seen her father regularly during this period.

On 25 April 1519, the infant Henri was baptised in front of the whole court. Henry VIII was to be the child's godfather, with Sir Thomas representing his sovereign lord by proxy. We can well imagine the eighteen-year-old Anne watching her father with some pride; it would not be the last time that the Boleyns were to be at the heart of royal pageantry.

During the same month, in *Letters and Papers*, we also read of discussions regarding the meeting between Henry and Francis, initially scheduled for the summer of 1519. In the end, politics would push the meeting back until June of the following year; it would eventually be immortalised as the famous Field of Cloth of Gold (see entry on Field of Cloth of Gold). During that summer of 1520, Claude was once again pregnant; it would be to St-Germain that the French court retreated after the summit was over, toward the end of June, for the queen's lying in. Here Princess Madeleine would be born on 10 August, the last French royal birth that Anne would be present to witness, for she would return to England by the end of the following year.

Visitor Information

Today, the only vestige of the palace that Anne knew remains behind in the form of the chapel (Sainte Chapelle). The medieval château has been largely lost. It was replaced by a later Renaissance palace built by Francis I after Anne had left France, and then subsequently altered further by successive monarchs. The baptism of the future Henri II took place in the chapel at St-Germain. In Anne's time, the chapel would have looked even more resplendent than it does today. Sadly, the great rose window, which measures over 100 square metres, is now blocked up and no longer allows the dance of coloured light to play upon the chapel's stone floors.

The château houses the Musée d'Archéologie Nationale (Museum of National Archaeology), a collection of artefacts from Paleolithic to Merovingian times. The rest of the building is not open to the public; however, luckily for us, the chapel is. The gardens surrounding the château are also worth enjoying, amounting to some 172 acres. There is a large forest and a delightful terrace with panoramic views over Paris and the Seine. To reach the palace of St Germain-en-Laye take the RER Ligne A – alight at Saint-Germain-en-Laye station; the château is across the road. The gardens are free, but there is a small charge for the museum.

Other Sites of Interest in and Around Paris

Although the court of Francis I was based in the Loire Valley for the first three years of his reign, Anne would have initially remained in Paris in the service of Queen Claude until April 1515, when Francis finally left the capital for the Château d'Amboise. She would return to Paris in the queen's entourage periodically thereafter, and so must have known the medieval city well.

Without turning this book into a complete guide to medieval Paris, there are one or two other notable sites that Anne would have seen, or perhaps visited, that remain behind to give us glimpses of the life she knew there.

The first of these is the Château de Vincennes, which lies to the east of Paris. Built in the fourteenth century and added to in the seventeenth, this grand medieval building was originally a hunting lodge, situated outside Paris's city walls in the Bois de Boulogne. In Retha Warnicke's *Rise and Fall of Anne Boleyn*, she postulates that when Anne first arrived in France, the young *demoiselle d'honneur* was sent to the royal nursery to attend on, and be a companion to, Renée, the younger daughter of Louis XII, who was lodged at the Château de Vincennes. However, Warnicke bases this assertion on Anne being only seven years old when she came to France. As the authors believe Anne's most likely date of birth was 1501, rather than 1507, we are more sceptical of this conclusion, but have included this location for completeness.

Another interesting vestige of medieval Paris is surprisingly to be found underground! Surely one of the great buildings of the age was the iconic Louvre. Before the current building existed, which was commenced by Francis I after Anne had left the French court, a massive medieval fortress existed in its place. It was a vast building and in its heyday housed the famous library – an enormous collection of 900 manuscripts that were ultimately dispersed during the chaos of the reign of Charles VI (the Mad) around the turn of the fifteenth century. Yet, the palace was also austere and damp on account of its location adjacent to the Seine. After Charles V built the Hôtel St-Paul, the ancient château was subsequently abandoned as his successors sought the cleaner air to be found on the east of the city. The old building was therefore doomed and eventually dismantled. However, the foundations of the original château, including the *Basse Halle* (Lower Hall) in the Sully crypt, are still to be seen beneath the present building. Standing in front of what is left of those huge stone walls gives us a feeling of the building that Anne would have undoubtedly seen dominating the western side of Paris's right bank. Note that you can also view parts of the original *Enceinte* Philippe Auguste in the large concourse area underneath the modern-day Musée Louvre.

Finally, in order to acquire a sense of the Gothic grandeur of the medieval palaces of Paris, do combine your visit to Notre Dame with the nearby Sainte Chapelle, the sole surviving building of the original royal *palais*. The palace was situated on the southern end of the Île de la Cité, with Sainte Chapelle constructed as both a chapel for the broader royal household (low chapel) and a high chapel (above) for use by the king, the royal family and other notables. The building is utterly breathtaking in its grandeur: the palate of vibrant colours, the gold leaf adorning the walls and the perfectly preserved medieval stained glass all combine to conjure up the dazzling spectacle of the Gothic royal court and help us visualise more easily how the other medieval palaces of the time, such as the Palais des Tournelles, might have appeared to Mistress Anne.

Sainte Chapelle is now surrounded by the buildings of the Palais de Justice and can be accessed from the Boulevard du Palais (nearest Metro: Cité)

The Loire Valley, France

Introduction

Two months after the Coronation of Francis I, the court left the capital and headed south-west toward the Château d' Amboise, sometimes travelling by horse, sometimes by boat. The new king would subsequently make this château his base for the first three years of his reign. On the way, the king and court rested at Melun, Fontainebleau, which was not the château we know today, but a small hunting lodge in the forest, then Montargis, Gien, Blois and Chaumont, before finally arriving at Amboise on 5 June. With the exception of Fontainebleau, which was completely rebuilt by Francis I from 1526 onwards, remnants of the royal lodgings that were undoubtedly used by the king and his entourage still exist today in all the above locations. This would have been Anne's first taste of an itinerant French court, which, over the following six years, would see her travel the length and breadth of France. The extent of these travels means that not all the locations will be covered in this guidebook, but we mention some of them should you wish to investigate them further for yourself.

Here we will concentrate on the key royal residences in the Loire Valley, which remained the centre of royal power during the early years of Francis's reign. These include the Châteaux d'Amboise, de Blois, de Chaumont, de Romorantin and de Chambord.

Le Château d'Amboise

Le cinquième jour de juin 1515, mon fils, venant de Chaumont à Amboise, se mit une espine en la jambe, dont il eut moult de douleur et moi aussi ; car vrai amour me contraignoit de souffrir semblable peine.

[On 5 June 1515, my son, while moving from Chaumont to Amboise, got a thorn in his leg, which caused him much suffering. And so did I suffer too, for true love compelled me to feel the same pain.]

Recorded by Louise of Savoy in her journal

On 5 June 1515 the redoubtable Louise of Savoy, mother of the new king, Francis I, recorded the above entry in her diary. Earlier that year on the 15 February, her beloved son had made his triumphant entry into Paris, following the death of his distant cousin, Louis XII, on New Year's Day 1515. The king and court had remained in Paris for the first half of the year, before finally leaving the city on 24 April and beginning its 90-mile journey south-west of the capital. Their destination was the Château d'Amboise in the Loire Valley; this was the much-loved childhood home of France's virile new king, who had been installed there with his mother and sister by Louis XII back in 1501.

Anne Boleyn was among only six English ladies that were allowed to remain in the service of his wife, Queen Claude. The rest had been sent home to England with Mary Tudor, the dowager French queen. By that time, Anne had been away from Hever for around a year and a half. The slender fourteen-year-old girl with dark, beguiling eyes and lustrous auburn-coloured hair must have been teetering on the brink of womanhood; her impressionable young mind had already been exposed to the powerful female role model of Margaret of Austria and, once in France, she must have soon met Louise of Savoy and her daughter, the future Marguerite of Navarre. Over the next few years, Anne would no doubt meet visionaries like Leonardo da Vinci, who would reside at Amboise from 1516 until his death in 1519, and be exposed to the thinking of French reformist writers like Jacques Lefèvre d'Étaples and Clément Marot, who was in residence at the French court during Anne's stay in France.

We must imagine her arriving at Amboise virtually fluent in conversational French and much at home in the sophisticated French court; it was a court that would soon become the epicentre of the Renaissance in Europe and would profoundly shape Anne's thinking and character, carving out her destiny as England's future queen.

The Château of Amboise is situated now, as it was then, on top of a high plateau overlooking the Loire. Travelling from the north with the rest of the court, Anne would have seen its silhouette painted dramatically against the sky. It was June, the days long and warm, the light airy rooms of the castle filled with the sweet scent of summer carried in through open windows on a gentle breeze. Perhaps Anne was struck, as the authors were, by the marked difference between homes of the English nobles, built to keep out the weather and keep warm, and those of their French counterparts, which seem to have been designed to let in the more benign weather of significantly warmer climes. Even today, it is clear how the chalky stone and white marble interiors create bright open spaces, while the exterior walls literally gleam in the summer sunshine.

Touring the Château
The original entrance to the palace was not where it is today, which was once the tradesmen's entrance, but via Porte des Lions, a small defensive fort whose remains

still stand on the eastern side of the plateau. A long, winding road, stretching for 4–5 kilometres, once wound its way up to this entrance and it is through this gateway that we can imagine Anne having her first glimpse of the place which would become her home for the next three years.

Sadly, only approximately 20 per cent of the sprawling complex of palatial buildings that Anne would have come to know intimately still exists today. However, luckily for us, two of those buildings are the Gothic and Louis XII wings. The latter is erroneously named as, in fact, it was built largely by Charles VIII but completed by King Francis during the first few years of his reign. These wings were subsequently used as the main royal lodgings for both Francis and his queen. Thus we can be quite sure that, when we walk through the surviving rooms of the château, we are walking through rooms that Anne once knew well.

The authors were there during a fine day in early September, when the château was set against a flawless sky and swallows swooped and dived from their nests tucked along the length of the string course, beneath the château's pitched, leaden roof. It was easy to imagine the splendour and insouciant nature of the French court; there is something about the place that speaks of carefree days, idle banter and playful flirtation. One can well imagine Anne dallying with the many *gentilhommes* of the court and honing the feminine guiles that would later so enrapture the King of England.

As you wander first around the Gothic, and then the Louis XII, wing, bear in mind the following:

The wonderful *Grand Salle* in the Gothic wing seems to have served a combined function equivalent to the English council chamber and presence chamber. So here Francis would consult, and hold audiences, with wider members of the court. It is also here that the banquet following the wedding of the Duke of Lorraine and Renée de Bourbon-Montpensier took place (see below). This is an authentic sixteenth-century room and is largely as Anne would have known it.

The private chambers of Francis I are situated on the ground floor of the same wing, just off the *Grand Salle*. In a similar vein to the arrangement of rooms in Henry VIII's palaces, we move from the largest room (similar to Henry's privy chambers – although this room also seems to have been accessible to wider members of the court) through to a slightly smaller room, which was the king's privy bedchamber, and finally a much smaller privy dressing room (the English equivalent of a raying chamber). These ground-floor apartments looked out over beautiful Italian Renaissance vegetable gardens, arranged by Dom Pacello da Mercogliano, who went on to work at the Château de Blois in 1517.

The ground floor of this wing has been restored to its sixteenth-century glory and is packed with Renaissance architecture, furniture and interior decoration. Thus, it provides a strong sense of how the château would have been experienced by the young English *demoiselle d'honneur*. However, you will need to take this memory with you as you head upstairs to the first floor. The suite of rooms that you find there follows the same pattern as the king's below, and was once occupied by the diminutive Queen Claude. However, they have been restored to a later period. Thus, we need to see past the nineteenth-century interiors and imagine the queen surrounded by her ladies, doing their embroidery, reading or catching up on court gossip. It is likely that a good deal of Anne's time at the château was spent in these rooms.

Events at Amboise

As mentioned earlier, sadly we cannot state with exact certainty any specific incidents that happened to Anne directly during this period of her life. However, we do know of a number of notable events that occurred at the Château d'Amboise during Anne's tenure at the French court. It is likely that she was present to witness the following:

On 26 June 1515, great celebrations were held as Francis claimed his right to the Duchy of Milan and began preparations for his campaign in Italy later in the year. The marriage of Antoine de Lorraine and Renée de Bourbon-Montpensier took place on the same day in the church of Saint-Florentin. This church once stood in the middle of the plateau, where the current bust of Leonardo da Vinci commemorates his initial resting place. The chapel was later destroyed during the French Revolution. Banquets, masques and tournaments followed. This included a famous incident where the wild boar that had been set loose in the grand courtyard for entertainment broke free and threatened the spectators watching in the galleries of the Seven Virtues. The king managed to kill the beast with his own dagger. It must have been quite a spectacle for the young Anne to witness.

The birth of three royal children: Princess Louise on 19 August 1515; Princess Charlotte on 22 October 1516 and then finally the long-awaited birth of the new dauphin, Francis, on 28 February 1518. Fabulous revels followed the baptism in the church of Saint-Florentin on the evening of 25 April 1518, with yet more dancing, masques and banquets. It was a double celebration, for the nephew of Pope Leo X, the Duke of Urbino, married a French princess, Madeleine de la Tour d'Auvergne, one week later on 2 May in the same church.

When we visit places like Amboise and begin to understand the key characters and events that surrounded Anne, we catch intriguing glimpses of those strong early influences that shaped her thinking in later life. We see her famed allure and grace forged amid the sophistication of the French court; we see her courage, strength and determination influenced by the formidable women that surrounded her; we see her flair for visionary thinking perhaps inspired by the likes of Leonardo da Vinci and Anne's interest in the new religion, undoubtedly ignited by reformist writers, whose works were widely read at the French court.

Le Château de Blois

> Blois, naissance de ma Dame,
> Sejour des Roys et de ma volonte …
> Habite Amour en ta ville a jamais.
> [Blois, birth of my Lady,
> Place of Kings and my will …
> Love lives in your town forever.]

Pierre de Ronsard, French poet

Anne's first sight of Blois must have come in late May or early June 1515, as France's new king passed through the town on his way to the Château d'Amboise. While Amboise was to be the centre of royal power for the first three years of Francis's reign, Blois was regularly frequented by the royal court during that period until 1518–9, when it became the king and queen's primary residence; that is until Paris eventually gained pre-eminence in the 1530s and 1540s.

Blois was a favoured residence of Francis I's wife, Claude, who had been brought up there from a young age. Anne's new mistress was the eldest daughter of Louis XII and his second wife, Anne of Brittany. In the summer of 1515, Claude was just fifteen years old, only two years older than her young charge. Noted for her kind disposition and sweet temperament, perhaps due in part to the very happy childhood she had experienced while growing up at Blois, it is not hard to imagine Anne warming to this gentle soul and learning well a queen's primary role: to bear children – and sons in particular. In the next nine years, Claude would endure seven pregnancies, giving Francis three healthy sons, before her death in 1524, a fact that would perhaps come to haunt Anne in future years.

The town was then, as it is now, built upon two hills and was surrounded by the Forêt de Russy, which no doubt provided fabulous hunting for the vigorous new monarch. It was also within easy reach of the châteaux de Romorantin and Chambord, which both belonged to Louise of Savoy, Francis's doting mother. In her fascinating journal, Louise records the king and court lodging at these châteaux as her guests on several occasions (see also notes below).

The Château de Blois itself occupies the summit of a triangular promontory, with far-reaching views over the River Loire to the south-west. Blois had been the centre of royal power during the reign of Louis XII, who had been born there, and was thus at the very heart of France. Anne Boleyn indeed arrived in the Loire at a fascinating time, for this was the dawn of the Renaissance – and it arguably began at Blois on account of Louis XII's successful campaigns in Italy. As a result of his contact with the country, Italian artists, architects and designers came to the French court; the king soon commissioned the work that would transform the Gothic château into a fine Renaissance palace. Francis I would later continue and accelerate this work, creating the fabulous Francis I wing, which incorporates the world-renowned external staircase that allowed the king to descend from his apartments in full view of the court. Blois truly was a theatre of history.

The sixteenth-century palace that Anne Boleyn knew when she first came to Blois is depicted in a drawing by Jacques Androuet du Cerceau. The château was built around a large, irregular, central courtyard, the Cour d'Honneur, which remains almost intact today. However, there are some notable differences between the château today and the château that Anne would have first known when she arrived in the summer of 1515.

The area immediately in front of the palace was once within its precinct and contained the Église Saint-Sauveur (St Saviour's church). Once within the central courtyard, the obvious alteration to the old château is the loss of the southern wing, which has been attributed to the end of the reign of Louis XII. This was replaced in the seventeenth century by the Gaston d'Orléans wing, which is quite obviously built in a later, classical style and is of no interest to those following in the footsteps of Anne Boleyn. Finally, outside the palace walls, to the east, was once a vast expanse of fabulous gardens containing symmetrical flower beds, a fountain, an orangery, an orchard, pavilions and courts for the playing of that beloved sport of French kings, *jeu de paume* or real tennis. These gardens were once accessed by La Galerie des Cerfs (The Gallery of Stags), so called because it was decorated with hunting trophies, befitting the fact that the king would go out to, and return from, his hunting trips via this building.

Although today a small park remains wedged in between the foot of the promontory overlooked by the majestic Francis I wing and the Église Saint-Vincent-de-Paul (church of Saint Vincent of Paul), busy roads now plough through this once-serene space and much of the gardens have long since been lost.

Touring the Château

The following areas are the main points of interest for the visitor interested in Anne Boleyn.

La Salle des États

This part of the château harks back to the feudal days of France's medieval history when the castle was commanded by the dukes of Blois. It was built at the beginning of the thirteenth century and was used as a hall of justice. While it has since been renovated, the hall is much as Anne would have known it, reflecting the Gothic style of the Middle Ages.

The Francis I Wing

Like Louis XII before him, when Francis set about building himself fabulous new royal lodgings at Blois in 1515, he built upon the existing Gothic façade. Work accelerated quickly between 1515 and 1519, although progress then slowed and it was only completed in 1524. By this time, Queen Claude was dead and Anne had been back in England for three years. Therefore, perhaps the most perplexing question at Blois is, 'did Anne ever spend time in this wing?' It would be wonderful to think so, for the interiors are so vibrant, opulent and beautifully preserved that one finds oneself wanting her to have seen the sights that so enchant the eye.

However, it seems that the wing was only fully occupied by Francis from 1523, when Anne had already left the French court. Thus, the authors suspect that Anne certainly did see this wing under construction, and may have visited it from time to time, but is unlikely to have spent her time attending on her royal mistress in its rooms.

Regardless of this, the Francis I wing is truly divine and surely presents one of the best-preserved examples of Renaissance interior decoration that you are ever likely to see. When we read of the palaces that Henry had refurbished for Anne, like Whitehall or her apartments at the Tower, we read of colourful tiled floors, gilded ceilings and grotesque work carved into wooden wall panelling. We know, for example, that at Greenwich Palace the ceilings of her bedchamber and presence chamber were latticed and decorated with gilded bullions. Expensive coloured floor tiles from Seville covered the area in front of the fireplaces, while the alcoves were tiled with plainer yellow and green tiles from Flanders. Whereas today much of this Renaissance splendour has been lost in the interiors of what remains of Henry's royal places, we can truly see it brought to life at Blois. Furthermore, we know that Anne played a very active part in the remodelling of Whitehall Palace; it is not hard to see from where she might have drawn her influences.

The Louis XII Wing

Shortly after he succeeded to the throne of France on 7 April 1498, Louis began work at Blois to build new lodgings for himself and his wife, the rather reluctant Anne of Brittany, who also happened to be the widow of Louis's predecessor. The wing that we see today is essentially unchanged from the one commissioned by the new king. Built of stone and brick, it is adorned with decorative motifs that pay homage to the Italian style while, over the main entrance, the visitor is greeted by an impressive statue of Louis on horseback; the king's emblem of the crowned porcupine is on prominent display, flanking his image.

In order to access the royal apartments, you sweep up one of two majestic stone staircases housed in separate towers that were built into either end of the wing. The staircases are wide and open to the outside elements, occasionally offering tantalising glimpses of rooms leading off them, or through the open balustrades of the comings and goings in the *cour d'honneur* below. The king and queen's apartments are situated on the first floor and accessed from a corridor that runs along the backbone of the wing, in its time an entirely new concept in domestic living, since previously rooms could be accessed only one from the other.

The rooms themselves are larger, perhaps more imposing than the privy chambers of the Francis I wing, the whole arrangement speaking of an earlier, more communal style of living that had not yet quite evolved to provide the royal couple with an entirely separate suite of chambers – often on different floors – that would become commonplace through the first half of the sixteenth century.

The number of rooms is limited; it seems the king had a bedchamber and privy chamber, *chambre de travail* (study), while the queen probably had similar at the opposite end of the wing. You will also find a larger room at the centre of the wing, which is thought to have been for conducting business of a more public nature.

Therefore, it was either in these rooms or those of the lost southern range that the young Anne would have most likely passed much of her time indoors doing embroidery or making conversation. Surely, she must have enjoyed the gardens at Blois, attending on the queen or passing time in the company of other *filles d'honneur*, such as her sister Mary Boleyn and her cousin Mary Fiennes, who, incidentally, would later become the wife of Sir Henry Norris.

Authors' Favourites

The Louis XII wing today houses a fine art collection. We have to confess, we paid little attention to the paintings. However, we certainly enjoyed sitting a while on one of the several seats provided, imagining Anne learning court craft at the feet of her mistress, the Queen of France.

In the Francis I wing, the queen's privy closet called 'the Studiolo' is the only room in the wing that definitely existed in that form during Anne's time. It can be dated prior to 1520. Like English privy closets, this room was for reading, writing and personal meditation. Alongside the oratory next door, these rooms provide perhaps the two finest examples of Renaissance interiors to be seen in the château.

Visitor Information

For further visitor information, please visit www.chateaudeblois.fr or telephone +33 2 54 90 33 32.

The Châteaux de Chaumont, de Romorantin and de Chambord

As mentioned earlier, other châteaux that are nestled in the heart of the picturesque valleys of the Loire and the Cher were frequented regularly by the king and court during Francis's reign. These trips served Francis's insatiable appetite for hunting, which he enjoyed to the full in the 2,000 hectares of rich forest that surrounded Blois and Amboise.

Thankfully, the journal of Louise of Savoy specifically locates the court at certain notable châteaux. We can assume that Anne too would have visited these places as part of the queen's household. We include three of the châteaux that feature prominently: Chaumont, Chambord and Romorantin.

Le Château de Chaumont

It is clear from Louise's diary that Chaumont was the final place of lodging for the royal court before arriving at Amboise, as it made its way from Paris following Francis's accession to the throne. By this time, Anne was certainly in attendance upon the new queen and would have lodged at the château.

Chaumont had been rebuilt between 1468 and 1510, after having been razed to the ground by Louis XI as a punishment against Pierre d'Amboise for rebelling against the Crown. So it was virtually new when Anne rode across the south-facing drawbridge and into the courtyard that overlooked the river below. Unfortunately, it has not been possible to identify exactly which chambers may have lodged the queen and her ladies. However, today this diminutive, but fairy-tale, castle perched above the Loire has a series of Renaissance-style chambers laid out in the east wing for the visitor to enjoy. Other rooms in later architectural style are also open to the public.

While not as grand or lavish as some of the other grand châteaux of the Loire, it has wonderful charm and can be less busy than other, better-known sites in the region. A word of caution, though: there is a climb on foot up to the château from the parking area over the road, along the riverbank. This seems to be the main parking area for the château. However, as we were leaving we located a second entrance, at the back of the château's grounds. You will need to drive uphill, away from the river, to locate it on the top of the plateau at the rear of the property. It avoids any strenuous climb. There is also little by way of refreshment, so perhaps it is an idea to have your own supplies with you that you can enjoy in its extensive and much-loved gardens.

Visitor Information

Please visit http://www.domaine-chaumont.fr for detailed information on opening times and admission prices.

Le Château de Romorantin

There are references in Louise of Savoy's diary to her son arriving at Romorantin on 30 June 1515 with 'toute sa compagnie' (all his company). At that time, Francis was on his way to Lyon, there to fight with the Duke of Milan over Francis's claim to the duchy. It is not clear whether the queen and her ladies accompanied him to Romorantin on that occasion. Queen Claude certainly did not progress to Lyon, for she would have been visibly pregnant and subsequently gave birth to her first child in Amboise on 19 August.

However, we can be more certain that Anne visited this château in January 1517, when there are records of jousts being held in front of the Château de Romorantin as part of the celebrations relating to the entry of several *chevaliers* (knights) into the Ordre de Saint-Michel. We can be almost certain that Anne was also there on 6 January 1521, when the court was gathered to celebrate the *jour de Rois* (Twelfth Night). A freak accident born of high jinks caused the king to be struck on the head, leaving him with a serious wound. Some three weeks later Louise of Savoy records that 'mon fils fut en grand danger de mourir' (my son was in great danger of death). One suspects that, due to this accident, the court remained at Romorantin for several days or possibly weeks, and that Anne would have borne witness to dark and dramatic days of uncertainty as the king's life hung in the balance.

The Layout of the Château

The Château de Romorantin was built in the fifteenth century by the counts of Angoulême and, typical of the region, it was constructed of brick used in perfect harmony with white stone. Of the original château, only two towers remain along with elements of the wall that once enclosed a vast central courtyard. On three sides of the courtyard were buildings of greater or lesser importance, while the fourth, to the west, constituted part of the rampart of the town. Four round towers were once situated at each corner of the courtyard, the ones in the west forming part of the defences of the town walls; it is thought that perhaps these predate the building of the château.

The apartments to the south, which adjoined the river, were used as the state apartments. This included the south-east tower, which was the largest and grandest of them all and, fortunately for us, still stands today. It consisted of four rooms, one on each floor, while an external staircase tower provided access to each level without compromising the space available to each room. Tradition has it that in 1499, when Louis XII and his court stayed as guests of Louise of Savoy at Romorantin, Anne of Brittany gave birth to the future Queen Claude in the first-floor room of the south-east tower. In honour of this event, the room is still called Salon Claude de France to this day.

Louise of Savoy and the Development of the Château de Romorantin

In 1487, the twenty-eight-year-old Charles d'Angoulême had married the eleven-year-old Louise of Savoy. Nine years later, having given birth to both the future Queen of Navarre and the future King of France, Francis I, Louise was widowed. In this way, Romorantin fell into Louise's sole possession and she lived there subsequently from time to time with her two young children.

In 1512, Louise set about enlarging the château: the southern wing was extended toward the west such that it tripled in length, while a vast park was laid out alongside the river. This was just as well, for when her son Francis finally became king he would thereafter visit his mother at the château with the entire court in attendance. Clearly, Francis had fond memories of Romorantin, for it is here that he first asked Leonardo da Vinci to conceive of a grand Renaissance château to rival all others. Sadly for Romorantin, the plans never materialised and Francis's dream was finally realised at Chambord, where da Vinci created a vast Renaissance palace which still stands today.

Visitor Information

The remains of the two towers can be viewed from public land. However, the old south-east tower where Claude was born is in private hands and cannot be accessed. The tower can be seen from the river, and is a stone's throw away from the central marketplace. If in doubt, enquire at the tourist information centre.

The address for the tourist information office is 32 Place de la Paix, Romorantin-Lanthenay. Telephone number: + 33 (0) 2 54 76 43 89.

There is also a museum in Romorantin–Lanthenay, called the Musée de Sologne. The museum houses some exhibits about the ancient château and you can see them at the following address: Moulin du Chapitre, Romorantin-Lanthenay. Telephone number: + 33 (0) 2 54 95 33 66. Email: museedesologne@romorantin.fr

Le Château de Chambord

Francis came often to Chambord as part of his hunting trips. Today, a magnificent château stands as a veritable jewel of the Loire Valley, a fabulous Renaissance creation of the young and energetic king. However, if Anne knew Chambord at all (and although this is likely, the authors have been unable to identify a specific date or event where we could be relatively sure of her presence there) it was not this château that she would have known. In 1519, the king began work on the new palace, demolishing a twelfth-century fortified tower, which had once been owned by the counts of Blois and later the dukes of Orléans. The new palace took many years to complete, with Anne long since returned to England before it was in use. There is nothing that remains to be seen of this medieval hunting lodge today.

The Field of Cloth of Gold, Pas-de-Calais

> I need not describe the magnificence of their dress, as their servants were so adorned that the meeting was named the Field of Cloth of Gold.
>
> Martin du Bellay, contemporary French chronicler

The Field of Cloth of Gold was exceptional in many ways, not least as it became legendary within its own lifetime. Within days of all the tents being packed away, leaflets commemorating the event were circulating round the streets of Paris and avidly consumed by all strata of society. It has been called the last great chivalric event of the medieval age, and surely to be one of the few thousand who flocked to an otherwise unremarkable spot between the border of Northern France and the English territory of Calais, was to enjoy a spectacle of a lifetime. Yet to be at the heart of it all, at the centre of one of the royal households, marked you out as being exceptionally privileged indeed. It was from this close vantage point that all modern-day historians place the nineteen-year-old Anne Boleyn in the household of Queen Claude, who was once again heavily pregnant, this time with Madeleine, the ill-fated future Queen Consort of Scotland.

It is not our intention here to set out the details of the complex political landscape that catalysed and bubbled away in the background of this meeting between two of the greatest Christian princes in Europe. There are many other books that would do justice to this aspect of the summit for, at its heart, the intention was to seal a pact of friendship and solidarity between the two ancient rival kingdoms of England and France. Rather, our intention is to conjure up the spectacle of the events to which Anne bore witness; to place the future Queen of England in relation to those events; and to help you follow in her footsteps should you choose to visit the location for yourself.

Preparations for the Event

The Field of Cloth of Gold was first talked about in 1514 during marriage negotiations for Princess Mary and Louis XII of France. However, six years elapsed before Wolsey, the main architect of the meeting, and his French counterpart Guillaume Gouffier, Lord of Bonnivet and Admiral of France, eventually brought it to pass.

In the run-up to the Field of Cloth of Gold, on both sides of the Channel, craftsmen, merchants and commissioners were tasked with designing, making, assembling and transporting vast quantities of costly objects, items of furniture and materials that would house and feed all those who were to attend the event. English chroniclers mention some 3,000 workers and craftsmen employed to complete the project and it has been recorded that, during the days before the meeting, French workmen toiled 'day and night' to finish the camp.

While Henry sailed from Dover to Calais in a fleet of sailing ships (the event is recorded in the enormous painting, *The Embarkation of Henry VIII at Dover*, which is on display at Hampton Court Palace), Francis made his way northwards from Blois on 18 April. On the same day the ladies set out for Paris. They arrived there on 5 May; the king arrived some time after on 17 May. Anne then must have travelled with the court to Abbeville, then to Montreuil (-sur-Mer) and finally Marquise. On 5 June the queen and her ladies followed Francis on the final leg of the journey to Ardres in preparation for the meeting of the two kings.

Henry and Francis were finally to greet one another on Thursday 7 June at around 6 p.m. About 1½ kilometres from Guînes, near Ardres, a gold canvas tent had been pitched between two man-made hillocks. Both kings left their attendants behind; meeting alone, they embraced as brothers. Oh, to be a fly on the wall of that particular conversation!

The following day, Friday 8 June, both kings met in the 'field' and an artificial 'tree of honour' was raised interlaced with the English symbol of hawthorn and the French raspberry bush. The tree carried three shields, each representing a part of the feat of arms: horseback jousting, open field tournament and foot combat. Each knight was required to touch the shield representing the competition he wanted to enter; around 200 knights all told took part in the feat of arms.

The Layout of the Field of Cloth of Gold

The camp was arranged in three distinct areas: the English were based at Guînes, the French at Ardres, and in between was the 'field' or '*champ*' (also meaning tiltyard) itself, a kind of 'no man's land', crafted into a tiltyard with viewing platforms, where the tournaments were to take place. Entrance to the French and English encampments was controlled by ticket. However, anyone who was dressed appropriately could watch the tournaments taking place on the 'field of arms'.

Being part of the French queen's household, we must assume that Anne was based with the French court at Ardres, visiting the 'field' with her mistress to watch the two kings fight as brothers-in-arms, both in the jousts and during foot combat. However, whether Anne travelled to Guînes to see the English camp, and the famous temporary palace that Henry had had erected there, is less clear.

The English Encampment at Guînes

The temporary palace erected by Henry VIII just outside the castle of Guînes has become the stuff of legend and was captured in all its magnificent glory as the centrepiece of the famous

Field of Cloth of Gold painting, which today hangs on display at Hampton Court Palace. *The Story of France* by Mary MacGregor captures its appearance in the following words:

> It was only a place of wood, yet when gilded with gold, it shone bright in the sunshine … Great gates of gold opened into the palace grounds, in which was a wonderful fountain that also shone as gold; while from the mouth poured … wine that sparkled crimson in the rays of the sun … Without the palace shone with gold, within it was hung with tapestries of gold and rich embroideries. Wherever one turned, one's eyes were dazzled with the gleam of gold and precious stones.

Described by Edward Hall as 'the most noble and royall lodging before sene, for it was a palays', the temporary construction contained lodgings for the king (four chambers), queen, Cardinal Wolsey and Mary, Duchess of Suffolk (three chambers each), as well as an enormous Great Hall, a chapel and covered passageway that linked the palace to the nearby castle – just in case! The interior was as sumptuous as the exterior was magnificent, being decorated with many fine tapestries spun with silver and gold thread. In fact, it is believed that the tapestry entitled *The Triumph of Fame over Death*, which now stands in the Victoria and Albert Museum, once hung in Wolsey's apartments. It is all the more likely as two of the characters depicted closely resemble the two monarchs in question.

The French Encampment at Ardres

Determined not to be outdone by his English 'brother', Francis I had commanded the erection of an enormous tent fashioned from cloth of gold. This marquee was 60 feet square and stood at the centre of a glittering town of tents, largely made from cloth of gold or silver. Inside, it must have appeared as if from a fairy tale; the roof was lined with a 'heavenly blue' cloth and sparkled with stars of gold under a gilded statue of St Michel. Throughout the eighteen-day meeting, protocol had determined that in the evenings the French queen and her court would play host to the English king and a number of gentlemen and ladies of the English court at Ardres, and Katharine of Aragon would reciprocate the honour to Francis at Guînes. With this in mind, it is entirely possible that Anne spent the first of her evenings dining and dancing under that star-spangled canopy with the cream of the English and French aristocracy. Indeed it would have been the first time that many an English gentleman would lay eyes on Anne's exotic allure and experience those bewitching black eyes 'that invited conversation'.

In both Guînes and Ardres dozens of tents had been pitched to accommodate each prince's retinue; this was estimated at some 6,000 alone for the English delegation and similar numbers probably made up the French court, for etiquette had been careful to craft a state of equality in all things. A French chronicler described the site at Ardres as a 'marvellous town of floating tapestries', fashioned from fabrics including canvas, taffeta and linen in a multitude of colours. However, typical of a northern European summer, wind and rain soon intervened to ruin the scene and many tents, including the French king's own, collapsed and had to be abandoned only four days after the start of the meeting. After this, the French court retreated to within the garrison town of Ardres, where they managed to provide new halls, a pavilion and a Roman theatre.

However, it seems most likely that it would be under the tent of cloth of gold on Sunday 10 June that Anne Boleyn laid eyes on her king for the first time as a mature woman of marriageable age. It is postulated that she had probably met Henry during his victorious Anglo-Imperial campaign in France in 1513, when the English forces had captured Therouanne and Tournai. Then Anne had been just a young girl of twelve in the service of Margaret of Austria. She had since been six years on the Continent, endowed with the self-confidence, manners and graces of a high-born lady of the French court. Did the pair meet, even dance together? Perhaps, but it seems that on this occasion it was Mary who caught the king's eye, for it is rumoured that it was at the Field of Cloth of Gold that the English king first set his sights on the elder Boleyn sibling.

A Family Reunion

We know that within the English delegation were Anne's parents, Sir Thomas and Elizabeth Boleyn. Sir Thomas had only four months previously relinquished his role as English ambassador to the French court to Sir Richard Wingfield. Professor Eric Ives also believed that Anne's sister, Mary, was indeed most probably there. She had been married to Sir William Carey in February 1520, and would have been present as a maid of honour to Katharine of Aragon. It is also postulated that Anne's brother, George, was also likely to have been in France, although unnamed, as one of his father's or mother's 'gentleman' attendants.

This must have been a happy time – not only a time of sumptuous festivities and thrilling tournaments, but one of reunion for Anne, who may well have not seen her mother since she left Hever in 1513.

In terms of chivalric entertainment and sheer opulence and splendour, the Field of Cloth of Gold would never be surpassed. Yet it was a political sham, and all too soon the two countries would be at war, precipitating perhaps the recall of Anne to England toward the end of 1521.

As the meeting drew to a close, the tiltyard was turned into a chapel and Wolsey sung a high Mass on Saturday 23 June. During the ceremony, the English flew a kite (some books say it was a firework) shaped like a dragon over the 'field'; this too is shown in the Hampton Court painting commemorating the event.

The Queen Mother of France, Louise of Savoy, who had been ever-present throughout, suggested a castle and church should be built on the spot where the field of arms had taken place, to immortalise the meeting, providing a place for the two kings to meet on an annual basis. It is such a tragic shame for the time traveller that this aspiration was never transformed into bricks and mortar, for today absolutely nothing remains on the ground to commemorate the twenty-four blustery days in June when history was made between two great nations and two rival kings.

Visitor Information

Visiting the Pas-de-Calais is a far cry from following in Anne's footsteps through the glamorous streets of Paris, or the opulent palaces of the picturesque Loire Valley. Like nearby Calais, there is little left to see that connects us directly to the sixteenth century and, in this case, those historic three weeks in June 1520, when the English Pale witnessed one of the most remarkable meetings in history. Therefore, perhaps this particular location is only for the most die-hard of Anne's loyal followers, determined to visit a place in which Henry first laid eyes on the mature woman who would eventually enthral his heart.

If you are visiting Calais, it is easy to combine a trip to the towns of Ardres, Guînes and the field outside the village of Balinghem (the site of the *lists* themselves). All the locations are within a few miles of each other and around fifteen–twenty minutes south of Calais itself.

Of the two main towns, Ardres and Guînes, the authors found the former was the more interesting of the two – somehow it also felt a little more welcoming. Public parking abounds, as do cafés, *boulangeries* (bakers) and *chocolateries* (chocolate/patisserie makers), where you can pick up delicious pastries and other waist-expanding delights! We recommend heading for the very centre of the town and the Place d'Armes (marketplace) next to the church.

The church itself was standing by the beginning of the sixteenth century and so it would have been a building right at the heart of the town that Anne must surely have seen daily. Also on the marketplace is the tourist information office (*office de tourisme*). We approached it with high hopes, having heard very good reports that the centre was a wealth of knowledge of the Field of Cloth of Gold. Unfortunately, on the day we were there, no-one spoke any English, so we came away with no information of use. Thankfully, with a book we found on sixteenth-century Ardres in a nearby shop and armed with our preparatory research, we managed to find what we were looking for.

Other than enjoying the delights of the church, the only other sixteenth-century survivor is one of the six bastions (stocky, defensive towers) once situated around the ramparts of the town.

Ardres was very much a military town in Anne's day, situated on the northern edge of France's territory. It had once belonged to the English and clearly there was no intention that this would happen again! To see what remains, head for the *hôtel de ville* just behind the Place d'Armes on the Rue de Lombards. At the back of it is a public park (*jardin public*). Once inside the park, walk ahead and into the garden until you can see the defensive walls. If you root around among the trees on the left-hand side of the park, you will also see the entrance to the underground tunnels that fan out underneath the bastion itself.

Having enjoyed a leisurely coffee break in the town (remember that in France most shops close for two–three hours from midday), jump back in the car and head along the D231 toward Guînes.

The marble monument that commemorates the actual site of the lists is to be found a couple of miles outside Ardres on the right-hand side of the road. However, don't expect to see any sign advertising its presence – low key is the order of the day! You will be upon it all of a sudden and there is only just room to pull over off the main road and admire, well, literally a field! Here, so many knights battled in *bonhomie* for the honour of their king and country.

We must admit that we were there on a very gusty day, not unlike the weather conditions of the time, by all accounts. Yet despite Mother Nature's assistance in creating a suitable ambience, it was difficult to sink one's imagination deep enough to recapture the moment with cars hurtling by on the adjacent road.

Afterwards, drive the short distance to Guînes, a town that has long since passed its glory days. However, you can still see the mound with a clock tower now surmounted upon it, the original motte of the town's castle. Around the town you will also come across the waters, fed by a natural spring, that once created the natural moats surrounding the fortifications and that are so clearly visible on the painting of *The Field of Cloth of Gold*.

All sense of the medieval square leading up to a rebuilt (and now crumbling) nineteenth-century church is lost. We were also disappointed to find that both the tourist information centre and the Tour de l'Horloge, a museum dedicated to the town's local history, were closed on a Saturday afternoon!

There is much debate among historians as to where Henry's temporary palace was actually situated. However, the UK television series *Time Team* identified its likely site on a special programme about the *Lost Palaces of Henry VIII*. They believe that it was situated behind the houses where the Rue Sydney Brown meets the Ruelle Mouchon. Of course, there is nothing to see there today, but it is fascinating to think that you are standing in a location depicted in one of the most famous pictures of the Tudor era.

Part 2
The Courting Years

Palace of Beaulieu (New Hall), Essex

> It is a fair old house, built with brick, low, being only of two stories, as the manner then was; the gate-house better; the court, large and pretty; the staircase of extraordinary wideness ... the hall is noble; the garden a fair plot, and the whole seat well accommodated with water; but above all I admired the fair avenue planted with stately lime trees, in four rows, for near a mile in length.
>
> John Evelyn, 10 July 1656

Conveniently located 27 miles from London and set amid vast hunting parks well stocked with deer, New Hall in Essex was one of only six royal houses in the 1520s that could comfortably accommodate the whole court. It had originally belonged to Anne's father, Thomas, who acquired it through his mother, Lady Margaret Butler, after the death of her father, Thomas Butler, Earl of Ormond. In 1516, Thomas Boleyn sold it to Henry VIII for £1,000. It is not known whether Anne visited the house in the days before her departure to the court of the Archduchess Margaret of Austria, when it was still in the hands of her Butler relatives, who entertained Henry VIII there in 1510 and 1515; however, it is almost certain that she was present when the court spent a month at New Hall in the summer of 1527.

Henry's purchase of the property in February 1516 coincided with the birth of Princess Mary. The king almost immediately ordered repairs to the new family home and purchased Flemish tapestries, hangings, beds, blankets and sheets to luxuriously furnish it, but by the end of the year new plans were in place. Instead of repairing New Hall he would rebuild it, and so Henry embarked on the first, and one of the biggest, building projects of his reign, completely transforming the former courtier's home into a magnificent royal residence between March 1517 and June 1521, at the huge cost of £17,000. He was so enamoured of his lavish new palace that in 1523 he renamed it Beaulieu, meaning beautiful place (although the name did not outlast Henry's death and reverted once more to New Hall) and visited it several times in the 1520s.

An Historic Tudor House Party – The Events of the Summer of 1527
In the summer of 1527, Henry stayed a month, surrounded by his closest friends and relations, including Anne's father and uncle. On this occasion, there was one notable

absence – Cardinal Thomas Wolsey. He was away on embassy in France and would return to find that his power – and favour – had greatly diminished and that Lady Anne Boleyn was a force to be reckoned with. On 31 July, Sir William Fitzwilliam, Treasurer of the Household and one of Wolsey's few remaining friends at court, wrote to inform him that

> the King is keeping a very great and expensive house, for there are lodged here the duke of Norfolk and his wife, the duke of Suffolk, the marquis of Exeter, the earls of Oxford, Essex and Rutland, viscounts Fitzwalter and Rocheford, both the ladies of Oxford, and others. He and the other officers intended to have reduced the expences this summer, but he does not see how it can be done. The King is merry and in good health, and hunts daily. He usually sups in his privy chamber with the dukes of Norfolk and Suffolk, the marquis of Exeter and lord Rocheford. Beaulieu, 31 July.

The king was spending much time behind closed doors with Anne's father, then known as Lord Rochford; Anne's uncle, the Duke of Norfolk; Henry's boon companion, Charles Brandon, Duke of Suffolk; and his favoured cousin, Henry Courtenay, Marquess of Exeter. All would prove themselves Wolsey's adversaries and, for the most part, support Henry's bid to annul his marriage to Katharine of Aragon. In the words of David Starkey, 'The house party at Beaulieu turned into an extended think-tank on the Great Matter.' It's difficult to not see Anne as part of these discussions or, at the very least, present. If we believe George Cavendish writing in the sixteenth century, Wolsey's enemies had joined forces and engineered his absence from court so that they might have 'convenient leisure and opportunity' to turn the king against his cardinal and he names Anne as their 'chief mistress'. This gathering would prove to be climacteric for Anne – and for England; by the end of the year, her relationship with the king would no longer be a secret and she would become Henry's acknowledged 'consort-in-waiting'.

Henry VIII's Palace of Beaulieu

In the meantime, the intrigue and politicking found a comely home in Beaulieu. Henry's stately red-brick quadrangle palace was approached from the south down an avenue lined with four rows of lime trees, almost a mile long. Visitors approached an enormous gatehouse, which was embellished with the carved royal arms of the king. Six large mullioned and transomed glazed windows stood out handsomely on the first floor of each of the flanking gateway towers, and richly carved chimney stacks promised luxury and comfort from afar. New Hall was a multi-courtyard palace, the Great Hall occupied part of the east range with a chapel in the west range. The royal apartments were probably located in the north range, which was rebuilt after 1573 by the Earl of Sussex and would have overlooked a large expanse of parkland. Henry's rambling palace also consisted of kitchens, a bakehouse, a scullery, pantries and stables in the east, and a tennis play built in a courtyard in the west. Henry was a keen tennis player and had been swatting balls from a very early age. Perhaps he showed off his skills during the month-long visit. He certainly impressed the Venetian ambassador to England, Sebastian Giustinian, who in 1519 claimed that it was 'the prettiest thing in the world to see him play; his fair skin glowing through a shirt of the finest texture'.

New Hall also boasted extensive formal gardens, an orchard and fishponds. In 1523, John Ryman was paid £60 'for making a garden at New Hall', referred to in 1530 as the 'great garden of Beaulieu'. On 15 November 1528, George Boleyn 'squire of the Body' was made 'keeper of the palace of Beaulieu', a position previously held by his brother-in-law, William Carey. George was also declared 'gardener or keeper of the garden and orchard of Newhall' and 'keeper of the wardrobe in the said palace or manor in Newhall'. These appointments entitled George to stay in chambers inside the house, or perhaps in a house on the grounds. When the court was not in residence, he had sole responsibility for the keys.

During the divorce proceedings, Princess Mary lived at New Hall for a time until she was ordered to remove to Hertford Castle, at which time George Boleyn took up residence. Chapuys related the event to Charles V on 16 October 1533:

> Nothing new has occurred except that the King has caused the Princess to dislodge from a very fine house [Beaulieu] to a very inconvenient one [Hertford Castle], and has given the former, I know not whether as a donation or otherwise, to lord Rochford, the lady's [Anne Boleyn's] brother, who has already established his household there.

After the royal party's protracted and lively stay in 1527, Henry appears to have lost interest in the house and rarely visited, if at all. Henry left the house to his daughter, Mary, in his will and it became one of her favoured residences. Early in Elizabeth's reign it was reported as being in poor condition and in 1573 was granted to Thomas Radcliffe, Earl of Sussex. John Evelyn, the English diarist, visited New Hall on 10 July 1656, noting that

> it is a fair old house, built with brick, low, being only of two stories, as the manner then was; the gate-house better; the court, large and pretty; the staircase of extraordinary wideness, with a piece representing Sir Francis Drake's action in the year 1580, an excellent sea-piece; the galleries are trifling; the hall is noble; the garden a fair plot, and the whole seat well accommodated with water; but above all I admired the fair avenue planted with stately lime trees, in four rows, for near a mile in length.

In the eighteenth century 'the fair old house' was greatly reduced in size, many of the wings were demolished including the 'noble' hall and chapel.

New Hall in the Twenty-First Century

Today, the children and young adults of New Hall School have taken over the site of Henry's 'Beautiful Place' in Essex. All that remain of the palace where Wolsey's enemies plotted to secure Anne's future are a fragment of wall, a stained-glass window from the original chapel (now at St Margaret's church, Westminster) and the arms of Henry VIII, which once adorned the enormous gatehouse and are now housed in the school's chapel. As toddlers through to senior-school students unfurl their dreams on the very site that once played a critical part in Anne's rise, it is tempting to hope that, with her love of learning and commitment to education, it's a scene she would be smiling over.

Visitor Information

New Hall School is not open to the general public. Researchers wishing to visit the site should contact the school direct via their website http://www.newhallschool.co.uk or by telephoning + 44 (0) 1245 467588. Alternatively, send an email to admin@newhallschool.co.uk. The school may be able to facilitate individual requests.

Postcode for New Hall: CM3 3HS.

Richmond Palace, Surrey

The King's goodly manour of Richemond, is sett and bullid betwene dyvers highe and pleasunt mountayns in a valley and goodly playnys felds, where the most holsem eyerys

Tudor herald, *c.* 1501

Richmond Palace in Surrey is perhaps best known to the Tudor enthusiast as the place where the first and last Tudor monarchs – Henry VII and Elizabeth I – took their last breaths, but it was also well known to Anne Boleyn, as it provided an opulent backdrop for a pivotal moment in her life, one that would establish Lady Anne as much more than just a passing fancy.

Mistress Anne and the Events of the Autumn of 1527

In late September 1527, Cardinal Wolsey returned from a mission in France. The original plan was that Henry would meet him on his journey across Kent where they would discuss the outcome of the embassy in private, just as they'd done after Wolsey's return from France in 1521. However, the original plan was discarded and instead Henry moved to Richmond with Anne, where a somewhat humiliated Wolsey arrived on 30 September. As reported by the Spanish ambassador, Iñigo de Mendoza, Wolsey immediately sent a messenger to inform the king of his return and to ask when and where they should meet for their customary private audience. The response no doubt rattled Wolsey, as it came not from the king's mouth but from Anne, who had been by Henry's side when the messenger arrived. 'Where else is the Cardinal to come?' Anne responded. 'Tell him that he may come here, where the King is.'

Mendoza remarked that 'the Legate, though extremely annoyed at a circumstance which boded no good to him, dissembled as much as he could, and concealed his resentment.' The tension in the king's privy lodgings, where the meeting presumably took place, must have been palpable and served as an ominous portent for Wolsey, who probably realised for the first time how much he'd underestimated Anne and Henry's relationship. The battle lines were drawn but it would be a few years before a decisive victor would emerge.

Rediscovering the Lost Palace of Richmond

The palace that bore witness to this showdown stood on the south bank of the River Thames, on a site formerly occupied by the Palace of Sheen, constructed by Henry V between 1414 and 1422 and largely destroyed by fire on the night of 22 December 1497. Henry VII rebuilt and renovated the palace, which dominated the surrounding countryside, as a monument to the Tudor dynasty and in 1501, when the main building works were complete, renamed it 'Rich mount'.

Approaching the house from the river, Anne would have seen the elegant façade of the royal apartments rising from the banks of the Thames, which according to Simon Thurley 'were built within the shell of the early fifteenth century donjon of the manor of Sheen'. The privy lodgings were three storeys high and built of white stone, enlivened by many octagonal and round towers, topped with cupolas and decorated with weather vanes. Each of the three floors contained twelve rooms built around an internal courtyard; the ground floor housed the household officials while the second and third floors were the king's and queen's richly furnished private apartments.

North of the lodgings, and accessible via a bridge over an inner moat, was a paved courtyard where in the centre stood a water fountain decorated with lions, Tudor dragons and other 'goodly beasts'. The courtyard was enclosed by the chapel to the east, a Great Hall to the west, an inner gatehouse to the north and a two-storey 'passage building', which connected the hall and the chapel, to the south. The stone chapel, which stood above the wine cellars, was 96 feet long and 30 feet wide. It was lavishly decorated and had a ceiling 'checkeryd with tymber' and embellished with roses and portcullis badges. On the west side was the king's privy closet, sumptuously furnished with silk hangings, carpets and cushions and on the opposite side was the queen's closet.

The equally impressive hall was also made of stone and was 100 feet long by 40 feet wide. Its timber ceiling was embellished with carved pendants and the interior adorned with statues depicting famous rulers of England, including Henry VII. To the west of the hall stood household offices, such as the pantry and larders and a freestanding kitchen, with a pyramidal roof that can be seen in Wyngaerde's view of the palace.

The inner gatehouse opened into the outer courtyard surrounded by red brick ranges in the east, west and north, which contained additional lodgings for officials and courtiers. The main gateway was in the north range and opened onto Richmond Green. The privy gardens and privy orchard lay to the east of the palace, surrounded by timber-framed two-storey galleries, the first of their kind in England, where Anne undoubtedly perambulated, admiring the knot gardens from above, and where were also found 'housis of pleasure', where visitors could pass the time playing chess, dice and cards. The galleries also linked the palace to the church of the Observant Friars that stood to the east. A Tudor herald described the gardens as 'most faire and pleasaunt' and noted that they contained 'many marvelous beasts, as lyons, dragons, and such othre of dyvers kynde'.

The palace, which also boasted a bowling alley, tennis plays and archery butts, was rarely visited by the court after 1530, as Henry preferred the comforts of Whitehall and Hampton Court Palace. In 1540 Richmond was given to Anne of Cleves as part of her divorce settlement and enjoyed something of a revival under Elizabeth I, who visited often and appears to have been genuinely fond of it.

All that is now left to see of Richmond Palace, where a young lady once outplayed a cardinal, is the main gateway and part of the outer range facing the green.

Visitor Information
Today, Richmond is a much sought-after residential location for well-heeled Londoners and subsequently is one of the wealthiest areas in the United Kingdom. Although now

part of suburban London, a little like Greenwich it maintains a 'village' feel with its own sophisticated style. Consequently, you will find plenty of restaurants, bars and boutique shops to indulge in once you have finished your Tudor adventure.

To begin this, make your way to Richmond Green. There is parking by pay and display around the green, although many locals and visitors to London will come to Richmond via the Tube (station: Richmond – District Line).

All that survives above ground of Henry VII's palace is the main gateway and part of what was once the palace wardrobe. Make your way to the west side of the park to view the typical red brick Tudor architecture that we have so come to associate with the period. A nearby noticeboard, opposite the gateway, helpfully provides an illustration of how the palace appeared in its heyday. Passing under this same structure, as Anne undoubtedly did on several occasions, notice Henry VIII's coat of arms above your head. You are now entering Old Palace Yard, originally part of the palace's outer court. In Anne's day, it was bounded by ranges of lodgings connected by galleries. Directly opposite the main gateway would have stood the middle gate building, which led through to the inner courtyard and the privy lodgings. This magnificent building once stood about halfway between the eighteenth-century Trumpeter's House, now a private residence, and the riverfront, its foundations buried beneath immaculately manicured lawns. Finally, you cannot miss the range of Tudor buildings lying to your left, originally part of Henry VIII's wardrobe.

Sadly, you can go no further here. However, if you retrace your steps and turn left, you can follow the road as it becomes Old Palace Lane. This brings you down to the river; 500 years ago, the river frontage of the palace, containing the king's lodgings, would have stretched away in front of you. You might even imagine Anne arriving at the palace with Henry by barge, brightly coloured flags bearing heraldry of the Tudor dynasty fluttering gently in the river breeze.

Before you leave Richmond behind you, consider heading to Richmond Park, situated about a mile away from the site of the old palace. This was originally part of the royal hunting park; a park that Anne would have known well. It still remains in royal hands today and forms the largest royal park in London, containing over 600 fallow and red deer. As you can imagine, it is very popular with locals, particularly when the sun is shining. You, too, can enjoy its charms. Of particular interest is King Henry's Mound, the highest point in the park. Legend has it that it is here that Henry heard the cannon of the Tower roar on the morning of 19 May 1536, a signal that Anne had been executed within the Tower precinct and that their extraordinary story was over. This is an interesting legend, but almost certainly untrue. Most modern historians agree that Henry VIII was at Whitehall Palace when he received news of Anne's execution, at which time he set off to visit Jane Seymour, whom he had lodged nearby, at Chelsea.

Postcode for Richmond Green: TW9 1QQ and for Richmond Park: TW10 5HS.

Windsor Castle, Berkshire

Calmly, from its hill-top, it enjoys the most delightful view in the world. It gazes down over the prospect of a wide and far-reaching vale, patterned with ploughland, green with meadows, clad here and there with woodlands, and watered by the softly flowing Thames.

Behind it the hills rise all round ... crowned with woods as though Nature herself has dedicated them to the chase.

Camden, English topographer

Windsor Castle was originally built by William the Conqueror as part of a ring of strategically defensive castles constructed around London shortly after the Norman invasion of England in 1066. Some 20 miles upstream from Hampton Court Palace, the mighty castle perches high on a chalky outcrop of the Chiltern Hills, almost 30 metres above the River Thames; it dominates the surrounding skyline.

Although the interior has been greatly altered over the centuries, its basic footprint remains almost completely unchanged since the original motte and bailey castle was established in 1070. Within easy reach of London, and surrounded by a royal hunting forest, Windsor quickly established itself as a much-favoured royal residence.

In external appearance, Windsor Castle certainly would have been recognisable to Anne, with one or two notable differences; for example, the central round tower was more squat than we see it today, the main exit on the southern side of the Upper Ward was from the south-west corner via a bridge crossing the original defensive ditch, while a tennis play clung to the foot of the central mound within the Upper Ward, close to the modern-day Engine Court.

Sadly, however, the Tudor interiors have been decimated in the remodelling/ refurbishment carried out by successive monarchs in the seventeenth, eighteenth and nineteenth centuries. To the uninitiated and unprepared, all trace of the Tudor apartments appear to have vanished, and it is easy to dismiss the interior rooms as irrelevant to Anne's story. Do not despair! Beneath the gaudy baroque grandeur are hidden gems of an earlier time, just waiting to be uncovered by the determined time traveller. So, with this book to hand, get ready to rediscover the lost treasures of Tudor Windsor.

The image of Windsor Castle by Hollar shows the castle as it would have looked in the sixteenth century, with the royal apartments on the north side of the Upper Ward, basically on the same footprint as the current State Apartments. The key difference between then and now was the existence of three internal courtyards, which have since been internalised within the structure of the modern-day building. The modern-day tour will take you through the following rooms. Our aim is to help orientate you to the lost chambers of the Tudor palace.

The Grand Staircase

This was the first open courtyard of the sixteenth-century castle, once known as 'Brick Court'. So, in Anne's time, you would have been standing in the open air. Once at the top of the grand staircase, you are now inside a wing of the building that ran perpendicular to the staircase on a north-south axis. Part of this wing was once occupied by the queen's watching chamber and it is within this chamber that you are now standing, although some of the walls have been taken down so it no longer appears to be a separate room.

The Waterloo Chamber

This was the second open courtyard of the Tudor royal apartments. You are now standing on what was the first-floor level in Anne's time. As you enter the chamber, imagine that running along the wall to your right was a gallery linking the queen's watching chamber to the king's watching chamber at the far end. To your left would have been two enormous oriel windows, which looked out from the king's presence chamber. This latter chamber was a key room in Anne's story – as you will discover in a moment.

The King's Drawing Room

This modern-day room was once Henry's privy chamber, the first of the private rooms to make up the king's privy lodgings. As you follow the modern-day tour of the apartments, you will pass through the king's bedchamber, once Henry's state bedchamber, dressing room and closet. All these rooms were originally part of Henry's privy chamber suite and were rooms that surely Anne knew well.

The Queen's Drawing Room and the Queen's Ballroom

These rooms have been extensively remodelled since the sixteenth century. In Anne's time, the northern end of the queen's drawing room seems to have been occupied by a chamber on the king's side, while the far end of the room was once part of Anne's bedchamber. So, in other words, this single room was once split into two. Some iconic Tudor portraits are not to be missed in this room. Once you are through into the current queen's ballroom, you find yourself in the main part of what was once Anne's privy suite. The northern part of the room, which you enter first, was occupied by the remainder of her bedchamber, and the southern end of the room comprised Anne's privy chamber.

The Queen's Audience and Presence Chambers

These two rooms originally made up a much larger, single presence chamber on the queen's side. Here Anne would formally receive guests, or hear petitions. If she were dining in public, she would do so in her presence chamber.

St George's Hall

This huge space was once divided into two. In Tudor times, the part that you enter on the modern-day tour would have been the Chapel Royal, while the second half of the room was occupied by the Great Hall, originally the main public space of the royal apartments.

The Grand Reception Room

This was once the site of the great staircase of Edward III's medieval palace. The chamber was later to become Henry's great watching chamber and, as you can see, was much bigger than its cousin at Hampton Court Palace. You can assume that it was through this room that Anne swept in regal splendour on 1 September 1532, as she made her way to the adjacent king's presence chamber. Here Anne was to receive her letters patent as the newly created Marquess of Pembroke.

The Garter Throne Room

So many lovers of Tudor history pass through this room blissfully unaware that it witnessed Anne at the zenith of her power. On 1 September 1532, she came before Henry and the court to be ennobled as Marquess of Pembroke. This elevation in her status was in preparation for the historic trip to Calais, when Henry and Anne would meet the French king, Francis I, in order to gain Francis's support for their anticipated, and imminent, marriage.

Led by Thomas Wriothesley, Henry's Garter King-at-Arms, Anne was followed by the fourteen-year-old Lady Mary Howard, Anne's younger cousin. Mary was carrying Anne's crimson velvet mantle, which was trimmed with ermine, and the gold coronet that would be placed upon her head. This day was clearly a family affair, for Anne was also accompanied by Eleanor, Countess of Rutland, and Dorothy, Countess of Sussex, both distant cousins on her mother's side.

Events at Windsor Castle

In February 1528, Anne returned to court after several months of self-imposed exile at Hever. On 25 February, Henry held a grand banquet in Anne's honour. From the *Letters and Papers of Henry VIII*, it seems that this banquet was held in 'the lodge in the little park' at Windsor. Anne no longer appears to have been in Katharine's service by this time, yet in 1528 the queen still presided at court. It is possible that Henry gave Anne private lodgings in one of the lodges in Windsor Park. There are records of such a lodge in what is now called 'Home Park', which stands close to the south-east corner of the castle, although sadly this lodge no longer stands today.

On 3 March 1528, Anne invited Thomas Heneage to sup with her in her lodgings. Thomas was Cardinal Wolsey's man and, during a dinner aimed at influencing the cardinal in a wardship dispute, she famously mentioned how much she would like carp and shrimp from the cardinal's fish pools at Hampton Court for Lent.

In June–July 1531, Henry left Katharine at Windsor and headed off on progress with Anne. He never saw Katharine, his wife of twenty years, again.

As we have already described, on 1 September 1532 Anne was created Marquess of Pembroke in a glittering ceremony in the king's presence chamber at Windsor Castle.

In July and August 1533, a heavily pregnant Anne was left behind at Windsor while Henry rushed off to Guildford to meet with George Boleyn. Lord Rochford had freshly returned from France with the news that Henry was being sidelined in discussions between the Pope and King Francis. This was a crisis meeting, and George was immediately dispatched back to France to give the Duke of Norfolk orders to return to England immediately. Shortly after Henry's return to Windsor, the couple headed back to Greenwich where Anne took to her chambers in anticipation of the birth of her son.

Authors' Favourites

Stand a moment in the Garter Throne Room and, in your imagination, watch the ceremony in which Anne's letters patent were read out to the court by Stephen Gardiner. In front of the throne, the king put an ermine-trimmed mantel of crimson velvet about Anne's shoulders and, befitting her newly elevated status, placed a golden coronet upon her head.

Visit the Chapel of St George and see the simple tombstone of Henry VIII himself set into the floor of the chancel. He is buried beneath your feet in the crypt below, alongside Jane Seymour. Don't forget to also locate the plain tombstone marking the burial site of Anne's long-time enemy, Charles Brandon, Duke of Suffolk, toward the south door of the chapel. The plain black marble gravestone carries the simple inscription 'Charles Brandon, Duke of Suffolk, K. G. Died August 24 1545. Married Mary, daughter of Henry VII. Widow of Louis XII, King of France.'

Also, while you are in the Windsor area, consider visiting the Ankerwyke Yew, near Wraysbury. Legend has it that Anne and Henry used to meet under its lugubrious branches during the halcyon days of their courtship. The yew tree is famous for its longevity. It is believed to be approximately 2,500 years old and stands in what were the grounds of the Priory of St Mary, which was later dismantled during the Dissolution of the Monasteries. It is a truly magical place, venerated over the centuries, and it is easy to imagine Henry and Anne stealing some private time away from the prying eyes of the wider court under its magnificent canopy.

Visitor Information
Windsor Castle is still owned by the Crown and is very much a royal family home to this day. Therefore, only some of the parts in which we are interested, including the state chambers, are open to the public. It is a popular tourist destination and so the castle and town can get very busy in the height of summer. If you want to avoid some of the queues, get there at opening time or book tickets in advance via the website: http://www.royalcollection.org.uk/visit/windsorcastle, or telephone +44 (0)207 766 7304.

Postcode for Windsor Castle: SL4 1NJ.

Beddington Place (Carew Manor), Surrey

a fair house (or palace rather) … which, by advantage of the water, is a paradise of pleasure.

In 1528, a besotted King Henry VIII poured out his heart in an amorous letter to Anne Boleyn:

Mine own Sweetheart, this shall be to advertise you of the great elengeness that I find here since your departing; for, I ensure you methinketh the time longer since your departing now last, than I was wont to do a whole fortnight. I think your kindness and my fervency of love causeth it; for, otherwise, I would not have thought it possible that for so little a while it should have grieved me. But now that I am coming towards you, methinketh my pains be half removed; and also I am right well comforted in so much that my book maketh substantially for my matter; in looking whereof I have spent above four hours this day, which causeth me now to write the shorter letter to you at this time, because of some pain in my head; wishing myself (especially an evening) in my sweetheart's arms, whose pretty dukkys I trust shortly to kiss.

Written by the hand of him that was, is, and shall be yours by his own will,

H. R.

As a result of the impending arrival of Cardinal Lorenzo Campeggio, the papal legate sent to hear the case for Henry's annulment, Anne had been sent, for propriety's sake, to her parent's house at Hever.

Although she had only been gone from court a couple of days, to Henry it felt like 'a whole fortnight'. David Starkey examines this letter in *Six Wives* and explains that the word *elengeness* means loneliness, dreariness or misery. Henry was missing Anne terribly and dreaming of holding her in his arms and kissing her 'pretty dukkys' (breasts).

He describes his only comforts at this desolate time being the 'book' he was writing (to help argue the case for his divorce) and the knowledge of their impending reunion: 'Now that I am coming towards you methinketh my pains be half removed.'

Henry had decided that, if Anne could not be with him in London, they would meet at Beddington Place, almost halfway between the Boleyn home at Hever and London. This was the home of Anne's cousin, Sir Nicholas Carew, one of Henry's young favourites and a member of his privy chamber. At Beddington, Carew built a 'fair house (or palace rather) ... which, by advantage of the water, is a paradise of pleasure.' A grand deer park was attached to the manor and, according to John Phillips, at its peak 'occupied almost all the land between London Road, Wallington and Beddington Lane. Its northern edge adjoined Mitcham Common and its southern edge ran along Croydon Road and then around Carew Manor and its gardens to Beddington Lane.'

Thomas Coryate in his *Crudities* of 1600 praised the water gardens as did the seventeenth-century diarist John Evelyn. In the diary of a young traveller, Baron Waldstein, recorded in 1600, the lush grounds of Beddington are brought to life in some detail:

> We made a four mile detour via Beddington in order to see a most lovely garden belonging to a nobleman called Francis Carew. A little river runs through the middle of this garden, so crystal clear that you see the water plants beneath the surface. A thing of interest is the oval fish pond enclosed by trim hedges. The garden contains a beautiful square shaped rock, sheltered on all sides and very cleverly contrived: the stream flows right through it and washes all around. In the stream one can see a number of different representations: the best of these is Polyphome playing on his pipe, surrounded by all kinds of animals. There is also a Hydra out of whose many heads the water gushes. The garden also contained orange trees that were covered by a removable wooden shed, or sheds, each autumn and heated with stoves over the winter to keep the frost at bay.

And so it was here – in Nicholas Carew's grand moated manor house, surrounded by a fine deer park and picturesque gardens, the predecessor to his son's famous Elizabethan gardens – that Anne and Henry retreated for four days of business and pleasure.

This is not the place to discuss in detail the events surrounding the legate's arrival in England, except to say (so that we might try to understand how they felt when reunited at Beddington) that Henry and Anne believed, or at least hoped, that with Campeggio's arrival there would come an end to their troubles. Frustratingly for the would-be lovers, his arrival heralded a period of immense irritation; Campeggio had been in England for five weeks at the time of their meeting and, rather than bring the case closer to a solution, was doing everything in his power to stall proceedings.

The exquisite gardens and park surrounding the house must have offered some relief, and the hunting a welcome distraction from the present situation. But it's clear that the couple did not completely ignore the business at hand, for when Henry returned to London on 14 November 1528, he was re-energised and armed with a fresh plan – he would send a new embassy to Rome headed by another Boleyn kin, Sir Francis Bryan.

The house that Anne knew no longer stands; the present house was rebuilt in the early eighteenth century and is today home to Carew Manor School. The only substantial remainder of the original house is a splendid Tudor hall, which boasts a fine early sixteenth-century arch-braced hammerbeam roof that rivals the magnificence of the Great Hall at Hampton Court Palace, although on a smaller scale.

Within the hall, Henry and Anne would have been lavishly entertained by their host and, although the interior has been much altered since Tudor times, it remains a very imposing space.

Authors' Favourites

Apart from the magnificent Great Hall, take your time exploring the grounds where other great Tudor personalities met for rendezvous. In May 1536, Jane Seymour took up temporary residence at Beddington Park and was visited by Henry discreetly under the cover of darkness.

Local legend has it that Elizabeth I and Sir Walter Raleigh used to take walks in the park and some even say that Raleigh's embalmed head is buried on the grounds!

What more could a Tudor enthusiast ask for?

Visitor Information

The Grade I-listed hall is open on select days. Tours run on Sundays only, a couple of times a year, and must be booked in advance. Telephone number: + 44 (0) 2087 704781.

Postcode for Carew Manor School: SM6 7NH.

Bridewell Palace, London

> Mademoiselle de Boulan is at last come thither [London], and the King has lodged her in a very fine lodging, which he has prepared for her close by his own. Greater court is now paid to her every day than has been to the Queen for a long time.
>
> Du Bellay, the French ambassador, 9 December 1528

On 9 December 1528, Jean du Bellay reported that Anne was back at court and lodged in splendour near to the king. Where this residence was is unclear; however, it has been suggested that the 'fine lodging' may in fact have been a suite at Bridewell Palace built from August 1515 onwards, on the west bank of the River Fleet, south of Fleet Street and adjacent to the Dominican House of Blackfriars. For several years after its completion in 1523, it was used as the king's principal London residence, as Westminster Palace had been devastated by fire early in Henry's reign.

The Arrangement of the Buildings at Bridewell Palace

The palace in Anne's day consisted of two brick courtyards; the inner court contained the royal apartments and was approached through a grand processional staircase from the outer court, which also housed the main gatehouse, possibly a chapel and kitchens. From the east side of the outer court, a 240-foot timber-framed covered gallery extended out over the River Fleet connecting the palace and Blackfriars. The southern range of the principal courtyard contained the king's watching chamber and the king's presence chamber, from where there extended south, towards the riverfront, a long gallery of about 200 feet, which commanded views over the privy gardens and terminated at two octagonal towers and a watergate on the River Thames. The king's lodgings appear to have been on the second floor in the southern end of the western range, and the queen's opposite the courtyard, on the first floor. Both were double height, undoubtedly luxurious and flooded by light pouring in through the tall windows.

In June and July 1529, Henry stayed at Bridewell often while the legatine court, charged with deciding the fate of his marriage to Katharine, was in session at Blackfriars. On 18 June, to the great surprise of all those present, Katharine of Aragon attended the opening of the court in person and on 21 June both Henry and Katharine were present. The French ambassador noted that the public, especially the women, were on Katharine's side. As the royal couple made their way from Bridewell across the gallery to Blackfriars, the queen was 'warmly greeted by immense crowds of people, who publicly wished her victory over her enemies'. Henry was enraged but there was little he could do to alter public opinion.

The Decline of Bridewell Palace

In 1529, Henry acquired Hampton Court Palace and Whitehall and lost interest in Bridewell, not using it at all after 1530 from when it became, primarily, a residence for the French ambassadors. Perhaps the palace's appeal had been marred by memories of the crowds that had gathered to cheer on a queen that Henry no longer wanted.

It has been suggested that Holbein's masterpiece, *The Ambassadors*, which depicts Jean de Dinteville, French ambassador to England in 1533, and Georges de Selve, Bishop of Lavaur, may have been painted at Bridewell.

In 1553, King Edward VI granted Bridewell to the City of London to house vagrants and homeless children. The site was subsequently used as a prison, hospital and a school. Much of the palace was destroyed in the Great Fire of 1666, partially rebuilt and finally demolished in the 1860s.

In 1978 part of the site was excavated when 9 Bridewell Place in London was demolished. Archaeologists uncovered the foundations of both sides of the southern end of the eastern wing of the inner courtyard, thereby pinpointing the exact location of the palace complex, which extended south to the area today occupied by the Crowne Plaza Hotel and Unilever House.

Visitor Information

A commemorative plaque on 14 New Bridge Street in London today marks the site of Bridewell Palace. The plaque reads:

Here stood the Palace of Bridewell built by Henry VIII in 1523 and granted by Edward VI in 1553 to the City of London to house Bridewell Royal Hospital founded by royal charter in the same year. The present building was erected in 1802 and in 1862 the Court Room of Bridewell Royal Hospital was incorporated therein.

Above the doorway of the office building is a relief portrait of Edward VI.

Postcode for Unilever House: EC4V 6JJ and for Crowne Plaza Hotel: EC4V 6BD.

Durham House, London

In July, 1536, Cuthbert, Bishop of Durham, granted to the king 'all that his capytall messuage … comenly called Durham Place, wyth all Houses, Buyldyngs, Gardeyns, Orcheards, Pooles, fysshyngs, stables and all other commodytes'.

On the late spring day of 29 May 1532, the king's watermen ferried Anne over the choppy, polluted Thames to visit her father, Sir Thomas Boleyn, at his London residence, Durham House. In almost exactly a year's time, she'd have no need of the king's barge – as queen she'd have her own – but today's family reunion was courtesy of the king. There is no record of their conversation, but the venue, at least, was a pleasant one.

Set back from the river, Anne's first glimpse of the grand home was of the Great Hall, described in around 1592 as 'stately and high, supported with loftie marble pillers', which abutted the river and was accessed via steps. It was said to 'standeth upon the Thamise [Thames] very pleasantly'. As the watermen drew closer, the gardens, stretching towards the riverfront, and orchards came into view. Its water features and fishponds would have appealed to the future queen's keen eye for aesthetics.

Durham House in the Strand was the London residence of the bishops of Durham and one of several palatial houses that lined the street. During the fifteenth and sixteenth centuries its richly furnished apartments were increasingly used as accommodation for royalty, foreign dignitaries and favoured courtiers, including Sir Thomas Boleyn and, towards the end of the sixteenth century, Sir Walter Raleigh. In the last decades of the seventeenth century, John Aubrey praised Durham House's inspiring qualities. While the property included the usual features of prestige homes – chapel, stables, cellars and 'other commodytes'– it was recognised as a scholarly retreat, as Aubrey's recollection of Raleigh's study highlights:

> I well remember his study, which was a little turret which looked into and over the Thames, and had the prospect which is pleasant perhaps as any in the world, and which not only refreshes the eiesight but cheeres the spirits and (to speake my mind) I believe enlarges an ingeniose man's thoughts.

In 1529, the house was temporarily under royal control – in February of that year, Thomas Wolsey had exchanged the Bishopric of Durham for the See of Winchester and a new bishop was not appointed until the following year. Four months later, on 14 June 1529, Henry wound his way along the Thames, travelling from Hampton Court Palace to Greenwich, and visited Thomas Boleyn on the way. According to John Foxe, a sixteenth-century historian and author of *Actes and Monuments*, Thomas Boleyn lived at Durham House in the summer of 1529. It seems likely that it was his city base until after his daughter's downfall: 'The King, coming by water, landed, in passing, at my lord of Rocheford's, with a small company of ladies and gentlemen, where he waited for the tide, and then went to Greenwich.'

Queen Katharine of Aragon had made her way to Greenwich by land and so was not present at this intimate gathering. Anne, on the other hand, almost certainly was. In July, Henry stayed at Durham House for almost two weeks, while the legatine court was being held at Blackfriars. The queen had removed to Greenwich and so it's likely that Henry and Anne sought refuge in the house, surrounded by their family and supporters.

Later in the year, once the couple had returned from their summer progress, John Foxe asserts that the king summoned Anne's father and asked him to 'let Dr Cranmer have entertainment in your house at Durham Place for a time, to the intent he may be there quiet to accomplish my request, and let him lack neither books nor anything requisite for his study'. The king had requested that Cranmer prepare a 'book' on the king's case for a divorce and so the weighty tome was penned, ultimately, under the guidance of Thomas and his daughter Anne.

Anthony Martienssen, Katherine Parr's biographer, went as far as to claim that Henry had put Anne in charge of the Durham House think-tank, not implausible when we consider that on 12 October 1529, du Bellay, the French Ambassador, reported that Thomas Boleyn had previously told him that 'none of the other [councillors] have any credit at all [with Henry] unless it pleased the Young Lady [Anne] to lend them some', a claim that the ambassador concluded was 'as true as the Gospel'.

The years that followed, like the roiling waters of the Thames, were turbulent and murky for the lady who'd so commanded the king's heart. In July 1536, with a meek new queen by his side, Henry acquired the property, then still described as 'late in the occupacyon of the Right Honourable Thomas, Erle of Wyltshyre', by exchange from Bishop Tunstall. Of this house that nurtured great scholars and sheltered an aspiring queen, sadly nothing remains. It was dismantled in the middle of the seventeenth century, but the Thames that drew Anne there still ebbs and flows, the beating heart of an ancient city.

Visitor Information

In the middle of the eighteenth century what remained of Durham House was demolished to make way for the Adelphi Buildings, a block of neoclassical terrace houses built by the Adam brothers (John, Robert, James and William) between 1768 and 1774 on the site formerly occupied by Durham House's buildings and gardens. Some of the large terraces were built parallel to the river, and others on two or three streets running at right angles to it. Sadly, all but one of the terraces was demolished in the 1930s to make way for an Art Deco building. Number 3 Robert Street, London, is the sole survivor and is today occupied by offices, namely that of the Chartered Institute of Public Finance & Accountancy (CIPFA).

Durham House stood between the river and the Strand, an area that today includes Robert Street, Adelphi Terrace, Adam Street and John Adam Street.

Postcode for CIPFA: WC2N 6RL.

Waltham Abbey, Essex

The xiiii day paied to one in rewarde for bringing home Ball the kings dog that was loste in the forrest of Waltham.

Privy Purse Expenses, May 1530

Layers of history jostle for attention in the small market town of Waltham Abbey in Essex, a place of pilgrimage and worship since at least the seventh century. It was founded in the eleventh century to house a miraculous cross brought to Waltham by Tovi the Proud, Marshall to King Cnut, and is said to be the burial place of King Harold II – the last Saxon king – whose body, it's claimed, was brought to Waltham after his death at the Battle of Hastings in 1066.

In the twelfth century, Henry II was required to found three new monastic houses as part of the penance ordained by Pope Alexander III for his part in the murder of Thomas Becket, Archbishop of Canterbury. He chose Waltham as one of those and in 1184 its status was altered to that of an abbey.

An intriguing backstory, but what of the town's connection to Anne Boleyn? Happily, it does not disappoint.

The Augustinian abbey at Waltham was one of the most prosperous of the country and a popular place for kings to stay during hunting trips in nearby Waltham Forest, known from the seventeenth century as Epping Forest. Henry VIII was a regular visitor and on several occasions was accompanied by Anne Boleyn.

A copy of the king's 1529 summer progress survives and confirms that the court arrived at Waltham on 2 August, shortly after the adjournment of the Blackfriars Court (where the case for Henry's annulment was being heard), remaining there for nine nights before leaving for Thomas Wolsey's residence at Barnet on 11 August.

Anne's presence can be taken for granted, as it's highly unlikely that the couple would have separated at such a crucial time and, furthermore, Eustace Chapuys, the Imperial ambassador to England, notes that Anne was with the king on progress the following month.

In September, the court visited Henry Carey's residence in Buckingham, the home of Anne's three-year-old nephew, who the year before had lost his father, William Carey, to the sweating sickness. This stop was surely the result of Anne's desire to visit her recently widowed sister, Mary Carey, and again attests to her being by Henry's side during this period.

The King's Secretary, Almoner and a Cambridge Scholar

As the abbey could not house the entire court, Stephen Gardiner, the king's secretary, and Edward Foxe, both educated at Cambridge, were accommodated nearby at the house of a Mr Cressy and there they were reunited with a mutual acquaintance, another Cambridge man, who unbeknown to them would go on to change the course of history and become one of Anne's most staunch supporters – the future Archbishop of Canterbury, Dr Thomas Cranmer.

It was at this historic meeting, during a discussion about the king's Great Matter, that Cranmer suggested a new way of resolving the king's present predicament: forget the legal case in Rome and instead canvass the opinions of theologians, as this issue, as far as Cranmer could determine, was moral rather than legal.

Although not a completely novel idea, when the king was told of Cranmer's view he was immediately intrigued and requested an interview with him that eventually took place at Greenwich in October 1529. From this moment on, Cranmer and the Boleyns were inextricably connected.

In September 1530, the court returned to Waltham Abbey and stayed from the 11th until the 20th. Anne's presence is confirmed by a record in the *Privy Purse Expenses*, detailing a payment made as compensation for a cow that was killed by two greyhounds, one of which belonged to 'my ladye Anne', the other to one Urian Brereton of the privy chamber, the brother of William Brereton who was executed in May 1536.

In September and October 1531, Henry made further visits. It's very likely that Anne was with him on these occasions as Katharine had been banished and Chapuys recorded that 'she [Anne] always accompanies the King at his hunting parties, without any female attendants of her own, while the Queen herself who used formerly to follow him on such expeditions has been ordered to remain at Vinsor [Windsor]'.

The next glimpse we have of Anne at Waltham comes in July 1532, when she and Henry stayed for five days. Gilles de la Pommeraie, the French ambassador, accompanied the couple over the summer and recorded in his correspondences that he hunted with Anne and spent time alone with her watching 'the deer run'.

During these visits the couple almost certainly stayed at the Augustinian abbey; unfortunately, the monastic buildings and part of the church were destroyed at the time of the Dissolution in 1540. The abbey lays claim to being one of the last monastic houses in the area to be dissolved and was leased to Anthony Denny in 1541.

The next ten years saw most of the abbey buildings demolished, with the exception of the nave of the Norman church and a fourteenth-century Lady Chapel and undercroft, both incorporated into the present-day church. In 1556 a tower was added at the west end of the church, using materials from the demolished abbey, and today dominates the building's façade.

Today visitors can also see the remains of the fourteenth-century gatehouse and bridge, and the walls of a house built after the Dissolution.

As to where Henry stayed during his visits, there is another possibility. Tradition has it that he possessed a small house in Romeland, to which he is said to often 'privately retire, for his pleasure'. One imagines that such a house would have afforded Henry and Anne greater privacy away from the leering eyes of the court. A later writer recorded that Henry made use of this house in 1529 when one would have expected him to reside at the abbey; this date fits perfectly with Anne's first visit and makes sense as the couple were, at this time, still attempting to maintain some semblance of discretion.

The building is no longer extant although excavation in the area has revealed a substantial fifteenth-century screens passage house, believed to have been the one leased by Henry.

Waltham Abbey has a fascinating story to tell; its rich history, not to mention its important Tudor connections, makes it an intriguing destination to explore.

Myth alert! Tradition has it that Henry VIII awaited news of Anne's execution at High Beach, a hamlet a few kilometres from Waltham Abbey. The story, as recounted by Winters in the *History of the Parish of Waltham Abbey* (1888), is that Henry wanted to be at some distance from London but still close enough to 'have the satisfaction of hearing the Tower guns fired as a signal of that awful tragedy being ended'. An interesting connection, but one that the authors have not found corroborated by any contemporary source. In fact, it's almost certain that Henry received the news of Anne's death at his Palace of Whitehall.

Visitor Information

To see all that Waltham has to offer the Tudor tourist, park your car at the far end of the Cornmill Car Park, cross over the stream by the wooden bridge and walk alongside the stream that Henry may have used to bring Anne into Waltham Abbey. Cross the road to Barge Yard and look at the landing site, also viewing the Olympic medal on the roundabout, which has Henry's head on it along with King Harold's.

From there, walk down Highbridge Street, passing the site of Henry's house in Romeland on the left. Continue past the tourist information centre and into the church.

Here look out for the marvellous late Elizabethan monument to Sir Edward Denny and his wife, Lady Margaret. The couple's ten children can be seen praying for the souls of their parents beneath the effigies.

From there ascend the steps to the fourteenth-century Lady Chapel, where on the east wall is a fifteenth-century Doom painting.

You might also like to visit the Epping Forest District Museum on Sun Street to find out more about the town's history. As a bonus, the museum is housed in a sixteenth-century building, and in the Tudor gallery visitors can see Tudor wall-panelling, originally from the Abbey House and built in the 1590s to the north-east of the present-day church.

And, of course, take your time exploring the park around the abbey where its ancient monastic past remains palpable.

Postcode for Cornmill Car Park: EN9 1RB.

Barnet Manor, Essex

The book of Statutes of the Household, signed by the King, is in the cofferer's custody, who has gone to his house in Sussex, and does not intend to come to the King before Bartholomew's Day. His books are in his house at London. Until the King comes to his standing house none can get at them but himself. If Wolsey wants it in a hurry, will send a servant to the cofferer to make him haste to London. Barnett, Tuesday.

Sir Henry Guildford to Cardinal Wolsey, 15 August 1525

In the eleventh century an important route north out of London to St Albans passed through Barnet, and on its fringes a town developed. As a result of the increased traffic, many inns sprung up with names like 'Red Lion', the 'Rose and Crown', the 'Antelope' and the 'Cardynalles Hat.'

The area, perhaps best known to the history enthusiast as the setting for the Battle of Barnet (fought on 14 April 1471 between the warring houses of Lancaster and York and decisively won by Edward IV), belonged to the Abbey of St Albans and remained the abbot's property until the Dissolution. With Wolsey acting as absentee abbot from 1522 to 1529, the manor was at his disposal.

It's no surprise then to find the court there in 1522, 1525 and 1529, making use of the cardinal's house, though Wolsey himself was not present on any of these occasions. In fact, there is no record of Wolsey having ever visited the manor.

On 11 August 1529, Henry VIII and Anne Boleyn arrived at Barnet. The very next day, Stephen Gardiner wrote to Wolsey that the king 'wishes Angus to come to Barnet this day at noon to take leave of him. Has spoken to Master Controller that Norfolk may tell him what inn to repair to. Gardiner would have come himself, but the King bid him stay. Barnet, this Thursday.'

Unfortunately there is no record of where the court stayed during visits and no surviving grand manor or local tradition to speak of. The lack of sources is further complicated by the fact that there is not just one Barnet but two. East Barnet is 2 miles south-east of Chipping Barnet, which is also known as High Barnet or simply Barnet.

It has been suggested that an ancient manor house once stood close to the church of St Mary in East Barnet, but no sources have yet come to light to substantiate the claim or confirm that it ever housed any royal visitors.

It seems that for now, the answers we seek remain frustratingly out of reach.

Tittenhanger House (Tyttenhanger), Hertfordshire

Since the King's coming to Tittenhanger he has been very well, and merrier than he was since his departure from Greenwich. He likes your house very well.

John Russell to Cardinal Wolsey, June 1528

Since at least the fourteenth century and up until the Dissolution, the Abbey of St Albans owned the manor of Tittenhanger, near Shenley, and there the abbots had a house that Wolsey acquired in 1522 when he became titular Abbot of St Albans. Very little is known of the appearance of the manor house, but it must have been fairly substantial, as it played host to many distinguished guests over the years, including Henry and Anne.

The house was originally constructed in the late fourteenth century and extended and altered by the successive abbots. In *A History of the County of Hertford: volume 2*, we learn that the manor was desirable because of 'the wonderful fertility of the soil, the beauty of the woods, and the plentiful supply of water for fishponds'.

In June/July 1528, an epidemic of sweating sickness in London drove Henry VIII and Katharine of Aragon to seek refuge there for a fortnight; Anne Boleyn was not with the king on this occasion, as she had retired to her parents' home at Hever.

Henry was clearly very impressed by what he saw and is described by John Russell, in a letter to Cardinal Wolsey, as being very happy there and liking the house 'very well'.

The court returned again for three days in August 1529; by this time Anne's influence was such that she – and her supporters – were almost constantly by the king's side. On at least two of the three days, Wolsey too was at court.

One imagines that the cardinal must have relished this time with the king, as his situation had become increasingly precarious and access to Henry, as Wolsey well understood, often meant the difference between life and death. Sadly for Wolsey, the respite was short-lived and things were about to get worse (see entry for Grafton Manor).

In 1539 the Abbey of St Albans was dissolved and the manor passed to the Crown. It remained the property of the king until 1547 at which time it was granted to Sir Thomas Pope, the founder of Trinity College in Oxford.

In around 1655, the medieval manor was demolished and a new building constructed in its place; this was further extended and altered in the eighteenth century and the result is the building we see today. It remained a family home until 1973 when it was converted to commercial offices and today is also a venue for corporate and special events.

While no image of the house that Anne visited survives, and no further details are known about her stay, the majestic splendour of the parkland that surrounds the house today hints at Tittenhanger's former charms.

Visitor Information

Tyttenhanger Park lies within sight of the busy M25 (London orbital motorway). To reach it, exit at Junction 22. Follow the signs to Colney Heath, along Coursers Road. The entrance to the park is the third turn on the left, just half a mile or so along the road.

Although the house that Anne once knew is long gone, it is thought that it stood just in front of where the current property is situated. Although pleasing to the eye in its own right, the symmetrical clean lines of the house, so typical of the later period in which it was built, may do little to stir the senses of a Tudor enthusiast.

Open days are usually held once a year in January. Please visit the Tyttenhanger Park website for more information at http://www.tyttenhangerpark.com. Alternatively, if you contact Paul at Weddings@TyttenhangerPark.com or call + 44 (0) 1727 744300, you can arrange to visit privately during office hours. A small charge of around £5–10 will be payable to cover costs.

If you need to take refreshments, you can always visit nearby St Albans, which is a city steeped in medieval and Tudor history. There are many restaurants and bars in this busy market town. Don't miss popping in to visit the cathedral and the adjacent Abbey Park, which contains the oldest pub in England: the Ye Olde Fighting Cocks Public House.

Postcode for Tittenhanger House: AL4 0PG.

The Old Palace of Woodstock, Oxfordshire

> In the afternoon we turned some 6 miles off our route to the Palace of Woodstock, which is a very extensive royal residence built by Henry the First. He gave it a large park surrounded by a stone wall ... The Royal domain lies in a valley where a brook wanders lazily through meadows, all very picturesquely; the palace itself is sited on a mound in order to give a better view of the surrounding hills and closely wooded country.
>
> Baron Waldstein, 15 July 1600

Perched regally on a hill in Woodstock, 8 miles north of Oxford, the Palace of Woodstock stood amid magnificent rolling parkland and ancient woodland. By the time Henry VIII ascended the throne, it had been a favoured royal retreat for over 400 years, visited by most English monarchs, including Queen Anne Boleyn.

Woodstock was one of only six royal residences in the 1520s that could accommodate the whole court and as such featured regularly on the king's itinerary, both in the summer and winter months. Anne accompanied the king on at least four occasions, the first being in late August 1529 when the couple spent six days there in the company of the cream of the English nobility, including the dukes of Norfolk and Suffolk, before retreating with a small entourage to the nearby satellite house at Langley, while the majority of the court, as recorded by Sir Brian Tuke, 'tarry here [at Woodstock] till he [the king] returns, which will be within two days'. Evidently, the king, almost certainly in the company of Anne, enjoyed the greater privacy afforded at Langley, as the stay was extended to four days. The couple returned to Woodstock on 4 September and remained there for a further five days.

In August 1531, we find the court again in residence, where Henry made the most of the diversions on offer, spending much of his time hunting, shooting, fishing and hawking. We can be certain of Anne's presence by Henry's side – Eustace Chapuys reported that she 'always accompanies the King at his hunting parties' – and imagine her, lean and graceful atop her mount, her laughter ringing out across the treetops, enjoying the sport just as much as the burly noblemen jostling for the king's favour.

The court returned in August 1532, Anne's joy plain for all to see, as she must have known how close she was to vanquishing her rival; plans for a visit to Calais were well in hand and her own elevation to Marquess of Pembroke only weeks away. In what must have been a heartbreaking contrast for Anne, when the court returned two years later the mood was more sombre. This visit was marred by the memory of the recent loss of her child in the final stages of pregnancy and her increasingly strained relationship with the king.

Woodstock: A Palace and a Prison

There were many reasons why Woodstock had lured royalty for centuries. It was a spacious double-courtyard mansion entered through a 'large, strong and fayre Gatehouse' decorated with the heraldic devices of Henry VII, which led to 'the great outer court', in 1650 recorded as measuring 'three roods and 12 perches' (3,339 metres squared). A fountain adorned with beasts stood in the centre of the courtyard. Opposite the gatehouse was the hall, approached by a flight of stairs, at the foot of which stood four beasts on pedestals and on the left of the hall was found the 'neat and stately, rich Chappel'. The outer court gave access to a smaller inner court, which measured '2 roods' (2,023 metres squared). The privy chamber overlooked the tennis play and the withdrawing and bedchambers boasted views of the privy garden. The principal rooms were plastered and heated by fireplaces, more than ninety of them according to a late sixteenth-century survey. Little else is known about the layout and appearance of the house that Anne knew.

During Henry VIII's reign, Woodstock was a place for sport and festivities but, under the rule of his daughter Mary, it was used as a prison for the teenaged Lady Elizabeth. She was held captive in the house for just under a year, after being implicated in the failed Wyatt rebellion of 1554. It is said that during her captivity she used a diamond to scratch these words of protest on a window:

Much suspected by me,
nothing proved can be,
Quoth Elizabeth prisoner.

The palace was already in decay at the time of Elizabeth's incarceration and was virtually destroyed during the English Civil War. All further traces were cleared when Blenheim Palace was built across the valley at the beginning of the eighteenth century.

Locating the Lost Palace of Woodstock

Today, thousands of people visit Blenheim each year; it is a World Heritage Site and the birthplace of Winston Churchill. The home was a gift from Queen Anne (last monarch of the house of Stuart) to John Churchill, 1st Duke of Marlborough, following his victory at the Battle of Blenheim in 1704. It is surrounded by 2,000 acres of landscaped parkland, beautiful formal gardens and a great lake. Sadly, the site of the Old Palace of Woodstock is away from the public path and so most passers-by remain oblivious to the significance of the site. It is a pity considering that the sheer beauty and tranquility of the surrounding landscape make it a perfect place to sit contemplatively in history's embrace beneath the shade of majestic maples and oaks. Listen to the ground and the rustle of leaves as they whisper to you of the lives of those whom time has stolen.

Visitor Information

In order to visit the site of the old Palace of Woodstock, you will need to purchase a ticket for the Park and Gardens, considerably less expensive than purchasing a ticket that includes access to Blenheim Palace (in 2013, £12 as opposed to a staggering £21 for a single adult). There is plenty of parking on-site, and you will be directed as to where to leave your car.

To find the site of the Old Palace of Woodstock, you need to make your way to the right of the main visitor entrance to Blenheim Palace. This will bring you round to the front of the house, which overlooks the lake. Turn your back on the spectacle of Blenheim and cross the grand bridge in front of you, heading away from the palace. You are making for the far side of the lake. Once on the other side of the bridge, veer off the path to your right, where a stone plinth, set above the lake on a broad plateau, marks the site of the palace that Anne once knew.

If you need rest and refreshments, Blenheim Palace has a café and toilets adjacent to the main house. Or instead you may wish to walk round the lake toward the entrance, flanked by a splendid arched gateway that leads directly into Park Street, the main street of Woodstock, a pretty little Oxfordshire town. Here you will find tea shops, pubs and restaurants galore. Our personal favourite is to do a very English thing and take afternoon cream tea in the Blenheim Guesthouse and Tea Room, just on your right as you enter Park Street.

Alternatively, to make the day complete for the more energetic among you, there are many beautiful walks around the parkland that can be downloaded from the Blenheim Palace website at http://www.blenheimpalace.com/thepalace/whattosee/parkandwalks.html.

Postcode for the Old Palace of Woodstock: OX20 1PP.

Grafton Manor, Northamptonshire

> the bravest and best seat in the kingdom, a seat for a prince and not a subject.
>
> John Bridges, *History of Northamptonshire*

To the uninitiated traveller, the sleepy hamlet of Grafton Regis, perched high on a ridge in the south of Northamptonshire, could easily seem nothing more than a quintessentially English rural idyll. Away from the busy Northampton Road, one is soon subsumed by quiet country lanes that wend their way by old, stone cottages toward the ancient heart of the village, all the time giving glimpses of the most splendid views across open countryside to the north and south. However, great history is belied by its sleepy charms, and Anne is found here alongside the king and at the centre of one of the most famous events in the king's reign – as we shall shortly hear. In all, we know that Henry VIII visited Grafton in September 1529, then again in September 1531, July 1532 and October 1534. All the evidence suggests that Anne was at the king's side on all four occasions.

The Story of the Manor of Grafton Regis

It would be easy to miss the fact that this tiny piece of England can lay claim to more than its fair share of history. For it is here at Grafton that Elizabeth Woodville, the mother of the Princes in the Tower, would be born in around 1437 and would later wed King Edward IV; Richard III would lodge at the manor in June 1483, and while Henry VIII would raise Grafton to the pinnacle of its glory during the Tudor period, the Civil War would finally see this most historic of houses consumed in flames by 1643.

There is much medieval history to be enjoyed here at Grafton, but our story begins in 1526 when a still energetic thirty-five-year-old King Henry VIII purchased 'the fayre manor place of Graftan and goodly parks and lands thereaboute' from Thomas Grey, second Marquess of Dorset. At the time, Grafton Manor was 'in great ruyne and decaye' and the king spent lavishly on its refurbishment, as he would continue to do consistently throughout his reign, creating what would essentially be a brand-new house, richly furnished in the height of contemporary taste.

Sadly, there are no known extant images of the manor house that Henry created, nor do any floor plans seem to have survived. However, in line with other fashionable royal houses of the day, records that were kept of the works undertaken at Grafton show that there was both a king's and a queen's side. On the king's side, chambers that are specifically mentioned in Colvin's *History of the King's Works* include a king's presence chamber, privy chamber, raying chamber, bedchamber, pallet chamber and closet. It is highly likely that the queen's side consisted of a similar arrangement. Certainly, there is mention of a queen's great chamber and raying chamber. Other notable buildings include 'the old chapel', which might encourage us to think that there was also a second, newer one, and a chamber for the Lord Privy Seal, which from 1530 to 1536 would have been Anne's father, Sir Thomas.

Grafton Manor and the Royal Progress

The royal court visited Grafton regularly after 1527, the king eventually conferring the additional suffix of 'Regis' in honour of its majestic connections. During Henry's reign, the court often lodged at the manor as a part of the summer progress, and the *Privy Purse Expenses* shows how Grafton was included in the *geists* as the king moved between Ampthill in Bedfordshire, to the south-east of Grafton, and Woodstock in Oxfordshire, to the south-west.

As we approach Grafton Regis today along the busy Northampton Road, which in Anne's day was the main London–Northampton road, we might pause to transport ourselves back to a gentler time, when the roar of the motor car was replaced by the sound of horses' hooves scuffing the earth, and birdsong filled the abundant hedgerows.

Set back from the main road to the east, there is something both serene and magnificent about the place, even though its glory days have long since passed. And on a fine spring day, such as the one on which the authors visited, it was easy to fall in love with the sweet, clean air and Grafton's gentle charms. In fact, we find ourselves wholly in agreement with Robert Dudley, Earl of Leicester, who at some point during the reign of Elizabeth I wrote to his royal mistress urging the queen to include Grafton in her forthcoming progress, saying that 'among meet places for you, I think none will be found more pleasant and healthful than this at Grafton'.

During the latter two of the three years that Henry and Anne lodged at Grafton together, extant privy purse expenses give us a tantalising glimpse of both the extraordinary and ordinary events at court. Thus in 1531, Henry first of all received the Hungarian ambassadors, who had lodged at the nearby staging post of Stoney Stratford, at the manor; he then healed a poor woman of her sickness and received pears and nuts from another 'poure woman' in the forest – presumably the royal party were out hawking at the time. The following year a monk is rewarded for bringing a purse to the king, and several park keepers are rewarded for their efforts in maintaining the many 'goodly parks' that covered the area. However, of all the visits that Anne made to Grafton perhaps it was the one of 1529 that is the most well known and to which we shall now turn.

The 1529 Progress: A King, a Cardinal and Mistress Anne

Thanks to George Cavendish, we have an account, in *The Life and Death of Wolsey*, of the historic events that took place at Grafton on 19 and 20 September 1529. We should remember that Cavendish was hostile to Anne and therefore was inclined to portray her in a negative light. Nevertheless, we are left with a rare insight into a defining moment that we can imagine literally unfolding right before our eyes on this remote Northamptonshire hillside.

The summer is 1529 and London has seen the collapse of the Blackfriars trial, much to the king's, and Anne's, disgust. Cardinal Wolsey was fast falling from favour, unable to secure the king his much-desired divorce. The story goes that when cardinals Campeggio and Wolsey arrived at Grafton from The More, so that Campeggio could take his leave of Henry and return to Rome, no chambers had been allocated to the king's first minister. However, Sir Henry Norris gallantly stepped in and offered Wolsey his rooms so that the cardinal could change from his riding attire.

Presently, Wolsey was conducted into the king's presence chamber 'where the lords of the council stood in a row, in order, along the chamber'. There had apparently been much speculation, and bets had been placed on whether the prelate would be received by 'his

Grace'. However, receive him Henry did, Wolsey kneeling before the king under his cloth of estate. Afterwards, Henry 'led him [Cardinal Wolsey] by the hand to a great window, where he [the king] talked with him' until dinner. The king then retired to his privy chamber to dine with a furious Anne. According to Cavendish, she berated him, 'as far as she durst', saying, 'There is never a nobleman within this realm that if he had done as he [Wolsey] hath done, but he were well worthy to lose his head.'

Despite Anne's ministrations, the king returned to his presence chamber, where Wolsey and all the lords of the council, including Norfolk, had been dining. The king resumed his conversation with the prelate until nightfall, when Henry bade his first minster goodnight and requested that he return in the morning so that they might continue their conversation. Wolsey was forced to leave Grafton for his lodgings, 3 miles from the manor at a place called Euston, only to return early the next day as the king had commanded. Yet it seems that there had been a change of plan. Henry had already granted Campeggio his leave and ordered Wolsey to return with the papal legate to London. Was the king being his usual capricious self, or had Mistress Anne intervened to finally turn the king against his minister? Cavendish suggests that 'the king's sudden departing in the morning was by the special labour of mistress Anne, who rode with him, only to lead him about, because he should not return until the cardinals were gone'.

Whatever happened overnight to bring about this change of heart in the king, when Henry and Anne rode out of the gates at Grafton Manor 'in sight of all men', Henry VIII never saw his first minister again.

It was a coup for Anne and the Boleyn faction. Within just two years, Anne Boleyn had almost single-handedly brought down the second-most-powerful man in the realm.

The End of Grafton Regis Manor
Elizabeth I visited Grafton Manor on three occasions, but by the reign of James I the house was falling into disrepair. In 1628, King Charles I sold the manor to Sir Francis Crane who was said to have partially demolished the house. In 1643, parliamentary forces took control of the manor, allegedly executing eleven people in the drawing room before setting it alight for the 'prevention of future inconveniences'. The existing manor house appears to occupy part of the original site, but according to Colvin this seventeenth-century building incorporates no recognisable portion of its fabric.

Visitor Information
The authors recommend parking just off the main Northampton Road, near the village hall, the second right turning into the village if travelling in a northbound direction, or first exit if you are heading southbound. Enjoy a pleasant five-minute stroll along a quiet country lane as you leave the busy traffic behind you and head eastwards towards the present-day manor and church. The views to the north are worthy of admiration.

At the bottom of the lane, another lane joins from the right and the road continues in an easterly direction toward the church. Directly to your left is a large gap in the wall; it is well covered with very tall trees. This, one presumes, was once the old entrance to the manor. However, the land today is privately owned and clearly enthusiastic historians are not warmly welcomed!

Nevertheless, stand back from the gate and perhaps imagine Henry and Anne sweeping out of the manor courtyard at the head of a hunting party, leaving a forlorn Cardinal Wolsey behind in their wake. After you have soaked up this piece of history, head down to the church. You will pass various red brick buildings. It has been hypothesised that some of these may have been part of the offices attached to the royal manor that were noted to have existed 'along the side of the road'. At its peak, sadly after Anne's time, Grafton was one of three of the king's lesser houses to incorporate a bowling alley, which is described in detail in Volume IV of Colvin's *History of the King's Works*. This abutted the pretty churchyard of St Mary the Virgin. The church is kept locked, a sad indictment of our times. So if you wish to visit, email ahead and arrange to meet a church warden, who will let you into the building. Email: churchwarden@grafton-regis.co.uk.

At the time of writing, 'Walks and Talks' covering the history of Grafton Regis are held four times a year by local history enthusiasts. Please check the Grafton Regis village website for 'What's On' at http://www.grafton-regis.co.uk.

Postcode for Grafton Regis: NN12 7SS.

Notley Abbey, Buckinghamshire

Of all the houses I've lived in over the years, Notley is my favourite. It was absolutely enchanting, and it enchanted me. At Notley I had an affair with the past. For me it had mesmeric power; I could easily drown in its atmosphere. I could not leave it alone, I was a child lost in its history. Perhaps I loved it too much, if that is possible.

Laurence Olivier

At the end of a magnificent tree-lined gravel drive, set amid romantic gardens on the banks of the River Thame in Buckinghamshire, lie the charming remains of Notley Abbey, a wealthy Augustinian monastery founded in the twelfth century.

Henry VIII visited regularly, and often stayed at religious houses during his summer progresses. This was the case when the court stayed at Notley between 25 and 27 September 1529. By this stage, Henry and Queen Katharine of Aragon were practically leading separate lives, although for the most part still residing under the same roof. Even though the two remained polite and courteous to one another in public, one can only imagine that the situation must have been anything but comfortable, especially considering that where Henry went, Anne Boleyn went too. Anne was no longer required to wait on the queen, and by December 1528 had her own sumptuous lodgings in London and a separate suite of rooms at Greenwich. By June 1529, she had separate apartments at Hampton Court Palace also.

On 25 December 1528, du Bellay, the French Ambassador, commented on the party of three: 'The whole court has retired to Greenwich, where open house is kept both by the King and Queen, as it used to be in former years. Mademoiselle de Boulan is there also, having her establishment (son cas) apart, as, I imagine, she does not like to meet with the Queen.'

What exactly the sleeping arrangements were at Notley is unknown but, like at other monasteries, royalty and distinguished guests usually lodged in the abbot's house and these lodgings survive, serving as the main residence today.

The Layout of the Buildings at Notley Abbey

The two-storeyed, L-shaped apartments were built in the fifteenth and sixteenth centuries abutting the west side of the cloister. In Anne's day it would have served as a combined abbot's house and guest accommodation.

As you approach the modern-day entrance to the house, the range directly in front of you, running east and west, is the fifteenth-century wing and contains an original fireplace on the first floor in the south-west corner. When first constructed, the first floor was divided into two rooms of unequal size and was open to the roof; the larger room, approximately 35 feet long, on the east, was probably the Great Hall, which would have been lit by a series of two-light windows, warmed by a fireplace and used by the abbot and his guests. It's almost certain that Henry and his court would have been entertained here. The smaller room, of about 20 feet squared, was probably the abbot's chamber.

The ground-floor rooms are likely to have served as the abbot's kitchen and offices and accommodation for servants. Today it houses a dining and withdrawing room, although the proportions of the rooms have been altered.

In the early sixteenth century it was decided to extend the abbot's accommodation and so another elaborate wing was added on the west (running north and south), almost at right angles to the fifteenth-century wing. On the first floor there were two rooms: a new chamber of grand proportions, with a newel staircase at the north-west corner linking it to the ground floor and a door leading to the outside; a second, smaller room, possibly used as a study or parlour, adjoined the chamber. The interiors were adorned with early Renaissance decoration and exquisite panelling of the highest quality. It was perhaps at this time that the earlier fifteenth-century chamber was converted into an anteroom or additional guest accommodation.

The ground floor had an independent entry and so was probably used to house special guests, but did it house the royal party in 1529?

Unfortunately, there is no definitive answer. It has been suggested that Robert Ridge, the last abbot of Notley (1529–39), may have been responsible for building the new wing. Five tiers of linenfold panelling from the sixteenth-century chamber that today line the walls of the Great Hall of Weston Manor, Oxfordshire, were probably made in around 1530 and bear his name on the wooden cornice. However, an entry in *Letters and Papers* confirming Richard Ridge's appointment is dated 4 August 1529 and the royal party arrived only seven weeks later. It is possible, though, that Ridge was not the builder – perhaps he only enhanced the wing in around 1530 – and so Anne may have spent time in this building during her visit.

Another possibility is that the thirteenth-century west claustral range (the abbey's original guest house), which today houses kitchens, offices and bedrooms, may have continued to function as guest accommodation even after the new fifteenth- and sixteenth-century lodgings were erected. This range was largely rebuilt after the Dissolution. However, the wall next to the cloister remains from the original building.

Notley Abbey: A Place for Romance

In around 1539 the abbey was dissolved, but the abbot's house was retained for use as a private residence. In the mid-1940s it became the home of Laurence Olivier and Vivien

Leigh. The famous acting couple lovingly restored it and regularly spoke of its powers to evoke times past and the spell it cast over them.

Today, Notley operates as a wedding venue and offers a romantic setting for modern-day lovers to nestle in. Perhaps Henry and Anne too sought solace in its beauty.

Visitor Information

Notley Abbey is not opened to the general public, nor can it be viewed from the road. For these reasons, we cannot recommend visiting it but have included it here for completeness. To enquire about having your wedding or banquet at Notley Abbey, please visit their website at www.notleyabbey.co.uk.

Postcode for Notley Abbey: HP17 8TN.

Bisham Abbey, Berkshire

> The evening light wears down from the Chilterns and veils both commentator and the Abbey. But tomorrow the place will come to life and make physical demands on those who seek to be expert at games, and whose shoes patter, as they serve or return a ball at tennis, over the dust of the man who made Kings, and of Earls who stood at bay on the fields of Crecy and Agincourt.
>
> Piers Compton, *The Story of Bisham Abbey*

As the maturing Thames sweeps down from its humble origins in Oxfordshire, the river carves a silent path between the two counties of Buckinghamshire and Berkshire. Opposite the town of Marlow, on the southern bank of that very same river, we find the medieval jewel that is Bisham Abbey, standing stately as an enduring witness to centuries of English history.

Existing records tell us that Anne only passed this way once. It was at a time when she was moving centre stage into the cut-throat world of court faction. Just over two weeks previously, Wolsey had been dismissed from the king's presence at Grafton Regis in disgrace. The king and Anne would never see the once-powerful minister again, and in this Anne clearly had a hand. It is interesting to muse upon her reception at Bisham, for it was owned at the time by Margaret, Countess of Salisbury, who was Princess Mary's governess and clearly a staunch supporter of Katharine and the conservative Catholic faith. We do not know if the countess was at home to receive her sovereign, as it seems she used Bisham only rarely. Perhaps for Anne's sake, we might hope that she wasn't and that Henry and Anne were able to enjoy their final night together on progress in peace, before heading back toward nearby Windsor Castle the following day.

The History of Bisham Abbey

Bisham Abbey, correctly pronounced 'Bizum', has stood sentinel on this site since the mid-thirteenth century, when a medieval hall of some grandeur was built for the ancient order of the Knights Templar. With the dissolution of that order, it briefly fell into the hands of the Crown before being conferred upon the earls of Salisbury, who established a priory of Austin Canons near to, but distinctly separate from, the medieval manor house.

The remains of the manor, which now stands amid lush green lawns, are essentially medieval but were much embellished through the mid-sixteenth century by the Hoby family. The house is a pleasing blend of golden stone, Tudor red brick and medieval features, like the remains of a cloister and the sweeping stilted arches in the thirteenth-century entrance porch, set against its distinctly Tudor heritage; mullion windows and the crenellated gable ends of some of the abbey's ranges.

The manor that Anne would have known from her brief visit in September 1529 was much larger than the house we see today, although there are distinct aspects of the extant building with which she would have been familiar. Luckily for us, a mid-sixteenth-century description of Bisham survives from a 1552 survey of the house, conducted before the Hobys set about their redevelopment of the manor. This, therefore, describes Bisham Abbey as Anne saw it in the autumn of 1529:

> The mansion howse there, wherein the sayde late Countes of Sarum [Margaret, Countess of Salisbury] sometime inhabited, is situate nere unto the Ryver of Thamys and adjoininge to the seite of the late monasteries there, being buylded partely of stone and partely of tymber and covered with tyles, wherein is conteyned a hall with a chembney [chimney], and at the lower end of the same is a pantery, a buttery, a kechyne [kitchen], a larder, and a lytell woodyarde. At the over [high] end of the same assendinge by a fayre half pace [staircase] is a greate chamber and loggings upon a quadrante, and underneath these chambers at the foote of the said half pace is a wyne sellar [and] a quadrant cloister with certeyne small loggings on every side of the same, the which cloister ledeth unto ij [two] lytell garden plottes.

What survives today is the western range of a building that once extended around a cloistered quadrangle, as referred to in the quote above. However, for now orientate yourself by standing in front of the medieval porch, knowing that north is directly in front of you. To the left is a building whose south gable is arranged in a distinctive chequerboard pattern made from flint; a fine plate-tracery window of high quality lights what was once the medieval 'solar' inside.

Dipping inside the cool shade of the elegant thirteenth-century stone porch, admire the original inner door before passing through the early Tudor screen that separated the main dining area of the Great Hall from the passageway leading directly through to the kitchens from its lower end.

This great chamber is probably the most intact of the sixteenth-century interiors and contemporary with Anne's visit. Surely Mistress Anne would have walked through this space to ascend the 'fayre half pace', or staircase, that would have taken her up to the manor's privy apartments.

Originally the hall had a central hearth, but it seems by the time of Anne's visit a fireplace was installed, although the fine version we see today dates from a little later in the century. Furthermore, Anne would have known a hall lit by windows on the northern, eastern and southern walls. But, with the addition of new chambers as part of the later Tudor embellishments, these windows were blocked off, as you see today. However, the wooden screen, through which one passes in order to enter the hall, and the gallery above it are fifteenth-century and so would have already been in place by the time of the visit.

Did minstrels once play to entertain the king and his lady as they dined at the high end of the hall? It is easy to imagine.

If you are lucky enough to gain permission, head to the door in the far left-hand corner of the hall, diagonally opposite where you entered. You will ascend a later version of the staircase that will take you up to the first floor. Turn right and enter the Elizabethan Conference Room. This was the 'great chamber' referred to in the 1552 survey and was originally approximately 67 feet long, with a raised dais at the high end. The authors suspect that this was a form of presence chamber, and certainly both Henry VIII and Elizabeth I were known to have held council in this room, hence the name.

Sadly, like many of the rooms at Bisham, the interiors are largely stripped out and have been divided up and turned into practical office and meeting spaces. However, if you look out of the main bay window, which was a Hoby addition and includes stained glass from the original priory windows, 500 years ago you would have been looking down into a pleasant cloistered courtyard, as described above. When you go back outside, do remember to take a look at what remains of this cloister, tucked underneath the great chamber range.

Thus, we can imagine the original house covering much of the lawn that lies immediately to the east of the current building. Just beyond, to the north-east, again under the current lawns, was the church of the Austin Canons Priory. It is often stated that its remains lie buried under the 'tennis courts'. It is easy to assume that these tennis courts were the current ones belonging to the Sport England campus. However, *History of Bisham Abbey* written in 1979 tells us that the imprint of the abbey used to be seen 'under the lawn in dry weather before the hard-core tennis courts were added'. A photograph included in this book shows these earlier tennis courts on the lawn immediately to the north-east of the current manor. These earlier courts are now gone. The authors believe that there has been a later misinterpretation of the original notion and that the priory, along with several notable persons from English history, including Warwick the Kingmaker, in fact lies under the current lawn near to the old abbey and not under the modern-day tennis courts.

Authors' Favourites

Over and above exploring the delights of Bisham Abbey, head on into the village and visit All Saints church. Here you will find a fabulous and rare obelisk memorial to Margaret, granddaughter of Mary Boleyn, who married into the Hoby family in 1596. The authors were lucky enough to be there as a church warden was arriving. However, it is clear that the church is usually locked. So if you wish to view the interior of the church, please contact the parish offices beforehand in order to arrange a visit. Email: parishoffice@marlowanglican.org

Visitor Information

Today Bisham Abbey is run by Sport England and what remains of the manor house serves as offices and a conference centre. It is also used as a venue for weddings and you may find the hall set out in anticipation of a reception. Generally, Bisham Abbey is not open to the public; however, if you email ahead you can arrange to visit privately by emailing Zoe Dixon, Head of National Centres on zoe.dixon@sportengland.org.

Postcode for Bisham Abbey: SL7 1RR.

Woking/Oking Palace, Surrey

a certain mansion there, sumptuously built with an orchard and garden, stables and other buildings adjoining the said mansion and its appurtenance.

Extract from a survey of the manor made in the second year of the reign of James I

Both *Privy Purse Expenses* and the *Letters and Papers of Henry VIII* attest to the presence of the court at Woking on one occasion when we know that Anne was close to Henry's side. The year was 1530; it would be the last summer progress that Anne would have to endure with Katharine still present at court. However, as the queen was still in residence, Anne would not yet be lodged in the queen's apartments.

Records suggest that the court stayed at Woking Palace from 11 to 21 July 1530. Ten days spent at one of Henry's lesser houses was quite considerable and clearly the hunting and hawking must have been pleasing, not least because we hear of the king receiving hounds from the Marquess of Exeter, no friend of Anne's, and Sir Francis Bryan, still very much a Boleyn creature at this time, and goshawks from 'my lorde Stewarde' and 'my lorde of Wiltshire'. Anne's father, by now a privy councillor, was clearly close at hand. However, even more interestingly, there is the payment to 'George Taylor, my lady Anne's servant ... for his half yeres anuytie', made from Woking.

In time, George Taylor would become Anne's Receiver General, or Treasurer, maintained on a substantial annual salary. It is widely acknowledged that he entered the service of the future queen at an early date and here we see the evidence for that. This entry in the *Privy Purse Expenses* tells us, however, that it was Henry who was paying his wages, not his mistress.

The Story of the Palace at Woking

The history of the old manor of Woking, or Oking as it is often called by Tudor scribes, goes back to the thirteenth century. Woking Manor was granted to Margaret Beaufort and Henry Stafford in 1466 and it was their principal home until Stafford's death in 1471. It remained in Margaret's possession until 1483 and was re-granted to her in 1485 by Henry Tudor upon his accession to the throne.

Henry VII took the manor into his own hands in 1503. In 1508, he commissioned the last major building project: that of the Tudor Great Hall, which was subsequently completed in 1511 by Henry VIII. Other building works by Henry VIII and subsequent monarchs were merely renovations and minor additions. In time, Woking became a much-loved royal palace, often used by the king.

The royal residence lay surrounded by Woking Park, half a mile downriver from Old Woking village. The earliest-known view of the palace comes from Norden's map of Woking Park, made in 1607. Even though this later map does not show the full extent of the palace in its halcyon days, as certain ranges had already been demolished, what we see is a charming arrangement of several buildings, including a Great Hall, all surrounded by a moat and adjoining the River Wey. While the buildings themselves covered 4 acres, there were also extensive formal gardens, orchards and a fishpond that covered an additional 4 acres. However, according to the Friends of Woking Palace, who have done much research into the site in recent years, 'Woking does not seem to have been a large palace and the king and queen would generally be accompanied by a "Riding Court" of perhaps forty to sixty people when they visited for a few days at a time.'

Nevertheless, a now-lost fourteenth-century survey confirms that, even in its early days, it was a manorial complex of some size including a hall, two chapels and many other rooms and offices. In the environs, there were also a corn mill, a fulling mill and separate stables for the king's and the queen's horses, as well as an extensive deer park, which by the Tudor period had extended to cover around 590 acres. The landscape in the park varied, no doubt contributing to its appeal for both hunting and hawking; it consisted of lightly wooded sections in areas that occupied the higher ground in the park, as well as large glades and 'lawns' for deer coursing. According to the Friends of Woking Palace, 'Access to the Palace was invariably by horse, despite the number of erroneous modern histories that state royal access was by barge up the River Wey from the River Thames.'

As a location, Woking was very often visited on the way to, or from, the king's lodgings at Guildford, another much-favoured residence (see entry on Guildford), and on occasion the magnificent Sutton Place, which had been granted to the family of the young Francis Weston by Henry VIII, who would later die because of his association with Anne.

The Lodgings at Woking Palace

Very little is actually known about the royal apartments at Woking, let alone any other lodgings in which Anne might have been housed. Archaeological evidence suggests that it is very likely that the royal chambers lay to the south and south-west of the Great Hall built in 1508–11, and incorporated buildings built over the preceding 250 years right up to the time of Lady Margaret Beaufort and Henry VII. We know from one reference that the queen's apartments were connected to the king's quarters by a gallery, an arrangement that was not uncommon in other royal palaces.

The *History of the King's Works* gives us many more tantalising glimpses into the other state chambers and privy lodgings that could be found at Woking during this time. These included those of key courtiers, who frequented the palace alongside the king and queen. Among these accounts, on the king's side we hear of a watching chamber, bedchamber and raying chamber, while on the queen's there is a dining room, the 'great bay window' in her privy chamber and a raying chamber. In 1534, plasterers were pargetting and whitening all the king's and queen's lodgings, the queen's maids' lodgings and the lodgings of the Duke of Norfolk, the Master Treasurer (at the time Sir William Fitzwilliam) and Sir Anthony Browne. At the same time, the talented Galyon Hone, the king's glazier, was mending and replacing glass in two bay windows in the queen's chamber, her privy chamber and also two more in the chamber of the 'queen mother'. This is a very rare reference to Elizabeth Boleyn, Countess of Wiltshire, who obviously had her own lodgings at the palace. Sadly, however, it seems that Anne was never to see this work.

Visitor Information

Only a few vestiges of this once-much-loved royal abode remain to be seen above ground. However, the surrounding moat and the River Wey mark out the footprint of the palace and its once tranquil gardens.

The Friends of Woking Palace have done a wonderful job in preserving what is left of the site. During the four years to 2012 they participated in an archaeological project led by Surrey Heritage, funded by both Woking and Surrey councils and Surrey Archaeological

Society and supported by the universities of Reading, London and Nottingham. An information board close to what was once the main entrance, via the gatehouse across the moat, contains information and a reconstruction of the buildings that Anne would have seen during her visit to the palace in the summer of 1530.

In March 2013, further funding was granted to the Friends by the Heritage Lottery Fund for a much wider three-year community project including the surrounding area and its park. Evidence gathered from the seasons of excavations, together with research into the landscape and documents, will help to shed more light on this fascinating site.

Across the moat from this main entrance, the royal apartments once extended away to your left with the Great Hall directly in front of you. However, the large wall still standing was not part of this structure, but another building that sat behind the hall. At the current time, its function is unknown, as is that of the building that stands directly to its left – the only roofed, although incomplete, building that remains on site. The King's Gardens lay beyond this wall, with additional gardens and fishponds in the copse, sited through a wooden gate over to your right.

It was a pleasant spring day when the authors visited, with a carpet of daffodils covering the woodland floor, while the screech of a bird of prey cut through the tranquillity of the place as she circled above us on the wing. Sadly, nearby electricity pylons and distant modern farm buildings keep you firmly rooted in the present. However, the open countryside and lazy, meandering river, set back from the full force of twenty-first-century life, preserve something of the haven that once served a king and his court. Certainly, it was not too hard to see Anne and her friends taking air in the gardens or to imagine the cacophony of sound coming from directly across the river, where the tiltyard is postulated to have been situated on what are now flat, open fields.

Woking Palace is owned by Woking Borough Council and it is surrounded by private land. Public access to the palace is restricted to three open weekends a year, held by the Friends of Woking Palace on behalf of the local council. Dates are set for May, July and September. During the open weekends, there are guided tours to learn about the history of the site and various displays. Full details are to be found on the Friends of Woking Palace website. Special group visits can also be organised via the same group.

Please note: no parking is available at Woking Palace or along Carters Lane leading to it, as this is private land. Access is by foot and cycle via a signed route (about 1 mile from Old Woking). Free long-stay parking is available in Old Woking in the larger car park (beyond the small short-stay tarmac car park) by the mini-roundabout in the High Street at the junction of the A247 and B382.

For more information on the palace, visiting the site or the excavations and further investigations of the site, please visit the Friends of Woking Palace website at http://www.woking-palace.org/. Telephone number: +44 (0) 7722 299026.

Postcode for High Street, Old Woking: GU22 9JH

College of Ashridge, Hertfordshire

A pleasaunter place than Ashrige is, harde were to fynde.

John Skelton, fifteenth-century poet

Henry VIII's privy purse expenses offer fascinating insight into Henry's relationship with Anne in the years preceding her elevation to the throne. The accounts demonstrate beyond doubt the depth of Henry's attachment to Anne and how intertwined their lives were. They're also a testament to the extensive amount of time the couple spent together – from late 1529 they were virtually inseparable.

In May 1530, 'the lady Anne Rocheford' was presented with all the accoutrements of archery, including bows, broad-head arrows, a bracer and a shooting glove. She was also set up to accompany the king on his travels – and in great style, one might add – receiving, among other tokens

> a saddle of the French fashion, with a pillow of down, covered with black velvet, fringed with silk and gold, the head of copper and gilt, graven with antyke works; one footstool, covered with black velvet, fringed with silk and gold; one saddle hose of velvet, lined with black buckram; one harness of black velvet, both fringed with silk and gold, with buttons pear fashion, and tassels of silk and gold; one great tuft of silk and gold upon the crupper, with buckles and pendants of copper and gilt; one slophouse of leather, lined with cotton; two girths of white twine; and two bits with two pair of gilt bosses.

Thus superbly kitted out, travel and hunt they did. On 17 and 18 August 1530, they were at the College of Bonshommes at Ashridge, near Berkhamsted on the Hertfordshire-Buckinghamshire border.

It was founded in 1283 by Edmund, Earl of Cornwall, and thrived as a seat of learning until dissolved by Henry VIII in 1539, at which time the monastic buildings were retained by the Crown and used as a royal residence.

The buildings were situated on high ground and surrounded by the Hertfordshire woods, a perfect place for the royal children – Mary, Elizabeth and Edward – to frequently reside. In 1551, Edward VI granted the buildings to his sister, Princess Elizabeth.

Little is known of the buildings prior to the Dissolution. Most information about the layout comes from a survey completed in 1575 when the estate passed from the Crown into the possession of Thomas, Lord Ellesmere, who restored the house.

The survey mentions that on the ground floor was the Great Hall, measuring 66 feet by 28 feet, and the Great Chamber, measuring 46 feet by 26 feet. On the first floor was the Chamber of Presence, measuring the same as the Great Chamber, and the Privy Chamber above 'a certain chapel', measuring 28 feet by 18 feet; the bedchamber, measuring an impressive 48 feet by 24 feet, lay beneath 'le Fermury'. It's possible that the infirmary had been on the second floor, thus allowing for the traditional sequence of presence, privy and bedchamber on the first floor. The aisled church and its cloister were also still intact.

It was while staying at Ashridge that an eleven-year-old Elizabeth began working on a new year's gift for her stepmother, Katherine Parr. It was an English translation of the French religious poem, *Le Miroir de l'Âme Pécheresse*, by Margaret de Angoulême, a woman whom Anne most certainly knew, perhaps even quite intimately, if a message that was sent to Margaret in 1535 is anything to go by, 'The Queen said that her greatest wish, next to having a son, is to see you again.'

Sadly, all that remain of the original college buildings that Anne visited are the fifteenth-century vaulted undercroft (formerly under the frater of the college buildings) below the dining and drawing rooms of the present-day house, and a medieval barn that was almost entirely rebuilt in 1816 and restored in 2002.

At the end of the eighteenth century, the college buildings were crumbling and so were partly demolished. Early in the nineteenth century the last of the buildings were dismantled, and the present structure, designed in the Gothic-revival style by architect James Wyatt, was constructed in its place.

Today, Ashridge House is home to the Ashridge Business School and so the tradition of learning established more than 700 years ago, and practised by Anne's daughter on those very grounds, continues to flourish.

Visitor Information

Visiting this location is a real treat, particularly if you love taking your dog along with you when you travel in the footsteps of Anne Boleyn. Most people will pass through the delightful, historic town of Berkhamsted before climbing up out of the valley and finding themselves driving through mile upon mile of the most glorious deciduous woodland, currently managed by the National Trust. Off in every direction, footpaths disappear into the forest. Then suddenly the woodland gives way to large, open spaces where dog walkers can be seen making the most of them. In fact, this is clearly a very popular leisure spot for walkers and bikers alike; there are many parking areas just off the main road where you can pull over and head off on your own woodland adventure.

It is immediately obvious why Ashridge was such a favoured royal residence. The countryside is breathtaking and the plentiful woodland must have made for excellent hunting. The country lanes seem never-ending, but you will not find yourself irritated by it on account of the sheer beauty that surrounds you. We recommend heading for the village of Little Gaddesdon, where you will pick up signs for Ashridge College. The road is marked as a private toll road. Do not let this deter you, for the site seems to be constantly criss-crossed by public traffic.

Continuing to pass along tree-lined avenues, and climbing ever higher, the sense of anticipation seems only to augment. Finally, when the college comes into sight, standing proud high up on a plateau, you will find yourself saying 'wow!' It is, of course, so sad that the original Tudor manor no longer exists, but since its replacement is in the Gothic style, it effortlessly defies time and manages to conjure up the grandeur of the lost building. We certainly found ourselves forgiving the fact that it is only around 200 years old.

We parked in the visitor car park in front of the college. As we visited on a blustery day with the rain beginning to come down just as we got out of the car, we had just enough time to take a few photographs before diving back inside for warmth. We imagine that on a sunny day this would be a pleasant spot to sit on the grass and let your mind wander to a time when Anne hunted in the forest that surrounds you, and later her daughter strolled amid its ancient cloisters, waiting patiently for the day that would see her finally become queen. There are no toilets or refreshments on-site, so do bring a packed lunch or head back toward Little Gaddesdon to The Bridgewater Arms, where lunch or light snacks are served from noon all day, every day.

The house is opened to the public at various times throughout the year, please check Ashridge College's website for further details: http://www.ashridge.org.uk or telephone + 44 (0) 1442 843491.

Postcode for Ashridge College: GU22 9JH.

Ampthill, Bedfordshire

The market town of Antehill is praty and welle favoridly buildyd, and is a quarter of a mile distant from the castelle: part of it standith on a hille, but the most and the best parte in a valley.

John Leland

The small town of Ampthill in Bedfordshire is well known today for its Georgian buildings; however, behind the sophisticated façade, there lies a more ancient history and one with a significant Tudor connection.

In the early part of the fifteenth century, Sir John Cornwall, Lord Fanhope, built himself a fine castle out of the spoils of the French Wars. The English scholar John Leland, who in 1533 wrote poems celebrating the Coronation of Anne Boleyn, travelled around England between 1535 and 1543, visiting the castle and recording his observations in his *Itinerary*: 'This Lorde Fannoppe buildid this castelle as it is now stonding stately on a hille, with a 4 or 5 faire towers of stone in the inner warde, beside the basse-courte, of such spoiles as it is saide that he wanne in Fraunce.'

The 'faire castle' was situated 40 miles from London in Ampthill, and enjoyed commanding views over the local lands. It was surrounded by a wooded park, and in 1524 became royal property. Henry VIII's intentions were 'to erect, build, and edifice upon his grace's manor of Ampthill, sumptuously, stately, beautiful and princely buildings', demonstrating his fondness for the location, where he is said to have enjoyed 'marvellous good health and cleanness of air'.

Henry VIII was a regular visitor and on a number of occasions Anne accompanied the king, and no doubt delighted in the bracing air and good sport afforded by the well-stocked deer parks that surrounded the castle. The couple were there in late August/early September 1530 and again in September 1531, when Henry purchased silks and 'a brooch with an amethyst in it' from William Lok, a London mercer. We can surmise that with Katharine shut away at The More, these lavish gifts may well have been for Henry's queen in waiting, Anne. In July 1532, the couple returned and there they remained for five or six days before moving to Grafton.

The following year, in March 1533, Katharine of Aragon was ordered to take up residence at the castle and was there the following month when she was summoned to appear before the Archbishop of Canterbury, Thomas Cranmer, at nearby Dunstable Priory.

There a court had been assembled to consider whether or not Henry was legally married to Katharine (even though he'd already been married to Anne since January). Katharine refused to attend and, on 23 May, Cranmer proclaimed Henry's marriage to Katharine null and void and five days later validated Anne and Henry's marriage.

Katharine remained at Ampthill until the end of July when she was ordered to move to Buckden in Cambridgeshire. On the day of her departure, the townspeople came out to bid farewell to Katharine, showering her with well wishes and very publicly pledging their support. In their eyes, Katharine was still their rightful queen and, according to Chapuys, some in the crowd even dared still call her that aloud, even though this had been expressly forbidden on pain of death. This must have lifted Katharine's ailing spirits and made the trip to Buckden all the more bearable.

But public protestation aside, Henry was now married to Anne and in June 1533 she was crowned Queen of England.

From 1534 onwards, Henry visited Ampthill frequently, attested by the many references to work carried out at the castle 'against his maiestie's comyng unto his said mannor'.

In the autumn of 1534, the floors in the king's and queen's chambers were repaired. Gaylon Hone, the chief glazier, supplied new glass for Anne's 'reaying chamber', closet and bedchamber. Hone also supplied four of Anne's falcon badges, which were installed in the windows of the king's dining chamber and bedchamber and Anne's bedchamber and 'reaying chamber'. In the Great Park, the queen's standing was also repaired and glazed ahead of the royal couple's arrival on 2 October 1534.

We know from Leland's account that the castle Anne stayed in had four or five towers in the inner court, although sadly nothing survives today and no image of the castle is known to exist. An Elizabethan plan, believed to be of Ampthill, made in around 1567 shows that the inner court was accessed via a large gatehouse and the hall and kitchens made up one side of the rectangular court, behind which stood a well, contained within a well house. A number of large bay windows and stair-turrets are also visible, perhaps these are the very 'faire towers of stone' noted by Leland?

By the end of the sixteenth century, the castle had fallen into ruin and by November 1649, was completely destroyed.

Today the only clue as to the site's Tudor connection is a stone cross, known as 'Katherine's Cross', erected in Ampthill Park in 1770 by Lord Ossory. Horace Walpole is said to have penned the inscription carved into the cross:

In days of old here Ampthill's towers were seen,
The mournful refuge of an injured Queen;
Here flowed her pure but unavailing tears,
Here blinded zeal sustain'd her sinking years.
Yet Freedom hence her radiant banner wav'd,
And Love aveng'd a realm by priests enslav'd;
From Catherine's wrongs a nation's bliss was spread,
And Luther's light from Henry's lawless bed.

It may be only Katharine's name etched in the stone cross at Ampthill, but its resonant grounds forever recall that *two* formidable queens once walked here.

Visitor Information
Today, the site of the old castle of Ampthill is located in Ampthill Park, which is owned and managed by Ampthill Town Council assisted by the Greensand Trust. It is another spot that is clearly popular with dog walkers as there are extensive areas of open grassland,

punctuated with woodland copses, all set on an undulating landscape and criss-crossed by paths that seem to lead in every direction.

To reach the central car park, you will need to head out of Ampthill on the B530 (Woburn Road) for about half a mile; the car park is clearly marked on your right. Parking is free. From the car park, pass to the left of the café and turn left toward the cricket pitch. Just before the green, head to your right through a gate and uphill to the summit of the ridge. At the top, bear left and this will quickly bring you in sight of two stone crosses. One is a war memorial; the other is Katherine's Cross. This marks the approximate site where the castle once stood at the top of the Greensand Ridge and offers majestic views over the surrounding countryside.

The authors visited on the anniversary of Anne's Coronation: 1 June. We could not help but think about Katharine staring out over the Bedfordshire countryside from the prison of her loneliness, while 40 miles away the bells of Westminster Abbey celebrated the anointing of England's new queen.

After sitting on the grass and looking out over those magnificent views for some time, we made our way back to the car park, not able to quite shake off the feeling that the plateau belonged to Katharine and that somehow, in Anne's name, we had been intruding upon her private grief.

As noted above, the café and toilets are located back at the car park where you started your journey. Alternatively there is free parking in Ampthill town centre and a number of tea rooms ready to quench your thirst.

You might like to plan your visit to coincide with the Aragon Day Festival, launched in 2003 to mark the anniversary of Katharine of Aragon leaving Ampthill after learning that her marriage to Henry VIII had been annulled. Each year, during summer, Ampthill turns back the clock and celebrates the town's rich history in grand Tudor style with displays of Tudor cookery, falconry and archery, storytelling and much more. Visit the Aragon Day Festival website for details of upcoming events: http://aragondayfestival. org.uk.

Postcode for Ampthill Park: MK45 2HX.

Hertford Castle, Hertfordshire

Went next [after seeing Lady Mary] to lady Elizabeth, who replied to the King's message with as great gravity as she had been 40 years old. If she be no worse educated than she appears she will be an honour to womanhood. Hartford Castle, Wednesday, 17 Dec.

Thomas Wriothesley, 1539

The history of Hertford Castle on the river Lea in Hertfordshire spans more than a millennium. It began its life on a site fortified by Edward the Elder in around 911 and by the time of the Norman Conquest consisted of a motte and bailey surrounded by a moat. From there it grew into a royal fortress and then a royal residence and remained so until after the death of Elizabeth I.

Henry VIII visited Hertford Castle occasionally during his reign, and in September 1530 spent four or five days at the castle with Anne Boleyn. The only details we have of the visit are surprisingly stripped of pomp and ceremony, hinting, perhaps, at happy domesticity. It's known that a James Hobart brought the king oranges and lemons and Jasper, the gardener, brought him herbs.

In 1523, a survey of the castle found that there were 'competant logyngs for his grace if his pleasure shalbe to lye ther for a season'. The unknown author of the survey also noted the 'fair court yarde' around which all the buildings stood.

These same competent lodgings would have accommodated Anne and Henry during their brief stay in 1530. Apart from the royal apartments, there were also a Great Hall, chapel, kitchens and offices all within the ancient curtain wall.

In around 1564, a partial plan of the castle was made by Henry Hawthorne and revealed that the domestic buildings within the castle were largely timber-framed. On the south side, the courtyard was surrounded by galleries, possibly made during the Tudor reign; however, most of the buildings probably dated from a reconstruction in the 1380s.

Although a royal residence, it was never the principal seat of any of the Tudor monarchs, and by the end of the sixteenth century was partially in ruins.

In December 1609, the castle was surveyed and still standing was 'one fayre gatehowse of brycke, one towre of bryck and the old walles of the said Castle'.

James I granted the castle to his son, Prince Charles, who in turn gave it to William Cecil, second Earl of Salisbury, bringing to an end centuries of royal ownership.

All that remain today of the buildings Anne would have seen are the formidable gatehouse – originally built by Edward IV as the castle's chief defence, although altered and extended in the late eighteenth to twentieth centuries – and the ancient flint walls dating to the twelfth century. The castle once occupied the enclosed ground behind the gatehouse but as the buildings were all timber-framed, no trace remains of their former grandeur.

Visitor Information

In our opinion, Hertford is a slightly frustrating town. Dotted among the imprint of its ancient streets are some real architectural gems of a bygone age, including a number of Tudor properties. However, while it is so close to being a charming medieval town, it falls short on account of a number of hideous, modern constructions that jar against what remains of its old-world charms. This is not helped by the fact that a number of the shops look run-down and neglected; graffiti and litter are too prevalent – perhaps a sign of the difficult financial times we live in. However, thankfully there is still much to please the eye, particularly in the castle gardens. It is probably best to park in one of the public car parks in the town (Gascoyne Way Car Park), as there is no parking on-site at the castle. It is a short walk through the town along Fore Street toward the castle. At the end of Fore Street turn right and you will see the entrance to the castle grounds on the other side of the road, just next to Hertford theatre.

You are entering via a gateway that did not exist in Anne's time. Plans of the castle show the main entrance was via the red brick gatehouse that is still standing. You will soon find yourself among charming gardens, which were bursting into blossom when we visited in May. Directly in front of you is an open area laid to lawn, which is surrounded by substantial remains of the castle walls. You are now within the inner bailey of the castle, where the royal apartments once stood. If you stand with your back to the sole survivor of the original castle, the gatehouse, the royal apartments would have covered the area directly opposite you, across the back of the inner bailey.

On the day we visited, a Tudor day, organised by the council, was in full swing with a falconry display taking centre stage. Guided tours were being held and we were lucky enough to briefly catch up with one of the Friends of Hertford Castle, who was conducting the tour. He explained that recent geophysics had shown up new buildings within the bailey, though no archaeological excavation of the site had taken place. Therefore the exact nature and layout of all the lodgings and offices within the courtyard area remain unclear. However, if you wish to see what is currently known of the layout of the castle, head inside the gatehouse; a map is hung on the wall to your left, just as you pass through the main doors.

Much of the building standing today is irrelevant to our story. However, it is worth heading upstairs to the Robing Room, which is contemporary to Anne's time and has some fine architectural features of the Tudor age.

Today Hertford Castle is home to Hertford Town Council and although not open to the general public, tours can be arranged. A number of its rooms are also available to hire for weddings, celebrations and corporate bookings. Various other events take place at the castle in the summer, sometimes incorporating free tours of the castle and grounds. For more information visit http://www.hertford.gov.uk. If you wish to visit this location, it is best to plan ahead. Entrance is free, although they do ask for a small donation to help with running costs.

Toilets are situated near the entrance to the castle gardens. The gardens themselves contain a pretty brook and are well tended, so make a fine place to rest and eat a packed lunch. Alternatively, there are plenty of bars and restaurants in the town. Hertford Castle can be easily combined with a visit to Hatfield House, which is about fifteen minutes away by car. Other sites within reasonable driving distance are Tyttenhanger Park and the College of Ashridge.

Postcode for Gascoyne Way Car Park, Hertford: SG14 1AB.

Farnham Castle, Surrey

> Our Sovereign had a short [number] of maidens over one of his chambers at Farnham while he was with the old lord of Winchester.
>
> *Letters and Papers of Henry VIII*

The summer of 1531 was a momentous one for Anne. Henry had cast his wife out of the royal household in July of that year, and Anne could finally enjoy her position at Henry's side as the king's uncontested consort in waiting.

On, or around, 29 July, the court had left nearby Guildford and travelled some 11 miles in a westerly direction to the small town of Farnham. There the grand episcopal palace of the bishops of Winchester dominated the town, as it had done since the early twelfth century when it was built by Henry of Blois, nephew of William the Conqueror and younger brother of King Stephen of England.

Perched majestically on the plateau of a hill to the north of the town, the entrance to the main gatehouse was one of pure theatre. Even early twentieth-century illustrations show how Castle Street steadily climbs in perfect alignment with Farnham Castle's main entrance. We can imagine the colourful cavalcade slowly making its way uphill through the town toward what had long been one of the most favoured residences of the bishops of Winchester.

The popularity of Farnham Castle lay both in its park, which was renowned for excellent hunting, and in its location roughly halfway between London and Winchester. This made it a perfect stopping-off point for bishops and kings on the move. The castle had grown in size over the centuries, from its early Norman beginnings to a sizable conglomeration of residential lodgings spanning the preceding four centuries. The most recent of these additions would have been the aforementioned gatehouse, a huge, red brick, block structure built by Bishop Waynflete between 1470 and 1475, alongside extensive alterations that had been made in 1520 by Richard Fox.

Both *Letters and Papers* and the *Privy Purse Expenses of Henry VIII* place Henry and Anne at Farnham toward the end of July and beginning of August 1531. First, there is the reward given on 2 August to the 'keepers of the park at Farnham', where the royal party had clearly been enjoying hawking or hunting, and secondly there is a grant made to a certain Richard Burton for lands previously owned by the disgraced Thomas Wolsey, dated 'Farnham Castle, 3 Aug.' It seems that Henry and Anne were at the castle, or in its environs, for a few days before moving on to lodge as guests of William, Lord Sandys, at The Vyne in Hampshire.

The Layout of Farnham Castle

The castle itself was essentially a motte and bailey structure with a fortified Norman keep rising up to surround the original motte. During the Tudor period, the keep was still in use, but it is much more likely that the royal guests and other nobles of Henry's court, including Anne, would have been lodged in the far more comfortable surroundings of the episcopal palace. The interior of the main palace buildings has been much altered over the years, so its original layout and appearance are often obscured. However, the main elements of any grand house of the time can still be identified.

Access into the archbishop's palace was via the outer gatehouse. This still stands, although it is not generally used for access onto the modern-day terraced gardens in front of Bishop Waynflete's Tower. The tower itself would have been the main point of access for the palace. Emery's *Greater Medieval Houses of England and Wales, Volume III* states that two flights of stairs led up to the Great Hall. Originally, the hall was a spacious room, 66 feet wide and 44 feet long with two rows of wooden pillars creating a central space and two additional outer aisles. It was probably lit by a series of windows running along both sides of the hall, but no evidence of these windows remains (note: the position of the current wall and fireplace cuts along the line of the original south arcade, thereby significantly reducing the size of the space that Anne would have known).

As was typical, a passageway at the low end of the hall led to kitchens, a pantry and buttery, and in this case also a Norman chapel, while at the high end, it seems that a vice stair, now part of the main entrance into the reception area, once gave access to the Great Chamber on the first floor. The east wing of the palace has 'suffered' more in the way of later remodelling than the west, so the original layout is harder to ascertain. However, in accordance with usual practice, it would seem likely that Henry occupied the bishop's state rooms and privy apartments when he was resident in the castle. It seems the main room here of interest to us in our story is now called the Bishop's Camera, essentially the bishop's main privy chamber. Here a fine bay window hints at an earlier, more lavish interior that has long since been lost to office modernity. The authors were lucky enough to meet with a local historian who has long been interested in the story of Farnham Castle. Together, we surmised that this room and the adjacent bishops' chapel probably once formed the mainstay of Henry's lodgings while at Farnham, although the authors stress that there is no definitive evidence of this.

However, where Anne was in all of this is harder to judge. Did she share these privy lodgings? It is possible, as she seems to have done so elsewhere. Was she actually lodged in the keep, which had access to the eastern wing via a flight of steps? Less likely, as the English Heritage brochure detailing specifically the history of the keep states that 'during the later medieval period ... the buildings in the keep were probably used as accommodation by the small group of retainers permanently based at the castle'.

Alternatively, perhaps she was housed in the Waynflete Tower. Emery's *Greater Medieval Houses of England and Wales* states that, although the pattern of accommodation in the tower is largely guess work,

> the first floor could have been an audience hall with a withdrawing chamber above for the bishop, although this would have been more convincingly built at the upper end of the hall range ... It is more likely, therefore, that this impressive tower provided suites of lodgings for honoured guests, including sovereigns, who were particularly frequent visitors during the fifteenth century.

Anne certainly could have been considered as one such honoured guest. Of the visit to Farnham in 1531, we know very little except that a hawk was delivered to the king, which makes it all the more likely that, it still being summer – the best hawking season, hunting with birds in the parks north of the castle provided the mainstay of daily entertainment.

Interestingly, in a later entry in *Letters and Papers*, we read of an interrogation of a John Hale, Vicar of Isleworth, in 1535, who had 'maliciously slandered the King and Queen and their Council'. In the report of the interrogation that took place in March of that year, Hale reported overhearing a conversation, in which it was said 'that our Sovereign had a short [number] of maidens over one of his chambers at Farnham while he was with the old lord of Winchester'.

The story, meant to illustrate popular issue with 'the king's marriage and other behaviours of his bodily lust', is sadly not dated, but reads as occurring during Henry's marriage to Anne. We know that Henry was at Farnham during the summer of 1534 during a period when he had left Anne, probably at Hampton Court, following the tragic stillbirth of their second child. Was this a wounded king consoling himself in the arms of pretty maidens, while Anne grieved for her dead child? We admit there is a good deal of conjecture in this, but it is certainly not beyond the realms of possibility.

Visitor Information

Today the bishop's palace is run as an International Briefing and Conference Centre.

Guided tours are held at the episcopal palace every Wednesday afternoon between 2 and 4 p.m. Booking is not essential but is recommended. Contact reception for further information. Telephone number: +44 (0) 1252 721194.

Please do note that these tours cover the whole history of the bishop's palace, and are neither specific to the Tudor period nor to Anne's visit, although the guides assure me that they do try and tailor each tour depending on the interest of those attending. Also bear in mind that the interiors have been heavily altered by successive bishops, so it is a location that, on the inside at least, requires much imagination!

The keep at Farnham Castle is maintained separately by English Heritage. Entry is free and details of opening times for both the bishop's palace and castle can be found at http://www.farnhamcastle.com/history/visit-farnham-castle.

Parking is available at the castle. There is a terraced area in front of the castle where you might enjoy a picnic and the views across the town are far-reaching. Perfect for a summer's day! Alternatively, if your legs can handle it, why not drop down into the town for some refreshments? Although, as you will find out, there is a stiff climb back up to the castle, if that is where you have left your car.

Farnham Castle is within relatively easy reach of a number of other locations in this guidebook including Woking Palace and Guildford.

Postcode for Farnham Castle: GU9 0AG.

Odiham, Hampshire

> He [Henry VIII] is tall of stature, very well formed, and of very handsome presence, beyond measure affable, and I never saw a prince better disposed than this one. He is also learned and accomplished, and most generous and kind, and were it not that he now seeks to repudiate his wife, after having lived with her for 22 years, he would be no less perfectly good, and equally prudent.
>
> Mario Savorgano's description of Henry VIII after meeting him in Odiham, August 1531

In August 1531, Mario Savorgano, a wealthy Venetian tourist and the son of a Venetian commander and aristocrat Girolamo, wrote about his meeting with Henry VIII in his travel diary:

> On the third day, I went to a park some 30 miles from London where the King was, taking his pleasure in a small hunting-lodge, built solely for the chase, in the midst of the forest. I saw the King twice, and kissed his hand; he is glad to see foreigners, and especially Italians; he embraced me joyously, and then went out to hunt with from 40 to 50 horsemen.

Savorgano reached London on 2 August and so 'the third day' was 4 August when we know from an entry in the *Privy Purse Expenses* that Henry VIII and Anne Boleyn were at Odiham Park.

The couple were en route to The Vyne and clearly enjoying the leisure and relaxation on offer, away from the prying eyes of Queen Katharine and her attendants, who had been left behind at Windsor in mid-July and ordered to move to The More shortly after.

The 'small hunting-lodge' that Savorgano refers to is probably Odiham Lodge, or Lodge Farmhouse as it is now called, built in the fourteenth century for Edward III and situated approximately a mile away from Odiham Castle, which had become ruinous by the late fifteenth century. It was built primarily to house the keeper of the king's park, an office generally granted for good and loyal service.

The lodge consisted of a cross-wing structure, approximately 5.2 m wide and 8.2 m long externally, and an adjoining hall. A solar occupied the entire first floor of the cross-wing – probably the principal private chamber in the house – with a divided service area on the ground floor.

When compared to other royal buildings, it was certainly a fairly modest structure and so in keeping with Savorgano's description. His comment about the lodge being 'in the midst of the forest' may be interpreted as hyperbole; however, Godson's map of Odiham drawn in 1739 confirms that in fact it was.

Records indicate that the lodge was almost entirely devoid of decorative features; there was no moulding or carving and no evidence of paintwork. Coupled with the obvious lack of space, this leads us to question whether or not this was a suitable place for the king and his fifty-strong riding party to take their pleasure.

Well, there's one other contender worth noting.

The Riddle of the Lodgings at Odiham

On the south edge of the park once stood a grand house called Odiham Place. Its appearance on Godson's map of 1739 suggests that it was a gabled mansion, built to an E-plan and thus typical of the Elizabethan period. In 1569, Elizabeth I stopped at Odiham for dinner while en route to Old Basing, further evidence of a substantial house in the area.

In 1575 the manor was granted to Elizabeth's Principal Secretary, Sir Francis Walsingham, who wrote letters from 'my house in Odiham', and in 1591 the Earl of Hertford's retinue stopped at the edge of Odiham Park while the earl himself went to meet the queen coming out of Odiham House.

It's clear then that by 1569 there was a house in the area suitable for entertaining royalty. It's possible that this house was then enlarged, or updated, by Walsingham in order to create the E-plan house visible on Godson's map and so its Elizabethan appearance doesn't preclude the existence of an earlier house on the site.

A brick barn, known today as The Cross Barn, built in 1532 may confirm the existence of this earlier house. The barn is the earliest agricultural building built of brick in Hampshire and so clearly constructed for someone of considerable affluence and standing. Its roof is made of top-quality oak and is a fine example of Tudor carpentry; it would not have been out of place built over a wealthy nobleman's house. This was a building erected to impress and its position at the entrance of a complex of buildings substantiates this.

It could be that the barn was among the last, rather than the first, buildings of Odiham Place to be erected and that the house to which the barn belonged may have been already standing when the king arrived in 1531.

With a barn of such quality one is left to imagine the magnificence of the principal buildings – certainly more appropriate as a stopping place for royalty than a modest, timber-framed hunting lodge?

The question though remains, would the Venetian tourist have referred to such a grand house as a 'small hunting lodge'? Its position on the south edge of the park also raises doubts and archaeological investigations in the area have not been able to shed any light on the matter.

Furthermore, as there is no suggestion that the royal party actually overnighted at Odiham, only that they enjoyed a day of hunting before moving on to the home of Lord Sandys, perhaps Edward III's lodge, although simple, sufficed.

The Remains of Odiham Lodge and Place Today

Today, the solar cross wing of Odiham Lodge survives, alongside fragments of the hall, which have been incorporated into Lodge Farmhouse.

As for the grander Odiham Place/House, the manorial barn (The Cross Barn) constructed after Anne's visit is the only survivor, albeit in a restored state. It is positioned less than 2 miles south of Lodge Farmhouse and can be hired for conferences and receptions.

Odiham Park is an important historic site because it's a place that Anne would have known and because of the rare, and possibly unique, survival of a medieval park lodge.

Visitor Information

Lodge Farmhouse is today part of a working farm, surrounded by concrete, modern barns and tractors, and is not accessible to the general public. The market town of Odiham is picturesque and hospitable; however, the sites associated with Henry and Anne's visit are on private land and so we cannot recommend visiting for this purpose alone.

The Cross Barn at Odiham, built in 1532, can be hired for conferences and private functions. More information about the facilities available and hire charges can be found by visiting http://www.thecrossbarn.org.uk.

The Odiham Society have published a number of circular walks around Odiham that may be of interest to those of you who would like to explore more of this historic town on foot. The walks vary in distance and difficulty and take in many sites of historic and general interest. The walks can be downloaded from http://www.odihamsociety.org/walks.html.

Postcode for Odiham Lodge Farmhouse: RG29 1HA and postcode for The Cross Barn, Odiham: RG29 1JX.

Havering-atte-Bower, Essex

> Havering-atte-Bower! The very name suggests the haunt of fairies and the songs of birds.
> Major Benton Fletcher, *Royal Homes near London*

It seems that the palace of Havering-atte-Bower was most often visited during the hawking season, which was between the months of September and April. During the summer of 1531, Henry finally banished his first wife, Katharine of Aragon, from court. Anne now reigned supreme and was never far from the king's side. Records show that Henry lodged briefly at Havering toward the end of October, when the royal couple broke their stay at Waltham Abbey to visit the Bower. On 23 October, the *Privy Purse Expenses* notes a sum of money given to a poor woman Henry healed at Havering; on the same day, there is also a record of Sir Henry Norris writing to the Vice-Treasurer of Calais, 'The King commands you, as soon as you have any leisure, to come over and bring with you all the King's money. Havering of the Bower. 23 Oct.'

However, Henry and Anne did not stay long, for by 25 October the court was back at Waltham Abbey.

The History of the Palace

There is something in the quote above that is perhaps not far from the truth. The Palace of Havering-atte-Bower, often also simply referred to as Havering, has ancient roots indeed. It was initially celebrated as a favoured royal palace during the Saxon period, when Edward the Confessor became the first king to be definitely associated with it. In fact, many believe that he died at the Palace of Havering and his body was taken from there to Westminster Abbey for burial.

Havering owed its popularity with its royal owners to the fact that it was delightfully situated: close enough to London to be convenient, but far enough away to provide clean air and respite from the demands of government. In addition, its position on high ground on the southern slope of a considerable hill overlooking the Thames Valley gave it, as Benton Fletcher describes, 'fine views and extensive prospects over a great part of Essex, Hertfordshire, Kent, Surrey and Middlesex'.

When Queen Eleanor was granted the palace, the park and village as part of the Queen's Dower in 1267, she inherited an estate of 16,000 acres of forest, woodland, pastures and marshes. At this point 'Havering' gained the suffix 'atte-Bower' and henceforth became the property of the queens of England, although it was largely still known as 'the King's House at Havering'. In this way the Palace of Havering was granted to Anne Boleyn after her marriage to Henry in 1533.

The Layout of the Palace Buildings

The palace that Anne inherited dated largely from the major building works of the thirteenth century. The plan was irregular, containing a Great Chamber (Great Hall), a presence chamber, royal apartments (privy chamber, withdrawing chamber, closet, and bedchamber), two chapels and various outbuildings. The royal apartments had views over the palace courtyard to the west and the gardens to the east.

The chapel on the southern side of the complex adjoining the Great Hall would have been accessible to anyone who was fit to gain entry to the palace precinct. It is the chapel that remained in use as a parish church until 1878, when it was finally demolished and replaced by the current church of St John the Evangelist. One imagines that the other chapel, being smaller and attached more closely to the privy apartments, was reserved for use by the king, queen, nobility and other favoured members of the royal circle.

Unlike the more fashionable houses of the day, the plans of the palace show no distinct king's and queen's sides. Thus, the building must have seemed cramped and very outdated by the early sixteenth century, perhaps explaining why it was used in the Tudor period largely as a hunting lodge only.

By Anne's lifetime, like its other medieval counterpart at Clarendon (see entry on the Old Palace of Clarendon), Havering was in decline, and by 1605 parliamentary surveyors reported that the former palace was 'a confused heape of old, ruinous, decayed buildings' fit only for demolition. Benton Fletcher adds to our understanding of its decline when he states that 'by the eighteenth century only parts of the walls were left to be seen' and by the nineteenth, 'not a vestige' remained. With the disappearance of these last remnants, around 800 years of royal history were subsumed into the earth, but in your imagination this ancient palace of queens lives on to whisper of its illustrious past.

Visitor Information

If you wish to visit the site of the old palace, you can park your car off the main road next to the village green. If you stroll down the lane that runs between the churchyard and the Havering Park Riding School, you will be walking over the site of the palace gardens, then across part of the palace that joined the Great Hall with the presence chamber to the north. The privy apartments of the palace were situated roughly where the current yard of the riding school can be seen to your right.

Sadly, the church was closed when the authors visited, but do remember that this is a nineteenth-century replacement for the earlier medieval building, which existed roughly upon the same site. Finally, ensure you explore the views both to the north and south across the city of London from either side of the ridge. The parkland surrounding it covered most of the former parish of Havering-atte-Bower west of the main road, now North Road, and was much more extensive than the current Havering Country Park, which covers the part of the former park adjoining the site of the palace.

Havering Museum, which contains many interesting facts associated with this period of history, is located in nearby Romford. Please visit the website www.haveringmuseum.org. uk, or email curator@haveringmuseum.org.uk for more information. Telephone number: +44 (0)1708 766571.

Postcode for Havering-atte-Bower: RM4 1PL.

Hanworth, Middlesex

About eight days ago, as the French ambassador was going to court, whither he had been summoned, to attend a dinner the Lady [Anne Boleyn] was giving to the King, at a manor-house, with which he has lately presented her [Hanworth], he happened to pass by my lodgings, and came in.

Eustace Chapuys, October 1532

In June 1532, Henry VIII bestowed upon his future wife, Anne Boleyn, the manor of Hanworth in Middlesex. The house had been extensively remodelled by Henry VII and subsequently maintained by his son. It stood on the site of an earlier house formerly owned by the Crosby family.

Located close to Hampton Court Palace, the moated manor house, surrounded by fine parks and gardens noted for their strawberries, also boasted an aviary, a pond, an orchard and a loggia in the park. The house was connected to the gardens by a bridge and extensively embellished and refurbished for Anne's use. Henry ordered furniture and joinery to be made at Hampton Court for various rooms of 'my Lady Anne's' house at Hanworth, including 'a table for the nether ende of my ladyes great chamber for my ladyes gentilwoman' and employed two Italians, Anthony Toto and John de la Mayn, to set up 'certen antique heds brought from Grenewiche to Hanworthe at the kyng's commandment'. These heads or roundels brought from Greenwich Palace were the work of Italian sculptor Giovanni da Maiano, and were similar to a set of eight terracotta roundels that Maiano had created for Cardinal Wolsey in the late 1510s to decorate the walls of Hampton Court, each representing the bust of a Roman emperor. Craftsmen were also engaged to decorate the roof of Anne's closet with battens and the exterior walls and chimneys with 'antike work'.

In this luxurious house, dressed in the latest Renaissance fashion, Anne hosted a dinner for Henry in September 1532, to which she invited the French ambassador, Gilles de la Pommeraie, who had accompanied Henry and Anne throughout the summer progress. Anne must have been feeling euphoric, as she'd only recently been elevated to the title of Marquess of Pembroke, an honour never before held by a woman and one that came with lands worth £1,000 per year. Soon she would travel to Calais to meet Francis I, as Henry's intended wife, her future as bright and shiny as the jewels – recently stripped from her predecessor – adorning her sumptuous gowns. As she dined with Henry and the ambassador, carpenters at the Tower of London were busy adding a new roof and floor to the queen's Great Chamber, repairing the dining chamber and 'a bridge in her garden' in preparation for Anne's forthcoming Coronation.

Unfortunately, nothing further is known of the layout or appearance of the house that held such triumphant memories for Anne, as it was largely rebuilt by Lord Cottington in the seventeenth century and destroyed by fire in 1797. It once stood south of the present-day St George's church, near to where Tudor House, built in 1875 and converted into flats, stands today. In the pediments of two Georgian lodges built on the site can be seen two terracotta roundels, almost certainly the same 'antique heds' brought from Greenwich in 1532 to beautify the walls of Anne's new residence. Some Tudor brickwork and two large kitchen fireplaces survive in the rear of an eighteenth-century stable block.

Much of the site has now been converted into housing estates and so is not accessible to the public. However, it is possible to visit the local parish church, rebuilt in 1808 on the footprint of the medieval church that stood nearby the royal manor of Hanworth. If you have time, take a turn around the grounds of Hanworth Park where Anne once hunted, secure in her happiness, by Henry's side.

Visitor Information

As mentioned above, the house that Anne knew was destroyed long ago and today a number of private housing estates stand on its footprint. Unfortunately, you cannot see any of the surviving fragments from the street and so we cannot recommend a visit for this purpose alone. Perhaps those of you wishing to drive past the site might consider combining this with a trip to Hampton Court Palace, which lies only 5 miles away from Hanworth.

Tudor House is on Castle Way in Feltham, Middlesex. If you are travelling south down Castle Way, you will pass St George's church on your right, followed almost immediately by the private entrance to Tudor House. The sign on the gatehouse will tell you that you are in the right place. Directly opposite the gate is a small turn off in the road where you can pull over briefly, but if you wish to explore the area more thoroughly and maybe take a walk in Hanworth Park, once a royal playground, you will need to find alternative parking. We recommend the Hanworth Park car park, which is free and located on Park Road in Feltham, postcode: TW13 6PN. It is opened from 8 a.m. until dusk every day.

Postcode for Tudor House: TW13 7QG.

Stone, Kent

> delivered to the king's grace at Stone which his grace loste at pope Julius game to my lady marques, mr. Bryan and maister Weston.
>
> *Privy Purse Expenses of Henry VIII*, 20 November 1532

The village of Stone lies just over 6 miles away from the north-west Kentish coastal town of Gravesend. If you had been a resident in this town on Friday 4 October 1532, you would have enjoyed the splendid sight of the king's ship being tethered at the shoreline, the royal standard fluttering in the breeze, thus signifying to all that the passengers contained therein were no ordinary travellers. In a letter to the Holy Roman Emperor Charles V, the Spanish Ambassador Eustace Chapuys explains why the king had not travelled overland, taking the usual route along the London–Dover road on the outbound trip to Calais: 'In order to avoid Rochester and other places where they are dying [of the plague], the King will go from Greenwich to Gravesend in his barge, and stay there for a day at the house du gentilhomme.'

The *gentilhomme* in question was Sir Robert Tyrwhitt, the third husband of Lady Bridget, née Wiltshire, sole heiress of her father, Sir John. She was a close friend of Anne's, and would later serve as the queen's Chief Lady of the Bedchamber. These were perhaps interesting times for the relationship between the two women. Anne had been on good terms with Bridget's second husband, Nicolas Harvey, who had been her loyal supporter. Sadly he had died on 5 August of that same year and, much to the scandal of the court, Bridget had remarried within weeks.

However, perhaps more problematically, her new husband, Sir Robert, was less well disposed to the new Marquess of Pembroke, being a lifelong friend of Anne's intransigent enemy, Charles Brandon. We can only guess at what events led to the following letter being penned to Lady Bridget by Anne sometime between 1 September 1532 and her marriage to the king the following January, when she no longer styled herself as 'Anne Rochford':

I pray you as you love me, to give credence to my servant this bearer, touching your removing and anything else that he shall tell you on my behalf; for I will desire you to do nothing but that shall be for your wealth. And, madam, though at all time I have not showed the love that I bear you as much as it was in deed, yet now I trust that you shall well prove that I loved you a great deal more than I fair for. And assuredly, next mine own mother I know no woman alive that I love better, and at length, with God's grace, you shall prove that it is unfeigned. And I trust you do know me for such a one that I will write nothing to comfort you in your trouble but I will abide by it as long as I live. And therefore I pray you leave your indiscreet trouble, both for displeasing of God and also for displeasing of me, that doth love you so entirely. And trusting in God that you will thus do, I make an end. With the ill hand of
Your own assured friend during my life,

Anne Rochford

The letter would be used in evidence against Anne at her trial in 1536, all part of Lady Bridget's supposed 'deathbed' accusations regarding the lax morals of the queen. What happened between them is a mystery. Did Bridget turn against the woman who had declared that, next to her mother, she loved no other friend more? Or did Sir Robert exploit a harmless altercation between the two women for his own ends? We do not know, but it does set an interesting context for this particular visit.

The Mystery of the Royal Lodgings at Stone

Yet the secrets surrounding Stone do not end there. Henry and Anne would visit the Tyrwhitts twice, once on their way out to Calais and the other on their return trip on 20 November 1532, when they played the card game, Pope Julius, as detailed above in the *Privy Purse Expenses*. It has traditionally been reported that when the royal couple stayed at Stone, they were lodged at the castle. This is a building steeped in 800 years of history, built between 1135 and 1140 and receiving several notable guests during its time, such as Thomas à Becket and the Black Prince. The castle later fell into disrepair and was rebuilt in the thirteenth or fourteenth century. All that remains today of the original structure is a 40-foot-high square tower made from flint and rough-cut blocks of chalk. The adjoining house is Georgian and was built onto the tower in 1825.

However, during research for this book, we uncovered another location of great significance, which appears to have existed on the same estate and has become largely forgotten: Stone Place. *The History and the Topographical Survey of Kent*, written by Edward Halstead in the eighteenth century, very clearly identifies this second residence, which at the time had been of 'repute for some centuries'. Halstead writes of the vestiges that remained:

The gate-house to this seat is still standing; the buildings appear to have been large and stately, the ceilings of several of the rooms are well finished with oak wainscot. Over the gate house, and on a stone chimney-piece in the parlour, are carved the arms of Wingfield, as above mentioned.

Richard Wingfield had been Bridget's first husband. And, like Nicolas Harvey and Robert Tyrwhitt who followed him, he had inherited her estates upon their marriage. As sole heiress, she and, therefore, her husbands in turn had inherited not only Stone Castle and Place, but also the other local manors of Littlebrook and Cotton. Halstead notes also that when Bridget's father, Sir John, had first come into possession of Stone Place sometime earlier, he had rebuilt a mansion upon the site. This very same mansion later played host to the imperious Cardinal Wolsey in 1527, who was at the time travelling on embassy to France in order to secretly urge the king's royal 'brother', Francis, to support Henry's annulment case. On this occasion he travelled in great pomp, accompanied by the Earl of Derby, the Bishop of London, Sir Henry Guildford and Sir Thomas More.

Thus, by the time Henry and Anne arrived there must have been a relatively newly built mansion on-site, which already had a pedigree with the Tudor court. It seems unlikely to us therefore, that the royal party would instead choose to lodge in the tower of a medieval castle. This is perhaps even more convincing after having talked with a local historian and curator of Dartford Museum, Mike Still, who suspects that until the later buildings were added, the tower of Stone Castle might have been the only substantial structure to have existed on the site.

For completeness we should also mention the existence of yet a third building to muddy the waters: Stone Court, which was about half a mile or so away from Stone Place. This is recorded as a distinctly separate building, which the antiquarian book called *Dartford and Neighbourhood* says 'seems to occupy the site of the old Bishop's Palace'. It is difficult to tease apart the entangled histories of these buildings. However, given the fact that Stone Place is recorded as clearly being used and favoured by eminent Tudor guests, our suspicion is that this is where Henry and Anne lodged too.

Anne at Stone Castle

The idyllic backdrop that Anne would have seen as she approached the Stone estate is long gone. The village of Stone is now close to the busy Dartford Crossing, as the M25 crosses the River Thames. Perhaps even more horrifying is the existence of the vast Bluewater Shopping Centre, lying a mere stone's throw away from what surely must have been a sleepy English village and leafy green parkland. So perhaps if you visit Stone in Anne's footsteps, you might prefer instead to think of how the estate would have appeared before the industrial revolution swept away a gentler time: '[Here] the ground rises, having Stone Castle about two fields from it, the prospects from which over the river are beautiful; behind which it stretches over hill and dale a long way southward.'

Visitor Information

Stone Castle and the site of Stone Place are only a mile or so apart. There is now nothing at all left of the latter. It seems that the gatehouse was at some point demolished and now all that remains to give a clue to the site is a street name – 'Stone Place Road' – surrounded by residential houses and open scrub land. From Stone Place Road, the views down over the Thames Estuary are impressive, and one can imagine why the site had been chosen. However, there is nothing left of its charm today. Sadly, Stone is set in a highly developed and somewhat run-down part of north Kent, its more illustrious past long since choked by modern suburbia.

The tower of Stone Castle is just a few minutes' drive from Stone Place Road. The front of it can be viewed from public land, as much of the surroundings are residential. Stone

Castle is now in use as offices, and the back of the castle grounds are marked as private. Access to view the exterior of both sites, including the front façade at Stone Castle, is open and unrestricted.

If you wish to find out more about the local history of the area, please contact the Dartford Borough Museum. Website: http://www.dartford.gov.uk/by-category/leisure-and-culture2/museums-and-galleries. Telephone number: + 44 (0)1322 224739.

Postcode for Stone Castle: DA9 9TW and for Stone Place Road: DA9 9BN.

Shurland Hall, Isle of Sheppey, Kent

A stately residence … a manor comparable to any gentleman in Kent.

Anon

Having left Stone on the morning of 5 October, Henry and Anne appear to have passed through Mote Park, near Maidstone, where they hunted and where 'my lorde of Rocheforde' was paid from the privy purse for a wager won against the king 'wt a brace of greyhounds'. Some time afterwards, they boarded a ship and crossed the water of the Thames Estuary, which separated the Isle of Sheppey, just off the north coast of Kent, from the mainland. The couple were some 46 miles to the east of London; perhaps the salty taste of the sea air carried itself on autumn's already chilly breeze.

They were to be guests of Sir Thomas Cheney, a distant cousin of Anne's through her father's side of the family, whose principal seat was the magnificent and recently refurbished Shurland Hall. The Cheneys had very much ingratiated themselves into the favour of the Tudor dynasty by their feats of loyalty and courage on the battlefield at Bosworth, and Thomas, of the next generation, had risen quickly first in Wolsey's household, then the king's, entering the privy chamber in 1520. However, despite the great favour that Henry showed toward Sir Thomas, Anne had nevertheless had to intervene for him during a wardship dispute over a Mistress Anne Broughton. The altercation was between the said knight and Sir John Russell. The year was 1528 and this must have been one of Anne's earliest forays into the dangerous game of political manoeuvring and court faction. However, Anne and Sir Thomas won the day eventually and Cheney married Anne Broughton – in the process Mistress Boleyn, as she was then known, made a life-long enemy of Sir John, who would speak viciously about her upon her downfall.

On the other hand, Thomas remained a steadfast and loyal servant of the king's and, as a friend of Anne and the Boleyns, no doubt fully supported Henry's plans for a forthcoming royal marriage. One can imagine, therefore, that Anne looked forward to this visit with relish, not least because Shurland had just been refurbished to a high standard. Thus, this was to be no fleeting, overnight stay; a full four days had been planned, with the new Marquess of Pembroke and the king as Sir Thomas's honoured guests.

King Henry and his queen in waiting arrived at Sheppey by royal barge on 6 October 1532 and were greeted with pomp and ceremony at Queenborough Castle, of which Sir Thomas was constable. When this ceremony was over, the royal party proceeded to Shurland Hall, escorted by many of Sir Thomas's servants. There were approximately 400 retainers and no doubt many more islanders, the majority of whom would have never seen their monarch before. Therefore, it must have been an impressive and joyful sight, full of colour and pageantry, as the cavalcade slowly wound its way through the parishes of Minster and Eastchurch on their way to the baronial hall at Shurland. As Daly describes in his *History of the Isle of Sheppey*, 'It does not require a very powerful imagination to picture this imposing procession winding its way over the hills of Sheppey, through a charming country, rich in its autumnal garniture, to the family mansion of the Cheneys.'

Shurland Hall was described as 'a stately residence', with a private chapel, stables, mews, kennels, offices and gardens. A contemporary plan, held today in the National Archives, shows it as an extensive red brick property, consisting of several large courtyards, some surrounded by walls, others offices and residential buildings. In Thomas Cheney's brief biography on Tudorplace.com, we hear of a building that

> apparently, [had] a wing on either side spread out from the central gateway ... with its flanking towers and ... new stairs ... Then came the banqueting hall on the east of the main court, the dormitories on either side, one court after another, till the whole range spread over several acres, comprising no less than nine quadrangles, enclosed within high stone walls with a chapel in the far south-east corner, the whole forming a worthy mansion.

Indeed, the layout of the principal building appears to have been similar to that at Hampton Court, whereby access was via an outer 'base' court before passing through a large gatehouse, the remains of which still stand today, to a second, inner courtyard. This second courtyard was flanked on all sides by lodgings, with a Great Hall lying directly ahead. Perhaps here we can imagine Henry and Anne dismounting, to sweep up a fashionable staircase into the largest public chamber – the hall – all the time admiring the sumptuous decoration that the king's patronage had, at least in part, enabled.

The royal couple spent four days at Shurland, eating, drinking and hunting with some coursing thrown in. The 36 square miles that made up the Isle of Sheppey were at that time covered in woodland and were ideal as hunting land. During the period that Henry and Anne were on the island, the *Privy Purse Expenses* gives us glimpses of some of the everyday events that occurred, including money paid to one of Master Cheney's servants who brought pheasants to the king and a sum of seven shillings and sixpence paid to the keeper of the park in which the king and Anne hunted prodigiously during their stay.

Shurland Hall Today

Shurland was neglected for many years and eventually fell into a ruined state. In the 1990s efforts began to preserve what was left of the buildings; these included the gatehouse range and part of the Great Hall. Then, in 2006, a grant of £300,000 was given to restore the façade of the hall and gatehouse. This work was completed in 2010/11.

Visitor Information

Visiting Sheppey is almost like descending upon another country as you drive over the Sheppey Crossing, a sweeping bridge that ascends to 115 feet before depositing you on an island that often feels remote and windswept. The island itself is small, so in a car it is easy to get around. One senses that the island might have enjoyed a more prosperous past and, as you drive around, it often feels as though the islanders are eking out a living on the edge of the mainland. Although there are pretty spots to be found, they are few and far between. The woodlands referred to during Anne's visits seem largely to have gone and the towns, in particular, seem to have fallen upon hard times.

In Queenborough there is nothing left of the castle, whose site can be tricky to locate. Do not expect any signs pointing the way! It was originally positioned where an open green area and playing field now stand, next to Queenborough railway station. There is an adjacent car park and commemorative plaque that gives some information about the castle. However, there is little to speak of its illustrious past and if you make the pilgrimage, you may find yourself leaving disappointed.

Shurland Hall has recently been sold and so is no longer overseen by the Spitalfields Trust. It is now in private ownership and the owners' attitudes to prearranged visits for those interested in its history are currently unclear. However, the hall can be seen from a distance and, should it become possible to visit this location in the future, these directions will help you.

Shurland Hall lies around ten–fifteen minutes' drive away from Queenborough, positioned on the edge of a small village called Eastchurch. On entering the village, continue along the high street to the far end. Where the road bends at a right angle, a small drive continues forward. At the time of writing, the red brick Tudor gatehouse is clearly visible at a distance down a quarter-of-a-mile-long drive, surrounded by fields. However, we must stress that this is private property and visiting permission depends on the inclination of the current owners.

The authors also made the ten-minute trip to nearby Minster, where an old Saxon abbey church sits proudly atop the highest hilltop on an otherwise rather flat island. It has been a site of worship for over 1,400 years. The owner of Shurland Hall, and Anne's host and client, Sir Thomas Cheney, is buried in the church of the former Minster Abbey in a tomb that has been greatly ravaged by time.

Postcode for Shurland Hall: ME12 4DA.

Canterbury, Kent

My wife is now near her lying in, so that I cannot remove her from Canterbury to any other place. I pray you, therefore, be content with the worst lodging that ever ye had in any poor friend's house. Canterbury, Michaelmas Day.

Sir Christopher Hales to Cromwell in a letter regarding Henry and Anne's visit to Canterbury in 1532

The ancient city of Canterbury played host to Anne and Henry twice in the autumn of 1532; the first time was on 10–11 October, when the royal party was on its way to Dover and then on to Calais to meet with Francis I, and the second on the return leg of the journey, lodging there overnight on the 17–18 November.

Tudor Canterbury

Canterbury is a medieval jewel, and in the sixteenth century was also a site of popular pilgrimage for those wishing to pay homage at the shrine of the martyred Thomas à

Becket in Canterbury Cathedral. Looking at a sixteenth-century map of the city by Braun and Hogenberg, we see Canterbury surrounded by a substantial circular wall and dominated by the cathedral that dwarfs a higgledy-piggledy complex of medieval streets and houses, some of which straddle the River Stour as it flows through the east of the city. Other than the cathedral itself, several notable locations visible on the map survive in various states of repair to this day: parts of the walls, North Gate, the castle, Dane John mound, the gatehouse of St Augustine's (Austin's) Abbey and the Cathedral Gate.

However, when it comes to identifying exactly where the royal couple stayed in Canterbury, we run into a frustrating puzzle that leads us almost to the front door of their lodgings – but not quite. Here we shall tackle the evidence that we have for each visit in turn.

The Visit of 10–11 October 1532

In anticipation of the coming visit, on 29 September Henry's attorney general, Sir Christopher Hales, wrote to his good friend Thomas Cromwell who, as ever, was right at the centre of organising the king's affairs. Sir Christopher was part of the Hales family, who owned land and property in and around Canterbury. They were undoubtedly one of the most powerful and pre-eminent families in the city. We shall allow Sir Christopher to speak for himself as he writes:

> I thank you for your last. I hear the King intends to be at Sherland, Mr. Cheyny's place, on Saturday next; but I hear not whether he proposes to be at Canterbury, nor the time of his coming ... You write to me of my new house at St. Stephen's, which you have heard say I shall have. I pray you help me thereunto. My wife is now near her lying in, so that I cannot remove her from Canterbury to any other place. I pray you, therefore, be content with the worst lodging that ever ye had in any poor friend's house. Canterbury, Michaelmas Day.

From this we learn that Sir Christopher was clearly looking to take a new property in the village of St Stephen's (Hackington), lying north of the city walls. It is just possible that this property was Place Hall, residence of the archdeacons of Canterbury, where the old William Warham had finally died on 22 August, just five weeks earlier. It is thought that Sir Christopher probably did eventually take ownership of Place Hall but most records, perhaps erroneously, guess that this was after the Reformation. Yet why would Hales need Cromwell's help if it wasn't to take over a major residence where controversy was involved? However, regardless of all this, it seems that the king and the new Marquess of Pembroke were to lodge in the city, in a 'poor house', as Hales's wife could not be moved due to her advanced state of pregnancy.

In a following letter to Cromwell, dated 7 October from Canterbury, Hales once again discusses the forthcoming visit by the king. He suggests to his friend that if he cannot be accommodated in the same house as the king, Cromwell could, as an alternative, be lodged at a nearby friend's house 'where no-one could disturb' him, 'or else at Christchurch', which must also have been nearby. Either way, Sir Christopher acknowledges that Master Cromwell needs to have daily access to the king. This gives us an indication that the lodging in which the king and Anne stayed must have been close to the centre of the city, near the cathedral, also known as Christ Church. In previous visits, Henry had lodged in the Abbot's Palace there, but no mention of it is made in these letters. Perhaps this was somehow on account of the recent death of the Archbishop Warham and the opposition by the Archbishopric of Canterbury to the king's divorce and to Anne; or perhaps it was to pointedly honour Sir Christopher, a loyal friend of the king's – and of Cromwell.

So all in all, the evidence points to the royal couple being lodged at Sir Christopher Hales's town house. This may have indeed been rather stately, despite the attorney general customarily referring to his house as 'poor'. Some twenty years later, records of Alderman Bunce referred to the fact that in 1554 the city wall at Worthgate and Riding Gate was repaired with stone 'from Mr Justice Hales's palace'. However, exactly where this palace was, or whether any part of it still stands today, could not be identified. Unfortunately, the *Privy Purse Expenses* doesn't really help us much as it simply records the payment made to the keeper of the house where the king stayed: 'Item the same day [11th October] paid to the keeper of the house that the king's grace lay in at Canterbury by way of reward – 7 shillings and 6 pence.'

The Visit of 17–18 November 1532

The first and only reference to where Anne and Henry lodged on the return trip from Dover to London is another entry in the *Privy Purse Expenses*. It states, 'Item the 18th day (November) paid to the keeper of my Lord Feneux house in Canterbury by way of reward – 7 shillings and 6 pence.'

Sir John Feneux of Herne, also Feneux and Fyneux, was Lord Chief Justice of England from 1495 to 1525, but had already died by around 1526 and was buried in Christ Church in Canterbury. He was a prominent citizen 'who had a fair habitation (house) in this City', according to Fuller's *Worthies of England*. Sir John Feneux's only surviving son and heir was William Feneux, who must have been the king's host in 1532. William's will reveals that among his many properties were lands at St Dunstan's and St Stephen's at Hackington.

Once again, we see the clearly fashionable district of Hackington making an appearance. Obviously, this was another influential and well-connected local family who had strong ties to the legal profession. Was this then Sir Christopher Hales's 'friend' referred to above, part of the Cromwell inner circle who secured Sir William a prestigious visit from Henry and his future queen? Unfortunately, no further information has been found on the reason for Henry and Anne lodging at 'my Lord Feneux's house', nor where it was located. The only other fragment of information is that on both stays in Canterbury the local waytes (musicians) seem to have provided entertainment, while the Abbot of St Austin's brought a book to the king.

The visit was fleeting, and soon Anne and Henry joined the main London–Dover road, taking their time as they wound their way back toward London.

Trivia: Sir Christopher Hales would lead the prosecution of Anne and George Boleyn at their trials in 1536. He is buried in the churchyard at St Stephen's church, Hackington.

Visitor Information

Canterbury is full of 'must-sees', including the surviving fragments of the city's wall and gates, the gatehouse of St Augustine's Abbey and, of course, the cathedral and its gatehouse.

Do remember to visit the back of the cathedral where you can wander through what remains of the rest of the original monastic buildings, which now lie partly in ruin following the Dissolution of the Monasteries. If you stay centrally, for pure convenience, we can recommend the Cathedral Gate Hotel right next to the Cathedral Gate; it is particularly atmospheric to wander the shadowy cloisters as night falls. Away from the cathedral itself, central Canterbury contains many architectural delights of the medieval and Tudor ages. Give yourself plenty of time, there is lots to see.

Visitor Information for the cathedral can be found at http://www.canterbury-cathedral. org/visit/. The local tourist information office, which will be able to help with booking accommodation, can be reached through http://www.canterbury.co.uk/.

Dover and Dover Castle, Kent

> Some time I fled the fire that me brent
> By sea, by land, by water and by wind;
> And now I follow the coals that be quent,
> From Dover to Calais against my mind.
>
> Thomas Wyatt, courtier and poet

Note: while we know Anne was at Dover, the castle is one of those locations that we cannot absolutely confirm that Anne visited. However, the balance of probability tips enough in favour of a royal visit to compel us to include this location. See below for further detail.

Whether arriving at Dover by land or sea, the eleventh-century Norman castle dominates the skyline above the harbour. The mighty fortress, perched atop of Dover's famous white, chalky cliffs, speaks of the castle's primary historic role in defending England against invasion from mainland Europe.

It is an impressive sight, defined in outline back in the late twelfth and early thirteenth centuries by an ambitious building project undertaken by King Henry II. This gave the castle its formidable central keep, as recognisable today as it would have been 800 years ago.

In size, might and its position upon a high, rocky outcrop of land, Dover may well remind the approaching visitor of Windsor Castle. Yet unlike Windsor, which in Anne's time – as it is now – was a much-loved and well-used royal abode, in the sixteenth century the accommodation at Dover had become outdated and was too inconvenient in its layout to be used regularly by the king and court. The interiors were largely medieval, with 6-foot-thick walls preventing any major redevelopment. Just as importantly, there were no extensive leisure facilities or fine gardens that one might find, say, at Greenwich, Hampton Court or Whitehall. As a result, outside of its main function of defending against war, by Anne's time the castle was essentially only used by the king for grand ceremonial purposes or for the occasional important visitor stopping off on their travels between England and the Continent.

Sixteenth-century pictures, such as the one by Antonis Wyngaerde entitled *A View of Dover from the Sea*, clearly show the topography of the land, the sheer dominance of the castle over the tiny port lying at the feet of its iconic white cliffs, its main western gateway, and a hint of the winding road leading down into the town.

In the intervening centuries, the town has gradually encroached upon the hillside to the west of the castle, the open countryside being replaced by roads, pavements and houses. But as the modern-day traveller makes their way up to the castle's main entrance, it is easy to imagine a train of baggage carts, horses and courtiers winding their way up from the harbour below. Of course, as we will hear in a short while, this is how we can think of Henry and Anne arriving at Dover Castle together in the autumn of 1532.

Two other sixteenth-century images tell us a little bit more about the appearance of Tudor Dover and its castle. The first is the *Embarkation of Henry VIII at Dover*. This famous painting is about 12 feet long and is now in the royal collection at Hampton Court. The picture depicts the king leaving England on 31 May 1520 with his then queen, Katharine of Aragon, and an enormous retinue of nobles, servants and horses. The view is taken from the south-west of Dover harbour, near the foot of Shakespeare's Cliff. The two forts, with their cannon giving the royal salute, are the Archcliff (you will still see this name referred to as you drive into the town on the main road from London today) and the Black Bulwark. Of particular interest is the appearance of Dover Castle in the top-left corner of the painting, once again showing the castle's main westerly gateways. What is more, the scene depicted gives a fantastic sense of how the harbour might have looked when Henry and Anne set sail for Calais on 11 October 1532, albeit on a slightly less grand scale.

The second image is a late sixteenth-century sketch of the inner bailey of the castle by John Bereblock. This valuable image gives us a wonderful record of the castle as Anne would have seen in it. The sketch depicts a series of crenelated walls, towers and gateways surrounded by a ditch and traversed by two bridges. Henry II's Great Tower dominates the image, and we also can see the lost corridor or 'pentice' that once linked the main keep to Arthur's Hall and the King's Lodgings to the north.

The Royal Apartments

Up until the early thirteenth century, the medieval royal apartments occupied the first and second floors of the main keep. The king occupied the second floor; the queen, the level below. This layout of rooms is very similar to other castles built during the same epoch, such as those in the White Tower at the Tower of London. Each floor comprised two large, vaulted chambers running side by side. One chamber was used as the Great Hall, or presence chamber, in which the king or queen held audience; the other was reserved as the privy chamber, allowing the monarch and his consort the opportunity to retire from the public gaze. Extending off these two great chambers is a series of smaller rooms built into the walls of the keep. These chambers were restored to their original medieval glory by English Heritage in 2008; they are fascinating in their own right for any lover of history and, in the authors' opinion, present the visitor with one of the finest medieval recreations you are likely to see in the country. However, as we are here to consider the Tudor castle, we will leave you to enjoy this delight and the fantastic costumed interpreters that bring it so wonderfully to life.

Was Anne Boleyn at Dover Castle?

As we mentioned at the outset of this entry, sadly it is impossible to irrefutably confirm that the royal couple lodged at the castle either on their way to, or back from, Calais.

However, the evidence weighs in favour of a visit. *The History of the King's Works, Volume III* states that in October 1532 the Constable of Dover Castle, Sir Edward Guildford, oversaw repairs to the castle's drawbridge and king's lodgings in advance of Henry's arrival on his way to his interview with Francis I. This seems definite enough. However, *The Letters and Papers of Henry VIII* are slightly less clear-cut, and we see Sir Edward writing to Cromwell and asking for confirmation that the king does in fact intend to stay at the castle. Perhaps Edward Guildford later received confirmation in the affirmative. We know that Anne and Henry certainly did lodge at Dover, both before and after their sea journey to and from Calais. However, there remains the possibility that, instead of making their way up to the castle, they were accommodated in the town; the two most likely alternative candidates for such lodgings are the Maison Dieu, whose remains stand today as part of Dover's old town-hall buildings, or St Martin's Priory. Three medieval buildings have survived from the latter site. These are now incorporated into Dover College: the original gateway to the priory is now the college library; the refectory is today the Great Hall; and what is thought to have been a guest house originally is now the college chapel.

If, however, we accept that the repairs did portend a visit then the question becomes, where exactly did the royal couple lodge?

In 1236, Henry III married the twelve-year-old Eleanor of Provence. The decision was taken to provide the bride with royal chambers in the Great Tower while the king moved into new lodgings in the inner bailey. The apartments were connected by the pentice described above. There are three possibilities: the first that, like her medieval predecessor, Anne was lodged in the main keep, while the king occupied the traditional king's lodgings in the inner bailey; secondly, that Anne lodged together with the king in the latter apartments; and finally, that both Henry and Anne lodged in the main keep, occupying the first and second floors.

Research that Gordon Higgott of English Heritage has recently concluded states that 'up to the early seventeenth century the chambers in the Great Tower were largely for ceremonial use'. Sadly, there is no specific information about the use of these rooms during the time of Henry VIII but, from accounts of the 1530s and early 1540s, we do know the names of the four main chambers:

> On the first floor the 'outer' (NE) room was the Queen's 'Reigning Chamber', while the 'inner' SW room was her Privy Chamber; on the second floor the 'outer' NE room was the King's Great Chamber or Watching (i.e. Guard) Chamber, while the 'inner' SW room was variously styled his Privy or Presence Chamber. This general arrangement seems to be confirmed by several references in the accounts for the refurbishment of 1625–6 to the king and queen's 'Presence' and 'Privy' chambers, which confirm that the first floor was regarded as the Queen's, and the second floor as the King's.

He also goes on to surmise that the king's lodgings, centred on Arthur's Hall in the inner bailey, would have provided the most comfortable accommodation for the royal couple. However, virtually nothing is left today to tell us how those lodgings were arranged.

The apartments in the Great Tower remain intact to this day, although the bare plaster walls would once have been covered in wainscoted panelling. The old king's lodgings were subsequently engulfed by the redevelopment of the old buildings into barracks in the eighteenth century. Yet the Great Hall, called Arthur's Hall, which was very much in use during Anne's lifetime, still exists and now houses the exhibition telling the story of royal Dover, although, as you will see, it has lost its undoubted former glory!

Events at Dover

Anne passed through Dover on four occasions: first on her way to and from the Continent as a young girl of twelve, when she was sent first into the service of Margaret of Austria in 1513; she returned in 1521, after six years spent at the French court. The second time was during the historic trip to and from Calais in the autumn of 1532, when Anne was at the zenith of her power and on the verge of her marriage to Henry of England. We know nothing of the former voyage, but of the latter we know considerably more. From wherever the couple did indeed lodge, they set out from Dover aboard the *Swallow* at 5 o'clock in the morning on 11 October. The wind was in their favour and they landed safely at Calais just five hours later at 10 o'clock (see the entry for Calais).

However, the couple were less fortunate on the return leg; severe gales had kept them holed up in Calais for two weeks longer than they had expected. Some ships that tried the return journey early were blown aground on the shores of northern France. A few were lost. Eventually, they boarded their ship at midnight on 13 November. After what must have been a rough twenty-eight-hour crossing, Henry and Anne arrived back in Dover at 5 o'clock on the following day, St Erkenwald's Day, 14 November. Henry and Anne then remained at Dover for two days, leaving on 16 November. The chronicler Edward Hall has suggested that it was in fact on this day that the couple were married. While most historians agree that the true date that Henry and Anne were married was 25 January 1533, some have postulated that perhaps, having consummated their relationship sometime during their time confined in the Exchequer in Calais, the two were finally betrothed after they arrived in England. If so, did the ceremony take place at Dover Castle? It is quite a romantic thought, for if this did indeed happen, Dover saw the first day of Anne as Henry's *de facto* wife and Queen of England.

Visitor Information

Dover Castle is managed by English Heritage. Please visit their website for visitor information at http://www.english-heritage.org.uk/daysout/properties/dover-castle/. Telephone number: + 44 (0) 1304 211 067

Postcode for Dover Castle: CT16 1HU.

Calais, France

Then shalle the Frenchman Calais winne, when iron and leade lyke corke shall swimme.

Inscription over the main Lantern Gate during the English occupation of Calais

In the first half of the sixteenth century, Calais was the only jewel of English sovereignty that remained as part of the French mainland. It was a remnant of the vast empire of England's Plantagenet dynasty, a dynasty that had once reigned across not only England, but much of northern and western France, as far south as Aquitaine.

Calais was part-garrison, part-trading town, the last outpost of English soil before reaching the rest of the Continent and beyond. Within its fortified walls was a grid-like network of narrow streets, packed tightly with fine medieval houses owned by affluent Calais merchants. Every so often, these streets would open up into spacious squares used for trading, recreation and the gathering of its townsfolk.

We can only assume that it was when travelling to take up her position as maid-of-honour to the regent, Margaret of Austria, in 1513 that the twelve-year-old Anne first came to Calais. Perhaps she was also there for the arrival of Mary Tudor on her way to be wed to the aging King Louis XII at nearby Abbeville. Unfortunately, we have no record of exactly where and when Anne joined the English contingent serving the new French queen. However, she most definitely would pass through the town again on her way back from France in the winter of 1521, no doubt a woman transformed by her social and religious education at the sophisticated French court.

Sadly, nothing is recorded of Anne's movements through the town during that time. Yet the same cannot be said for her only other visit in the autumn of 1532. Anne would return in triumph at Henry's side as the newly created Marquess of Pembroke; she was at the pinnacle of her power and influence with the king. The trip was planned as a great celebration, during which the French and English kings would reaffirm their pact of mutual support against Charles V, and Anne would be formally received by Francis, thereby effectively endorsing her position as Henry's queen in waiting.

Tudor Calais – Rediscovering a Lost Town

Tragically, the bombing of Calais during the Second World War destroyed virtually every remnant of the town's medieval grandeur. However, due to the efforts of English antiquaries in the nineteenth century, we do know something of the buildings that had survived over the intervening 300 years. Combined with contemporary accounts of the town and its history, the modern-day time traveller can yet walk in Anne Boleyn's footsteps and gain some satisfaction by seeing beyond its unexciting modern-day façade to once more recreate the sixteenth-century town in their mind's eye.

Perhaps the best way to begin this tour is to approach Calais as Anne must have done initially in 1513 and then again with Henry in October 1532 – by boat. A ferry leaving from Dover on a clear day will soon reveal the shores of France looming on the horizon. Imagine the excitement of the twelve-year-old Anne setting out on a journey of incomparable adventure, or in eager anticipation of her triumphant return in 1532.

A view of the town as it was in the sixteenth century, taken from the *Chronicle of Calais in the Reigns of Henry VII and Henry VIII*, shows the skyline of Calais as Anne would have seen it approaching across the English Channel from Dover. The town was fortified by enormous city walls. Along its length, a series of towers provided a mixture of both accommodation and defence. The Lantern Gate, in the centre of the picture and standing roughly at the point of the intersection of the modern-day Boulevard des Alliés, the Boulevard de la Résistance and the Rue de la Mer, was the principal gate of the town; like all the gates of the city, these were locked during an elaborate ceremony every night. Beyond the city walls, follow the long-lost outline of four key buildings which made up the town's impressive skyline: the churches of Our Lady to the left and St Nicholas to the right, while the exquisite medieval structures of the Town Hall and Staple Hall stand centrally, directly to the south of the Lantern Gate.

As you dock at Calais today, you will see the gnarled remnants of the old Rysbank Tower over to your right. The ruins of the fortifications are still signposted from within the town itself, over the Pont Henri Henon. Modern-day ferries moor to the east of the town centre. If you had been travelling aboard the *Swallow* with Anne in 1532, your ship would have taken you directly past the Rysbank Tower to dock against one of Calais's many quays and jetties, lying directly in front of the old city walls.

Find your way from the ferry to the site of the now-vanished Lantern Gate, whose position is as described above. To enter the town, follow in Anne's footsteps and make your way down Lantern Street, now the Rue de la Mer, and you will find yourself standing in what was once the footprint of the main marketplace, now the Place d'Armes. Only two ancient buildings remain to be seen today in Calais. The first of these is on the south side of the Place d'Armes; the Tour du Guet is a rare survivor from the Middle Ages, once standing behind the medieval, thirteenth-century town hall that was destroyed during the Second World War. The surviving tower certainly would have been a building that Anne would have seen, albeit not quite in this derelict state!

On arriving here, the royal party turned right and headed down what was once called the High Street, the then main road heading east-west through the town, now called the Rue d'André Gerschel. Henry and Anne made their way toward the now lost church of St Nicolas, where a service of thanksgiving was held for their safe passage across the Channel. Thence they went on to their lodgings at the Exchequer, situated directly opposite the church. Here Anne was lodged in a suite of seven rooms, in splendour befitting a queen. Sadly, the church of St Nicolas and the Exchequer are both long lost. The two buildings were situated in the western quarter of the old town and their precise location is difficult to fathom. However, they were oriented facing each other, perhaps somewhere close to where the Rue André Gerschel intersects the Rue de la Victoire.

Next, head down the modern day Rue Royale until you come to an intersection with the Rue du Duc de Guise. It is difficult to believe it now, but at the intersection of these two streets once stood the most magnificent residence in Calais – the Staple Inn. Like many of the grand buildings of Calais its architecture combined Tudor and Flemish styles, and it was the residence for Henry VIII in 1520 when he travelled to the Field of the Cloth of Gold, as well as Francis I in 1532. It was indeed here, in the sumptuous rooms of the palace, that Anne made her grand debut in front of Francis during the Calais trip of 1532. Along with six of her ladies, she danced for him and the French and English courts at a masque held at the Staple Inn on Sunday 27 October.

If you turn out of the Rue Royale and into the Rue du Duc de Guise, you will soon come across Rue Marie Tudor on your right; across the entrance to this street once stood the original gateway.

Your next stop is the only other survivor from Tudor Calais: the church of Notre Dame, or 'Our Lady', as it was known in Anne's time. You can reach it by walking right the way along the Rue du Duc de Guise, until you join the Rue du Seigneur de Gourdan. Unfortunately, when the authors were there, the church was closed for extensive renovation. However, it is worth a visit, just knowing that many kings and queens of France and England have prayed here in centuries gone by. Also of particular note to the Tudor enthusiast is the sixteenth-century tomb of John Bourchier, 2nd Baron Berners, who is buried in the church choir. Baron Berners was the Lieutenant of Calais until he died in 1533, and so it was he who welcomed Henry and Anne when they landed from Dover in 1532.

Events at Calais: 11 October–12 November, 1532

By ten o'clock on the morning of 11 October 1532, Anne and Henry had arrived on board the *Swallow* from Dover. The couple spent a little over a month in Calais. Henry left the town on 21 October to meet with his royal 'brother', before being escorted to lodge at the expense of the French king in nearby Boulogne for six days, returning on 27 October. Meanwhile, Anne was lodged magnificently at the Exchequer. This was a grand building, which encompassed two privy gardens enclosed within two central courtyards, a tennis play and a delightful Long Gallery.

After the official royal visit was over, fierce storms broke out in Calais. Some of the English court had already set sail to return; many ships were blown off course and some were shipwrecked. However, with decreased numbers of courtiers present, Henry and Anne remained lodged, one imagines, with a greater degree of privacy than was usual. Professor Eric Ives describes it as a sort of honeymoon for the couple. The trip had certainly been an outstanding success. Assured of Francis's support, was it at the Exchequer that Anne finally surrendered herself and slept with Henry for the first time? It is certainly a delicious possibility to consider. Perhaps it is because Anne must have been at her happiest here that Calais holds such a fond place in the authors' hearts – even though much of the town that Anne knew is now lost.

Sandwich, Kent

> paied to the friers at Sandwiche by way of rewarde XV crowns.
>
> *Privy Purse Expenses of Henry VIII*

The *Privy Purse Expenses of Henry VIII* makes it clear that Henry and Anne left Dover two days after their arrival, on 16 November 1532. Ordinarily, one might have expected the royal party to make their way directly toward London along the ancient highway known as the Dover Road; this stretched for around 70 miles between England's most significant embarkation point for the Continent and the country's capital. However, following the triumph at Calais, it seems that they were in no hurry and instead headed northwards for just over 12 miles toward another ancient port on the Kentish coast, Sandwich. The reason for this detour is unknown.

The couple lodged merely one night in the town, which today has been called the 'most complete medieval town in England'. The only clue to their possible lodgings is an entry in the *Privy Purse Expenses*, which details that a payment of fifteen crowns was made by the king to the 'friers at Sandwiche' by way of reward. As it was common for such a payment to follow in recognition of hospitality received, it is quite probable that they lodged in the Carmelite Friary on the southern edge of the town. This theory is also supported by the fact that the friary was probably the only lodging in the town large enough to accommodate a royal retinue.

The friary had been founded in the late thirteenth century, and then enlarged to eventually cover a site of around 5 acres between New Street to the east, Cattle Market to the north and the town ramparts, known as The Rope Walk, lying to the south.

Crossing the main entrance, which was off Cattle Market, Anne would have been faced with the sight of the friary church. Beyond this, to the south of the church was a large central cloister surrounded by buildings. Other than the friary church, only a refectory and possible guest house have been tentatively identified following the four archaeological digs that have taken place at the site. Of course, there would also have been a prior's house as part of the complex, which was a common lodging for a king and queen when they visited religious houses. In addition, in 1416, when Henry V stayed at the Whitefriars around 100 years earlier, he was noted to have held a meeting in 'an outer chamber'. Clearly there was accommodation suitable for a king, his lady and the court.

Surrounded by ditches, which drained the marshy land upon which the friary had been built originally, the enclosure included a dovecote, fish pools, fruit gardens and an orchard. Furthermore, we know something of what the court might have eaten that night, for the town council had provided 'two couple of fat oxen, twenty fat wethers and twenty couple of fat capons'.

But Anne's brush with Sandwich was fleeting; the following morning the royal party were on the move, the king paying for a boat to 'take him over the water at Sandwiche' before heading eastwards toward the great and venerated city of Canterbury. By the way, 'over the water' does not mean out to sea. There were, and still are, a large number of inland waterways surrounding Sandwich and these would have had to have been crossed before reaching Canterbury, lying further inland.

The end of the friary came in 1538 when it was dissolved and subsequently passed into Crown hands.

Note: if you are wandering around Sandwich and enjoying its many charms, you may read on one of the informative history boards located around the town that a building on Strand Street called The King's Lodgings was actually where Henry [and Anne] lodged during their visit of 1532. Although it would be lovely to add such a location to the list, it sadly does not stand up to scrutiny, and historian Helen Clarke, who has done much research on the town, explains,

> Despite all our best efforts, the signboards around the town still carry well-worn urban myths. The house today called King's Lodgings was never anything of the kind. It was built as a merchant's house in the fifteenth century and then became an inn – The White Hart. It subsequently became known as The Old House, and the present name is a very recent attribution. There was a King's Lodging (in a different location on Strand Street), but it has long gone. It was where Queen Elizabeth stayed in 1572.

8. Blickling Hall, Norfolk. Blickling was home to the Boleyns for over a century and is traditionally said to be where, in around 1501, Anne Boleyn was born. The manor today dates mainly to the seventeenth century; however, it was built on the footprint of the house that Anne would have known.

9. Detail from a tapestry hung at Hever Castle entitled *The Marriage of Louis XII and Princess Mary in 1514*, c. 1525. It has been widely postulated that Anne is depicted in this contemporary artwork. If so, this might be one of the few true likenesses of the future queen. Nobody knows if this is indeed the case, but it is fun to guess which figure might represent her. Our favourite candidate is seen in the top left-hand corner of this picture, the woman second along from the left on the top row, clearly engaged in conversation with two gentlemen. Is one of them Sir Thomas, her father? What do you think?

10. *Hever Castle* by Edmund John Niemann, 1858. This mid-nineteenth-century painting of Hever shows the external appearance of the castle before extensive internal and external renovations were undertaken by the Astors in the early twentieth century. Here we can more keenly appreciate the original, rather rugged-looking surroundings of the castle, including the marshy area in front of the main gatehouse. We can also see the dense forest of *Andreswald* that once surrounded Hever, infamous during the medieval period for its lawlessness. The Manor of Polebrooke can just be seen in the background, rising up behind the crenelated turrets of Anne's family home.

Above left: 11. Hever Castle, Kent. Anne is thought to have come to Hever first as a small child of around four or five, after her father inherited the castle in 1505. Thomas Boleyn, an aspiring and gifted courtier, immediately undertook major alterations to bring the new Boleyn family home in line with fashionable standards of the day. He created a fabulous Long Gallery over the Great Hall and an impressive staircase gallery that connected the east and west wings of the castle at first-floor level.

Above right: 12. Anne Boleyn sculpture at Pashley Manor, 2012. There are a number of sculptures on display in the gardens of Pashley Manor, including this very moving sculpture of Anne Boleyn by Philip Jackson, made especially to commemorate the link between the Boleyn family and the house.

Opposite bottom: 16. Conjectural drawing of Rochford Hall, Essex, by Norman Barnes. This drawing, which hangs in the Rochford Hundred clubhouse, shows what Rochford Hall may have looked like in the sixteenth century and gives a good sense of its former grandeur. The only surviving turret is the one in the foreground.

13. St Peter's church, Hever, 2009. The church, which dates back to the twelfth century and is located in the centre of Hever next to Hever Castle, is best known for being the final resting place of Anne's father, Sir Thomas Boleyn. On 12 March 1539, he died at Hever Castle.

14. Pashley Manor, Ticehurst, 2012. The manor is located on the Sussex and Kent border, around a one-hour drive from Hever Castle. Sir Thomas Boleyn, Anne's father, owned the house in the early sixteenth century, giving rise to the local legend that Anne visited the house as a child, plausible considering its proximity to Hever Castle, the Boleyn family home.

15. Rochford Hall, Essex, 2009. The manor came into Boleyn ownership in 1515 and today operates as a golf club. The grand turreted and moated manor house that Anne would have known is now greatly altered. In its heyday, it was one of the largest houses in the county but a disastrous fire in 1760 reduced it to what we see today.

Above: 17. The palace of Margaret of Austria, Mechelen. 2013. The Renaissance palace built for Margaret of Austria was home to Anne for around a year following her arrival there in the summer of 1513. The building now functions as the city's courts of justice.

Opposite bottom left: 18. The east end of the Rue St-Antoine, looking onto the Place de la Bastille in Paris's 4th *arrondissement*, 2013. The column at the centre of the *place* commemorates the 1830 July Revolution. In the sixteenth century, from this spot, Anne would have seen the fortress of the medieval Bastille itself dominating the eastern gateway to the city. It was here that the French played host to the English delegation sent to seal the betrothal of the two-year-old Princess Mary to the French dauphin in December 1518. Anne's services as an interpreter would have been greatly in demand.

Opposite bottom right: 19. Vintage postcard of the Hôtel de Cluny from 1909 showing the main gateway through into the courtyard. The *hôtel* appears much as it did in Anne's day; the main building with two wings flanks a courtyard that once faced onto the Rue Mathurins St-Jacques.

Top right: 20. The *cour d'honneur* (central courtyard) of the Hôtel de Cluny, 2013. This picture is taken looking in through the main gateway. The building is probably one of the best-preserved examples of medieval architecture of its type in the city, and was built by the abbots of Cluny around the end of the fifteenth century/the beginning of the sixteenth.

Bottom right: 21. The Basilica of St-Denis, Paris. The basilica became the traditional theatre for the coronation of French queens after Anne of Brittany's took place there in 1491. In Anne's day the church was part of a flourishing Benedictine abbey that lay some 6 kilometres to the north of Paris. She may well have been here for the Coronation of Mary Tudor on 9 November 1514, and there is no reason to question her presence two years later, when Claude was crowned Queen of France on 10 May 1516.

Above: 22. The Cathedral of Notre Dame, Paris. Anne would have visited here in the entourage of Queen Claude of France following the latter's Coronation at the Basilica of St-Denis in May, 1516. A solemn Mass of thanksgiving was the culmination of the queen's ceremonial entry into the city of Paris. We do not know if Anne also accompanied Mary Tudor to Notre Dame under similar circumstances following her Coronation two years earlier.

Left: 23. Vintage Postcard of the High Chapel at La Sainte Chapelle. La Sainte Chapelle was originally part of the medieval Palais-Royal on the Île de la Cité, Paris. Today it is one of the last vestiges of this once-great royal abode, surrounded by the modern-day Palais de Justice. Although the palace was no longer in regular use during Anne's time in France, La Sainte Chapelle is worth visiting to see the Gothic style of architecture that would have dominated Paris's other royal residences in the early part of the sixteenth century, before the Renaissance swept through France.

24. The Gothic and Louis XII wings of the Château d'Amboise, in the Loire Valley, 2013. Anne arrived here with the French court in May 1515, after King Francis I moved the court from Paris. These two wings represent around 20 per cent of the original royal château that has survived. On the left is the Gothic wing, with the sixteenth-century *Grand-Salle* on the ground floor. On the right is the Louis XII wing, with the restored Renaissance lodgings of Francis I on the ground floor, and those of Queen Claude stacked directly above.

25. The Louis XII wing of Château de Blois from the site of the original forecourt (*avant-cour*), 2013. Anne would have stayed here regularly from June 1515 until her return to England in 1521. Here we see the north-east façade of the Louis XII wing; it is thought that the king's chambers were to the left at first-floor level and the queen's to the right. The main entrance to the inner *cour d'honneur* is surmounted by a statue of Louis XII on horseback.

26. The Church of Notre Dame, Ardres, 2013. In the sixteenth century, Ardres was a fortified town, lying just outside the English Pale. It was home to the French king and court during the Field of Cloth of Gold. The church lies at the centre of the town and is one of the few buildings surviving from the period.

Above left: 27. The Château de Romorantin, Loire Valley. The château was owned by the Queen Mother, the powerful Louise of Savoy. It is likely that Anne spent time here in 1515 and 1517. This image of the south-east tower shows the best-preserved remains of the Château de Romorantin. Here, on the first floor, the future Queen Claude was born in 1499.

Above right: 28. Illustration of *The Field of Cloth of Gold* taken from *The Story of France* by Mary MacGregor. The picture shows King Henry VIII and King Francis I on horseback and, although fictional, conveys the colour and splendour of the occasion. A sea of tents, pitched to house the thousands who accompanied each royal retinue, was described by one French contemporary chronicler as a 'marvellous town of floating tapestries'.

Below: 29. The site of the Field of Cloth of Gold, 2013. This marble monument marks the site of the original list (tiltyard) where combat took place between the English and French delegation of knights. In the far distance, on the ridge of the hill, is Ardres, the site of the French encampments.

Right: 30. Richmond Palace Gatehouse, 2012. The gatehouse, with Henry VIII's coat of arms, and part of the outer range of Richmond Palace are all that survive above ground of the palace that once bore witness to the famous 1527 encounter between Anne and Cardinal Wolsey after he returned from his embassy to France.

Below: 31. The Henry VIII Gateway, Windsor Castle, 2007. Windsor Castle featured prominently in Anne's story. It was here that King Henry VIII welcomed Anne back to court with a grand banquet given in her honour after her protracted stay at Hever over the winter of 1527/28. It was also here that Henry set out with Anne on the summer progress of 1531, leaving Katharine of Aragon behind never to see her again. Finally, in a glittering ceremony in the king's presence chamber (today the Garter Throne Room), Anne was ennobled as Marquess of Pembroke.

Top: 32. New Hall School, Essex. The school occupies the site of Henry VIII's Beaulieu Palace, which the king purchased from Thomas Boleyn in 1516. The northern range, pictured here, was rebuilt in around 1575 and altered over the centuries; it probably originally housed the royal apartments. Much of the Tudor house was pulled down between 1737 and 1764 during the ownership of Lord Waltham.

Above left: 33. The royal arms of King Henry VIII, New Hall School, Essex. This once adorned the enormous gatehouse of Beaulieu Palace and is now housed in New Hall School's chapel. It is one of only a few survivors of the original residence and one that Anne would have seen as she arrived at the house in the summer of 1527.

Above right: 34. Carew Manor School, Surrey, 2012. In the sixteenth century, Beddington Place was the home of Anne Boleyn's cousin, Sir Nicholas Carew. His grand moated manor house was the setting for a romantic rendezvous between Henry and Anne in late 1528. The only substantial remainder of the original house is a splendid Tudor hall; the rest of the house was rebuilt in the early eighteenth century and is today home to Carew Manor School.

Above: 35. Bridewell Palace, London, *c.* 1660. A view from the Thames of Bridewell Palace as it appeared around the year 1660, with the entrance to the Fleet River and part of the Dominican House of Blackfriars visible. For several years after its completion in 1523, it was used as Henry VIII's principal London residence. In June and July 1529, Henry visited regularly, as the Legatine Court, charged with deciding the fate of his marriage to his first wife, Katharine of Aragon, was in session at Blackfriars. From 1530 onwards, the house was used primarily as a residence for the French ambassadors.

Below: 36. View showing Durham House, Salisbury House and Worcester House (in 1808), all of which once stood on the Strand backing onto the Thames in around 1630. From 1529 onwards, Durham House appears to have been the London residence of Anne's father, Thomas Boleyn. Anne visited her father there on a number of occasions and Thomas Cranmer resided there for a time in 1529.

Right: 37. Waltham Abbey, Essex, 2012. Henry VIII was a regular visitor to Waltham Abbey and on several occasions was accompanied by Anne Boleyn. During one of these visits in 1529, an historic meeting took place between Edward Foxe, Stephen Gardiner and their mutual acquaintance, Thomas Cranmer. The King's Great Matter was discussed and Cranmer suggested a new way of resolving the king's predicament that would change the course of history. All that remains of the Augustinian abbey where Henry and Anne would have stayed is the abbey church, seen here in the background. The Tudor lady is author Sarah Morris.

Above: 38. The village of Grafton Regis, 2013. On the left of the image is a white picket fence, which marks the original entrance to the manor. The original building was burnt to the ground during the Civil War. Today a seventeenth-century replacement stands on its footprint, tucked well back from the road. Note the tower of the parish church of St Mary the Virgin in the background. This church would have been standing during Anne's three visits to Grafton. Along this road, various red brick buildings can be seen and are thought to have once been offices serving the royal manor.

Middle: 39. Notley Abbey, Buckinghamshire. In the sixteenth century, Notley Abbey was a wealthy Augustinian monastery and one regularly visited by Henry VIII. In 1529, Henry and Anne sought solace in its beauty and in the twentieth century it became the home of another famous couple, Laurence Olivier and Vivien Leigh. Today, Notley operates as a wedding venue.

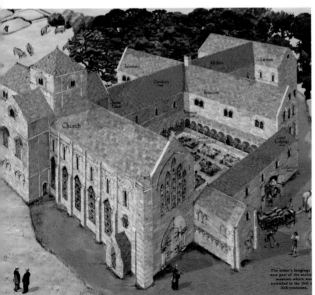

Bottom: 40. Notley Abbey, Buckinghamshire, as it would have appeared in the thirteenth century. This reconstruction by Madeleine Smith shows the abbey's original guest lodgings, which were extended in the fifteenth and sixteenth centuries and now form part of the modern-day house.

41. Bisham Abbey, Bisham, 2012. Only part of the sixteenth-century house that Anne visited remains extant today. Here we see the southern gabled end of a chequerboarded building that once contained the medieval solar, on the left. In the centre of the picture, a Tudor frontage now covers what would have been the exposed southern wall of the Great Hall. Its red-tiled pitched roof and tall chimneys remain visible from the outside. On the right of the picture, facing us, is the gabled end of the western range of a lost cloistered courtyard. Here, the first floor contains a much-remodelled 'council chamber' contemporary to Anne's visit.

42. Reconstruction of Woking Palace as it would have looked in the sixteenth century. The entrance into the courtyard, across the moat, remains the principal access point to the site today. The Great Hall lies directly opposite the gatehouse, while the royal apartments are shown over to the left of the picture. Service buildings are shown in the foreground and to the right of the picture. The buildings that remain standing today are not shown here, as they stand behind the Great Hall.

43. Ashridge House, Hertfordshire, from the north, c. 1761. The gatehouse and the windows of the Great Hall are clearly visible. Early in the nineteenth century, the house that Anne visited was dismantled and the present-day structure, designed in the Gothic revival style by architect James Wyatt, was constructed in its place.

Above left: 44. Katherine's Cross, Ampthill Park, 2013. Katherine's Cross in Ampthill Park marks the approximate site where Ampthill Castle once stood at the top of the Greensand Ridge, and offers majestic views over the surrounding countryside.
Above right: 45. Hertford Castle gatehouse, Hertfordshire. This is all that remains of the buildings that Anne would have known and is today home to Hertford Town Council.

Above: 46. Odiham Park Lodge, or Lodge Farmhouse as it is now more commonly called. Odiham Park Lodge was built in the fourteenth century for Edward III and is situated approximately a mile away from Odiham Castle. Anne and Henry hunted in the park in 1531 and made use of the lodge, where Henry met Mario Savorgano, a wealthy Venetian tourist who recorded details of the meeting in his travel diary. The little building on the left with curved braces is the only part that would have been standing in 1531.
Left: 47. Farnham Castle, Farnham. Illustration by James Ogilvy taken from *A Pilgrimage in Surrey*, 1914. Here we see the Episcopal Palace from Castle Street in the town of Farnham. The late fifteenth-century Waynflete's Tower is clearly visible in this picture.

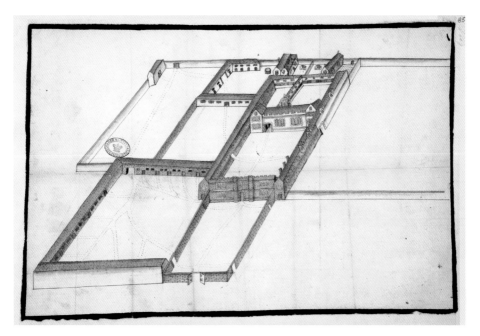

48. Shurland Hall, the Isle of Sheppey. This contemporary plan of Shurland Hall shows the house accessed via an outer court, surrounded by a red brick wall. The main gatehouse range shown in the image still stands today, and has recently been completely renovated to its former glory. A secondary or inner courtyard leads to an off-centre square archway, giving access to the Great Hall (the white building running parallel to the main gatehouse). The chapel can be seen in the background, identified by the cross on its roof. It is easy to see its similarities to the style and layout of Hampton Court Palace, one of the most fashionable houses of the day.

Above left: 49. Stone Castle, Stone, Kent, 2013. It was once part of the estate inherited by Lady Bridget Tyrwhitt (née Wiltshire) and her three husbands in turn. Part of the castle (to the left of the picture), contains the medieval square tower, original to the time of Henry and Anne's visit in 1532. Although this has long been held as the place in which the couple lodged as they made their way to and from Calais, the authors believe it was more likely to be nearby Stone Place, a sumptuous Tudor residence situated half a mile away on the same estate.

Above right: 50. Butchery Lane, Canterbury, Kent, 2013. We do not know the exact locations of the townhouses in which Henry and Anne stayed in autumn 1532, but letters suggest a central location near to Christ Church on their outward journey to Calais. Butchery Lane runs straight to Cathedral Gate (seen in the distance), and is a fine example of the type of medieval passageway that would have made up the ancient city at the time of the royal visit.

Above: 51. Dover Castle, Kent: early twentieth-century postcard. The castle sits high above the town in a perfect defensive position overlooking the English Channel. Henry II's central keep is easily visible, towering above the turreted curtain wall. This view gives a feel for its once-isolated position.

Below left: 52. The *Hôtel de Ville* and Tour du Guet, Calais. This coloured engraving shows Calais as it looked before Second World War bombing destroyed much of its surviving medieval charm. The image is painted from the high street, looking toward the southern end of the marketplace (now Place d'Armes), with the town hall in the background and Tour du Guet in the foreground. The latter was once part of the Staple Hall, one of the major buildings in medieval/Tudor Calais. Upon their arrival in 1532, the couple rode through the marketplace, turning into the high street toward their lodgings at the Exchequer.

Below right: 53. Rope Walk, Sandwich, Kent, 2013. This raised walkway runs around part of this ancient town. These walkways are the vestiges of the medieval ramparts, built to defend a town that was often raided by foreign powers. The area (off to the right of this picture) was once occupied by the Carmelite friary, more commonly known as the Whitefriars. This is probably where the royal court lodged overnight on 16 November 1532.

Bottom right: 54. The Red Lion, Sittingbourne, Kent, 2013. The Red Lion was once the pre-eminent coaching inn in Sittingbourne. It lodged kings, cardinals and emperors in its heyday, and on 19 November 1532 played host to Anne and Henry on their return journey from Calais. The modern-day inn has some wonderful Tudor features, notably in the buildings facing onto the courtyard garden.

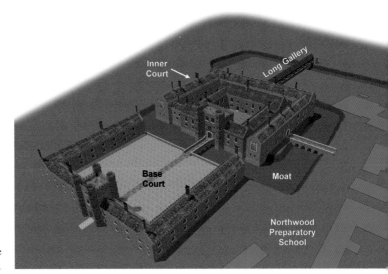

55. Reconstruction of The More, Hertfordshire, 2011. This image shows how The More would have appeared in the sixteenth century.

56. Aerial view of the site of The More, 2011. The manor house, near Rickmansworth in Hertfordshire, once stood on the grounds today occupied by Northwood Preparatory School. Nothing survives above ground; the foundations of the house once deemed more magnificent than Hampton Court Palace lie buried beneath the school's sports field.

57. Greenwich Palace, Kent. Here we see the king's lodgings facing the River Thames. Left to right: the chapel (with its pitch gabled end), the privy chamber, presence chamber, kitchen and massive central donjon with some of Henry's most private chambers, including a library on the top floor. Anne was conveyed to the Tower for her coronation celebrations in May 1533, and then again to her prison in 1536, from the steps in front of the palace.

Left: 58. Reconstruction of Greenwich Palace, Kent, by Peter Kent (2002). This wonderful reconstruction shows the palace complex during its heyday. Running alongside the river are the king's lodgings, with the chapel at the left-hand side of the wing. Directly opposite, across to the south of the inner court, were the queen's lodgings. The tiltyard and its towers, the place that Anne last saw Henry, are also clearly shown.

Middle: 59. The route of Anne Boleyn's walk to the scaffold, adapted from an engraving by G. Haiward and J. Gascoyne, 1597. When Anne Boleyn emerged from the royal apartments on the morning of 19 May 1536 under heavy guard, she walked first from the Inner Ward, through the Cold Harbour Gate, before passing northwards to the site of the scaffold. This was not on Tower Green as is often cited, but in front of the current Waterloo Barracks.

Bottom: 60. The route of Anne Boleyn's coronation procession. This annotated map shows the route of Anne's coronation procession, taken on the afternoon of 31 May 1533. A: the Tower; B: Fenchurch Street; C: Gracechurch Street; D: Cornhill; E: Poultry; F: Cheapside; G: St Paul's Cathedral; H: Ludgate; I: Fleet Street; J: Temple Bar; K: the Strand; L: Charing Cross; M: the Holbein Gate; N: Whitehall Palace; O: Westminster Hall.

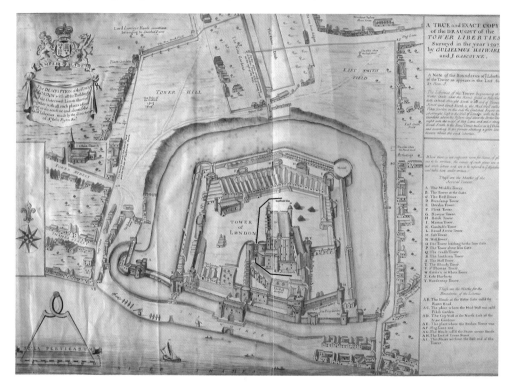

Above: 61. The Tower of London as viewed from near the main western entrance, 2012. In the right-hand corner is the Byward Tower, which in Anne's day led to a series of gatehouses and drawbridges that comprised the main land entrance from the city. The outer defence was the Lion Tower, now demolished, the outer wall of which stood just in front of the present-day Tower shop. Anne would have emerged from here on her way to Westminster for her Coronation and George Boleyn, Henry Norris, Francis Weston, William Brereton and Mark Smeaton would have been escorted out of the Tower via this same route and led to their executions on Tower Hill.

Right: 62. The site of the Palace of Whitehall, Whitehall, 2013. This picture is taken looking south, down the modern-day Whitehall at the heart of the City of Westminster. The banqueting house (from where Charles I was led out to his execution) seen on Hollar's engraving still stands, almost unaltered, to the left of the picture. The Holbein Gate once stood roughly aligned and to the left of the statue of George, Duke of Clarence, on horseback (seen in the centre of the road). Over on the right of the picture was the Palace of Whitehall's leisure complex, which Henry and Anne designed together, including tennis courts, a tiltyard and a cockpit.

Below: 63. Reconstruction of Westminster, *c.* 1530. This bird's-eye view of the ancient City of Westminster shows the abbey in the foreground, its precinct entered via a gateway on its northern side. The old Palace of Westminster fronts the River Thames on the right of the picture. We can see clearly the route Anne must have taken from Westminster Hall to the abbey for her Coronation on 1 June 1533, going first from Westminster Hall, across the paved yard, under the Great Gate, through the gateway into the abbey precinct and then on to the main west doors of the abbey church.

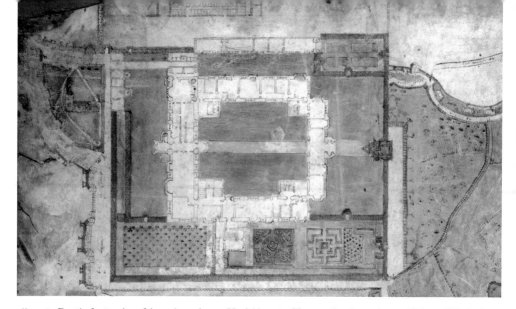

Above: 64. Detail of a site plan of the early gardens at Hatfield, *c.* 1608. This site plan shows the royal Palace of Hatfield as it appeared prior to its partial demolition in 1608, and is much as Anne Boleyn would have known it. The west hall range on the left, containing Bishop Morton's Great Hall, solar, kitchens and butteries, is all that survives of this once-grand house. The gatehouse visible to the north-west (left of the surviving range and just behind the church) still stands, albeit in a heavily restored state. During her visits, Anne was probably lodged in the south wing, which overlooked the formal gardens.

Below left: 65. Reconstruction of Eltham Palace, Kent, *c.* 1605. Eltham Palace was one of Henry VIII's 'Great Houses' capable of lodging the entire court of around 1,000 people. This reconstruction shows the palace largely as Anne would have known it. A: gatehouse; B: Green Court; C: chancellor's lodgings; D: inner courtyard; E: courtier lodgings; F: chapel; G: queen's lodgings; H: gallery; I: king's lodgings; J: Great Hall.

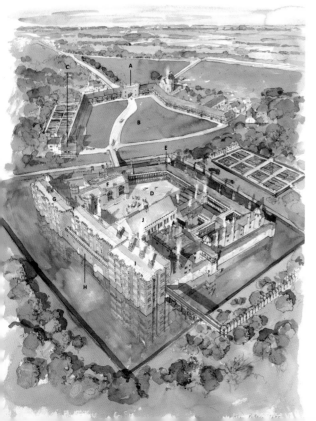

Below: 66. Hatfield House, Hertfordshire. A short distance from the present Jacobean Hatfield House once stood the royal Palace of Hatfield. Princess Elizabeth lived at Hatfield from December 1533 to March 1534, where Anne visited her in the spring of 1534. All that remains of the house that would have witnessed many tender moments between mother and daughter is the west hall range, pictured here.

Above: 67. The west front (main entrance) of Hampton Court Palace, as viewed from Trophy Gate, 2012. The palace was originally built for Cardinal Wolsey as a house for entertaining royalty, foreign ambassadors and dignitaries. Henry VIII stayed at Hampton Court often before taking full possession of it in 1529 and beginning an enormous building campaign that would transform it into one of the most magnificent palaces of Tudor England. Anne visited both before and after becoming queen, and had her own lodgings there as early as June 1529.

Right: 68. Antique print of Anne Boleyn's Gateway, Clock Court, 1920. This charming old engraving of Anne Boleyn's Gateway, Hampton Court Palace, depicts the building as viewed from Clock Court.

Below: 69. The Great Hall at Hampton Court. This is perhaps one of the most impressive survivors of the Tudor age. Although it is not quite in its original splendour, having lost, for example, its brightly painted and gilded ceiling, it is a chamber that looks much as it did when it was remodelled by Henry VIII in the early 1530s.

70. The remains of the moat that once surrounded Guildford Manor, Guildford, Surrey, 2013. This is all that is left of the royal abode that once occupied a corner of the Royal Hunting Park at Guildford.

71. Reading Abbey gatehouse, Forbury, 2013. In the sixteenth century, Reading Abbey was one of the sixth-wealthiest monasteries in England and one of Henry VIII's favourite monastic houses. Anne Boleyn visited the house on a number of occasions, both before and after becoming queen. The abbey gatehouse and the main building of the hospitium, a guest house used mainly by pilgrims, are all that survive of the monastery, which featured regularly on the itinerary of Tudor kings and queens.

72. The remains of Ewelme Manor, South Oxfordshire, 2013. In the fifteenth century, the Duke and Duchess of Suffolk, William and Alice de la Pole, enlarged and improved the manor house at Ewelme, of which this building, originally part of one of the outer ranges, is all that survives. The range is likely to have originally stood within the base court and probably adjoined a brick gatehouse. Henry and Anne visited in August 1531 and 1532. In 1535 Henry acquired the property in exchange for land elsewhere, utilising Ewelme as a lesser house to where he would retreat for greater privacy with a small group of friends and attendants. Today the house is privately owned and can only be viewed from the street.

73. Abingdon Abbey gatehouse, Oxfordshire, 2012. At the time of its dissolution, Abingdon Abbey was one of the wealthiest Benedictine abbeys in England. Only a small fragment of a vast complex of buildings, courtyards and gardens survives today, including this fifteenth-century gatehouse.

Above left: 74. Sudeley Castle, Gloucestershire. A view of the Queens' Garden at Sudeley Castle in Winchcombe, which today occupies the site of the original Tudor parterre where four queens of England have walked – Queen Anne Boleyn, Queen Katherine Parr, Lady Jane Grey and Queen Elizabeth I.

Above right: 75. The site of the manor of Langley, Oxfordshire, 2012. A view of what was once the formal gardens of the manor of Langley looking across to Langley Farmhouse. This building incorporates some fifteenth- and sixteenth-century fabric and occupies part of the site of the former royal residence. Throughout the sixteenth century, Henry VIII stayed at Langley when hunting in Wychwood Forest and often used the house as a satellite to Woodstock Palace. Copies of two of Anne's letters survive written from 'my Lord's manor of Langley.'

76. Aerial view of Sudeley Castle, Gloucestershire. To the left of the formal gardens once stood the lavish east range where Anne Boleyn stayed during her visit in 1535. The now-vanished south range would have contained the Great Hall, and a cross range, now lost, once separated the two courts. In Anne's day the castle was approached through a gatehouse in the north, originally protected by a moat and drawbridge. The refurbished fifteenth-century church, north of the formal gardens, is the final resting place of Henry VIII's sixth wife, Katherine Parr.

77. Tewkesbury Abbey, Gloucestershire, 2013. Henry and Anne would have made an offering at the church before being escorted to their accommodation, almost certainly the abbot's house within the abbey precincts.

78. Abbey House, Tewkesbury, 2013. Most of Tewkesbury Abbey's claustral buildings were destroyed after the Dissolution, with the exception of the abbot's lodging, which was retained and forms part of what is now Abbey House. The house is located next to the west front of the church – note the impressive oriel window built in 1509, the year of Henry's accession. To the right of Abbey House can be seen the main abbey gateway, used by the court when coming and going from the abbey precinct.

Above: 79. View of Painswick Lodge from the nearby road, Painswick, 2013. This was the main manor house of the day, lying just outside the main village. Only two ranges of the original courtyard house survive. Note that in the background there lies the wooded escarpment called Longridge. For a long time after Anne's visit, it was called The Queen's Wood on account of Anne's presence hunting there during the stay. The house today is privately owned.

Right: 80. The South Porch at Gloucester Cathedral, 2013. It is here that Anne and Henry were received by Abbot Parker upon their arrival at Gloucester Abbey in 1535. Within the porch, we hear that 'both kneeled down and kissed the crosse with greate reveraunce, and then went up to the highe alter, and so from thens [there] to there [their] lodgynges'.

Below: 81. Prinknash Abbey, 2013. In the sixteenth century, Prinknash served as a country residence and hunting lodge for the abbots of Gloucester. Situated just 5 or so miles south of the city, it would have been a perfect place for the royal hunting party to take rest and refreshment before moving on to nearby Painswick. In appearance, it is typical of grand, medieval Cotswold manor houses, fashioned from distinctive yellow Cotswold limestone. Today Prinknash is a working Benedictine monastery and this building is not generally open to the public.

82. The old priory of Leonard Stanley, 2013. This image shows the south side of the old priory church of Leonard Stanley, which now serves as the parish church. You can clearly see the blocked-up doorway that once led into the cloisters. The building to the right is the later manor house, which stands over where some of the conventual buildings would have once stood. Just on the left of the picture is the end of the original Saxon chapel, where legend has it that Henry and Anne were received by the abbot during their overnight stay in the summer of 1535.

83. Thornbury Castle, south Gloucestershire. On the edge of the Cotswolds, Thornbury Castle is the only Tudor castle to be opened as a luxury hotel. Pictured here is the double-storey south range of the inner court, which originally housed the Duke of Buckingham's own lavish suite on the upper floor and on the ground floor those of his wife, Eleanor Percy, Duchess of Buckingham. It was also in these apartments that Anne and Henry stayed during their visit in 1535. Anne's bedchamber was on the ground floor of the south-west tower and Henry's directly above; both overlooked the magnificent privy gardens.

84. Brockworth Court, 2013. Brockworth was once the private country residence of the prior of Lanthony Priory. Rumours of a visit from Anne Boleyn have existed for generations. This could very well tie into the itinerary for 3 August 1535, when the royal party did indeed head in this very direction en route to Coberley.

Above: 85. The west front of Thornbury Castle, south Gloucestershire. This range was only partially completed at the time of the Duke of Buckingham's execution in 1521. Only the south-western tower and adjacent turret were finished as per the original plan, the remaining buildings only rising to two storeys, rather than the intended four.

Middle: 86. Acton Court, Gloucestershire. In the sixteenth century, Acton Court, on the outskirts of the village of Iron Acton, was home to Nicholas Poyntz who spent nine months – and a huge amount of money – adding a new wing to his moated manor house in anticipation of a royal visit that would last just two days. Today, Poyntz's extravagant east range comprises much of what remains at Acton Court.

Bottom: 87. The 1535 'Holbein Frieze', Acton Court. This frieze is found in the central room of the royal apartments at Acton Court and is named so because it is believed that Hans Holbein was the mastermind behind the design.

88. Little Sodbury Manor, Gloucestershire, 2012. In the sixteenth century, Little Sodbury Manor was the home of Sir John and Lady Anne Walshe who played host to Anne and Henry for three days in late August 1535. The sixteenth-century south range with its magnificent oriel window, from where Anne is said to have watched the entertainments on the terrace below, survives. Today the house is privately owned and not accessible to the public.

89. Wolfhall Manor, Wiltshire, 2013. This largely eighteenth-century red brick house roughly occupies the site of Wolfhall, which in the sixteenth century was the home of Sir John Seymour, whose eldest daughter, Jane, would become Henry's third wife.

Below left: 90. Spye Arch Lodge, Wiltshire, 2013. This Tudor gatehouse once served Bromham House, the home of Anne Boleyn's vice-chamberlain, a long-time favourite of Henry VIII, Sir Edward Baynton. Beneath the splendid oriel window can be seen the arms of Henry VIII flanked by fine carved panels, and the arch spandrels are decorated with the arms of Sir Edward Baynton and his first wife, Elizabeth Sulliard.
Below right: 91. The church of St Peter and St Paul, Thruxton. In September 1535, Henry VIII and Anne Boleyn stayed at Thomas Lisle's house in Thruxton of which nothing remains; however, it once stood adjacent to the village church, which welcomes visitors.

92. The ruins of Bishop's Waltham Palace, Bishop's Waltham, 2013. Anne stayed at the Bishop of Winchester's palace, here in Bishop's Waltham, for a week at the end of September 1535. On the right, we see the remains of the west tower, which once contained the bishop's privy lodgings. It is almost certain that the king and Anne lodged in this part of the palace complex, with a privy chamber on the first floor, then two further chambers, stacked one on top of the other. Perhaps the king's bedchamber occupied the larger of the two chambers on the second floor, with Anne's bedchamber directly above it.

Above left: 93. Winchester Cathedral, Hampshire, 2012. On 19 September 1535, Winchester Cathedral witnessed the consecration of three newly appointed reforming bishops, Edward Fox, Hugh Latimer and John Hilsey. Henry VIII and Anne Boleyn were present for the ceremony, which was performed by the Archbishop of Canterbury, Thomas Cranmer.

Above right: 94. Bargate, Southampton, 2013. Medieval Bargate was once the main defensive gateway providing entry to the city from the north. Anne and Henry must have passed under its stone arches on their arrival from Winchester on 30 September 1535.

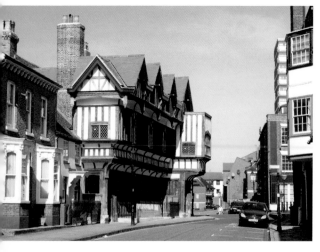

95. Tudor House, Southampton, 2010, one of the rare survivors from Tudor Southampton. There is a local legend that Anne and Henry stayed, or were received, in this sumptuous town house that was once owned by Henry's Lord Chief Justice of England, Sir Richard Lyster, and his wife, Isabel.

96. Portchester Castle, 2011. Here we see the medieval keep of Portchester Castle from outside its defensive walls. However, the rear of Richard II's privy lodgings, to the right of the main tower in this picture, contained the most comfortable apartments at the castle. It is likely that the king and queen stayed in Richard II's privy lodgings for their brief visit in October 1535.

97. Crane House, Church Street, Salisbury, 2013. In early October 1535, Anne and Henry were guests of John Tuchet, 8th Baron Audley, at his town house on Crane Street. The house has been enlarged over the centuries, and later remodelling has stripped out almost all its original interiors. However, much of the north range fronting onto Crane Street, as shown in the picture, is original to the fourteenth century. The corner of the building in the foreground of the picture housed the main solar, and is highly likely to have been part of the royal lodgings.

Above: 98. The Vyne, Hampshire. At the time of Anne's visits, The Vyne was the home of William, Lord Sandys, one of Henry's leading courtiers and Lord Chamberlain of the Royal Household. The South Front, pictured here, was probably part of the private apartments of a substantially bigger house. As was the fate of so many grand Tudor houses, The Vyne was drastically reduced in size, altered and modernised by subsequent owners, thereby much of Lord Sandys' house lies today buried beneath the lawns north of the present house.

Below left: 99. The chapel, The Vyne, Hampshire. Most of the interior decoration has been altered over the years; however, there are a few important exceptions, including the beautifully carved choir stalls, which are Tudor and largely unaltered, as is the stained glass in the east window, which is among the finest examples of painted glass of the Renaissance period in England. This glass was originally commissioned by Sandys for the Chapel of the Holy Ghost in Basingstoke and moved to The Vyne during the Civil War.

Below right: 100. The Oak Gallery, The Vyne, Hampshire. The richly decorated first-floor Oak Gallery is one of only a few surviving from the first half of the sixteenth century. At the time of Anne's visit it was sparsely furnished, as the showpiece was the exquisite floor-to-ceiling linenfold panelling, decorated with heraldic carvings, which was installed between 1518 and 1526. These panels still line the walls today.

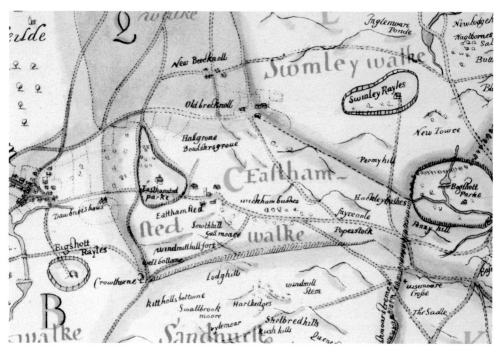

Top left: 101. Bramshill House, 2013. Anne and Henry visited Bramshill on 19 October 1535. At the time it was owned by Lord and Lady Daubeney, Lady Daubeney being Anne Boleyn's aunt. The house we see today is a Jacobean replacement, incorporating the earlier house. This pathway was once the main entrance through the gatehouse into the inner courtyard, which has largely long since been lost.

Top right: 102. A replica of Anne Boleyn's Portrait Medal made by stone carver Lucy Churchill, as it would have looked when struck. The original medal of Anne Boleyn, inscribed A. R. THE MOOST HAPPI ANNO 1534, was made as a prototype in 1534 to commemorate the anticipated birth of a son, but tragically Anne lost the baby late into the pregnancy, explaining why multiple copies of the medal were not commissioned. Although the original, which is housed in the British Museum, is badly damaged, it is still of great importance, as it's the only undisputed contemporary likeness of Anne Boleyn.

Above: 103. Detail from John Norden's map of Berkshire showing Easthampstead Lodge and Park, 1607. The image shows clearly the imparked area surrounding the lodge of Easthampstead, which was visited on a number of occasions by Anne during her lifetime, including on and around 8 August 1531 and 22–6 October 1535. Its proximity to Windsor Castle, and the fine hunting to be had in the park, made it a popular hunting lodge during Henry VIII's reign.

Visitor Information

Although New Street and Cattle Market, which together formed the north, east and western boundaries of the friary lands, remain to this day, there are no extant vestiges of the friary itself. The remains of the buildings now lie under an entirely ordinary residential area only a street name, Whitefriars Way, acknowledges its historic past. Taking a stroll along Rope Walk, accessed from the main central car park next to the Guildhall and Whitefriars site, you can look over the area that was once occupied by this ancient monastic house.

All round it is an entirely agreeable town with some beautiful medieval buildings and plenty of places to rest and take refreshment. There are also a tourist information centre and the Museum of Sandwich located in the nearby guildhall, which provide more information on this lovely, historic town. As the museum closes for the winter period, it is best to check up-to-date opening times via their website at http://www.sandwichtowncouncil.gov.uk/guildhall/museum.htm. Telephone number: + 44 (0) 1304 617197.

Postcode for Whitefriars Way, Sandwich: CT13 9AD.

Sittingbourne, Kent

> paied to the wif of the lyon in Sytingbo'ne by way of Rewarde.
>
> *Privy Purse Expenses of Henry VIII*

Having left Canterbury on 19 November 1532, the royal party joined the old Dover Road, continuing their journey toward London. It is worth pausing to consider the history and decline of this most eminent of thoroughfares. Its significance is captured beautifully in the elegant words of a nineteenth-century book, *The Old Dover Road* by Charles Harper. He surmises in the preface that 'it would be rash to declare that more history has been enacted on this road than on any other, although we may suspect it; but certainly history is more spectacular along these miles. Those pageants and glittering processions are of the past.'

Henry and Anne no doubt made up one of those 'glittering processions'. We can imagine travellers lining the streets to get a glimpse of the king and the woman who had supplanted Katharine in Henry's affections. The pair and their entourage continued to wend their way along what had once been a Roman road, making their way from Canterbury toward London. Their destination was a further 13 miles in a north-westerly direction; they were headed for the Kentish town of Sittingbourne. Early November 1532 was noted for its storms and flooding, so perhaps progress was slow on a road that had been churned up into a sea of unyielding mud.

Situated roughly halfway between London and Dover, Sittingbourne had been a major staging post since medieval times – and indeed continued to be so until the advent of the railway. Looking at old images of Sittingbourne from later years, we see that the high street, which once formed the London–Dover road, was a particularly wide thoroughfare, hinting at its earlier significance and the relative weight of traffic that must have passed along it.

During the halcyon days of the coaching inn, the town itself was reported as not being large, but 'had an astonishing number of hotels, inns, and beer-houses'. This helps us account for just how the huge retinues associated with a travelling court were able to be lodged in just one place, and why clearly this destination was such a favoured stopping off point for kings, emperors, cardinals and other notables. Of all these inns, though,

> the 'Red Lion' was undoubtedly the chief inn at Sittingbourne from a very early time, and it kept its good repute for centuries; for here it was that Henry the Eighth stayed when 'progressing' along the Dover Road in 1541, and here he held what in those autocratic times answered to our present Cabinet Councils … In the sixteenth century, then, Emperors and Kings were the usual guests of the 'Red Lion'. The landlord at that time sniffed at Princes and Archbishops, and turned away such riff-raff as Dukes and Earls.

Over and above Henry's stay in 1541, we know the king had also been there on at least one previous notable occasion. This was in May 1522, when Henry stayed at the inn with his royal 'brother', the Emperor Charles V, bringing with them a massive combined retinue of about 2,000 souls. It seems therefore that the king knew the place well. Furthermore, we know that in between these two dates he stayed with Anne on the evening of 19 November, for the *Privy Purse Expenses* notes a payment, this time to the wife (landlady) of 'The Lion' for four shillings and eight pence; not bad value considering they were entertaining a king!

The first floor of the Lion contained the banqueting hall in addition to its many bedrooms, and we know that this hall ran from the front of the hotel towards the back. In time, with the decline of the coaching inn, the old Lion Inn was divided up into smaller private tenements, such that the Red Lion that stands on the High Street today only reflects the central portion of the original inn; the adjacent buildings to the right and left were also once part of this most historic of buildings.

Interestingly, in 1934 during the course of costly repairs to the old inn, which at the time was decaying with woodworm, a series of impressive Tudor murals was uncovered (Internet search 'The Sittingbourne Murals' for more information).

Henry and Anne only lodged at the inn for one night; the next day, with their bags packed, they continued their progress toward Stone, the home of Sir Richard and Lady Bridget Tyrwhitt.

Visitor Information

Sittingbourne is hardly your usual tourist destination. Sadly, it is not located in one of the more affluent or well-manicured parts of the 'Garden of England' (as Kent is often otherwise known). Any romanticism needs to be firmly set aside for this pilgrimage for, apart from the fact that the high street is unusually wide – reflecting the fact that the road passing through the town was once one of the most important in the realm, there is nothing to speak of its significant past. However, once you have located the Red Lion on the High Street, it is most definitely worth a peek inside. The front of the pub in particular retains huge oak beams, and somehow the voices of its historic past still whisper their stories in your ear. It is warm and welcoming and easy to sit a while and enjoy an English pint or a glass of wine, as so many countless thousands of people have done before you. Now you can number yourself among kings and princes! By the way, make sure to look down the side of the pub into what was once the old yard. Beautiful Tudor architecture is still visible in the external brickwork and timber framing.

Postcode for the Red Lion at Sittingbourne: ME9 0RT.

The More, Hertfordshire

Wolsey's favourite country house, and du Bellay [the French Ambassador] thought it more splendid than Hampton Court.

A. F. Pollard

The More was a manor house, near Rickmansworth in Hertfordshire, that in 1527 the French Ambassador, Jean du Bellay, deemed more splendid than Hampton Court. It once stood on the grounds today occupied by Northwood Preparatory School and was one of five properties that Henry VIII appropriated after Cardinal Wolsey's fall. Like Hampton Court Palace, it had been conveniently enlarged and beautified by the cardinal, before falling into royal hands in 1531.

Anne Boleyn visited on 23 September 1530 as part of the annual summer progress but appears not to have returned until after becoming queen. In the winter of 1531/32 Katharine of Aragon was sent to live there, during which time the house, like its abandoned royal mistress, was rather neglected and in April 1532 Thomas Heritage (a royal chaplain) complained of the dilapidated state of the park and gardens. The following year, the park received some attention but it wasn't until 1534 onwards, that a large amount of money was spent repairing and embellishing the principal buildings of the house and tending to the surrounding parkland, home to a herd of up to four or five hundred deer.

In the summer of 1534, in anticipation of a visit by the king, the staff occupied themselves by 'mowng and clensyng of gresse and weeds in and about the pownds and in the moote for the kyng's grace to fysche'.

The moated mansion that Anne knew, described by a visitor in 1525 as a 'sumptuous building', was constructed from the fifteenth century onwards primarily of brick. On arrival, Anne would have passed under the outer gateway, into the Base Court, which consisted of four towers and three sides of lodgings. From there she would have proceeded into the moated inner courtyard via a second gateway, where the royal apartments stood on either side of the courtyard, divided into the customary king's side and queen's side.

On the north side of the house, a fine, 253-foot-long gallery extended out into the garden, overlooking the elegant knot gardens below.

In 1534, Anne's apartments consisted of the usual sequence of watching chamber, presence chamber, privy chamber, bedchamber, raying chamber (a dressing room) and closet, identical to the layout of Henry's lodgings, with one exception: Henry also had a dining chamber that lay between his privy chamber and bedchamber.

Several of Anne's rooms were adorned with gilded badges, 'antike' heads and borders, the work of John Hethe, a painter from London. The walls of the queen's watching chamber were plastered, whitened and painted in yellow ochre as were two of the staircases in her apartments.

As well as fishing, the royal couple may have enjoyed other outdoor pursuits including hunting and coursing deer. In inclement weather, the generous and luxurious Long Gallery would have provided a warm and comfortable retreat in which to pass the time. Henry was even known to practise shooting (probably with a crossbow) in the gallery!

The end of the reign of Edward VI heralded the demise of The More. From there on, it was virtually abandoned and left to decay. At the beginning of the reign of Elizabeth I, it was estimated that to make it habitable again would cost £1806 13s 4d.

It seems no one was up for the challenge – or the substantial cost – and so by 1598, only 'the anncient ruynes of Morhouse' remained.

Today, nothing of The More survives – those 'ancient ruins' lying buried beneath the sports fields of the Northwood Preparatory School.

Visitor Information

Northwood Preparatory School is not open to the general public. Researchers wishing to visit the site should contact the school direct via the school's website http://www. northwoodprep.co.uk or by telephoning + 44 (0) 1923 825648.

If you have prearranged your visit, you will need to make your way to Sandy Lodge Road in Rickmansworth. Turning off the A4145 (Moor Lane), you will see that the road is marked as private and cameras record vehicle registration numbers as they come and go. It is immediately obvious that this is an affluent area, as you will see by the large detached arts and crafts (1920s and 30s) houses, sitting behind immaculately tended gardens. Indeed, Sandy Lodge Road is one of the most expensive residential roads in the country. However, don't be put off, public access is allowed. Make your way down the lane and before the road goes under the railway line you will find the discreet entrance to Northwood Preparatory School on your left.

It is likely that you will be shown around by the school archivist, Suzanne Smith, who will meet you at the gates and subsequently escort you on a tour of the grounds and show you the four surviving pieces of carved stonework that once adorned the palace gatehouse.

However, do note that if you are not there during school opening hours, the buildings are locked and there are no toilet facilities on-site. Nearby shops can provide refreshments.

Postcode for Northwood Preparatory School: WD3 1LW.

Part 3
Anne the Queen

Greenwich Palace (The Palace of Placentia), Kent

I was creuely handeled a … a Greweche [Greenwich] with the Kynges consell with my lord of Norfolke, that he sayd Tut, [tut, tut!], and shakyng hyr[his] hed[head] iii. or iiij. Tymes

The words of Anne Boleyn, reported by Sir William Kingston following her arrest at Greenwich Palace, *The Letters and Papers of Henry VIII*

In around 1501, the old Manor of Pleasaunce, which had originally been built by Duke Humphrey of Gloucester, was demolished by King Henry VII. In its place a fine red brick palace rose up on the southern banks of the Thames at Greenwich. In time, this new palace would become one of Henry VIII's most favoured 'great houses', particularly during the early years of his reign. On account of this, it is probable that Anne spent more of her time here than at any other royal abode.

Sadly, nothing at all remains of Greenwich Palace today, except ghosts and the imprint of the historic events that unfolded upon its glittering stage. On account of all this, the site of Greenwich Palace is a 'must-see' for anybody wanting to follow in the footsteps of Anne Boleyn. Just remember to take your imagination with you!

The Palace Buildings
Greenwich Palace was highly innovative in design at the time it was built, being a courtyard house, built of brick and without a moat. A seventeenth-century painting of the palace by an anonymous painter shows the fine river frontage, which comprised the kitchens to the west; the king's lodgings, including the magnificent five-storey donjon containing the king's privy bedroom, library and study in the centre; and to the east the Chapel Royal. Running parallel to this range on the opposite side of a grand courtyard were the queen's apartments, which looked out over the Great Garden, orchard and Greenwich Park beyond.

The complete arrangement of the west wing is not entirely known. However, it seems that a privy gallery connected the king and queen's sides; and the queen's bedroom, Anne's bedroom, seems to have been accessed from this gallery. To the east were the king's and the queen's great watching chambers – the most public rooms of the royal apartments after the Great Hall. These chambers were connected to the hall via a central staircase.

Visiting the Site of Greenwich Palace

One of the best ways to arrive at Greenwich is to follow in Anne's footsteps and arrive by boat. Take a river cruiser from Westminster Pier past the site of Whitehall Palace, Baynard's Palace and the Tower, eventually arriving at Greenwich. You will be greeted by the sight of the old Royal Naval College; this eighteenth-century building stands squarely on the site of the old Palace of Greenwich, which first fell into serious decay during the English Civil War and was demolished shortly thereafter. With this guide in hand, take a walk through the grounds of what is now a college of music; stand on the site of the old king's apartments fronting the river; imagine the great courtyard and its central conduit; cross the modern-day Romney Road that bisects an area that once separated the queen's apartments from the orchard and Great Garden beyond. As you walk along the path cutting across the National Maritime Museum Gardens, look to your left and imagine the two elaborate Tiltyard Towers rising up from the ground and looking down on the tiltyard that lay to the east; see the May Day jousts of 1536 taking place, and imagine Anne's last moments by her husband's side.

Events at Greenwich Palace

Some of the most momentous events in Anne's life occurred while she was resident at Greenwich Palace. The most significant of these are described below.

In 1528 Anne and Henry received Dr Edward Foxe on his return from his embassy to the Pope. Anne was lodged in the magnificent Tiltyard Towers at the time, avoiding an outbreak of what was probably measles in the main palace complex. It seemed initially that the embassy to obtain a decretal commission from the Pope and have Henry's divorce heard in England was a success. Sadly, this was not to be. Stephen Gardiner and Edward Foxe had missed a loophole inserted by Pope Clement VII that rendered the document virtually useless.

Just a month later, it was at Greenwich that one of Anne's maids fell ill with the sweating sickness, a virulent disease of unknown aetiology that often killed its victims in hours. This event is reported in a letter from Jean du Bellay, the French Ambassador, on 16 June 1528. The outbreak caused panic at the palace and prompted Henry to flee to Waltham Abbey, leaving Anne alone to make her way back to Hever.

Then in 1533, at around five–six months pregnant, Anne set off from Greenwich along the Thames toward the Tower. She was to lodge there for two days before making her ceremonial entry into the City before her Coronation. Anne was at the pinnacle of her power, travelling amid a great river pageant, which saw mechanical dragons belching fire, sweet music, pageantry and endless salvoes of cannon fire, all saluting England's new queen.

On 7 September 1533, as the Duke of Suffolk married his second wife, the young and intellectual Katherine Willoughby, in the same building Anne gave birth in her privy apartments to the future Elizabeth I.

Finally, on 1 May 1536 while watching the annual May Day joust, the king fatefully received a note. This probably conveyed details of Mark Smeaton's 'confession' following his interrogation at Cromwell's house in Stepney. Henry stalked off, leaving Anne behind him, never to see her again. The following day, she was ordered to present herself before three members of the Privy Council while watching a game of real tennis in the palace grounds.

After being questioned, Anne was confined to her privy chambers before finally being formally arrested and conveyed by barge to the Tower. It was thus at Greenwich that Anne had her last taste of freedom.

Authors' Favourites

We highly recommended starting your visit by heading for the Discover Greenwich Museum (part of the old Naval College and near to Greenwich Pier). There are excellent models of both Henry's palace and his tiltyard, which will help fire your imagination before your wander round the site of the old palace itself. There is a section that includes several artefacts from the original palace, such as the green and yellow tiles that were excavated from the site of the Chapel Royal in the 1970s. There is also a replica of Anne's coat of arms, fashioned from stained glass, that would have decorated many of the palace's fine mullioned windows.

However, one of our favourite things is to make our way through Greenwich Park, which lies to the south of the old palace. Climb up to the top of Castle Hill, where the Greenwich Observatory now stands. In the exact same spot once stood Duke Humphrey's Tower, a miniature castle where Henry is said to have kept his fine wine and mistresses – including Mary Boleyn and possibly Anne! Look back down upon the old Naval College and take a moment to imagine the pitched roofs, barley-twist chimneys and pleasant gardens of the sixteenth-century palace laid out below you.

Visitor Information

You are welcome to roam the grounds of the current music college, upon which the palace once stood, at any time. Discover Greenwich, part of The National Maritime Museum, houses a small exhibition about the lost Tudor palace, as described above. The museum is open 10 a.m.–5 p.m. daily. Entrance is free. For further information visit the website on: http://www.ornc.org/visit/getting-here/opening-times.

Alternatively, if arriving by car, you might wish to park in the large public car park at the top of Castle Hill, adjacent to the observatory. From here, you can walk down the hill to the site of the old palace.

Postcode for the site of Greenwich Palace: SE10 9NN and postcode for Greenwich Park Car Park: SE10 8QY.

The Tower of London, London

It comes to a thousand days – out of the years. Strangely just a thousand. And of that thousand – one – when we were both in love. Only one when our loves met, and overlapped and were both mine and his.

> Maxwell Anderson: Anne's fictional speech from the
> Tower in *Anne of the Thousand Days*, 1948

Of all places associated with Anne's story, there is nowhere more poignant perhaps than the Tower of London, that mighty Norman fortress first constructed by William the Conqueror shortly after the said Duke of Normandy invaded England in 1066. Situated in Central London on the north bank of the River Thames, it has looked over the City of London for over 900 years and has served as a royal palace and fortress, prison and place of execution, an arsenal, a royal mint, a royal menagerie and jewel house.

Within the shadows of its walls, Anne experienced both the pinnacle of her triumph – as she lodged at the Tower with Henry in sumptuous splendour prior to her Coronation in 1533 – and the darkest days of her cataclysmic downfall almost 1,000 days later in May 1536. The only other time that we know that Anne visited the Tower was during the first week of December 1532, shortly after she and Henry had returned from Calais.

During that visit, the king and Anne, then Marquess of Pembroke, inspected the new queen's lodgings, which were being constructed for Anne in advance of her Coronation the following year. At the same time, the king showed Anne the interior of the Jewel House, which once abutted the southern wall of the White Tower. This was a great honour indeed. Many items of gilt and partially gilt plate were transferred to adorn Anne's increasingly lavish household during that December; did the royal couple select the items from here? We can only begin to imagine what sights Anne laid eyes on for the first time that day, as the Jewel House was then used to house the Crown Jewels and coronation regalia, later to be used in her own coronation ceremony on 1 June 1533 (see also 'Westminster Abbey').

And so no Tudor pilgrimage is complete without a visit to the Tower, but, with its complex and varied history spanning almost 1,000 years, it's easy to miss some important Anne connections. Let's explore these highlights together!

St Thomas's Tower

Much of the medieval palace was restored in 1532 in preparation for Anne's Coronation the following year. St Thomas's Tower was at this time largely rebuilt and provided accommodation for two of Henry's senior household officials, the Lord Great Chamberlain and Lord Chamberlain, who were responsible for orchestrating the magnificent coronation ceremonies. It's still possible to see the fortified beck and timber walls that Henry had installed for this extravagant event. They certainly needed to be strong to withstand the weight of the ceremonial guns. According to Tudor chronicler Edward Hall, Anne's arrival was marked by the firing of 1,000 cannon!

The Wall Walk

You exit the Wakefield Tower via a spiral staircase, which leads you to the South Wall Walk. Continue along this stretch of walk towards the Lanthorn Tower and pause about halfway. Look out towards the open grass area in front of the White Tower; this area was once enclosed and contained a Great Hall, where Anne and George Boleyn were tried in 1536, and the queen's lodgings, specially built for Anne's Coronation (see below, The Royal Apartments). In a merciless twist of fate, she would spend her final days and darkest hours in the very same apartments that only three years earlier had played host to such revelry and lavish celebrations.

Continue along towards the Salt Tower, used as a prison in the Tudor period, and follow the wall walk until you reach the Martin Tower.

The Martin Tower

As you enter, look out for the carving that reads 'boullen'. George Boleyn may have carved it, as tradition has it that he was imprisoned here. Although there is no conclusive evidence to prove it, it's plausible, considering the Martin Tower did house prisoners in Tudor times.

From 1669, it's where the Crown Jewels were displayed and today houses an exhibition – 'Crowns and Diamonds: the making of the crown jewels'. Sadly, none of the jewels have an Anne connection.

From the Martin Tower you descend into the inner ward; from here make your way towards the Beauchamp Tower and another Boleyn carving.

The Beauchamp Tower

This time the carving is of Queen Anne's falcon badge – minus its crown and sceptre – and can be found etched in a first-floor cell of the thirteenth-century Beauchamp Tower. There it competes for space with a sea of graffiti left by Tudor prisoners.

The Beauchamp Tower's spacious accommodation and proximity to the constable and his deputy made it a perfect place to house prisoners of high rank. In Mary I's reign John Dudley, Duke of Northumberland, and his five sons were all imprisoned here.

This tower is also home to another important Tudor graffito; the name 'Jane' is roughly carved into the stone of the upper chamber. It is thought that Lady Jane Grey's distraught husband, Guildford Dudley, inscribed it during his imprisonment in 1553–4. But what of Anne's carving?

Did one of the men arrested alongside her hastily scratch her uncrowned falcon badge into the wall as a final display of loyalty to a queen they knew to be innocent? It's possible. And the fact that Anne's falcon has been stripped of its royal regalia, like its mistress, is most poignant.

As you leave the building and cross Tower Green take note of the scaffold site on your left but keep in mind that although it's a touching memorial, it is not the site of the scaffold upon which so many notable Tudor personalities, including Anne, lost their lives (see below, Anne's Final Walk to the Scaffold Site). Make your way now to the oldest of all the medieval buildings and perhaps the most imposing, the White Tower.

The White Tower

There is much of interest for the Tudor enthusiast in this ancient structure, begun by William the Conqueror in the 1070s, including a wonderful display from the Royal Armouries' collection on the ground floor (don't miss the suits of armour belonging to Henry VIII and his son, Edward).

Much of the interior was refurbished for Anne's Coronation, as the White Tower played an important role in the coronation rituals. On Friday 30 May 1533, eighteen Knights of the Bath were created and each candidate was required to take part in an overnight vigil in various chambers in the White Tower.

On the first floor, the Chapel of St John the Evangelist is a must-see, as it's said to be one of the best-preserved Norman chapels in the world. It's not known whether Anne visited the chapel for certain but it remains a distinct possibility.

Let's now turn our attention to these once-grand apartments that saw both triumph and tragedy.

The Royal Apartments

From Thursday 29 May to Saturday 31 May 1533 and from Tuesday 2 May to Friday 19 May 1536, Anne was accommodated in the queen's lodgings, part of the royal apartments, which were situated in the south-east corner of the Tower. She was not, as a Victorian myth later propagated, accommodated during her imprisonment in the Queen's House, which was built several years after Anne's execution and can still be seen overlooking Tower Green today.

There had been royal apartments on that site, in one form or another, since 1220. During the reign of Henry II, a permanent inner ward was created and separate lodgings for both the king and queen were constructed, including a Great Hall (later to bear witness to the trials of Anne and George Boleyn). At the turn of the sixteenth century, Henry VII significantly enlarged the king's lodgings, with the addition of a tower (containing the king's library and closet) in 1501, with a gallery bisecting the new privy gardens following in 1506.

Then, in 1532, Henry VIII ordered Cromwell to organise the construction of a whole new suite of rooms, in order to honour Anne as his queen-to-be. The additional space was also necessary to house the entire court during the two days of festivities and to provide a majestic backdrop to the opulent ceremonies that took place in the Tower prior to Anne's ceremonial entrance to the City on Saturday 31 May.

An engraving of the Tower made in 1597 shows the lodgings as Anne would have known them. Unfortunately, today they are all but lost, except a few foundation stones that give us an inkling of their former existence. However, if you find the south lawn, directly south of the White Tower, you will be looking over what was once the tower's inner ward, as described below. Here, once again, you will need your imagination!

The entrance to the inner ward was through the mighty Cold Harbour Gate. Remnants of the gate can still be seen abutting the west wall of the White Tower today. Once inside the inner ward, in front of you would have been a complex of buildings arranged around an irregular triangular 'courtyard'. Running diagonally from the Cold Harbour Gate toward the Great Hall was a line of brick-built Tudor lodgings/offices; the thirteenth-century Great Hall occupied the southernmost aspect of the courtyard (roughly where the modern-day café and bookshop are situated), while a series of buildings ran at right angles from the hall toward the south-east corner of the White Tower and the Wardrobe Tower, thereby completing the far side of the courtyard. These latter buildings formed the newly built queen's apartments. Finally, abutting along the southern wall of the White Tower was the Jewel House, referred to above.

Anne's new suite of rooms was palatial, consisting of six chambers, including a 70-foot by 30-foot great watching chamber, a presence chamber, privy chamber, closet/oratory, bedchamber and another large chamber (possibly a dining chamber). All rooms were decorated in the most fashionable Renaissance style. A flight of stairs led down directly from Anne's privy rooms into the courtyard. It seems that it was down those stairs that Anne was led to first her trial and then, three days later, to her execution.

Read more about Anne's final walk to the scaffold in the Myths section below and let's now proceed to where Anne's physical remains were buried.

The Chapel Royal of St Peter ad Vincula

On the morning of 19 May 1536, Anne Boleyn went bravely to her death in a private execution at the Tower of London.

It took only one stroke of the executioner's sword to sever her delicate neck, the very same neck that the poet Thomas Wyatt had once praised as 'fair' in one of his admiring verses. It was then left up to her ladies to move and prepare her body for burial.

Anne's head was covered in a white cloth and carried by one of her attendants. Her body was undressed and 'wrapped in a white covering' and placed in an old elm chest that had been used to store bow-staves. Although only a short while ago Anne had been queen, loved and desired by a king, no provision had been made for a proper coffin.

Anne's women carried her body approximately 65 metres to the royal chapel of St Peter ad Vincula, passing the newly filled graves of Norris, Weston, Brereton and Smeaton, who had been buried in the churchyard adjacent to the chapel only two days earlier. There, Anne's ladies buried their mistress in the earth beneath the chancel pavement in an unmarked grave (see Myth Five below).

Only three years and thirty-seven days after she'd first dined lavishly as Queen of England, she now lay dead and all but forgotten by those at the English court who now chose to turn their back on the past.

It's possible to visit Anne's final resting place and pay your respects. The chapel can be accessed through a yeoman warder tour (check the daily programme on arrival) or in the last hour of standard opening time, usually from 4.30 p.m.

Other notable Tudor personalities are also buried within the chapel, including George Boleyn, Jane Grey, Catherine Howard, Lady Rochford, Thomas More, John Fisher and Edward Seymour.

Before exiting the Tower complex, head to the Bell Tower, unfortunately not opened to the public, but important as it's here that the poet Thomas Wyatt spent his imprisonment in May 1536.

The Bell Tower

The Bell Tower was another place regularly used to house important prisoners. Notable personalities like Sir Thomas More and Princess Elizabeth were at one time imprisoned here, and tradition has it that the poet Sir Thomas Wyatt witnessed the gruesome execution of the men accused alongside Anne from his prison in the Bell Tower (or somewhere nearby). He was so deeply affected by what he saw from his cell that he responded by writing a poem about the fate of those who rise and fall at court, *Innocentia Veritas Viat Fides Circumdederunt me intimici me*, where he emphasised that

> The Bell Tower showed me such sight
> That in my head sticks day and night.

What exactly was the 'sight' that so affected Wyatt? To follow this trail we need to exit the Tower and visit the site of the scaffold on Tower Hill.

The Scaffold on Tower Hill

On the morning of Wednesday 17 May 1536, George Boleyn, Henry Norris, Francis Weston, William Brereton and Mark Smeaton were led out of the Tower under close guard and beheaded on a high scaffold on Tower Hill. Large crowds, including many courtiers, had gathered to see the bloody end of these once-great men.

It was reported that all five men died in a dignified manner and observed scaffold etiquette by confessing their faults and confirming the justness of their punishments in their farewell speeches. What they did not allude to though were the specific crimes that brought them to this terrible fate.

The highest-ranking, George Boleyn, faced the axe first but only after he had delivered a very long speech, of which several versions survive, but which commenced:

> Christian men, I am born under the law, and judged under the law, and die under the law, and the law hath condemned me. Masters all, I am not come hither for to preach, but for to die, for I have deserved to die if I had 20 lives, more shamefully than can be devised, for I am a wretched sinner, and I have sinned shamefully.
>
> I have known no man so evil, and to rehearse my sins openly it were no pleasure to you to hear them, nor yet for me to rehearse them, for God knoweth all. Therefore, masters all, I pray you take heed by me, and especially my lords and gentlemen of the court, the which I have been among, take heed by me and beware of such a fall.

Norris, Weston, Brereton and Smeaton soon followed.

Smeaton, a lowly ranked musician, was the last to die. The sight that lay before him must have been horrendous: the block floating in a sea of red surrounded by butchered bodies and heads. Yet still he managed to find the courage to utter a few words before laying his head on the blood-soaked wood.

The mutilated corpses remained there until Tower officials stripped them of their clothes and piled them onto a cart that transported them to their final resting places: the Chapel Royal of St Peter Ad Vincula for Lord Rochford and the adjacent churchyard for Norris, Weston, Brereton and Smeaton. In the sixteenth century the churchyard extended out to the area now occupied by the Waterloo Barracks.

Today a small square marks the spot of the scaffold on Tower Hill where more than 125 prisoners, including five of Anne's loyal subjects, lost their lives.

The court attempted to turn its back on these bloody events; however two poems, attributed to Thomas Wyatt (although not all historians agree with this attribution), *In Mourning wise since daily I increase* and *Innocentia Veritas Viat Fides Circumdederunt me intimici me*, ensured that they would not be forgotten.

In the latter, Wyatt reflects on the fate of those who rose high at court and experienced a reversal of fortune. He ends each verse with a Latin phrase that roughly translates as 'Thunder rolls around the throne'. Verse three speaks for itself:

These bloody days have broken my heart.
My lust, my youth did them depart,
And blind desire of estate.
Who hastes to climb seeks to revert.
Of truth, *circa Regna tonat.*

Common Myths about Anne Boleyn and the Tower
Myth One: Anne Boleyn and Traitor's Gate

On 2 May 1536, Queen Anne was arrested and transported from Greenwich to the Tower of London in full daylight. It is often said that Anne entered the Tower via Traitor's Gate, the gate below St Thomas's Tower, but this is incorrect.

In Charles Wriothesley's *A Chronicle of England during the Reigns of the Tudors, from A.D. 1485 to 1559 Vol. 1*, he states that

> Anne Bolleine was brought to the Towre of London by my
> Lord Chauncelor, the Duke of Norfolke, Mr. Secretarie, and
> Sir William Kingston, Constable of the Tower; and when she
> came to the court gate, entring in, she fell downe on her knees
> before the said lordes, beseeching God to helpe her as she was
> not giltie of her a accusement, and also desired the said lordes
> to beseech the Kinges grace to be good unto her, and so they left her
> their prisoner.

Court Gate was also referred to as Towergate and if we look closely at the plan of the Tower of London labelled *A True and Exact Draught of the TOWER LIBERTIES, survey'd in the Year 1597 by GULIELMUS HAIWARD and J. GASCOYNE*, and compare it to a plan of the Tower of London today, it is clear that the building that is labelled 'The Tower at the Gate' is today known as the Byward Tower.

In the fifteenth and sixteenth centuries, when arriving at the Tower, royalty often used this private entrance, which gave access to the Tower from the wharf.

Although originally constructed by Edward I, the gate through which Anne passed dates from the fifteenth century and this and the drawbridge can still be seen today.

After disembarking the boat and climbing the stairs (today called the Queen's Stairs) on to the wharf, Anne would have crossed the drawbridge – necessary as the moat was filled until 1843 – and entered the Byward postern gate, exiting onto Water Lane. From here it is unclear exactly what route she took but it would have only been a short walk to the entrance of the royal lodgings where she would spend her imprisonment.

Anne was not the only high-ranking prisoner said to have entered via this gate. Her daughter, Princess Elizabeth, followed in her mother's footsteps when she arrived at the Tower as a prisoner on 18 March 1554. Her mind must have been plagued with thoughts of her mother's dreadful end only eighteen years earlier.

Myth Two: Where Was Anne Imprisoned in the Tower?

Contrary to recent popular films and television series about Anne and the Tudors, Anne Boleyn was not kept in a cell during her imprisonment. Quite befitting her status as queen, she was housed in the same considerable splendour she had known in 1533, occupying the same queen's lodgings as have been described above for the entire duration of her stay at the Tower.

Myth Three: Anne's Final Walk to the Scaffold Site

When Anne emerged from her lodgings early on the morning of 19 May 1536, resplendent in a grey damask gown lined with fur and an English gable hood, she was probably led down a flight of steps that appears to have stood in the north-east corner of the inner ward leading directly down from Anne's privy rooms. Headed by Sir William Kingston – and with a guard of 200 of the king's bodyguard in attendance – Anne made her way along a path in front of the Jewel House (this no longer exists, but once abutted the south wall of the White Tower) toward the Cold Harbour Gate. Swinging right and passing under the shadow of the gate, Anne continued her walk northwards to the scaffold site.

Again Victorian myth leads many visitors to believe that the original scaffold site is on the current site of Tower Green in front of the Beauchamp Tower. This is erroneous and not helped by a poignant monument to the executed, which was unveiled there in 2006. However, to stand on the site of the original scaffold you need to head across the parade ground (on the north side of the White Tower) toward the entrance to the Waterloo Barracks and the exhibition of the Crown Jewels. There, roughly in front of the entrance, was the site of the place where Anne died at the hands of the Sword of Calais, the French executioner from St Omer.

Myth Four: Anne Saw George's Execution

As we have already established, Anne Boleyn was detained throughout her imprisonment at the Tower in the queen's lodgings, situated in the south-east corner of the Tower precinct. Given the topography of the place and the position of the scaffold on Tower Hill to the north-west of the fortress, it becomes clear that it would have been impossible for Anne to witness the execution of her brother and the other four men who suffered with George Boleyn on the scaffold that day. The only way this might have been possible would have been if Anne had been escorted to one of the towers on the north or west side of the Tower, specifically to watch the men die their bloody deaths. The only hint we have that the condemned queen might have been forced to watch the men die comes from Chapuys in one of his dispatches, although Ives in his biography of Anne dismisses this on account of the logistics involved in moving such a high-profile prisoner.

Myth Five: Is Anne Buried Beneath Her Memorial Plaque?

There exists some debate as to exactly where in the chancel Anne's body was buried. In October 1876, the chancel was restored with Queen Victoria's approval as part of a larger restoration project that hoped to address the dilapidated state of the chapel and bring it back to its original condition.

It was known that Queen Anne Boleyn, George Boleyn, Lady Rochford, Catherine Howard, the dukes of Somerset, Northumberland and Monmouth and the Countess of Salisbury were buried there, and so work proceeded with great care under the supervision of a team of six people including the Resident Governor of the Tower. The findings were documented by Doyne C. Bell in *Notices of the Historic Persons Buried in the Chapel of St. Peter Ad Vincula in the Tower of London* (1877).

The team claimed to have consulted various historical sources and from these documents produced a plan showing where they believed the persons had been originally buried.

On 9 November 1876, the pavement above the spot marked on the plan as the final resting place of Queen Anne was lifted and the earth removed to a depth of 2 feet. Here the bones of a female were found and, after a thorough examination, all present were convinced that the remains they had uncovered were those of Anne Boleyn who, according to Bell, was recorded as being buried in front of the altar by the side of her brother George.

George Boleyn's remains were not discovered during the restoration and so were either removed or buried further towards the north wall, an area that remained undisturbed.

The description offered by Dr Mouat (Local Government Inspector), who examined the bones, is very much in keeping with what we know of Anne's appearance with the exception of one comment – 'a rather square full chin'. The bones were also identified as belonging to a female of between twenty-five and thirty years of age, perhaps another discrepancy; however, the debate about Anne's year of birth is not one to explore here!

In addition, the committee also recorded that they had uncovered the remains of Lady Rochford and Margaret, Countess of Salisbury, near the south wall. Bell recorded that the bones believed to belong to Lady Rochford were of a female of 'rather delicate proportions' of between about thirty and forty years of age.

Catherine Howard's remains were not found and the explanation offered was that, because she was so young at the time of death, her bones were not yet hard and so the lime used in the interments turned her bones to dust.

Historian Alison Weir offers an alternative explanation. She believes that the bones identified as belonging to Anne Boleyn might in fact be those of Catherine Howard, who was aged between sixteen and twenty-three years when she was executed and whose miniature by Holbein may show her with what could be described as a square chin.

Weir also argues that the remains identified as Lady Rochford by the Victorian committee are in fact those of Anne Boleyn. It's an interesting theory; however, as this has only been intended as a brief overview of the case, you can examine it in more detail by reading Doyne C. Bell's findings and Alison Weir's arguments in *The Lady in the Tower: The Fall of Anne Boleyn*.

Anne's death did not bring about an end to the controversy that surrounded her in life and, after almost half a millennium, continues to trail her in death.

What is certain is that in the end, on 13 April 1877, the remains of those exhumed from the chancel were reinterred where they had been found and there they remain until this day, marked only by a Victorian memorial plaque.

Each year on 19 May, the muted hues of the marble pavement in front of the altar accentuate the beauty of the red roses sent by anonymous admirers to commemorate the life of this remarkable woman.

Authors' Favourites

Before visiting, we strongly urge you to watch a brilliant video on YouTube by Historic Royal Palaces; it will help you visualise Anne's apartments at the Tower. It charts the process of the digital recreation of Anne's Boleyn's lodgings (Search on YouTube for 'Anne Boleyn's apartments – HM Tower of London')

Sadly, you cannot actually walk in Anne's footsteps from the site of her lodgings to the scaffold. However, do find the real site of the scaffold and go and stand there. Take a look around and you will see, almost unchanged, the last sight that met Anne's eyes before she was executed.

Finally, if you ever get chance, travel to the City of Winchester and see an extant Great Hall, built at the same time as the one at the Tower by the same king – Henry III. It probably looks very similar to how the Great Hall at the Tower once looked. Standing under its cavernous, vaulted roof, gives you a very good idea of the size, grandeur and acoustics of the hall and how Anne might well have felt at her trial in 1536.

Visitor Information
The Tower of London is managed by Historic Royal Palaces. For more information on how to reach the Tower and its opening hours, visit the Historic Royal Palaces' website at http://www.hrp.org.uk/TowerOfLondon, or telephone + 44 (0) 2031 666000.

Postcode for the Lower Thames Street Car Park (Tower of London): EC3R 6DT.

Anne Boleyn's Coronation Procession, London

On Saturday, the last day of the month [May], also in the afternoon, she [Anne] passed from the Tower to Westminster, with very great pomp, clad in silver tissue, with her hair over her shoulders, and a coronet (coronella) on her head; being carried on a chair of cloth of gold, between two mules, which were also covered with silver damask, and under a canopy of cloth of silver, accompanied by the greater part of the nobility of this kingdom, with the utmost order and tranquillity, all the streets and the houses being crowded with persons of every condition, in number truly marvellous; and in many places there were triumphal arches, pageants, and other decorations, as usually made on similar occasions.

Caelo Capello, Venetian ambassador, 7 June 1533

At around 5.00 p.m. on Saturday 31 May 1533, a fine summer evening, Anne Boleyn emerged from the Tower of London where she had been comfortably lodged since Thursday. She was dressed in the French fashion, 'filmy white, with a coronet of gold', and her loose dark hair flowed luxuriously down to waist length. She rode in a litter drawn by two palfreys – small dainty horses – draped in white damask.

For the citizens of London, this was their first glimpse of the woman who had changed everything, from the succession to the way they worshipped. For Anne, the coronation procession was her first glimpse of the City and her citizens. Some reports say she had a lukewarm reception with sullen crowds failing to remove their caps and Anne complaining to Henry with the words, 'Sir, I liked the city well enough but I saw a great many caps on heads, and heard but few tongues.' Eric Ives believed the crowds were 'more curious than either welcoming or hostile' and he gave little credit to hostile reports. Whatever the truth, one can only imagine how Anne felt that May evening as she began her journey through the crowded, noisome streets. Was she nervous, joyful, defiant or proud? A mixture of emotions is likely. But it's not within the realms of fantasy to imagine her breathing a sigh of relief as the procession cleared the city boundaries at Temple Bar and continued on its way to Westminster where she would finally be crowned.

So what do we mean by the City? Well, being the oldest part of London, it's a magical place. For a history buff with a keen sense of the past it's difficult not to feel a shiver as you wander around the winding lanes and streets, literally following in the footsteps of all those who have gone before us – right back to the Romans who founded London in AD 50. It's thanks to the Romans that the city is nicknamed 'The Square Mile' because it was they who first surrounded London with a great wall that made up approximately 1 square mile. The City of Henry VIII's reign was mostly confined to that small area with a substantial population of approximately 100,000 people.

Traditionally the City is the centre of business and finance, still dominated by trade guilds and livery companies, which elect the Lord Mayor annually. Anne Boleyn's coronation procession was significant because monarchs did not (and do not) enter the City uninvited. Since the days of William the Conqueror, the City has retained its independence from royal interference. Anne's passage through the streets was therefore an occasion to show herself to the people.

This guide is intended to help you retrace her progress through the City of London, allowing you to follow the same streets and get an idea of what Anne saw on the day. Although the City still has its basic medieval street plan, it is much changed today due to disasters such as the Great Fire of London and the Blitz. Therefore, as you walk the route (or read it!) imagine how much narrower the streets were in 1533 and how much darker it would have been with the overhanging roofs blocking the sunlight. Think also of the how the ground was sprinkled with grit to stop the horses slipping and imagine beautiful timber-framed buildings adorned with tapestries, carpets and fine cloth.

Walking in the Shoes of a Summer Queen

Tower Hill – if you're arriving by tube, as you exit Tower Hill Station, you will see the great Norman fortress over the road to your left. Anne arrived at the Tower on Thursday 29 May after sailing down the Thames from Greenwich in a lavishly decorated barge. During her forty-eight-hour stay, eighteen courtiers were made Knights of the Bath, including Francis Weston who was later destroyed along with Anne when her enemies struck in 1536.

Walk straight ahead into Trinity Gardens and follow the stone pathway on your left. It will bring you to the site of the Tower Hill scaffold with a poignant plaque remembering those who died there. Sir Thomas More and Bishop Fisher are named, but curiously absent are George Boleyn, Francis Weston, Sir William Brereton, Sir Henry Norris and Mark Smeaton who also lost their lives at this spot.

But this was three years into the future and Anne would have had no sense of impending disaster as her procession skirted Tower Hill on its way to Fenchurch Street. Continue along the path and exit the garden through the gate at the top of the gardens, crossing the road onto Cooper's Row. Walk down into Crutched Friars (named for the monastery) and then go up Lloyd's Avenue until you reach Fenchurch Street.

Fenchurch Street – Fenchurch Street was probably named for the fen or moor it was built upon and the church (St Gabriel's) that stood there until the Great Fire of 1666.

St Gabriel's was situated in the middle of the road and Anne's procession stopped here for the first entertainment of the day. Built up against the eastern wall of the church was a tableau designed to celebrate Anne's French links and her friendship with France. The tableau included children dressed as merchants who welcomed Anne to the City in both English and French. Interestingly, the procession was headed by twelve servants belonging to the French ambassador Jean de Dinteville who is depicted in Holbein's masterpiece *The Ambassadors*. It was a huge compliment to France to be featured so prominently – not to mention a snub to the Emperor!

After enjoying the tableau, the procession split around the church and continued on its way down Fenchurch Street, Anne's scarlet-clad ladies riding along behind their mistress.

Continue down until you reach the corner of Fenchurch and Gracechurch Street.

Gracechurch Street – in Saxon times it was known as Grass Church Street after the corn market that was held here. By the sixteenth century, however, it was sometimes known as Gracious Street. It was here that Anne was faced with her first reminder of her reasons to be gracious – and grateful.

She was six months pregnant. An exhausting time for any woman perhaps, but for Anne, carrying within her belly all the hopes and expectations of king and country, the next tableau reminded her of the enormous responsibility.

On the corner of Fenchurch and Gracechurch Street she was shown a tableau designed by Holbein. No words were spoken but the meaning would have been very clear to the pregnant queen as she read the Latin verses held aloft by actors representing the classical figures of Calliope, Apollo and the muses of art and learning:

> Anna comes, the most famous woman in all the world,
> Anna comes, the shining incarnation of chastity,
> In snow white litter, just like the goddesses,
> Anna the queen is here, the preservation of your future.

No pressure then!

The group was seated upon a model of Mount Parnassus and its sacred fountain. Above Apollo's head there was an eagle, which the Imperial ambassador Eustace Chapuys believed had been placed there by the German Hanse merchants (who paid for it) as a malicious reminder of the Emperor, Charles V. But as Eric Ives stated, the Emperor's eagle was two-headed and 'according to the classical story the eagle was blinded by Apollo's brilliance – hardly a compliment to Charles V!' Whatever the truth, we can imagine the eagle being quite lost on ordinary Londoners as they tucked into all the free Rhenish wine pouring from the fountain.

Turn right up Gracechurch Street and continue on until you reach the entrance to Leadenhall Market on the right hand side.

Leadenhall – there has been a market on this site since the fourteenth century. The earliest market (and the one Anne would have seen) was a large stone building with a lead roof, hence the name Leadenhall! Today's market is a wonderful piece of Victoriana designed by Sir Horace Jones in 1880.

With her pregnancy advancing and the whole court eagerly expecting a male heir, the next tableau was designed to reinforce the message. Backing onto the entrance of

Leadenhall Market, Anne saw an open castle painted inside with clouds, angels and cherubs. Seated on top of a green hillock within the castle were figures representing St Anne (the mother of the Virgin Mary) and her descendants, including Jesus.

The message was clear. Anne the queen would rival the maternal success of Anne the saint.

For a Tudor detour, walk straight through the cobbled street of the market and out the other end, passing Lord Rogers' Lloyds Building on your left. Follow the curvature of the street round to the left and cross Leadenhall Street to the little stone church of St Andrew Undershaft. Built in 1522, this little church miraculously survived the Great Fire of London and the Blitz. Its strange name comes from the fact that it was constructed next to a huge maypole, which dwarfed the church. St Andrew was quite literally under the shaft!

Retrace your steps to the entrance of Leadenhall and cross Gracechurch Street, turning left onto Cornhill.

Cornhill – the name Cornhill continues the reference to the corn market, which was probably centred around Leadenhall. Today it's a modern city street that hides a labyrinth of ancient alleyways to its left.

Tucked away in a little alleyway just off Cornhill (Corbet Court) you will find an interesting lady. She is a 'Mercer's Maiden' and this is the badge, or symbol, of the Mercer's Company, the richest of the City Livery Companies. Anne's great-grandfather was a member of the Mercer's Company. Geoffrey Boleyn became Lord Mayor in 1457 and was knighted by Henry VI. He seems to have been a fair-minded individual – on two occasions during his mayoralty he allowed people to forgo their jury service on the grounds of ill health or age. But he could also be firm – he once had to order a fishmonger to burn his wooden bowls because they were sappy and ruined the fish.

But back to Cornhill. In Anne's day there was a conduit here, which carried water down from the springs in the hills above London. It was at the conduit that the next tableau was staged. Figures representing the Three Graces waited to greet the queen, each announcing themselves as 'Glad Heart', 'Stable Honour' and 'Continual Success'.

As she processed down this scarlet-and-crimson-draped street, imagine Anne nodding her thanks to the Three Graces and enjoying a moment of quiet pride in her achievements so far.

Continue down Cornhill, crossing Bank Junction, and turn right onto Cheapside.

Cheapside – in Anne's day, Cheapside was the widest of the City streets and the focus of pageants, public gatherings and, of course, coronation processions. It was also a major shopping centre, the word 'Cheap' coming from the old English word for market. As you walk down Cheapside, look out for the names of the little streets and alleyways running off it, which remind us of the commodities on sale here: Milk Street, Bread Street and Honey Lane are a few examples.

Standing at the eastern end of Cheapside you will see a big, modernist red brick building on your left. This is Number One Poultry and was completed in the late 1990s but incorporates an interesting frieze showing the coronation processions of Edward VI, Elizabeth I, Charles II and Queen Victoria. This detail shows Elizabeth in her litter.

For Anne's coronation procession, the buildings were draped in a magnificent display of cloth of gold and velvet. She was greeted by all the livery companies standing on one side of the street and the general citizens on the other.

Opposite Honey Lane she was treated to Latin speeches and music; static displays and heraldic devices. She then moved to the Eleanor Cross, which was located opposite the church of St Mary le Bow, where the Aldermen presented her with a gold purse containing 1,000 marks.

For a detour, step into the entrance of Ironmonger Lane and see more examples of Mercer's Maidens at the Mercer's Hall. Continue up the winding lane and cross Gresham Street into Guildhall Yard. The imposing Gothic Great Hall standing before you is where the Lord Mayors have been sworn into office every year since it was built in 1430. Geoffrey Boleyn would have been very familiar with it.

Retrace your steps and continue down Cheapside, turning left onto New Change, and cross the road onto Carter Lane. St Paul's Cathedral is now in front of you to the north.

St Paul's – Carter Lane is named for the carters who dropped their passengers off at the many coaching inns that lined this long, winding lane. The paved area in the centre of Carter Lane demonstrates how narrow it was and how congested it would have been! The lane backed onto St Paul's churchyard, and near here Anne saw her next entertainment.

At one of the gates to the churchyard, she saw an empty throne mounted high ready for its new occupant. Three elaborately dressed women waited below, the central figure holding aloft the cheerful message, 'Come my love, thou shalt be crowned.'

The watching crowd was thrown wafers bearing the words, 'Queen Anne, when thou shalt bear a new son of the king's blood, there shall be a golden world unto thy people.'

It's at this point that we get a touching insight into Anne's mood on this special day. After watching a sweet display of 200 children reciting Latin poems to their new queen, she said 'Amen' with a 'joyful, smiling face'.

For an interesting detour, continue down Carter Lane for 200 yards until you reach the gloomy-looking alleyway called Church Entry on your left. Walk down the hill to the bottom and turn left again until you see the little ruined churchyard. Walk up the steps and see the dilapidated old stonework near the entrance. This formed part of a church located in the centre of the Blackfriars monastery that played host to Katharine of Aragon's divorce hearing in 1529.

The monastery housed around 400 monks who were presumably pensioned off when it was dissolved in 1538. The building was sold off piecemeal and if you retrace your steps back into Playhouse Yard, you will be standing roughly where Shakespeare's company operated their famous indoor Blackfriars playhouse in the monks' refectory.

Anne Boleyn's procession continued down Fleet Street and out of the City through Temple Bar on its way to Westminster. She would have had no inkling of the tragedy that lay ahead of her but, for those of us who admire the courage and intelligence of the woman who 'set our country in a roar', it's a comfort to know that she always remained true to herself and to her firmly held beliefs.

With thanks to Zoe Bramley from London History Walks for kindly contributing this entry. Visit www.tudorfiction.com to find out how to join a guided walking tour of Tudor London.

Whitehall Palace (York Place), London

> to please the lady [Anne] who prefers that place for the King's residence to any other.
> The Spanish Ambassador writing about Whitehall Palace, Christmas/New Year, 1529/30

Whitehall Palace surely holds a special place in the story of Anne Boleyn, for it was here that we see the young, twenty-one-year-old Anne, who was newly returned from France, make her first recorded appearance at the English court, taking part in a masque called the *Château Vert*, during which she rather prophetically played the part of 'Perseverance'.

At the time, the palace was part of the Archdiocese of York and was occupied by the king's powerful and wealthy first minister, Cardinal Wolsey. However, by 1526, Henry had fallen head over heels in love with the captivating Mistress Boleyn and Wolsey's world was about to be turned upside down. Unable to secure the king his divorce, Wolsey fell into disgrace after the collapse of the Blackfriars trial of 1529. Then on 22 October 1529, he pleaded guilty to charges of *preamunire*. In an effort to gain mercy from the king, Thomas Wolsey surrendered all his property and goods into the king's hands. Among the spoils was the fabulous York Place, a sumptuous palace positioned conveniently on the western bank of the Thames just half a mile north of Thorney Island, which formed the old City of Westminster, then the seat of government in England.

We know that just two days later, Anne accompanied the king from Greenwich, along with her mother, Elizabeth, and Sir Henry Norris. The king found the present 'more valuable than even he expected'; it included a glittering array of silver-gilt and gold plate, some encrusted with precious stones, much of it laid out in the eponymous Gilt Chamber, Wolsey's private study that overlooked the Thames.

Henry and Anne were by this time at the centre of the storm that was 'The King's Great Matter', with the king utterly resolved to set Katharine of Aragon aside and take Anne as his new wife. York Place, as it was still known, soon became the favoured residence of the two lovers; having no queen's side, Henry could lodge Anne at the palace away from the withering disapproval of the king's discarded wife. York Place, or Whitehall as it was later to be known, was to be a glittering new Renaissance palace, which Anne and Henry set about designing together over the Christmas of 1529.

Whitehall was to be much enlarged, encompassing the buildings of York Place within its core. Added to the existing kitchens, service buildings, Great Hall, watching, presence and privy chambers and Long Gallery would be an entirely remodelled and augmented queen's side incorporating many of Wolsey's original rooms; a 100-foot-long privy stair that projected out into the Thames for private use by the king and queen; an entire privy gallery range containing the king's most private apartments; and the Holbein Gate, which marked the entry and exit point from the royal enclave of Whitehall and Westminster. It also connected the palace's lodgings to its new leisure complex that lay on the far side of King Street, now the site of the modern-day Whitehall. Land was also reclaimed to the south of the palace in order to augment the gardens, making a vast orchard/garden and, north of the new privy gallery, an additional privy garden with surrounding loggia was also created.

While sadly the palace is entirely lost, with the exception of some underground corridors and fireplaces that are not accessible to the public, a good deal of contemporary descriptions and illustrations survive to give us a good idea of its external and internal decoration in the sixteenth century.

The complex itself was truly enormous, a staggering 23 acres compared to the rather paltry 6 acres that defined the footprint of Hampton Court; at the same time, its edifice extended 200 feet along the western bank of the Thames. The palace was bisected by King Street, a busy thoroughfare which allowed Londoners to pass from Charing Cross at its northern end down to old Westminster Palace. To the west of King Street, Henry and Anne planned a marvellous recreation complex, including a tiltyard and viewing gallery, four tennis courts, a bowling alley and cockpit, all backing onto the pleasant park of St James's, which provided the couple with excellent hunting.

The east side of the palace contained the state and privy chambers; here very little brickwork was visible. Instead, the timber framing was left exposed throughout, producing a grid-like pattern extending across the whole face of the building. Between these grids, plaster panels were painted decoratively with grotesque work. Rather vividly and in contrast to this, the Great Hall was painted in chequerwork while the privy kitchen was inlaid with bands of galleting. All this gave Whitehall an entirely distinctive appearance. Henry had been keen that in every way it should embody the best of Renaissance architecture; all about it were symbols of chivalry and heraldry, creating forms that were painted in bright colours and that cast strong silhouettes against the London skyline.

Inside, there are records of the giant fresco depicting Henry VIII's Coronation painted along one wall of the Long Gallery overlooking the Great Orchard; a newly built, wide, processional vice-stair that led up to the queen's apartments from a cloister connecting this stair to the Great Hall; the 150-foot queen's privy gallery that so impressed Sir Thomas More that he is said to have told Wolsey of his distinct preference for it over that of the privy gallery at Hampton Court. And if you want a visual impression of the interior of Whitehall, then look at Henry VIII's dynastic portrait, called *The Family of Henry VIII*, painted retrospectively in around 1545: this probably depicted both the interior and exterior aspects of design at Whitehall. You can see the richness of the grotesque work, gilding, wood carving and elaborate carving of heraldic symbols of the Tudor dynasty on the ceiling, and get a sense of the vivid colours that adorned every great Tudor palace.

Events at Whitehall Palace
Several key events unfolded at the Palace of Whitehall:

On 29 January 1533 a pregnant Anne is said to have married Henry in the upper chamber of the Holbein Gate in a secret, pre-dawn ceremony.

On 31 May 1533, Anne would have passed down King Street and under the Holbein Gate on her way from the Tower to the Old Palace of Westminster; here she was formally received in Westminster Hall. With this ceremony complete, Anne slipped out of the back of the old palace via the queen's privy stair and travelled downstream the half a mile to lodge with the king at Whitehall prior to her Coronation the following day.

It was at Whitehall that elaborate celebrations were held for several days following Anne's Coronation at Westminster Abbey. This included a spectacular tournament held on the tiltyard, now Horse Guards Parade.

It is reasonable to suppose that Anne was also with the king at Whitehall when Parliament met to debate and pass two crucial Acts that touched greatly on Anne's position and future as Henry's consort. The *Act of Restraint of Appeals*, which effectively barred Katharine from appealing to Rome in the case of her divorce from the king, came first in the spring of 1533 and then, in 1534, the *Act of the Succession* was passed, which placed the inheritance of the English throne solely in the heirs of Anne's body, thereby disbarring the Lady Mary from the succession.

Authors' Favourites

There is nothing above ground to be seen of the old Tudor palace and, we admit, busy traffic roaring incessantly along modern-day Whitehall makes it difficult to find the inner space to imagine Henry's magnificent palace sprawled across both sides of the road. However, taking a trip down Whitehall from Charing Cross takes you in Anne's footsteps as she processed, in a fabulous litter draped in white cloth of gold, from the City to Westminster on Saturday 31 May 1533.

Just before the Banqueting House is Horse Guards Avenue; this roughly marks the spot of the main street-side entrance to the palace. Beyond Banqueting House, but on the same side of the road, a hideous concrete building called Wales' House stands roughly over the original site of the Great Orchard. Then, on the other side of the road is the arch that leads through to Horse Guards Parade ground, the original site of the palace's tiltyard, while the statue of George, Duke of Cambridge, on horseback is the original position of the Holbein Gate.

Continue down Whitehall to visit two other historic sites associated with Anne: Westminster Hall and Westminster Abbey.

Visitor Information

Whitehall is always accessible to the public, except during exceptional state occasions (e.g. royal weddings, funerals etc.) and on Remembrance Sunday, when it is closed for the morning.

Postcode for Whitehall: SW1A 2ER.

Westminster Hall, London

Come my love, thy shalt be crowned!
Written into the St Paul's pageant for Anne Boleyn's coronation procession

As far as we know, Anne Boleyn only visited Westminster Hall in relation to one occasion: her Coronation. She was thirty-two years old and carried within her belly Henry's hopes and aspirations for a son and heir to continue the Tudor dynasty.

England's new summer queen was around six months pregnant on 31 May 1533, when she processed from the Tower through the City of London on her way to Westminster. Dressed in white cloth of gold, a purple mantel edged with ermine around her shoulders and a golden coronet set upon her flowing, auburn-coloured hair, she must have looked celestial, almost divine.

Once at Westminster, Anne lodged overnight with the king and court at Whitehall, ahead of the appointed day of her Coronation, which was set for Sunday 1 June. In a ceremony steeped in ancient rites that stretched back to the dawn of England's recorded history, Anne was finally crowned queen on Whit Sunday by her old friend, Thomas Cranmer, Archbishop of Canterbury. After the Coronation, Anne processed on foot back to Westminster Hall, where she presided over a great banquet held in her honour.

A week of celebrations then followed. These included jousts, masques and banquets, all of which took place at Whitehall Palace, and which were dedicated to paying homage to Henry's 'most beloved' wife. It had been a long road that had transformed the slight, twelve-year-old child, who left Hever behind for foreign shores, into a powerful and influential *feme sole* who was, by degree, influencing the course of England's religious and social landscape. However, the transformation was now complete; years honing her political acumen, grace and accomplishments at the Hapsburg and French courts had finally paid off – Anne had reached the pinnacle of Tudor society.

Exploring King Street and Westminster Hall

If you have just visited the site of the old Palace of Whitehall, then continue walking southwards along the eponymously named road, which 500 years ago was called King Street. Having passed the original site of the Holbein Gate, you are now walking within the old royal enclave of Westminster and following the final stages of Anne's journey from the Tower.

At the bottom of Whitehall, you will be standing at the north-east corner of Parliament Square. On most ordinary days, your senses will be assaulted by the noise and smell of the busy traffic, and you will be jostled among the throng of tourists. Imagine these reminders of a busy twenty-first century melting away to leave the abbey and palace dominating a peaceful landscape surrounded by open, green spaces, wide thoroughfares and pretty ornamental gardens.

The towering edifice of Westminster Abbey lies directly in front of you, stretching away to your right, while over to your left, nestled in among the Victorian grandeur of the remodelled Houses of Parliament, you will notice the much older Westminster Hall, once part of the original medieval Palace of Westminster.

In the sixteenth century, the City of Westminster was, as it remains today, the seat of English government and power. Although we can no longer see evidence of it, the Collegiate Church of St Peter in Westminster (Westminster Abbey) and the old Palace of Westminster stood on an island, called Thorney Island, with the River Tyburn and one of its tributaries flowing into the Thames on either side of the site; presumably these are now underground. Thus, Westminster was connected to the mainland on the north, south and west by several bridges, being encircled on three sides by open countryside and abutted by the River Thames the east.

At the bottom of modern-day Whitehall, there would have stood another gatehouse; this two-storey crenelated building opened up into an area called the Outer Yard or Old Palace Yard. The Outer Yard was a huge courtyard that ran from the King's Steps by the river on the east to the Great Gateway on the west. In the centre was a conduit, while the whole area was enclosed by stone, brick and wattle-and-daub buildings along its northern edge, with the magnificent façade of Westminster Palace running along its southern side. These latter buildings were fashioned from white stone, the roofs being pitched and crenelated in parts, chimneys and turrets rising into the sky. Along this range of buildings, between England's office of the Auditors of Foreign Accounts and Westminster Hall, was a further gateway. This would have straddled part of the modern-day road that runs between the Abbey and the Houses of Parliament. It once led through to the palace's inner ward and the entrance to the privy palace apartments.

The Great Hall of Westminster was virtually rebuilt by King Richard II in the late fourteenth century. At 240 feet long, nearly 70 feet wide and just under 100 feet tall at the centre apex, the hall dwarfed many of the buildings surrounding it in its day. Now it stands as an integral part of the Houses of Parliament, cast in the shadow of Big Ben. However, this *grande dame* of English history seems indomitable, enduring despite the fire that burnt much of the original medieval palace to the ground in 1834 and even surviving heavy bombing by the German Luftwaffe during the Second World War. Today Westminster Hall remains as a priceless relic of England's medieval history. It has borne witness to many momentous occasions, including the trials of Sir Thomas More and the four men accused with Anne – Smeaton, Brereton, Weston and Norris; the 'Coronation' of Oliver Cromwell; and, over the centuries, countless dignitaries and world leaders have passed through its doors.

Stepping Back in Time: 1 June 1533
Now, let's slip back in time for a moment and imagine the scene as it looked on 1 June 1533: the day of Anne's Coronation. From seven o'clock in the morning, lords, ladies, aldermen of London and other dignitaries had been gathering in Westminster Hall, awaiting Anne's arrival. She rode from Whitehall Palace to Westminster in the royal barge, a journey of only about half a mile. Once at the Palace of Westminster, Anne alighted via the queen's stairs. She therefore must have slipped through the queen's apartments to reach Westminster Hall through its southern entrance.

The hall itself was bedecked with expensive tapestries and rich fabrics. At the high end, a dais was raised twelve steps above the throng of courtiers and officials of London. This is where Anne would later sit to preside over the coronation banquet. As tradition dictated, the queen in waiting was dressed in a purple velvet gown furred with ermine, set against a kirtle fashioned from cloth of gold; her hair was loose about her shoulders and upon it was the same coif and coronet that she had worn the day before. Down the centre of the hall was a blue carpet, railed on each side; it extended the 700 yards between the dais of the hall and the high altar of the abbey. We do not know if Anne walked those 700 yards barefoot in the traditional act of humility associated with the crowning of a new monarch. However, Anne was escorted by a procession of the great and the good of the land: men from the King's Chapel, the monks of Westminster and divers bishops and abbots, gentlemen, squires and knights, followed by the aldermen of the City and judges, all dressed in their scarlet robes. Barons and viscounts in their scarlet parliamentary robes followed, with England's nobility coming behind, walking side by side in pairs; earls, marquesses and dukes in their crimson robes of estate, all furred with ermine and powdered according to their degrees.

Anne walked to the abbey beneath the same gold canopy of the Cinque Ports that had been carried over her the day before, John Stokesley and Steven Gardiner taking up the traditional positions of bishops of London and Winchester on either side of their queen. In front of Anne, the newly married Henry Grey, Marquis of Dorset, carried the sceptre of gold, while the twenty-one-year-old Earl of Arundel held the sceptre of ivory topped with a dove symbolising the Holy Spirit. Finally, immediately in front of Anne came Charles Brandon, carrying the crown of St Edward. A train of Anne's ladies and gentlewomen variously dressed in scarlet velvet gowns, some furred with ermine, followed on behind. The Dowager Duchess of Norfolk had the honour of holding the long train of Anne's purple velvet surcoat; Lord Burgh, the queen's chamberlain, supported the train in the middle.

Thus, Anne set out in procession to the abbey, there to be crowned as Queen of England.

Authors' Favourites

Once you have passed through the security checks at the Houses of Parliament, you will cross over the threshold of the hall's enormous north-facing doors and into its cool, shady interior. As you step through those doors, you will be following directly in Anne's footsteps, as she was received into the heart of the Palace of Westminster on 31 May 1533. Here, Thomas Cranmer described what happened next in a letter written to the English ambassador to the Spanish court: 'A certain banquet was prepared for her, which done, she was conveyed out of the back side of the palace into a barge and so unto York Place, where the King's Grace was before her coming.'

Even stripped bare, as it is today, be ready to have your breath snatched away by the sheer grandeur of the space and the utter magnificence of the largest hammer-beam roof in England. To explore the modern-day interior, pay particular attention to the following:

The plaque on the floor commemorating the fact that great state trials were held here, including that of Sir Thomas More.

Somewhere near the foot of the steps at the southern end of the hall, which lead up to St Stephen's Chamber, was the position of the dais that Anne sat upon beneath a rich cloth of estate as she presided over her coronation banquet, although there were no such steps in Anne's day.

Finally, make your way to the foot of those steps and with your back to the north doors, look up to the second window along from the southern end of the hall. Here there was a gallery and a 'window' where Henry was able to look down upon the celebrations below. As custom dictated, the king stayed out of sight during the entire coronation festivities. The day was Anne's alone.

Visitor Information

UK residents should contact their local MP or a Member of the House of Lords in order to arrange a tour. There is no charge for tours booked in this way. UK residents can also visit on Saturdays and during the summer recess (see notes for overseas visitors below). Tours must be booked in advance with bookings open up to four months ahead. Demand is high, so early booking and flexibility regarding dates and times are an advantage.

For further information visit http://www.parliament.uk/visiting/visiting-and-tours/ukvisitors/tours/.

Overseas visitors (and UK residents) can buy tickets for a tour of Parliament on most Saturdays throughout the year and six days a week during the summer opening period. Foreign language tours in French, German, Italian and Spanish are available at various times on all days. There are no tours on Sundays or on Bank Holidays. For further information visit http://www.parliament.uk/visiting/visiting-and-tours/overseasvisitors/summeropening/.

Postcode for Westminster Hall: SW1A 0AA.

Westminster Abbey, London

And so she [Anne] was brought to St Peter's church at Westminster, and there set in her high royal seat ... and there she was anointed and crowned.

Edward Hall, English chronicler

The origins of the Collegiate Church of St Peter in Westminster, or Westminster Abbey, are obscure. Nobody knows exactly when this mighty building was founded. However, Edward the Confessor certainly built a magnificent Saxon church upon the site, and William the Conqueror sealed its place in English history by having himself crowned at the abbey following the conquest of England, on Christmas Day in 1066. Subsequently, virtually every English monarch has been anointed and crowned here.

The abbey is arguably one of the most historic and important buildings in England. It is steeped in centuries of English history and has steadfastly born witness to profound social and religious change. Thousands of notable figures have passed through its doors and many now lie buried within its grounds. These include the founder of the Tudor dynasty, Henry VII, and his wife Elizabeth of York, who lie in eternal repose at the heart of the sumptuous Henry VII Chapel. Indeed, there is much to be seen by the Tudor enthusiast, not least the grave of Anne of Cleves, who lies interred to the right of the sacrarium close to the high altar. Then, of course, there are the fabulous marble tombs of Mary I; Mary, Queen of Scots; and Anne's own daughter, Elizabeth.

However, as we are following in Anne's footsteps, we will leave you to explore in full the delights of Westminster Abbey in your own time, while we turn our attention to the events that unfolded beneath its soaring, vaulted ceiling on Whit Sunday, 1 June 1533.

Stepping Back in Time: 1 June 1533

Once inside the abbey, make your way to the main west doors. If you wish to follow in the footsteps of Anne Boleyn, then pick up the coronation procession as Anne steps through those very same doors and into the heart of this most sacred of buildings. Continue at your own pace walking down the abbey's central nave toward the quire and the high altar, which lies beyond. Imagine the church packed to capacity with the great and good of the kingdom, all gathered to witness the crowning of England's new queen. The abbey would have been ablaze with colour and filled with the sound of its heavenly choir, calling to God to witness the coming forth of a new English monarch. Stop and reflect for a moment on how Anne might have felt, just one mortal woman about to kneel at the feet of God and be anointed with immortality.

As you make your way forward, look up to admire the vaulted ceiling of the nave that towers above over you at over 100 feet high. While heavily influenced by French design, the Englishness of the abbey is apparent in the elaborate mouldings of the main arches, the use of polished Purbeck marble for the principal pillars and the fine overall sculpted decoration.

Keep moving forward until you pass through the screen that separates the quire from the rest of the nave. The way through from the body of the nave to the quire may be locked and you might have to make your way back round to the quire via the outer aisles. Beyond the quire is the high altar at the heart of the sacrarium, the part of the abbey which has become colloquially known as the 'theatre of coronation'. For it is here, in front of the high altar, that this most sacred of ceremonies takes place.

According to tradition, directly before the altar a scaffold would have been erected. This was covered in expensive arras. At its centre stood the 500-year-old wooden coronation chair of King Edward the Confessor, see below. Upon this chair, Anne would be anointed and crowned. Thus, she herself would be following in the footsteps of all the Saxon and medieval kings who had come before her, enshrouding her evermore in the mystique of monarchy.

In front of Anne, the high altar would have been resplendent, adorned with gold, and perhaps the medieval *Westminster Retable*, which can be seen downstairs in the museum, would still have been in place. Somewhere above your eyeline, in the gallery overlooking the sacrarium the king sat behind a grill and alongside his guests, the French and Venetian ambassadors, their presence an outward display of acceptance of Anne as Henry's rightful wife and queen.

The coronation ceremony itself has changed little over the centuries. During Anne's time, when the country was still Catholic, the ceremony was set within the context of a solemn Mass and would have lasted several hours. The ceremony of coronation is a complex one with many ritualistic parts symbolising the monarch's God-given right to rule, while also invoking qualities of fairness, justice, devotion and duty to the people in the new king or queen. It is not our intention to describe this ceremony in full here; it has been well documented elsewhere. However, in brief, Anne would have been presented to the north, south, east and west as their new and rightful queen, before taking the coronation oath. Then, as Cranmer wrote, 'divers ceremonies were used about her'. This would have included being anointed beneath a canopy, with the Archbishop of Canterbury using a golden ampulla and spoon for the purpose before setting 'the crown upon her head'. A *Te Deum* followed and, after that was sung, a solemn Mass. All the while Cranmer describes Anne sitting 'crowned upon a scaffold which was made between the High Altar and the quire in Westminster Church'.

There are two notable points that relate to Anne's Coronation in the context of coronation history as a whole. Firstly, Anne Boleyn was the last queen regent to be crowned independently. Jane Seymour should have followed in Anne's footsteps, but died after giving birth to Henry's longed-for son, Edward, before the ceremony could take place. Secondly, most unusually,

Henry insisted that Anne be crowned with the crown of St Edward the Confessor. This crown is usually reserved only for the reigning monarch. It was a great honour and surely a sign of Henry's determination to have Anne accepted as lawful Queen of England.

Sadly, all the Crown Jewels and coronation regalia that would have adorned Anne that day have subsequently been lost, much of it sold off or melted down during the English Civil War. There is no evidence that the medieval spoon used during the anointing ceremony today was used until after the restoration of the English monarchy. However, an image of the pre-Reformation Crown Jewels can be seen in the wonderful portrait of Charles I painted by Daniel Mytens in 1631, which now hangs in the National Portrait Gallery.

Following the ceremony, Anne would have received pledges of fidelity from both clergy and noblemen, Thomas Cranmer declaring on behalf of all the clergy to be faithful and true according to the law, then according to rank England's nobility would have done the same, sinking down before her on one knee to declare before all that in God's name they were Anne's 'liege man of life and limb, and of earthly worship, faith and truth; that they would bear unto themselves, to live and die against all manner of folks' should anyone challenge Anne's right to be queen. One can only imagine that a number of the men who were present that day took that oath through gritted teeth!

Finally, Anne would have passed behind the high altar to pray at the shrine of St Edward the Confessor. This still stands behind the high altar today. It is easy to forget that Anne Boleyn was nearly six months pregnant when she was crowned at Westminster Abbey. She must have been elated at the great honour to which God had raised her, and also full of emotion and a certain degree of physical discomfort which is often associated with this second trimester of pregnancy. No doubt on account of the length of the service, during this time of brief respite out of sight of the public, the new queen would have been offered refreshments and an opportunity to use her closed stool in a nearby private room.

Eventually, with the service complete, Anne processed back towards Westminster Hall, still 'going under the canopy, crowned, with two sceptres in her hands'. Leading Anne from the abbey was her father on one side and the young Lord Talbot, the Earl of Shrewsbury's son and heir, on the other. Several hours still stretched ahead of Anne, as she was to preside over a banquet, which according to the chronicler Edward Hall was 'the most honourable feast that has been seen'.

However, on that day, Anne left Westminster Abbey an anointed queen, and as such only death could now intervene to take that status away from her.

Authors' Favourites

The coronation chair of St Edward the Confessor: this precious artefact is currently kept behind glass at the west end of the abbey. It was made on the orders of Edward I in 1300–1 and would have been used by Anne for her Coronation in 1533.

Stand in front of the high altar and, if it is uncovered, admire the medieval *cosmati* pavement upon which the Coronation of Anne Boleyn took place.

Visit the Pyx Chamber and undercroft and see a number of precious Tudor artefacts, including the head of Mary I's funeral effigy and the so-called 'Essex ring' belonging to Elizabeth I. However, the *Westminster Retable* is perhaps one of the most precious items.

It was painted in around 1270 and donated to the abbey by Henry III. It is thought that the *Retable* was set upon the high altar up until the Dissolution of the Monasteries. If this is the case, then we might also assume that Anne's Coronation was the last coronation to which it bore witness.

Visitor Information
Westminster Abbey is usually open to visitors from Monday to Saturday throughout the year. On Sundays and religious holidays, such as Easter and Christmas, the abbey is open for worship only. All are welcome to services. For more information visit http://www. westminster-abbey.org/visit-us/opening-times/general-opening-times.

Postcode for Westminster Abbey: SW1A 3PA.

St James's Palace, London

[The king] has newly builded St James in the Fields, a magnificent and goodly house.
Thomas Cromwell, 1536

Despite the fact that it is widely held that St James's Palace was built for Anne, there is very little evidence that she lived there, or even visited; although being so close to Whitehall we might well assume she did, and that she was very familiar with the place. It is often said that Anne resided at St James's after her Coronation, on the evening of 1 June 1533. However, the account of Anne's coronation festivities, written as a contemporary account by Wycken de Worde, actually reads that after the ceremony 'her grace retourned to Whyte Hall [Whitehall]', where jousts took place the following day. We have found no contemporary evidence to suggest that Anne was anywhere but at Whitehall on the evening following her Coronation, and dismiss this assertion as a well-propagated myth.

In order to see St James's Palace as Anne would have known it during the 1530s, we must sweep away the elegant rubble of suburbia and imagine a very different landscape indeed. Today, what remains of the diminutive, red brick Tudor palace is somewhat dwarfed by the swanky Georgian façades that surround it, its once-serene grandeur now struggling to maintain its composed presence amid the roar of the motor car, as a constant barrage of traffic sweeps endlessly past the palace's north-facing chapel and iconic five-storey gatehouse. However, 500 years ago Anne would have experienced a very different ambience.

The Palace of St James was once a leper hospital, the site no doubt chosen as it was a long way away from habitation, with few, if any, dwellings situated close by. Lying within the old parish boundary of St Margaret's, Westminster, it was surrounded by fields in a bleak spot on the edge of low-lying marsh. After drainage was put in place by Henry VIII, this area later became known as St James's Park. Away to the north of the hospital, the land rose to a ridge, along which passed one of the main routes out of London to the west, roughly along the road that is today known as Piccadilly. About a mile away to the south was the great Abbey Church of St Peter (Westminster Abbey), while lying a similar distance to the east was the new palace of Whitehall with all its glorious leisure facilities.

A view of St James's Palace and Westminster Abbey from the village of Charing shows the palace's once-rural location, surrounded by open fields; the lofty roofs of Westminster Abbey and Hall lie due south on higher ground. We can see an uninterrupted view over Westminster and St James's Park and it is clear that in its time, the palace was indeed a stately residence, a country seat that dominated the surrounding landscape.

In October 1531, Henry acquired the hospital and a good deal of land beside, such that he owned around 144 acres south of Pall Mall and west of Whitehall Palace; the area was almost twice the size of the current St James's Park. He immediately demolished the hospital and began to build a new palace in quintessential Tudor style. One of the interesting, and perhaps debateable points, is why? Traditionally, it has always been said that the palace was built for Anne. This is probably because building began in 1531 at the height of the royal romance. In addition, intertwined lovers' knots, with the initials 'H' and 'A', can still be seen in an extant Tudor fireplace located in a room that was once the presence chamber of the palace. However, Kenneth Scott, in *St James's Palace: a History*, argues that it was more likely that the palace was built as a court for Henry's illegitimate son, Henry Fitzroy, who some believed was being groomed as heir presumptive by the early 1530s, and that the entwined initials would have been common decorative practice, saying nothing about whether the queen ever actually lived there. I suspect we will never truly know the truth of the matter. Certainly Henry Fitzroy was to die there in 1536, but that does not prove anything of the motivation behind the building of the palace.

The Palace Buildings

It has been suggested that Cromwell, and perhaps Holbein, had a hand in the design of the palace. Although sadly we have no record of what the palace looked like in Henry's time, we can form a general idea of the layout. Scott describes this in the following way:

> The main entrance was through the Gatehouse to the north, and this led into a large courtyard, now called Colour Court, much of the brickwork of this is original. To the west of the Gatehouse is the Chapel Royal, possibly built on the site of the principal hall of the old hospital … To the south of Colour Court were two smaller courtyards, around which, on the first floor were the Royal Apartments overlooking the park, which were probably the first parts of the palace to be built.

These two smaller courtyards were at one time merged and now form 'Friary Court', an open courtyard that can easily be viewed from Marlborough Road, which runs by the east of the palace.

Visitor Information

St James's Palace is within walking distance of three other locations in this guidebook: Whitehall Palace and Westminster Abbey and Hall. If your walking legs permit, why don't you combine a circular walk between them, perhaps including a stroll through St James's Park, a place that Anne must have known intimately, although its manicured gardens are probably much changed today from the open fields and woodland in which the royal couple once hunted.

Of all the locations featured in this guidebook, St James's is unique in that it still retains its mantel of royalty, serving as the official residence of the British monarchy. The palace is often in use for official engagements, and a number of offices attached to the monarchy are based there. Therefore, the interior of the palace is not open to the public, although you can view its exterior from the roadside. Church services in the Chapel Royal are also open to the public on Sundays. Please check the following website for the most up-to-date information: http://www.royal.gov.uk/TheRoyalResidences/TheChapelsRoyal/Services. aspx.

Postcode for St James's Palace: SW1A 1BS.

Royal Palace of Hatfield, Hertfordshire

> The King's mistress, having gone to visit her daughter (Elizabeth), sent a message to the Princess, requesting her to visit and honour her as Queen which she was. Should she do so (the message bore), she would be as well received as she could wish, and it would be the means of her regaining the good pleasure and favour of the King, her father, and of her being treated as well or perhaps better than she had ever been.
>
> Eustace Chapuys, 7 March 1533

A short distance from the present Jacobean Hatfield House in Hertfordshire once stood the Royal Palace of Hatfield. Cardinal Morton, Bishop of Ely, built the grand russet-brick courtyard house, surrounded by an extensive deer park, in around 1480 and each of Henry's children – Mary, Elizabeth and Edward – resided there at various times in their lives.

In a survey completed in 1538, the year that Henry acquired the estate by exchange, the palace is described as 'a very goodly and stately manor place … constructed alle of brykke, having in the same very stately lodgynges with romes and offices to the same very necessary and expedient, albeit in some places it ys oute of reparaciones'.

Hatfield: A Royal Nursery

In this 'very goodly' home Anne Boleyn's daughter, Elizabeth, was sent to live in December 1533, when she was just three months old. It was the little princess's own private household, managed by a staff of nurses, courtiers and tutors, and there she remained until the end of March 1534 when she was moved to her father's childhood home at Eltham.

As one household rose, another fell. At this time, Elizabeth's now-illegitimate half-sister's household was dissolved and the Lady Mary was forced to join Elizabeth at Hatfield. In charge of this new joint household were Sir John and Lady Shelton, Anne's aunt and uncle.

In the spring of 1534, Queen Anne made the 20-mile journey from London to visit her beloved Elizabeth at Hatfield. It's easy to imagine that the joy at seeing her infant daughter again must have been marred by the obvious tension that existed between the now-illegitimate Lady Mary and her 'step-mother'.

During the visit, Anne extended a hand of friendship to Mary, promising to welcome her and reconcile her with her father if she would only accept her as queen. Mary's response caused outrage, as she stated that she knew no queen but her mother; however, would be grateful if 'madame Anne de Bolans' would intercede with her father on her behalf.

Regardless of the rebuke, Anne attempted once more to be gracious but Mary remained unmoved; in the end the queen departed Hatfield vowing to 'bring down the pride of this unbridled Spanish blood'.

The Appearance of the Old Palace

What of the house that Anne would have known? It was certainly a substantial building, consisting of four wings enclosing a courtyard. These four wings encompassed a Great Hall, a solar room, withdrawing rooms, bedrooms, kitchens and butteries.

Of this, only the west hall range, containing Bishop Morton's Great Hall, solar, kitchens and butteries and a gatehouse, much altered, to the north-west, survive, as the rest of the building was demolished in 1608 to make way for the present-day Hatfield House, constructed in 1611 by Robert Cecil, 1st Earl of Salisbury and Chief Minister to King James I.

Today, a visit to the sunken gardens on the east side of the old palace reveals traces of the demolished wings, once surrounding the present-day Old Palace Garden. The state apartments, where Anne would have been lodged during her stay, were likely to have been in the now-lost south wing, overlooking formal gardens.

Hatfield later became Elizabeth's principal seat, and today an oak tree in the park marks the place where it's said the twenty-five-year-old flame-haired Tudor first heard of her accession to the throne on 17 November 1558. Although the story is most likely apocryphal, it remains a wonderful spot to just sit and ponder those famous words, 'This is the Lord's doing, and it is marvelous in our eyes.'

On 21 November 1558, Elizabeth's first council sitting took place in the Great Hall and on this great occasion she appointed William Cecil Secretary of State. It is his ancestors that still reside at Hatfield today.

The beauty of the gardens, the fresh country air and deer park made Hatfield an attractive destination in the sixteenth century, but perhaps Elizabeth's fondness for the palace stemmed not just from these attributes but from the knowledge that when she first came to live there, she was the anchor of a family on the cusp of a joyous and promising future.

Authors' Favourites

Very near to the remains of the old palace there is a wonderful sculpture of Elizabeth I and her courtiers. It's a lovely place to sit and imagine Queen Anne walking in the gardens with her ladies, perhaps with an infant Elizabeth in tow.

We also recommend taking a stroll in the park. Walk up Queen Elizabeth Avenue until you locate the Queen Elizabeth Oak, where legend has it Elizabeth first heard of her accession to the throne. This is another picturesque place to pause and think of all that has passed in this historic location.

When touring the Jacobean house, be sure to keep an eye out for the *Rainbow Portrait* of Elizabeth I by Nicholas Hilliard and the exquisite *Ermine Portrait* of the queen by Isaac Oliver. Hatfield House is also home to a hat, silk stockings and pair of gloves said to have belonged to Elizabeth, but perhaps the most fascinating item is a richly decorated parchment roll tracing the ancestry of Elizabeth I back to Adam and Eve.

Visitor Information

If you wish to arrive at Hatfield Palace the way Anne would have no doubt done, then ignore the main, modern-day tourist entrance. Instead, follow signs to Hatfield 'Old Town' and park your car somewhere near the bottom of Fore Street. You can now meander on foot up the old medieval high street. This once led up to the main entrance to the old palace. It is a quiet but charming street, full of quaint medieval and Tudor houses.

At the top of Fore Street (once part of the Great North Road from London), you will find St Etheldreda's parish church where Lady Frances Brandon – daughter of the Duke of Suffolk and Mary Tudor, and mother of Lady Jane Grey – was christened on 17 July 1517 in the presence of a 'Lady Boleyn'. Given the date, and her appearance at another great banquet at Greenwich only ten days earlier, this almost certainly was Anne's mother, Elizabeth.

Beside the church you will find the old palace gatehouse, formerly part of the west entrance range of Bishop Morton's palace, although now changed, as it was altered in the seventeenth and nineteenth centuries.

The history, exquisite gardens – some dating from the seventeenth century – and vast parklands make this a must-see destination. Just as Elizabeth held Hatfield so dear, so do we, and the fact that we have such few vignettes of Anne's time with her daughter makes Hatfield a location to treasure.

For more information on how to reach Hatfield House and its opening hours, which are seasonal, visit the Hatfield House website at http://www.hatfield-house.co.uk, or telephone + 44 (0) 1707 287010. Please note that the inside of the Old Palace can only be seen from the viewing bay. When a private function is taking place the tower will be closed. Visitors particularly wanting to see the inside are urged to call or email ahead to avoid disappointment.

Postcode for the Royal Palace of Hatfield: AL9 5NQ.

Eltham Palace, Kent

> I went to see his Majesty's house at Eltham, both palace and chapel in miserable ruins, the noble woods and park destroyed.
>
> J. Evelyn, diary entry for 26 April, 1656

Eltham Palace has its origins in a manor house owned by Odo, who was the Bishop of Bayeux, Earl of Kent and younger brother of William the Conqueror; it was first mentioned in the Domesday Book of 1086.

Early in the fourteenth century, the manor passed into royal hands, and it soon became a favoured residence of the king and court. During its glory days in the fourteenth and fifteenth centuries, Eltham witnessed much of England's turbulent history and was treasured by its royal owners as a palace of pleasure, nestled among some of the finest hunting ground in the country. Successive monarchs subsequently enlarged the buildings so that Eltham's importance grew until, by the reign of Henry VIII, the Palace of Eltham, as it was by then known, was considered one of the king's five 'Great Houses', comparable in size to Windsor Castle, Greenwich or Hampton Court.

Although she could not have known it, Anne bore witness to the beginning of the end of Eltham's place as a royal abode. Indeed, quite poignantly, its fate mirrors her decline. Earlier in Henry's reign, the king had commissioned new works at the palace including the building of a new, permanent tiltyard to the east of the palace moat; the construction of new privy apartments for himself in the western range, while also making alterations to the queen's lodgings; and finally, he commanded the construction of a new brick-built chapel in the central courtyard. However, despite this large investment in the fabric of the building, its use as a palace was already in decline. For lying just 2 miles to the west was Greenwich Palace, constructed by Henry VII at the turn of the sixteenth century. When Henry VIII succeeded his father in 1509, Greenwich quickly assumed far greater importance than its medieval royal cousin. As a consequence, Eltham was increasingly confined to being used as a nursery for royal children, a place of entertainment for important visitors or as a simple hunting lodge.

Then, in the 1530s its decline accelerated; with the development of Hampton Court and Whitehall, the court began to move evermore westwards, leaving Eltham to slip further into decay. By the seventeenth century the palace was falling into ruin, and for 200 years after the Civil War it was used as a farm. In the 1930s Virginia and Stephen Courtauld saved the building from complete ruin. Thanks to their efforts, fans of Tudor history are today able to visit the salvaged Great Hall, originally built by Edward IV in the 1470s, which had almost been lost to the ravages of time.

Anne at Eltham Palace

We can only pinpoint Anne's presence at Eltham once she became firmly established as Henry's consort in waiting.

Thus, we can say with certainty that 'my Lady Anne' stayed at Eltham alongside the king and court in June–July 1532, when we read of Anne receiving sumptuous gifts of fabrics from the king's privy purse including 'blacke satin for a Cloke', 'blac vellute for edging of the same Cloke', 'blac vellute to lyne the colar', 'blac satin to lyne the sleves', 'blac satin for a nightgown', 'and black taffatta to lyne the same gown'. One suspects that Anne was being dressed as a queen, preparing her wardrobe for the historic trip to Calais later that year.

The couple were then back at Eltham on 24–5 November of the same year, when they lodged there on their way back from the aforementioned meeting with Francis I. They must have been jubilant; the trip was being heralded as a triumphant success. Francis had acknowledged Anne's position as Henry's consort and pledged to support them in their petition to the Pope, urging the Holy Father to have Henry's marriage to Katharine annulled. What is more, most historians agree that at some point during their stay in Calais, or on their way back to London, the couple slept with each other for the first time. One cannot help but imagine that this must have been one of the happiest times in Anne's life; everything that she had been striving for over the previous six years was finally coming to pass and the world must have seemed to lie at her feet.

Then, after Anne became queen, Eltham was one of the palaces to be used as a royal nursery for the infant Princess Elizabeth, born on 7 September 1533. Thus, the court was there at both Easter 1534 and three months later in July. On both occasions, Anne, who was ever a doting mother, must have been happy to be in the company of the little princess. However, it was during the first of these visits that Anne and the king's contumacious elder daughter Mary infamously quarrelled after the two ladies had found themselves hearing Mass at the same time in the chapel at Eltham. The story goes that Mary curtsied toward Anne before leaving to return to her rooms. Anne did not see the gesture, but it was subsequently reported to her. Interpreting it as a rare show of goodwill, Anne sent a conciliatory message returning the courtesy along with a friendly missive that was no doubt meant to be an olive branch of peace. However, when the message was relayed to Mary at dinner, she was reported to have replied rudely,

> The Queen could not have possibly sent it; nor is it fit that she should, nor can it be so sudden, Her Majesty being so far from this place … you should have said that the Lady Anne Boleyn had sent it for I can acknowledge no other Queen but my mother, nor esteem them her friends who are not hers … as for the reverence that I made, it was made only to her [the Lady Anne] maker and hers alone, and that she had been deceived to think otherwise.

Anne was undoubtedly hurt, frustrated and furious. Following on from a similar incident at Hatfield only a few months earlier, the queen once again threatened to bring down Mary's high spirit.

Finally, the king and court spent Christmas at Eltham in 1535. Once more, Anne must have been both relieved and overjoyed, as by that time she knew that she was once more pregnant. Only five months later, the court and City of London would be scandalised to hear the allegations that Anne had had sex with her brother at Eltham during that festive season; shocking enough, but even more repulsive given the fact that the queen was *enceinte*.

Visiting Eltham Palace

When making a pilgrimage to the remains of Eltham Palace today, the street names around the main gate whisper to visitors of its ancient past, such as Court Yard and Tilt Yard Approach. The former alludes to the fact that the area lying outside of the moat, directly in front of the main gates, was once occupied by a huge outer courtyard called The Green Court, which was flanked on north, east and west sides by service buildings. The second refers to the aforementioned tiltyard, lying to the east of Green Court. Note that just before you cross the bridge to your right is an extant building from the earlier palace. This building is called The Chancellor's Lodgings, where Chaucer, Wolsey and Thomas More are known to have stayed in their time.

The north stone bridge, built originally by Richard II in 1396 and enhanced in brick by Edward IV in the fifteenth century, is enchanting and conveys a sense of the grandeur of the palace that once existed; its four stone arches span one of the widest moats in England, reaching nearly 100 feet across on the south side.

Many people come to Eltham to visit one of the finest art deco houses in the country. These buildings sit roughly on top of what was once a vast range of courtier lodgings running around the north-east edges of the original Great Court. You might want to start here and, although the art deco house is interesting, as a Tudor enthusiast you will no doubt be making a beeline for the restored Great Hall. While not quite as grand, it is certainly reminiscent of the Great Hall at Hampton Court Palace. Many a king and queen have feasted here, and you might imagine Erasmus arriving to be greeted by the young and precocious Prince Henry in 1499.

Once back outside, make your way to the Courtauld's turning circle, outside the house, which roughly marks the centre of the original inner court. In front of you lies the Great Hall. While facing the hall, turn to your right; close to where you are standing would have been the east end of the chapel in which the famous incident between Anne and the Lady Mary took place in 1534. A tree now stands on the lawn over the site of its remains.

If you walk over to your right, you will come upon the exposed remains of the west range, which once contained the queen's privy apartments to the north (the end of the range closest to where you entered the turning circle from the main entrance) and the king's to the south. Therefore, standing in the north-west of the inner courtyard means we are looking down on the remains of Anne's apartments. We know something of her taste at Eltham, for in 1534 we hear of preparations being made 'against the coming of a Prince' with the redecoration of the suite in yellow ochre, interestingly mirroring the decoration we have already heard about in the French palaces that Anne knew in her youth.

As you stand there, you will notice that the palace stood proudly atop of some of the highest ground in the neighbourhood – excepting nearby Shooter's Hill. Views from the royal apartments must have been magnificent, looking down across a broad and beautiful landscape that stretched out to the west. In the distance 2 miles away would have once been the bold and finely wooded outline of Greenwich Park, while further in the distance, it was possible to trace out the spire of the Gothic cathedral of St Paul's and the lofty roof of Westminster Abbey.

Eltham Palace has an easy charm and it is delightful to imagine Anne spending treasured time with Elizabeth in the royal nursery or in the pleasant south-east facing gardens. Somehow, even though London stands silhouetted against the horizon just a mile or so away, it is easy to feel that you are tucked away in a peaceful idyll that somehow, despite the neglect and abandonment by its former royal patrons, still speaks easily of happier times at the centre of English sovereign power.

Visitor Information

Eltham Palace is managed by English Heritage. For more information on how to reach Eltham Palace and its opening hours, which are seasonal, visit the English Heritage website at http://www.english-heritage.org.uk/daysout/properties/eltham-palace-and-gardens/, or telephone + 44 (0) 20 8294 2548.

Postcode for Eltham Palace: SE9 5QE.

Hampton Court Palace, Middlesex

> This is the most splendid and magnificent royal palace that may be found in England or indeed in any other kingdom.
>
> Jacob Rathgeb, 1592

To walk the grounds and corridors of Hampton Court Palace is to walk in the footsteps of all of the Tudor kings and queens. Within the Tudor palace's russet-coloured walls, the present fades into the brickwork and the past emerges to greet us.

Hampton Court Palace is a place that Anne Boleyn would have known well, both before and after becoming queen. Although much of the Tudor palace has, over the years, been modified or demolished and replaced with William III and Mary II's baroque palace, the buildings that survive propel us back through the years to a time when Hampton Court was one of Henry VIII's most beloved palaces, at the centre of court life and politics.

A Brief History of Hampton Court

Originally built for Cardinal Wolsey as a house for entertaining royalty, foreign ambassadors and dignitaries, its magnificence reflected his status as Cardinal and Lord Chancellor of England. Wolsey built new kitchens, courtyards, lodgings, galleries and gardens, and began work on the chapel. He also built luxurious apartments for Henry VIII, Katharine of Aragon and Princess Mary on the site of the present-day Cumberland Suite, part of the later Georgian Rooms.

Henry VIII took full possession of Hampton Court in 1529 and embarked on an enormous building campaign attested to by the 6,500 pages of building accounts that survive in the Public Record Office.

Anne's Apartments at Hampton Court

Anne had her own lodgings at Hampton Court as early as June 1529, where it is said Henry kept her 'more like a queen than a simple maid'; unfortunately the precise location is unknown. What we do know is that Henry and the newly crowned Queen Anne visited in July 1533 when the queen's new lodgings, designed expressly for Anne, were only just being excavated. These lavish apartments were to be built on the east side of a new courtyard, overlooking the park. Beneath the lodgings would be a wardrobe for Anne's clothes, a privy kitchen and a nursery for the prince they hoped Anne was carrying.

The external appearance of these new rooms can be seen on a number of early views of the east front of the palace; they stood in the area now known as Fountain Court but were demolished in the late seventeenth century to make way for Sir Christopher Wren's baroque palace. Given that the apartments were not completed until early 1536, it was necessary for Anne to stay in the old queen's lodgings, those built by Wolsey for Katharine of Aragon, from where she would have been able to see how the work was progressing on the new wing.

The royal couple visited again in December 1533, in the early summer of 1534 and again in July 1534, the same month that George Boleyn was asked to 'repair to the French king with all speed' to defer a meeting between Henry VIII and Francis I because Anne was 'far gone with child' and not able to travel. However, as we shall now explore, all was not as it appeared.

The Tragedy of July–August 1534

It is likely that Hampton Court was the backdrop to one of the most emotional and dramatic moments in Anne's life. But to understand this connection, it's important to look at what we know of Anne Boleyn's second pregnancy.

As early as January 1534, Anne is reported as being 'again in the family way'. Her receiver-general recorded in late April that the queen had a 'goodly belly'. Then on 26 June, we hear in a further letter, this time sent from Sir Edward Ryngeley to Lord Lisle, that the couple were 'merry'. No doubt the king was hunting daily, while Anne was careful to take rest; at between seven and eight months pregnant, she would soon be expected to be taking to her chambers.

However, quite suddenly, on 2 July, the king seems to have left Anne behind and moved to The More, where he summoned Anne's uncle, the Duke of Norfolk, and Thomas Cromwell to meet him on 5 July. Shortly thereafter, it was announced that the trip to Calais to meet with the French king, which had been long arranged for the forthcoming autumn, was cancelled. Almost immediately, George Boleyn was ordered to go to France in all haste, in order to delay the planned meeting with Francis I, using the excuse that Anne's advanced pregnancy prevented her from travelling overseas.

The only historian that the authors have come across who has gone into these perplexing events in any detail is Rethe Warnicke in *The Rise and Fall of Anne Boleyn*, who postulates that sometime between 26 June and 2 July Anne was delivered of a stillborn child. The king, who was no doubt both devastated and furious at Anne's failure, summarily left her at Hampton Court. No longer able to face Francis, who was already the father of three healthy sons, a cover story was created to save face and the whole event swept under the carpet. In the end, we even hear through Chapuys that rumour had it at court that Henry had begun to doubt whether the queen had ever been pregnant. The king had been misled and was free of all stain – how convenient!

It's conceivable, then, considering that Henry and Anne were at Hampton Court in late June to early July, that she was at Hampton Court when she lost the baby, remaining there to rest and recuperate while Henry commenced his summer progress.

In mid-March 1535, the couple returned. Unbeknown to Anne, this visit would be her last, for the following year, in May 1536, Anne was charged with twenty-one acts of adultery. One of these was alleged to have taken place at Hampton Court Palace on 8 December 1533, with a gentleman of the King's Privy Chamber, William Brereton. This is not the place to discuss Anne's fall except to say that historians over the years have successfully demonstrated that the case presented by the Crown in May 1536 against Anne and the five men accused with her is, at best, flimsy and under close analysis collapses.

After this final visit in March 1535, and probably as a result of the massive building works taking place, Henry absented himself and appears not to have visited at all between April 1535 and May 1537. He would return on 8 May 1537 with his third wife, Jane Seymour.

The queen's new lodgings were not in full use until October 1537 and so Anne Boleyn, like her successor Jane, did not live to enjoy her lavish new apartments.

Visiting Hampton Court Palace Today

The main entrance is via the west front, begun by Cardinal Wolsey and completed for Henry VIII. Wolsey's gatehouse was originally five storeys high, rather than the three that we see today, but was found to be unstable and so reduced in the eighteenth century.

On the turrets either side of the gatehouse are terracotta roundels with the heads of the Roman emperors Tiberius and Nero. These were found in a cottage in Windsor Park by the Victorian surveyor Edward Jesse, and were probably originally from the Holbein Gate at Whitehall (see Whitehall Palace entry), where in an upper chamber over the gate Anne Boleyn married Henry VIII in January 1533 (see Hanworth entry). Two similar roundels survive from the now-lost Hanworth Manor, bestowed upon Anne in 1532.

The bridge leading to the central gateway is lined with ten heraldic beasts supporting the royal arms, including the Tudor dragon and the queen's lion. These are modern replacements of the originals that once stood here. Look up above the central gateway and on a carved panel are the arms of Henry VIII.

Stepping into base court feels very much like time travel. It is much as it was when Wolsey built it as a place to house his guests and large household; Anne would certainly recognise it today. Each of the thirty double guest lodgings had an outer room and an inner room with garderobe (toilet) and fireplace. The epitome of sixteenth-century luxury!

The 4-metre high, recreated Tudor wine fountain that you see in this courtyard is built on the very spot where Henry VIII's octagonal fountain once stood and testifies to Hampton Court's role as a pleasure palace. The design is based on the fountain visible in the *Field of Cloth of Gold* painting that hangs in the 'Young Henry VIII' exhibition and is actually engineered to serve real wine on special occasions.

Those of us in search of the last vestiges of the reign of Queen Anne Boleyn should proceed to Anne Boleyn's Gatehouse.

Anne Boleyn's Gatehouse

This name dates from the nineteenth century when the vault beneath the gateway was reconstructed. The ceiling is decorated with Henry and Anne's entwined initials and Anne's falcon badge; sadly these are not original, rather Victorian replicas. The good news is that there is a stone falcon badge from the original vault on display in the Great Hall, where you should proceed to next.

The entry to Henry VIII's state apartments is up the staircase under Anne Boleyn's Gateway, which takes you into the magnificent Great Hall. The doorway leading into the buttery, just before the hall, is decorated with Tudor roses for Henry VIII and Spanish pomegranates – Katharine of Aragon's personal badge.

The Great Hall

The Great Hall is majestic and breathtaking. The splendid hammer-beam roof is decorated with royal arms and badges and a series of carved and painted heads. In Anne's day, the floor would have been paved with tiles and the roof painted blue, red and gold.

The hall today is hung with priceless Flemish tapestries of the *Story of Abraham*, commissioned by Henry VIII and woven in the 1540s with real silver and gold thread. A series of six hangs in the Great Hall, one of which – *The Oath and Departure of Eliezer* – was hung in Westminster

Abbey for the Coronation of Elizabeth I. The tapestries have faded over time, but you can still get a sense of how vibrant and splendid they would have been when first woven.

Anne took a great interest in the building works at Hampton Court and on the ceiling you can still see Henry and Anne's entwined initials and Anne's falcon badge. The wooden screen behind you as you enter the hall is carved with Anne and Henry's interlocking initials – all serving as a poignant reminder of her brief reign. After Anne's arrest and execution, Henry ordered all of her badges removed and replaced them with those of Jane Seymour. Luckily for us, in the frenzy to eradicate all memory of Henry's fallen queen, those less accessible were overlooked.

The great watching chamber was originally the first of Henry VIII's state apartments and its principal function in Henry's reign was as a dining room for household officials. The door at the far end of the room once led to the king's presence chamber and state apartments, sadly now lost. This door would have been heavily guarded and only those close to the king, including Anne, would have been permitted entry.

The stained-glass window in this chamber, although beautiful, is not original, and the Tudor fireplace and great heraldic frieze that once decorated the walls above the tapestries are long gone. However, the splendid ceiling, decorated with the arms of Henry VIII and Jane Seymour, and the tapestries, are original.

The Horn Room, the Council Chamber and the Haunted Gallery

The Horn Room was originally used as a waiting area for servants bringing food from the Tudor kitchens directly below up to the Great Hall and great watching chamber. The balustrade is Victorian; however, the original Tudor oak steps survive.

Further down the gallery is King Henry VIII's council chamber, opened to the public for the first time in April 2009. It is worth pausing here for a moment to consider that in this very room Henry VIII discussed and debated important matters of state, making many historic decisions within its four walls. Like so many of the chambers at Hampton Court, the energetic imprint of those who have passed through here – Norfolk, Suffolk, Cromwell, Thomas Boleyn and Henry himself – is tangible; you can almost hear their voices speaking to you across time. When we were there, a brief glimpse out of the window into the courtyard below catapulted us back in time. For there, walking through the gardens, were two Tudor noble ladies (part of the Past Pleasures re-enactment group). It was quite disorientating but a wonderful snapshot of a lost era.

From here proceed to the upper chapel cloister, better known as the Haunted Gallery (see author's note below), built by Cardinal Wolsey to connect the chapel to the rest of the palace. It is home to some wonderful tapestries and paintings including *The Family of Henry VIII* by an unknown artist dating from around 1545. Look closely at the 'A' necklace adorning the neck of the Princess Elizabeth, as it's said to have belonged to her mother. From the Haunted Gallery you can access the royal pew; here Anne would have sat and looked down into the body of the chapel.

In Tudor times, the king and queen had separate rooms in the royal pew, with windows looking down into the choir of the chapel. Henry VIII installed the magnificent vaulted ceiling that you see today in 1535–6, replacing an earlier ceiling added by Cardinal Wolsey who built the body of the chapel.

Originally, there would have been a great double window at the east end filled with stained glass. In October 1536 the window was reglazed to remove the figure of St Anne, the mother of Mary, originally installed as a way of linking Queen Anne with the Virgin. In the eighteenth century, the glass was removed and the window hidden.

It is in this chapel that Prince Edward, Henry VIII's long-awaited son, was christened in October 1537. In the king's closet, within the Chapel Royal, Henry married his sixth and final wife, Katherine Parr, in the presence of his two daughters, the princesses Elizabeth and Mary. If only walls could talk!

As you exit the chapel into the north cloister, take note of Henry VIII and Jane Seymour's coat of arms flanking the chapel door. Although almost certainly moved from another part of the palace, these two heraldic plaques once held Cardinal Wolsey's arms and hat, which were repainted by Henry VIII after 1530.

Henry's Lost Privy Apartments – The Cumberland Suite

The Georgian Rooms may seem like they have nothing to offer the Tudor enthusiast but, as mentioned earlier, it is precisely on the site of the present-day Cumberland Suite that Wolsey built part of the state apartments that Anne and Henry stayed in while awaiting the completion of their new lodgings. Remember the door at the far end of the great watching chamber? This once opened into Henry's presence chamber. This led on to his private apartments, with Anne's apartments positioned directly above the king's, on the second floor.

The three-storey range was originally designed to house Princess Mary on the lower level, Henry on the first floor and Katharine directly above him. The queen's apartments contained three large rooms, the entrance to which still survives, although sadly it is not accessible to the public. A surviving doorway on this level depicts Wolsey's arms on one spandrel and the royal arms on the other. Within, exist a few more remnants of its Tudor past: a large chimneypiece containing Wolsey's badges and mottoes and a door leading to a closet.

In 1537, Jane Seymour occupied the same 'old lodgings' as her two predecessors and gave birth to Prince Edward in one of the rooms. She would never recover from the birth of her precious son, and twelve days later died. Perhaps this is the same room in which Anne was delivered of a stillborn baby in late June/early July 1534.

This range was entirely rebuilt in the eighteenth century; only Wolsey's great spine wall with its fireplaces and closets remains. Make your way into the room, which contains a large bed set back into an alcove. Over in the far corner is a bricked-up doorway that once connected the king's privy chambers directly with Wolsey's gallery and apartments. If you are lucky, and ask nicely as we did, one of the guides may show you the surviving Tudor spiral staircase that once led to Henry VIII's wardrobe. Every morning, Henry's clothes would be brought up these stairs from the wardrobe below and handed to the gentlemen of the privy chamber, who were responsible for dressing the king.

The Wolsey Closet and Rooms

The Wolsey Closet beyond the Cumberland Suite gives visitors a good idea of what a small closet might have looked like during Anne's reign. Although heavily restored in the nineteenth century, conservation revealed that part of the ceiling, dating from the late 1530s, has remained *in situ*. The ceiling is decorated with gilded Renaissance motifs and badges incorporating the Tudor rose.

Further evidence of Hampton Court's Tudor past can be found in the Wolsey Rooms, believed to have been Wolsey's private lodgings in the 1520s. It is also thought that Princess Mary (later Queen Mary) and Katherine Parr may have also stayed or entertained here.

Like so much of Hampton Court Palace, the rooms have been modified and altered over time, but some original Tudor features have survived: sixteenth-century linenfold panelling lines the walls of the two smaller rooms, the plain Tudor fireplaces date from Wolsey's time, the ribbed ceilings in the two main rooms incorporate early Renaissance motifs and the ceiling of the end room incorporates Wolsey's badges.

The Renaissance Picture Gallery and Wolsey Rooms house many sixteenth- and seventeenth-century paintings, including a portrait of Anne Boleyn said to be 'a copy of a contemporary portrait, probably painted in the late 1500s'.

The Palace Kitchens and the Tiltyard

No visit to Hampton Court Palace is complete without a tour of the Tudor kitchens. Built partly by Lord Daubeney, who owned Hampton Court before Wolsey, and extended by Henry VIII in 1529, they were designed to feed the royal household, which in the wintertime could number up to 800 people, dining in the Great Hall and the great watching chamber twice a day.

Today, the smell of woodsmoke from the fire burning in the great kitchens awakens memories of a distant past. The throngs of tourists that pack the kitchens during peak times evoke a sense of the hustle and bustle of the 200-strong staff that manned this vast operation during Henry's reign.

Royal dishes were prepared in a separate or privy kitchen by the king and queen's own cook and personnel. From 1529 until 1537, Henry's private kitchen was situated beneath his lodgings and survives, albeit in a much altered state, on the ground floor below the Wolsey Closet.

And while on the topic of food … the Privy Kitchen (a café) is housed in what was once Elizabeth I's private kitchen. It's easy to miss this gem, home to some interesting artefacts, including a large plate marked with the crowned ostrich feathers of Arthur, Prince of Wales.

The Tiltyard Café is the only surviving tower from five built by Henry VIII for use as viewing platforms, where dignitaries and courtiers watched tournaments in the tiltyard.

The Gardens

There are also over 60 acres of stunning gardens waiting to be explored at Hampton Court Palace. Cardinal Wolsey was probably the first to build ornamental gardens on-site, but it was Henry who established the magnificent gardens that the palace would subsequently become renowned for, gardens that surpassed in beauty and size those of all other royal residences.

The sunken pond gardens, once Wolsey's fishponds, look and smell exquisite in early summer, when they are bursting with blossom and overrun with flowers. In March 1528, Anne Boleyn dined with Thomas Heneage at Windsor and commented on these very fishponds, saying how pleasing it would be during Lent to have some freshwater shrimps or carp from Wolsey's famous ponds.

To get a sense of what the gardens were like in Anne's day, be sure to visit the recreated gardens in Chapel Court, inspired by those visible in the background of *The Family of Henry VIII* that hangs in the Haunted Gallery. The gardens are planted with flowers and herbs that would have been available in the sixteenth century, enclosed by green-and-white-striped low fencing and guarded by heraldic beasts on poles.

Apart from the impressive gardens, when completed Hampton Court Palace boasted tennis courts, bowling alleys, a hunting park and even a multiple garderobe. All of Henry's children spent time indulging in Hampton Court's splendour, both as heirs to the throne and in their own right as Tudor kings and queens.

Elizabeth I, like her mother, visited Hampton Court Palace not long after her Coronation. It is here that her first official summer progress concluded in 1559. One wonders whether Elizabeth took note of her parents' entwined initials in the Great Hall or thought about her mother's first triumphant visit to the palace as queen, when she – and not the expected male heir – was safely cradled in her womb.

For those of us wanting to follow in Anne's footsteps, or more generally for the Tudor enthusiast, Hampton Court has no equal. So much of Henry VIII's private drama – from heartbreak to triumph – played out within its walls. Listen closely, as they echo with the footsteps of its past inhabitants and play back the memories of those distant, cataclysmic, events.

Authors' Favourites

Would it be cheeky of us to say the entire palace? Hampton Court Palace is by far one of our favourite places in the world. Not only does more survive of Hampton Court than of any other Tudor palace, it is also home to some incredibly authentic, costumed, live interpretations that help bring the palace, and its stories, vividly to life.

To see what the palace looked like in Anne's day and beyond, we recommend watching a very useful video, which at the time of writing was being shown on the ground floor of the Wolsey Rooms as part of the 'Young Henry VIII' permanent exhibition. The video reconstructs and compares Wolsey's palace of 1528 with Henry VIII's palace of 1545 and shows how the palace evolved under royal ownership.

Don't forget to try and find a quiet moment in the Haunted Gallery, said to be rife with ghostly goings on. The palace is home to a myriad of ghost stories, but perhaps the most famous is that of Catherine Howard's screaming spectre.

On 2 November 1541, Archbishop Cranmer informed the king of Catherine's extramarital dalliances while he was at Mass in his Privy Closet. Legend tells that Catherine, knowing that her husband was at Mass in the chapel, escaped her captors and ran screaming through the gallery in a final attempt to plead for her life. She was quickly restrained and dragged back to her apartments only to face the executioner's block on 13 February 1542 at the Tower of London.

Tradition has it that her ghost replays, again and again, this final desperate dash for mercy in the gallery at Hampton Court. We love a good ghost story but it seems that there is no documentary evidence to confirm that the event ever took place. In fact, after hearing the devastating news, Henry left Hampton Court and his young wife was confined to her apartments, where she remained until she was moved to Syon House on

14 November. However, the truth doesn't detract from the eerie atmosphere of the gallery, as no doubt you'll find out…

From its beginnings as a palace built to impress to its present-day role as a magnificent time capsule, Hampton Court remains, after almost 500 years, a wonder without peer.

Visitor Information

Hampton Court Palace is managed by Historic Royal Palaces. For more information on how to reach Hampton Court and its opening hours, visit the Historic Royal Palaces website at http://www.hrp.org.uk/hamptoncourtpalace, or telephone + 44 (0) 2031 666000.

Postcode for Hampton Court Palace: KT8 9AU.

Guildford, Surrey

> The King is now at Oking, and comes hither on Tuesday, and will tarry here and at Eltham
> till Friday, when he will meet with the Queen at Guildford.
>
> Letter written by John Husee the Younger to Lady Lisle on 18 July 1534

Guildford is the county town of Surrey and is situated 27 miles south-west of London, midway between the capital and Portsmouth. It is another English town that is deeply steeped in royal history, frequented regularly by medieval and Tudor monarchs, no doubt on account of the very fine hunting to be had in Guildford's Royal Hunting Park.

Shortly after the conquest of England in 1066, it is thought that King William was responsible for building the town's castle, the remains of which can still be visited today in a beautifully landscaped garden. If you visit during the summer, as the authors did, you will be delighted by a profusion of blossom and vibrant colours packed into the many flower beds surrounding the ruined central keep; a great place to enjoy a packed lunch while you are on your tour, it is also a stone's throw from the museum mentioned below.

Then in 1274, the dowager queen, Eleanor of Provence, established Guildford's Dominican friary in the centre of the town in memory of her grandson, Prince Henry, who had died at the castle on 20 October 1274.

Although the castle was in decay by the early sixteenth century, and was no longer being used as royal accommodation, this does not diminish the significance of Guildford in Anne's story. It seems likely that Anne was alongside the king when he arrived at Guildford on 23 July 1530, as by this time the two were virtually inseparable; and then again on 29 July the following year. However, as we shall shortly hear, the town also bore witness to a dramatic time in Anne's life; a time that must have been particularly devastating for the queen.

Events at Guildford, July 1534

It was the summer of 1534; Henry and Anne were jubilant. The queen was heavily pregnant for the second time in a year and the royal couple were expectantly awaiting the arrival of Henry's longed-for son. They were whiling away the height of summer together at Hampton Court Palace. Then a strange sequence of events occurs. The events surrounding the stillbirth of Anne's second child are so shrouded in mystery and secrecy that their significance seems to have almost been lost to time. We have described these events in the previous entry for Hampton Court Palace. However, here, at Guildford, we can pick up Anne's story.

Having conferred with his most trusted ministers at The More about the fate of the forthcoming Calais meeting, it seems that the wounded king proceeded on a mini progress, lodging at Chenies Manor, Woking and Eltham Palace before meeting with the queen (who seems to have been left behind at Hampton Court Palace) at Guildford; this reunion occurred sometime toward the end of July or the beginning of August. By that time, Henry and Anne had been apart for about one month, one of the longest periods of separation since 1528, when Anne had left the court in anticipation of Campeggio's arrival and the Blackfriars hearing.

It is not too hard to imagine how strained such a meeting must have been, not least since Anne would have still been grieving for the loss of her child. However, the icy chill of the king's obvious displeasure must have made the situation almost unbearable; Anne had failed her dead child, her family, her husband, her king and the country. Such were the heavy expectations laid upon the shoulders of a sixteenth-century queen.

So when we visit Guildford, we do so knowing that on her last visit to the town Anne Boleyn must have been deep in grief, made all the worse by Henry's clear condemnation of her failure to deliver on her side of the bargain – a healthy son and heir.

Where Did the Royal Couple Lodge?

As the authors have already mentioned, by Anne's time, the castle was falling into ruin and no longer in use as a royal abode. Two other possibilities exist according to local historians: the Dominican friary, mentioned above, and the Manor House, located within the royal hunting park. It is also worth noting that the towns of Guildford and Woking are close to one another. As the lodgings at Guildford were quite small, it would be quite feasible for some of the king's courtiers to be based at Woking, while the king resided at Guildford.

Regarding the lodgings at Guildford, we certainly know that Henry was at the friary during the visit of 1534, for on 2 August the king signed a treaty with the Scots, dated at the 'Black Friars, Guildford'. It was signed in the presence of the Abbot of Kinlos, Ambassador of Scotland; Sir Thomas Audeley, Chancellor; Stephen, Bishop of Winchester; Thomas, Duke of Norfolk; Henry, Earl of Northumberland; Henry, Earl of Cumberland; Thomas Cromwell, the King's Secretary; Sir William Fitzwilliam, Keeper of Guildford Park; Edward Fox, the King's Almoner; and Richard Sampson, Dean of the Chapel Royal.

The king seems to have held the friars in high esteem, although that did not stop the friary being dissolved in 1538, and had built himself a 'house of honour' within its precincts. It is possible that it was here that the king and queen lodged. Sadly, there is nothing left to see of the building. The friary was dismantled over the centuries and today the modern-day Friary Shopping Centre/Mall stands directly on the site of the medieval buildings.

The second possibility is that Henry and Anne lodged themselves at the moated Royal Manor House, which was situated in the south-west corner of the royal hunting park, adjacent to the town.

Guildford Park had been part of the medieval royal forest of Windsor since it was created by Henry II around 1154. According to local historian Helen Chapman Davies, the park 'contained 1,620 acres of reasonably good ground enclosed by a pale'. Since these earliest times, a manor house had been maintained by the king, although a keeper of the park often lived at the manor in the king's absence. In Anne's time, this was a man who would play a significant part in orchestrating her downfall: Sir William Fitzwilliam.

The manor house is believed to have consisted of a number of gabled buildings around a courtyard, with one side having a gatehouse tower. It incorporated the following rooms: a hall, four chambers, a chapel, the king and queen's dining chambers, privy chambers and bedchambers and a separate kitchen. An artist's impression of how the manor might have looked during the sixteenth century is included in the images section.

Since the creation of the Surrey Sports Park by the University of Surrey, access to the site is now fairly easy. It is a scheduled ancient monument, so although you should not walk on the exact site, you can view part of the moat that once surrounded the position of the former hunting lodge via a public footpath that runs close by.

Visitor Information

The sites mentioned are on public ground and open to the public, without charge, seven days a week at reasonable hours. If you are interested in exploring this site further, Dragon History Tours offers a bespoke guided local history walk to the site of the manor house. Telephone number: + 44 (0) 1483 537551.

Guildford Museum and the Surrey Archaeological Society are other sources of information on the local area. These are located in the same building, on the corner of Quarry Street and Castle Hill, Guildford, GU1 3SX. Telephone + 44 (0) 1483 444 751 for opening hours.

Postcode for Surrey Sports Park: GU2 7AD; for the Friary Shopping Centre: GU1 4YT and for Guildford Castle: GU1 3SY.

Part 4
The 1535 Progress

Introduction

> Anne Boleyn was not a catalyst in the English Reformation; she was a key element in the equation.
>
> Professor Eric Ives

A little later than scheduled, on 8 or 9 July 1535, Henry VIII set out from Windsor Castle in Berkshire on what would become one of the longest and most politically significant progresses of the king's reign. Anne, still the king's 'most dere and entierly beloved lawfull wiff', was at his side. Cromwell, the king's wily secretary, joined them two weeks later on 23 July. *Letters and Papers* setting out the king's 'geists', or itinerary, show that the king and queen had planned to travel through the West Country to Bristol, before circling back to arrive at Windsor on 1 October. In the end the royal couple did not make it to Bristol, due to an outbreak of plague in the city. Furthermore, they were to delay their return by almost one month, enjoying the hunting and hawking in Hampshire so much that they did not arrive back at Windsor Castle until Monday 25 October, altering the final leg of their intended route in order to avoid the plague around Farnham and Guildford in Surrey.

However, this progress was intended to be much more than merely 'pastime with goode companie'. It was to have huge political significance. Were Henry and Anne making a point when they departed from Windsor just days after the execution of Sir Thomas More? Bishop Fisher was already dead and the new Pope, Paul III, left outraged at Henry's conduct, the king having executed Fisher only days after he had been created a cardinal by the Holy See. Certainly, their itinerary sought to honour those landed gentry and courtiers who were known reformists and had showed strong support for the king's second marriage.

To underline the way in which Henry's will was clearly bent, a ceremonial centrepiece of the trip had been masterminded. This was no doubt heavily influenced by a determined collaboration between Anne and the king's principal minister, Thomas Cromwell; it was to be the consecration of three hand-picked reformist bishops – Foxe, Hilsey and Latimer – at Winchester Cathedral on 19 September 1535. All were staunch supporters of Anne.

A little while afterwards, Cromwell left Anne and Henry to their pursuit of pleasure; he returned to London, the royal couple dallying in Hampshire among some of the best hunting ground in the country. And take pleasure they seemed to do; three separate letters note that 'the King and Queen are merry'. And indeed, if we calculate backwards from Anne's fateful miscarriage on 29 January 1536, we find ourselves somewhere between The Vyne and Easthampstead in the latter part of the 1535 progress. Exactly where is impossible to pinpoint, and is made even more muddied by two different accounts. Wriothesley records that Anne felt that she was about fifteen weeks pregnant at the time of her miscarriage; the Imperial Ambassador, Eustace Chapuys, stated that the aborted foetus looked to be about three and a half months gestation, in other words about fourteen weeks. This would bring us to a date of conception between 16 and 23 October, placing Anne at either at The Vyne, Basing House, Bramshill or Easthampstead. Clearly, during their time away from London, Henry and Anne had regained some level of intimacy, despite Anne's second pregnancy ending in a devastating stillbirth the preceding summer.

In this section, we will follow Henry and Anne's progress, recapturing lost locations and setting the scene by touching on key events as they unfolded during this historic fourteen-week royal tour.

Note: where possible, exact dates of the progress from one location to another will be given. However, sometimes there are gaps in contemporary records or last-minute changes of plan, which appear to put one piece of information in direct conflict with another. This is particularly true during the second half of the progress. So, in some cases it is not possible to be absolutely certain of precise dates. In these instances, the closest approximation will be given.

Reading Abbey, Berkshire

The Abbey is situated on a gravelly eminence, hanging over the river Kennet on the south, and on the north commanding a view of the Thames and Caversham in Oxfordshire. The outer wall now encloses a green, called the Forbury.

Observations made by Sir Henry Englefield in 1779

On 8 July 1535, Henry VIII and Anne Boleyn left Windsor Castle bound for Reading Abbey. The twelfth-century monastery was founded by William the Conqueror's youngest son, Henry I, and was the first stop on a summer progress to the West Country and Hampshire and, at only a day's ride away from Windsor, it was a very convenient staging post.

Henry VIII often stayed at monastic houses during his progresses, as they were expected to provide hospitality; feeding the hungry and sheltering the wayfarer were two of the seven Acts of Mercy and fundamental Christian obligations.

During Henry's reign, Reading Abbey was one of the six wealthiest monasteries in England and one of Henry's favourites, featuring regularly on his itinerary. This was not the first time that Anne had visited either; she had accompanied the king and court in July 1529 and August 1532 when they lodged at the abbey on their way to Woodstock and Windsor, respectively.

Hugh Faringdon was the Abbot of Reading at the time of Anne's visits. His responsibilities varied greatly and, apart from looking after the spiritual and material needs of the monks, included maintaining the monastery buildings, running the town, collecting taxes and administering justice. Another responsibility of the abbot was to offer hospitality to the monarch and his retinue.

Important guests were lodged in the abbot's house; at Reading this stood beside the inner gateway that is still extant today, within the monastic 'inner-sanctum' where the general public was not admitted. There, in 1535, Anne would have been housed in one of the sumptuous guest rooms reserved for the king and queen. Members of the court that could not be accommodated at the abbey would have stayed in the town.

The once-splendid abbey church today lies in ruins – a distant echo of its magnificent former self. At only 50 feet shorter than the present-day St Paul's Cathedral in London, the abbey church was a vast structure, taking up most of the south-east corner of today's Forbury Gardens. We can imagine that during Anne's visits her gaze would have been drawn to the eight massive round pillars that supported the roof on either side of the nave, and the richly decorated altars that lined the walls. The summer light would have trickled through the stained-glass windows and caressed the flagstone floors, as flickering candles made shadows dance on the painted walls, and the smell of incense filled the air.

The monks of Reading Abbey spent most of their time in the church tending to their religious devotions; this included attending eight services every day, each up to two hours long, composed mainly of singing. When not in the church, daily life centred on the cloisters and consisted of private prayer, meditation, reading and writing.

In 1539, this tranquil existence was brought to a brutal end; the last abbot, Hugh Faringdon, despite having had a good relationship with Henry, was executed for treason in front of the abbey gate and the majority of the buildings dismantled.

Among the few buildings untouched was the abbot's house, which was converted into a royal residence used by Henry as early as 1540, suggesting that the alterations required were minimal.

Edward VI, Mary and Elizabeth I all stayed at Reading, and during the reign of Elizabeth the principal buildings were noted as being the great gate, the hall (probably the former refectory), the kitchen, the great chamber, presence chamber, privy chamber, bedchamber, raying chamber and gallery.

Unfortunately, the exact position of the abbot's house where Anne stayed is now uncertain; it survived the Dissolution only to be destroyed in 1642 at the end of the Civil War. A survey of the property made in 1650 suggests that the house lay on the west side of the former cloisters inside the existing abbey gateway, with the adjoining refectory serving after the Dissolution as a Great Hall.

Today the romantic ruins are in the Forbury Gardens and are looked after by Reading Borough Council. This area was formerly known as the Forbury and was located within the main abbey walls. In Anne's day it was a large open space, which the public was permitted to access. It was often the site of markets, fairs or religious celebrations where the monks and the townspeople could interact freely, and remains today a public park.

The abbey gateway and the main building of the *hospitium*, a guesthouse used mainly by pilgrims, survive, albeit in a heavily restored state.

Before touring the site of the ruins, visitors today should commence their stay with a trip to the Museum of Reading accommodated within Reading Town Hall, where objects from excavations in the area are displayed in the People and Place Gallery and in the Window Gallery. The abbey ruins were stripped of their stone facing and thus lack any of their former decorative embellishments; however, a number of very beautifully carved fragments from the abbey are housed at the museum and give a sense of the richness of the buildings that Anne would have seen.

At the foot of the main staircase in the People and Place Gallery, in the Bayeux Gallery and on the first floor of the Town Hall, you will also find displayed a set of twentieth-century paintings commissioned by Dr Jamieson Boyd Hurry, a local doctor with an interest in Reading, that depict important events in the abbey's history.

Although Henry and Anne's visit is not among them, there is a painting of interest to the history enthusiast, one that records another important royal visit by a couple whose marriage caused a storm of controversy, not unlike the one that raged around Henry and Anne's nascent relationship.

On St Michael's Day, 29 September 1464, King Edward IV introduced his new bride, Elizabeth Woodville, whom tradition states he'd married secretly on 1 May 1464, to a somewhat surprised royal council, and all present publicly acknowledged her as Queen of England.

Another painting in the collection shows the execution of Hugh Faringdon, the last Abbot of Reading by the west front of the abbey church. His 'trial' is believed to have taken place in a room above the inner gateway.

While in town, a visit to St Laurence's church is also suggested; situated alongside the site of the abbey, it was originally constructed in the early twelfth century to serve the people of the town and today houses some interesting historic items, including a font said to have been made in 1522 by a master mason from Hampton Court Palace. It is an interesting blend of the ancient and very modern, a rare survivor from the original abbey complex and certainly a building Anne would have seen.

Elizabeth I paid several visits to the church and the novelist Jane Austen worshipped there daily when she attended the Abbey School for girls, housed in the abbey gateway.

There is much to see and explore in this historic town, where ancient monastic ruins still sing to us of its glory days.

Visitor Information

Today, the remains of the once-mighty Reading Abbey are located in the heart of a sprawling metropolis. Reading is a busy city and if you are arriving by car, a satellite navigation system will be helpful in steering you to the right place. The closest parking is on Valpy Street, just 50 metres or so away from the entrance to Forbury Gardens. However, parking there is very limited, so you may prefer to park at nearby Reading railway station, where there is a multistorey car park that lies about five minutes' walk away from the site.

Sadly the authors visited on a rainy day in May, which took away somewhat from the pleasant surroundings of the very well-tended gardens that were once part of the abbey yard, lying to the north-west of the main abbey complex. If you enter the gardens from Valpy Street, walk diagonally through the gardens until you see the inner gateway. This originally led through into the monks' inner sanctum, including the cloisters, refectory, dormitory and abbot's lodgings. Standing in front of the gateway on Abbot's Walk, these buildings would have been on its far side to the south-east, now entirely covered by later Georgian properties and other, modern office blocks. At the time of our visit in 2013, the gateway was looking rather neglected and partially obscured by scaffolding. Thankfully, conservation of these historic ruins is most certainly on the agenda, with an application submitted by the local council to the Heritage Lottery Fund for £4.3 million. The five-year scheme principally aims to conserve the gateway and abbey ruins, both of which are currently on the English Heritage 'at risk' register, and redevelop the whole abbey quarter for a better visitor experience.

If facing the abbey gateway, turn to your left and continue walking along Abbot's Walk, taking a walkway that lies on your right just before you reach the end of the street. You will find yourself in front of some gardens with a view of the abbey ruins behind them. You are roughly standing in the area that was once occupied by the cloisters of the abbey; perhaps this is reflected in the rather haunting sculpture of a figure in monk's clothing, to remind us of those who went this way before us.

Access to the ruins is currently only possible during a limited number of Heritage Open Days held throughout the year. Nevertheless, if you arrive as we did outside of these times, you can still get a reasonable view of what remains behind of the south transept of the abbey church and the chapter house.

On the west side of Forbury gardens, back along Abbot's Walk, lies the medieval church of St Laurence. In 2001 it was given a new mandate: 'To see young people come to faith and to build new forms of church with them.'

If the weather is in your favour, why not sit a while in the gardens and allow the hustle and bustle of twenty-first-century suburbia to melt away, and imagine in its place the sounds of the medieval abbey transporting you back in time to the prosperous religious house that Anne would have known.

At the time of publication the abbey ruins were closed for conservation work; however, it's possible to join one of several hard-hat tours held throughout the year. Keep an eye on the 'What's On?' page of Reading Museum's website for details: http://www.readingmuseum.org.uk.

For information on how to reach St Laurence's church, visit the church's website at http://www.saintlaurencereading.com, or telephone + 44 (0) 1189 571293.

Postcode for Valpy Street Car Park: RG1 1AF; for Reading train station: RG1 1LZ and for Forbury Gardens: RG1 3EH.

Ewelme Manor, Oxfordshire

> The maner place of Ewelme is in the valley of the village: the base court of it is fair, and is buildid of brike and tymbre.
>
> John Leland

In the fifteenth century the Duke and Duchess of Suffolk, William and Alice de la Pole, enlarged and improved the manor house at Ewelme, which after the execution of their grandson Edmund de la Pole, Earl of Suffolk, in 1513 was forfeited to the Crown. The majority of the earl's confiscated estates and his titles were re-granted in 1514 to Charles

Brandon, newly created Duke of Suffolk and one of the king's favourite companions. Twelve years later, in 1525, Henry VIII granted the manor of Ewelme to Charles and his wife Mary, the king's sister.

Henry and Anne visited on 13 August 1531, en route to Woodstock, and again on 27 August 1532 as they made their way back to Windsor at the conclusion of the summer progress. However, by 1535 Suffolk's lack of enthusiasm for Henry's marriage to Anne Boleyn was repaid with his temporary fall from favour; thereby, Henry asked for the property back in exchange for lands elsewhere and during the course of the 1535 progress, on 12 and 13 July, he and Anne inspected the manor.

The duke claimed to have spent £1,000 on Ewelme but the property failed to impress the royal couple. It was noted that when 'the King himself viewed Ewelme when lately there', he found the manor 'in great decay' and in need of large sums of money in order to repair it. Even so, Ewelme once more became a royal residence and was used by the king as a lesser house, a place where he retreated for greater privacy with a select group of friends while on hunting trips.

Minor repairs carried out at the time of Henry and Anne's visit provide some clue as to the layout of the buildings. There were the customary king's and queen's apartments, with the queen's side consisting of the watching chamber, presence chamber, bedchamber and chapel. The king's apartments contained a watching chamber, presence chamber, dining chamber, privy chamber and bedchamber.

Leland's account of Ewelme, recorded in 1542, testifies to its grandeur:

> The maner place of Ewelme is in the valley of the village: the base court of it is fair, and is buildid of brike and tymbre. The inner part of the house is sette with in a fair mote, and is buildid richely of brike and stone. The haul of it is fair and hath great barres of iren overthuart it instede of crosse beames. The parler by is exceeding fair and lightstum: and so be al the lodginges there. The commune saying is that that Duk John [John de la Pole] made about the beginning of King Henry the vij [VII] tymes most of the goodly buildings withyn the mote.

In the early years of the reign of Elizabeth I, the residence was said to have been in such a sorry state that demolition was thought to be the only solution. However, some minor repairs were carried out that extended the life of the house, and the queen visited Ewelme on a few occasions. But the minor alterations were not sufficient to save the house, and by the reign of James I, the 'capital mansion' was completely ruined.

The Remains of Ewelme Manor

In 1612, a survey of the remains recorded the existence of a gatehouse outside the moat. It also mentioned several brick buildings, one of which held the monthly Court of the Honor. This range survived into the eighteenth century and was engraved by Samuel and Nathaniel Buck in 1727. It probably originally stood within the base court and is likely to have adjoined the brick gatehouse. It consisted of six chambers on the ground floor and five on the first, a lower hall and an upper hall, all heated by fireplaces. It was partially demolished sometime after the engraving was made; however, the walls of the hall and its roof still survive, now incorporated into a house that is largely Georgian in appearance.

Set back from the street, this house sits behind a low brick wall and is surrounded by open fields. At a glance it looks like a simple nineteenth-century farmhouse but its angle buttresses reveal something of its ancient past.

This is not the only building of interest in Ewelme. William and Alice de la Pole were also responsible for rebuilding the church, establishing the almshouse and founding the school over a twenty-year period, all of which still stand as a testament to the splendour of the de la Poles' former estate.

Visitor Information

We visited the small Oxfordshire village of Ewelme at about the prettiest time of the year. Surely, there are no two months more delightful in England than May and June, when nature's mantel is in full bloom and vibrant colours and the sweet scent of fragrant blossom fill the air.

The village is another perfect rural idyll, although sadly generations of established families are dying out and, as well-heeled commuters buy up the ever more expensive local property, children whose forefathers have lived in the area for generations are forced to move elsewhere. Today successful businessmen, statesmen and landed gentry keep immaculate houses that front onto quiet village lanes.

We recommend that you head uphill toward the church and park directly outside the gate. As the village sits snugly on the side of a hill, when you look out over the churchyard you will already have a feel for just what an agreeable spot this is. It is not hard to see why a palace grew up here, surrounded by parkland for hunting, alongside a plentiful supply of water, which runs along the bottom of the valley, close to where the old palace once stood.

The current parish church lies half a mile or so uphill from the original manor but, as the house that Henry and Anne stayed in had its own private chapel, it is difficult to say with certainty that the royal couple visited here in person, although they no doubt saw it as they passed to and from their hunting trips.

Nevertheless, the medieval gems inside are not to be missed, in particular the stunning marble *memento-mori* tomb of Alice de la Pole, Duchess of Suffolk. The wall paintings in St John's chapel have been restored in more recent times, but are true to the original decoration of the chapel. In the central aisle of the knave, you will also find the brass plaque marking the site of the tomb of the five-year-old Edward Norris, son of Sir Henry, who was once bailiff and keeper of the park at Ewelme.

Outside head to the west doors; you are now standing in the short gallery that leads to and from the almshouses. The door leading to the almshouses is often shut, but our local guide assured us that the public do have access, so make sure you push it open and head down the short flight of stairs. These stairs have seen countless generations of almsmen trek up and down to St John's chapel inside the church in order to say prayers for the soul of Lady Alice. Although, of course, this tradition has long since been lost, the almshouses today continue the tradition of sheltering elderly inhabitants. Standing inside the small, galleried courtyard, you will soon be planning how you could move in yourself! It is a haven of tranquillity and perfectly maintained.

Continue round the gallery, heading out via a corridor on the right. This leads you into the formal garden. Enjoy its charms before turning left and walking down to the road. Here you will find the other great medieval survivor of the village – the school.

The original aim was to take the brightest boys from the estate in order to educate and prepare them for a university place at nearby Oxford. The school continues to serve as such and is in immaculate condition; the coats of arms of the founding family can be seen on the side fronting the road. Next, turn right heading down High Street, back through the centre of the village. Just after Parson's Lane, opposite Ewelme Preschool, is a red brick wall marking the boundary of the current manor house; close to its main entrance once stood the manor of Ewelme. We were lucky enough to be there on Spring Bank Holiday when the village fete was being held in the manor grounds; a worthy stop for tea and home-made cakes alone! In the adjacent field the vague imprint of the moat is still visible. However, generally speaking the manor house is privately owned and not accessible to the public.

If you wish to take rest and refreshment, retrace your steps for a few metres before turning left up Parson's Lane by King's Pool, reputedly called so because Catherine Howard once playfully pushed Henry into it. We wish we could have seen that one, or perhaps pushed him in ourselves! Anyway, plotting revenge aside, continue up the lane back toward the church until you find Ewelme Stores where you may finally take your ease.

As a side note, leading historian David Starkey believes that it's likely that Henry VIII was conceived at Ewelme on account of his parents, Henry VII and Elizabeth of York, spending much time at the manor house in late September and early October 1490 (Henry was born on 21 June 1491).

Postcode for St Mary church: OX10 6HP and for Ewelme School: OX10 6HU.

Abingdon Abbey, Oxfordshire

> I wrote to you that you should provide crimson velvet for three countesses. The King's pleasure now is that no robes of estate shall be now made but only for my wife. I send you the pattern. Garter must be at Abingdon on Saturday. Langley, 21 Aug.
>
> Duke of Norfolk to Thomas Cromwell

On 14 July 1535, Henry VIII and Anne Boleyn made the 10-mile journey from Ewelme to Abingdon en route to Langley. This was not the first time that the couple had relied on the hospitality of this great monastic house, as they had spent time there in late August 1532.

We can imagine the royal party approaching the town across Abingdon Bridge, which would have offered them a good view of the spire of the nearby, late medieval St Helen's church that still dominates the skyline of the town. They may also have been able to glimpse the towers of the abbey church from the causeway.

Abbot Thomas Rowland would have received his royal guests with great pomp and ceremony and accommodated them in the abbot's house, a large mansion with sumptuous guest chambers, halls, offices and its own kitchen. Although nothing today survives of this once-grand establishment, a few buildings remain that Anne would have seen.

Touring the Abbey Remains

The main abbey gateway was rebuilt in around 1450 and is still standing. When facing the gateway, St Nicholas's church, originally constructed in 1184 for the abbey's servants and lay tenants, stands on the left and the former St John's hospital, founded in the twelfth century as a lay infirmary, on the right. The latter was built in around 1130 and is one of the oldest buildings in Abingdon. After the Dissolution, the old hospital ward became a courtroom and is still used by the Magistrates Court today. The old Abbey Grammar School, refounded by John Roysee in 1563, used part of the site until it moved to its present place adjacent to Albert Park in 1870. Anne would have seen these buildings as she approached the gateway.

As you walk through the gateway, pause for a moment beneath the central arch and imagine Anne and Henry riding in followed by their large and eye-catching retinue. Heavy wooden doors, which have long since disappeared, would have secured the gateway; you can still see one of the original hinges.

You now emerge into what was once Little Court. From here abbey visitors could proceed via gatehouses into the base court and the inner court. The latter was where the abbot's lodgings once stood.

Continue along the path to the Victorian round garden. In the open grass area beyond this site once rose the west end of the Norman church built by Abbot Faritius in the early twelfth century. By the sixteenth century, it is said to have resembled Wells Cathedral in Somerset. Although there are no visible remains, its outline is marked out in stone on the grass. Look out for crosses on marble slabs too, as they mark the probable locations of the high altar of the Norman church and an earlier Saxon church.

Locate the stone plinth that displays a plan of the medieval abbey, just outside the park, and close to the river. Note that to the south of the church were the cloisters, around which all the other buildings were constructed. To the west of the cloister was the abbot's hall and lodgings, which originally consisted of a parlour on the ground floor and a chamber and chapel above it, later extended into the large house described above, where important guests, like Henry and Anne, were entertained.

The standing ruins within the abbey gardens occupy the site of the abbot's house where Anne stayed; however, they are not ruins of the abbey. A former owner, Mr Trendell, built these picturesque remains out of pieces of stone and coffins that he found when laying the gardens in the mid-nineteenth century. To this he added pillars and windows sourced from local churches undergoing restoration and with the various building materials created a folly.

The Domestic Buildings of the Abbey

A second group of buildings that were standing in Anne's day are on Thames Street by the Millstream and consist of the bakehouse, the Checker Hall and the Long Gallery. These were all part of the domestic buildings around the base court, and were accessed via a gatehouse near the west end of the street.

What was originally part of the monastic bakehouse is now the office of the Friends of Abingdon, the group responsible for saving these ancient buildings from demolition, restoring and maintaining them.

The Checker Hall was described in 1554 as the 'Granatory or Garner' suggesting that it may have been the residence of the granator or his granary. It was originally connected to the mill via a loft over the gateway and, prior to the Dissolution, may also have been used as accommodation. Today it houses an Elizabethan-style stage and is home to the Unicorn Theatre. Be sure to visit the small paved court to the north of the Checker Hall, as this is the best place from which to see Checker chimney, said to be one of the finest thirteenth-century chimneys in England.

An internal stone staircase from the Checker Hall leads into the upper chamber of the checker, once the business centre of the abbey. The checker undercroft is a fine vaulted chamber that was probably being used as a wine cellar around the time of Anne's visit. Undoubtedly, the staff were kept very busy!

The superb partly stone, partly timber-framed Long Gallery was built in the late fifteenth century and since then the layout has been altered many times. The space was originally partitioned and thought to have been used to house guests or visiting clerks. Keep an eye out for an Elizabethan wall painting on the plaster above one of the crossbeams, a sure sign that at one time its inhabitants were quite prosperous.

The Demise of the Abbey

When Henry VIII decided to suppress the monasteries, Abingdon Abbey – one of the wealthiest Benedictine abbeys in England – surrendered 'voluntarily'. Henry considered converting some of the buildings into a royal house but after Sir Richard Rich surveyed the vast complex of buildings, courtyards and gardens, he wrote to Cromwell saying that he wished him to 'signify to the King's Majesty that the most part of the houses of office therof be much in ruin and decay except the church ... and as concerning the abbot's lodgings, I think it is not like for an habitation of the King's Majesty, unless his Highness will expend great treasure'.

Within a few weeks a team of thirty-two men arrived to remove the lead and stone from the abbey church, and from there the majority of the buildings were demolished.

Although not much remains of Abingdon Abbey today, the surviving buildings and ancient grounds hark back to much happier times, when Abingdon was one of the greatest monasteries in England and Anne Boleyn, the king's most beloved wife.

Visitor Information

The domestic abbey buildings are open from 1 May to the end of September, 2–4 p.m. daily except Wednesdays. The buildings are often in use for private functions so it is recommended that you call before visiting: + 44 (0) 1235 525339 or visit the Friends of Abingdon Civic Society's website for more information: http://www.friendsofabingdon.org.uk.

The abbey gardens are open to the public at all reasonable times.

Postcode for Abbey Close Car Park (Abbey Gardens): OX14 3JE and for the abbey buildings: OX14 3HZ.

The Old Palace of Langley, Oxfordshire

The ruins of King John's Palace, which was inhabited by the royal family till the beginning of the reign of Charles I, are still to be seen in the edge of the forest at a place called Langley; these vestiges of the palace remain: The Queen's garden, park pool, the slaughter-house, the park closes with stone walls ten feet high, a barn and a farm-house with Gothic arches and windows. The prospect is extensive and beautiful.

Warton, 1815

Perched on high ground to the south of the village of Shipton-under-Wychwood is the small hamlet of Langley, locally famous for being home to a site where it's traditionally said once stood King John's Palace. This legend is shaky, but that ancient Plantagenet king is not the monarch whose footsteps we follow at Langley; we're on the trail of a Tudor queen and on this rare occasion, we find the evidence penned in Anne's own delicate hand.

In the fifteenth century, the manor of Langley belonged to the Nevilles. It passed with Isabelle Neville to her husband George, Duke of Clarence, and became Crown property upon his death in 1478.

Henry VII was a regular visitor and from 1496 onwards was responsible for much of the building works. Like his father, Henry VIII clearly favoured Langley, as shown by the number of recorded visits.

On 18 July 1535, Queen Anne Boleyn wrote a letter to Thomas Cromwell from 'my Lord's manor of Langley':

As you have heretofore been good to Robt. Powre whom we put to you in service, and have granted him the nomination and preferment of an abbacy for his friend, we request you now to help his said friend to the preferment of the abbey of Wallryall, in Lincolnshire (Cheshire), of which the abbot is lately deceased.

The court had made the 12-mile journey from Abingdon Abbey, arriving on 16 July and staying for five days before proceeding to Sudeley Castle near Winchcombe on 21 July. Anne's brother, Lord Rochford, and her uncle, the Duke of Norfolk, were among the royal entourage.

From Langley, Anne wrote a second letter to Cromwell concerning the wardship of a child, 'Poyns', which had been granted to her by the king. It's clear that there was a matter that needed addressing; however, Anne did not want to trouble the king and requested that Cromwell deal with it:

Mastar Seretery, I pray you despache with spede this matter, for myn honneur lys mouche on ytt, and wat should the Kynges attornne do with Poyns hoblygassion [obligation], sens I have the chyld be the Kynges grace gyfte, but wonlly to trobe[l] hym her haffter, wyche be no mens I woll soffer, and thus far you as well as I wold ye dyd. Your lovyng mestres Anne the Quene.

This was not the first time that Henry and Anne had visited Langley. In September 1529, the majority of the court was left behind at Woodstock, 9 miles away, while the king and a small party moved to this place, one of Henry's lesser houses. Although there is no way of knowing for certain whether Anne was part of this intimate retinue, the greater privacy afforded by such a visit makes it highly likely.

The royal party returned again in August 1532, when Henry VIII was given 100 crowns to play at dice; this amount and more he lost to a 'maister weston', almost certainly Francis Weston, who had been made a gentleman of the privy chamber earlier that year. A servant of 'my lady Russelles' was on the same day rewarded for bringing a stag and a greyhound to Anne, which she then gave to the king.

In September 1534, the court was again at Langley and later that month the house was considered as a residence for the one-year-old Princess Elizabeth. On 20 September 1534, Sir John Shelton, Anne's uncle through marriage, wrote to Cromwell: 'I received your letter on Sunday afternoon of the Princess's removal to Langley or Knebworth I know not in what case those houses stand, and whether they be meet for her Grace and her household. Hunsdon, St. Matthew's eve.'

This was not the only time that Langley would be named in connection with the princess. On 9 October 1535, Sir William Paulet informed Cromwell that

the King having considered the letter to Cromwell from lady Brian and other of the Princess's officers, has determined that she shall be weaned with all diligence, and that Langley shall be put in readiness. Sends letters to them, and one from the Queen to lady Brian. The King desires the commissions for the despatch of the ambassadors to be shortly sped, and Cromwell to return to him. Salisbury, 9 Oct.

Throughout the sixteenth century, Henry stayed at Langley when hunting in Wychwood Forest, and the house was often used as a satellite to Woodstock.

Recreating the Lost Palace

Occasional repairs were made to the manor house during his reign; however, very little documentary evidence exists, making it difficult to build a thorough picture of the buildings.

In 1536, the accounts of James Nedeham, as Clerk of the Works, show that work was done to the king's and queen's wardrobes and lodgings, including new plastering. The account provides us with other fleeting glimpses of the buildings that Anne would have known. We hear about stairs going from the king's lodgings to the hall, from the queen's apartments to the inner court, and a flight of stairs leading directly to the 'king's garden'. In 1539, the roofs of 'divers lodgings' in the inner court were repaired, as were the roofs of the king's apartments.

The overall picture is fragmentary and not helped by the fact that only a portion of one wing of the manor house survives, incorporated into a nineteenth-century farmhouse. The evidence does, however, seem to indicate that this was only a small part of a much larger house, confirmed by the complex of earthworks that surrounds it. Clearly it was comfortable enough to frequently entice the court and to be considered fitting for a young Princess Elizabeth. Tradition has it that Charles I and his court resided there as late as 1614.

The site is now called Langley Farm and, although extensively remodelled in 1858, incorporates fifteenth-, sixteenth- and eighteenth-century fabric, including Tudor walls on the north and west and a lovely bay window of two storeys. It's still possible to see the initials H E, for Henry VII and Elizabeth of York, on a stone panel at the front of the farmhouse.

The house is privately owned and so can only be viewed from the street. The now-empty field, littered with cow patties, is a far cry from the splendid sight that must have greeted Anne, but it's easy to summon an image of her, sumptuously attired, strolling with her ladies in the manicured pleasure gardens, breathing in the scents of summer, auburn highlights in her dark hair catching the sun and her black, profound eyes gleaming with hope.

Visitor Information

In our opinion, Langley is a haunting place. It is a location whose significance is virtually lost, even to the local population. One of the authors, who happens to live just a few miles away, was entirely unaware of its presence until researching this book.

In Anne's day, it may well have been surrounded by the extensive Wychwood Forest, which remains in pockets around the nearby town of Charlbury. But today the location sits isolated and forgotten on a ridge close to the town of Shipton-under-Wychwood. Langley Farm stands as the only witness to the site of a once much-loved medieval palace.

Finding the location can be a bit tricky and you will probably need a map. Perhaps the easiest way is to locate the B4437 that runs between Charlbury and the A361, near Shipton-under-Wychwood. Look out for a crossroads that signposts Swinbrook 2½ miles to the right, as you head toward Charlbury. The first turn on your left is signposted Fordwells. Take this turn and continue along the road until you come to a farmhouse. This is Langley Farm, comprising a main house fronting the road and a number of farm buildings straddling the lane. A sign, Langley Farm, on one of them tells you that you are in the right place.

You can pull over here and wander along the deserted lane. You may even meet the owners of the farm, as we did the day we were there. Having explained what we were doing, they were very hospitable and showed us around the exterior of the house, which incorporates fragments of the old hunting lodge. Sadly, you cannot get a good view of all these pieces from the road, and the property is on private land so cannot be accessed ordinarily. However, in the field to the left of the house as you stand facing it, you will clearly see earthworks of a ditch, which presumably was once a moat. The field then levels to a plateau; it was on this plateau that the formal gardens of the palace were once laid out for pleasure.

For rest and refreshment, nearby pubs can be found in Swinbrook – the Old Swan, owned by the Dowager Duchess of Devonshire, or The Shaven Crown at Shipton-under-Wychwood, once part of an old monastic complex, hence the rather unusual name! Another location within easy driving distance is the Old Palace of Woodstock.

Postcode of Langley Farm: OX29 9QD.

Sudeley Castle, Gloucestershire

> There is a particular time in the evening when the light is at a certain level … there is this sense of timelessness here, I can't really explain it but one merges into it.
>
> Lady Ashcombe

Nestled deep in the Cotswold Hills, close to the ancient town of Winchcombe, lies beautiful Sudeley Castle. Its mere mention evokes images of Henry VIII's sixth wife, Katherine Parr, who lived through elation and despair within its rooms that still pulse with the energy of Tudor personalities and intrigues of the past. Lady Jane Grey and Thomas Seymour are among those who've called Sudeley home, and Queen Anne Boleyn once roamed its enchanting grounds.

On Wednesday 21 July 1535, Anne and Henry made the 14-mile journey from Langley to Winchcombe in Gloucestershire. There they lodged at Sudeley Castle with their immediate retinue, while the rest of the court stayed at nearby Winchcombe Abbey.

Cromwell Joins the Progress and the 'Visitations' Begin

Thomas Cromwell joined the court on or near 23 July and it was while staying at the Benedictine abbey that he began the process that would eventually lead to the destruction of England's monasteries.

While under the abbey roof, he met with his agents, known as visitors, and briefed them on the new injunctions – created in consultation with the king – that were to be issued to the monks after each abbey inspection. From Winchcombe, Cromwell's agents fanned out and 'visited' a number of monastic houses while Anne's disapproving gaze fell on a nearby religious house, called Hailes Abbey.

According to Anne's chaplain, William Latymer, the queen, like her husband, fully supported the new campaign. One of the injunctions prohibited the display of 'relics or feigned miracles', and it was while staying at Sudeley that she sent her chaplains, Latymer and probably John Hilsey, to the nearby abbey, which lay only 2 miles to the north-east of Winchcombe. Their mission was to investigate a renowned relic of the Holy Blood of Christ that had transformed the abbey into one of the most popular places of pilgrimage in late medieval England. According to Latymer, Anne, 'mistrusting that which afterwards she approved to be trew, sente thither certeyn of her chappellayns and others, straightly commaunding them truely and faythfully to vewe, searche and examyn by all possible meanes the trueth of this abominable abuse'.

What her chaplains reported was that the famous phial said to contain the blood of Christ 'was nothing els but the bloode of some ducke, or as some saye, red waxe'. Anne is reported to have gone directly to Henry and requested that the relic be removed, which Latymer claimed it was, although it seems that he was either mistaken or this was only a temporary removal, as it was again at Hailes in 1538, when it was investigated by Hugh Latimer and Richard Tracy. This time it was found to contain not duck's blood, as noted by Anne's chaplain, but rather a gum-like substance.

Apart from sending their representatives, Henry and Anne planned to visit the abbey, although it's uncertain as to whether or not this visit ever took place.

The Tudor Layout of Sudeley Castle

The castle we see today is mostly Elizabethan, built in the later sixteenth century by Baron Chandos and partially restored by the Dent family in the mid-nineteenth century. However, the castle as Anne knew it had been constructed in the mid-fifteenth century by Ralph, Baron Boteler, and in the 1470s by Richard, Duke of Gloucester.

Boteler constructed a large, double-courtyard residence between the years 1441 and 1458. It was constructed from local honey-coloured Cotswold stone. He then added a private chapel outside the moat of the castle in the early 1460s, the shell of which survives today. The detached chapel was connected to the main building via a covered gallery, which extended from the south side of the church.

The castle was approached through a gatehouse in the north, originally protected by a moat and drawbridge. The outer court of lodgings and perhaps offices, gave way to an inner court, accessed via an internal gatehouse. On the opposite side stood a grand banqueting hall, flanked by square residential towers, one of which survives today. The west range of the inner court housed the kitchens, services and offices while the opposite east range probably housed the living quarters.

The two courts were originally separated by a cross range that no longer exists; however, the two towers that once stood at either end of the range still stand, albeit in a restored state.

Part of Boteler's outer court – namely the gatehouse and a segment of outer wall; a section of his inner court; a barn, now in ruins, and the chapel are all that survive from this first phase of construction.

The three ranges that today line the outer court were almost entirely rebuilt in 1572. It seems that the more lavish apartments, where it's almost certain Anne stayed, were in the now-ruined east range of the inner court thought to have been built by Boteler's successor, Richard, Duke of Gloucester, to replace the original residential range.

Gloucester's lavish east range overlooked formal gardens and consisted of a suite of three apartments on the ground floor and first floor, both similar in plan. The rooms were lit by a sequence of magnificent windows glazed with stained glass and warmed by elaborately decorated fireplaces. It is in these sun-lit rooms, decorated with fine tapestries and ornate ceilings, that we can imagine Anne spending her time. The long summer evenings would have provided ample opportunity for Anne to walk with her ladies in the formal gardens; The Queens' Garden today occupying the site of the original Tudor parterre.

The now-ruined east range, draped with clematis and roses, is a truly magical place and you would certainly be forgiven for thinking that, at any moment, Anne might emerge from the ruins.

Sudeley Castle exudes a sense of timelessness that is rarely felt elsewhere. Within its idyllic grounds, its past inhabitants appear almost tangible, as the present fades to reveal an intriguing past.

Authors' Favourites
Sudeley is by far one of our favourite places in the world because of its serene and magical atmosphere and also for the many Tudor treasures housed there.

To make the most of your day at Sudeley, begin at the Visitor and Plant Centre adjacent to the car park and make your way to the ruins of the fifteenth-century tithe barn built by Boteler and now home to a romantic garden, abundant with wild roses, hydrangeas and wisterias. Breathe in the beautiful scents as you take in the stunning view of the castle.

From here follow the path to the entrance to the exhibitions in the original fifteenth-century west wing of the castle to learn more about Sudeley's past residents, in particular

Katherine Parr who, after the death of Henry VIII, lived at Sudeley with her new husband, Thomas Seymour.

Be sure to visit the 'Six Wives at Sudeley' exhibition that houses replica Tudor costumes from David Starkey's television series *The Six Wives of Henry VIII.*

The 'Katherine Parr' exhibition is also a must-see, as it offers a unique opportunity to see personal items belonging to Henry's sixth queen, like a prayer book, letters and even a lock of her strawberry-blonde hair! Throughout the exhibition you can hear more about Katherine's story in a film presented by David Starkey – *The Life and Loves of Katherine Parr, Queen of England and Mistress of Sudeley.*

The story of Katherine's life continues in a new exhibition in the South Hall that begins in the Knot Corridor with a display of Tudor jewellery. There you have the opportunity to see a copy of the National Portrait Gallery's full-length portrait of Katherine, before visiting her private apartments.

From there, cross the garden to St Mary's church; this was standing at the time of Anne's visit. Although the church was left in ruins after the Civil War and restored in the nineteenth century, it retains much of its original shell. The church is best known for being the final resting place of Katherine Parr, who died at Sudeley in September 1548 after complications following the birth of her daughter, Mary. The interior of the church, including Katherine's grand tomb, is Victorian.

Be sure to leave yourself sufficient time to explore the medieval ruins and lose yourself in the numerous stunning gardens, including the Tudor physic garden.

We guarantee that Sudeley will remain in your thoughts long after the visit has come to an end.

Visitor Information

For information on how to reach Sudeley Castle and its opening hours, which are seasonal, visit Sudeley Castle's website at http://www.sudeleycastle.co.uk, or telephone + 44 (0) 1242 604244 (during open season only). Those wishing to tour the family's private apartments must join an organised house tour on Tuesdays, Wednesdays or Thursdays during open season, as access is not permitted at any other time. At the time of writing, Sudeley Castle also holds a number of 'Tudor Fun Days' on Sundays throughout the summer months. You may just bump into the one of the authors in costume, strolling through the grounds with other members of the Boleyn family, bringing the castle's rich Tudor Heritage back to life. Please check the Sudeley Castle website for further information.

Postcode for Sudeley Castle: GL54 5JD.

Tewkesbury Abbey, Gloucestershire

> I thank you for your goodness at my preferment, and your loving commendations to the King when he was at Tewkesbury, as yet undeserved of me.
>
> John, Abbot of Tewkesbury, to Cromwell

On Monday 26 July 1535, the royal party left Sudeley Castle and made the 7-mile journey north-west to Tewkesbury. They were three days behind schedule but in no rush to try and make up the time; instead they proceeded, thus far, to all scheduled stops remaining roughly for the time specified in the original 'geists', which meant four days at Tewkesbury.

In keeping with protocol for all royal arrivals, the mayor and other dignitaries would have received the king, queen and their retinue just outside the town, with the two parties merging to travel in procession to the cathedral or abbey church. After making an offering at the church, Henry and Anne would then have been escorted to their accommodation, probably at the abbey, as a letter written by Thomas Cromwell on 29 July and signed from 'The Monastery of Tewkesbury' seems to indicate.

The abbey was founded in 1087 but work on the buildings that Anne saw did not commence until 1102. It was originally built to house Benedictine monks and was near completion when consecrated in 1121.

The Royal Lodgings at Tewkesbury

As at Reading and Abingdon, it's likely that Henry and Anne were accommodated at the abbot's house within the abbey precincts, as this was the only building suitable to house such distinguished guests. Unlike many of the other monastic buildings, this had been rebuilt in the early sixteenth century and so was fairly new at the time of Anne's visit. The marvellous news for those of us on the trail of Anne Boleyn is that, although most of the claustral buildings were destroyed after the Dissolution, the abbot's lodging was retained and forms part of what is now Abbey House. The house is located next to the west front of the church – note the impressive oriel window built in 1509, the year of Henry's accession – and is today home to the vicar of Tewkesbury Abbey, the Reverend Canon Paul Williams.

Abbey House sits close to the main abbey gateway, as this position allowed the abbot to greet all his guests, including Anne when she arrived there in 1535. The gateway, consisting of one large room at first-floor level, accessed via a spiral staircase, was built around 1500 and it too survived ruination in 1540. The building is currently leased by the Landmark Trust and available to rent as holiday accommodation.

Exploring the Abbey Church

The splendid abbey church still stands, as parishioners saved it from destruction by purchasing it from the Crown. At the time of Anne's visit, its walls were covered in biblical scenes, and its fourteen enormous Norman pillars, which today stand bare, were dressed in bold patterns and vivid colour.

Keep an eye out for the magnificent vaulted roof of the choir, with its gilded Suns of York installed after Edward IV's crucial victory against the Lancastrian forces in 1471 (see below). The church is also renowned for its medieval stained glass – added to its seven quire windows in the fourteenth century and among the most outstanding survivors of their kind in Europe. No doubt Anne admired them during her visit.

In the north ambulatory is a cenotaph often said to commemorate John Wiche/Wyche, later known as John Wakeman, the last Abbot of Tewkesbury and the abbot at the time of Anne's stay. However, the monument is now known to predate Wakeman's lifetime by around 100 years. The grisly cadaver monument, designed as a reminder of the mortality of man, depicts his decaying corpse being devoured by a worm, a frog, a mouse and a snail.

At the west end of the church, you will find the Holy Cross Chapel, originally reserved for the private worship of the abbot and thought to have been connected to his lodgings by a covered walkway. Keen eyes will also spot the unique collection of early fourteenth-century bosses, representing the life of Jesus, that adorn the roof of the nave.

As you head toward the exit of the church, take note of the unique Norman arch that soars almost 20 metres high. Once outside, wander round to the south side of the abbey, fronting the River Swilgate, where the cloisters, one of the busiest parts of the abbey precincts and the monastic buildings, once stood. These are now all now lost in time.

The Mystery of Forthampton Court

As to where the royal party stayed in Tewkesbury, the abbey is the most likely contender; however, there exists another location worth mentioning and one that we are grateful to Richard Sermon for bringing to our attention.

At Winchcombe, while Henry and Anne stayed at Sudeley Castle, Thomas Cromwell stayed at Winchcombe Abbey and so it's feasible that once more they were lodged separately; but with no royal castle in the immediate vicinity, where might this alternate accommodation have been?

A clue exists in the transcription of the marginal notes of the original itinerary where after 'Sedley to Tewkesbury' we find noted '... gtor the ... ttes place'. Local Tewkesbury archaeologist, Richard, has suggested that the first fragment may have been incorrectly transcribed and is more likely to have been originally written as '…gton', which makes sense as the common English place name element '…ington'.

The village of Forthampton, in the past also called Forthington, lies just 3½ miles from the abbey, just over the River Severn, and was once home to Forthampton Court, the country residence of the abbots of Tewkesbury who owned the manor from the twelfth century to the mid-sixteenth century. It was a large house consisting of several wings, a Great Hall, a solar and a chapel and described by John Leland sometime between 1535 and 1543 as 'a faire place'.

The Great Hall, 16 metres by 6½ metres, although curiously narrow was particularly large for an abbot's country house; this and its proximity to the abbey suggest that it was probably used for entertaining and, in the words of Anthony Emery, used to 'vie with comparable episcopal halls'.

In light of this, even if Anne and Henry did not stay at Forthampton Court and instead remained at the abbey with Cromwell, it's still possible that, at some point, they were entertained at the house by the Abbot of Tewkesbury. It was certainly not uncommon for the king and queen to use an abbey as their central base, from where they would venture out on day trips in the surrounding area. While on progress, they were regularly wined and dined by influential people, including abbots, and on one recorded occasion stayed out until after dark, requiring the assistance of torchbearers to guide them home (see entry for Gloucester).

On 24 October 1535, Abbot John Wiche, later Wakeman, wrote to Cromwell to thank him 'for your goodness at my preferment, and your loving commendations to the King when he was at Tewkesbury'.

Wakeman evidently remained on good terms with Henry, who took possession of Forthampton Court and granted it to him after the dissolution of the abbey in January 1540. The following year, Wakeman was appointed the first Bishop of Gloucester after which time he made improvements to the house using stone from the demolished Tewkesbury's Lady Chapel.

Over the centuries, Forthampton Court has been altered and extended; however, later additions have retained and incorporated the medieval Great Hall, a first-floor chapel and various other fifteenth- and sixteenth-century walls. Today, the house is privately owned, but a self-contained, nineteenth-century wing of the house can be rented out to holidaymakers.

Visitor Information

Tewkesbury is a charming English market town of considerable medieval heritage. Its main street is full of wonderful timber-framed buildings, making it hard to keep your eyes on the road when you first drive into the town! There is ample parking in a pay-and-display car park just off Gander Lane, directly adjacent to the east end of the abbey. From here you can access the abbey and grounds, taking your time to explore its fabulous Norman architecture, as you follow in Anne's footsteps up the central aisle to stand in front of the high altar. A plan of the medieval abbey before the Dissolution is hung on the wall in the north ambulatory, to the right of the high altar as you stand facing it.

After leaving the abbey, walk a short distance around the corner to your left and you will soon come across the fine building that was once the old abbot's lodgings. That beautifully carved, stone oriel window will be one of the first things to draw the eye. The carvings are somewhat worn, but one can clearly see inscribed the date of 1509, coinciding with the year of Henry VIII's accession to the throne. Continue further along until you come across the gatehouse, the main medieval entrance to the abbey precinct. Hear the clatter of horses' hooves as the royal party swept in and out of their lodgings.

Before you leave Tewkesbury, do take some time to enjoy its medieval charms, particularly the Merchant's House on Church Street. This range of timber-framed buildings has been converted into a museum, recreating the interior of a typical merchant's house of the Tudor period. This is affiliated with the John Moore Museum next door. Further information on opening times can be found on their website, http://www.johnmooremuseum.org.

Tewkesbury Abbey is opened all year round; please visit http://www.tewkesburyabbey.org.uk for opening times. Entry is free; however, visitors are asked to leave a donation towards the upkeep of the abbey. Any questions can be directed to office@tewkesburyabbey.org.uk, or call + 44(0) 1684 850959. The abbey has tea rooms in its grounds, a convenient place to rest and take refreshments.

To enquire about staying at the Abbey Gatehouse please visit http://www.landmarktrust.org.uk. Alternatively, you can call + 44 (0) 1628 825925 or email the booking office at bookings@landmarktrust.org.uk.

For more information on staying in the modern wing of Forthampton Court visit www.ruralretreats.co.uk. Alternatively, you can call + 44 (0) 1386 701177 or email info@ruralretreats.co.uk.

Postcode for Tewkesbury Abbey: GL20 5RZ.

Gloucester and Environs, Gloucestershire

Later, Anne Boleyn, newly a queen, smiled through our green woodlands while hunting in the [former] Park and Longridge Wood with her terrible master, and they were accompanied by Sir John Dudley, afterwards Duke of Northumberland and father-in-law of Lady Jane Grey.

Welbore St Clair Baddeley, from *A Cotswold Manor Being the History of Painswick*

Overview

It was the height of summer when the king and court took leave of the Abbot of Tewkesbury and headed the 12 miles or so southbound toward the city of Gloucester. Thankfully for us, long-overlooked records of the Corporation of Gloucester, found in the Duke of Beaufort's papers, provide us with a detailed account of this visit. This was the 'first commyng [of the king – and Anne] to Gloucester, after his Graces Coronacion'. These records give us an unsurpassed insight into the pomp and ceremony that must have accompanied the royal couple whenever they visited a major town or city and, on account of this and its uniqueness for those particularly interested in Anne Boleyn, we shall be covering its contents in some detail.

31 July 1535: The Arrival at Gloucester

From the account we know that, on Saturday 31 July, Henry and Anne were met by the Mayor of Gloucester, John Falconer; aldermen; sheriffs, Thomas Payne and Richard Edwardes; and about 100 or so burgesses of the 'town of Gloucester'. The greeting party rode out in their scarlet gowns and velvet 'typpettes', while the burgesses were attired in 'cootes of musterdevillers', a type of mixed, grey woollen cloth. They met the king and queen at 'the grene at the hether end of the lane athisside [this side of] Brickehampton's brigge' or bridge, now Down Hatherley village, where they made their obeisance on horseback, offering the king their right hands in turn. The mayor then kissed the mace of the town and said to the king,

Thanks be to God for your Grace's health and good prosperity, which God long continue! That all such liberties, privileges, customs, and grants as your Grace and other your noble progenitors heretofore have given unto the Mayor and Burgesses of this your town of Gloucester, as we deliver up unto your Grace, trusting that your Grace will be as good and gracious Lord unto us now as you have been heretofore. And furthermore, I hereto present myself unto your Grace as Mayor of your said town of Gloucester, certifying that all your burgesses there be ... at your Grace's commandment, and heartily thank your Grace for such liberties, privileges and grants that your Grace has given unto us, beseeching you of your gracious aid and assistance hereafter in the execution thereof in doing justice. [Spelling modernised]

The king then took receipt of the mace, immediately delivering it back to the mayor with his continued blessing. With the first formalities completed, a procession then formed, led by the burgesses, aldermen and sheriffs. Then 'alle gentilmen, esquyers, knyghtes, lords, and other greate men' followed. Before the king and queen came the mayor, still carrying the mace, escorted by sergeants-at-arms. Behind Anne followed her ladies and gentlewomen and other 'sondry persons folowyng the Courte'.

The royal entourage then passed by Whitefriars (now the bus station!) immediately outside the city walls to the north-east, before arriving at the medieval Northgate, positioned at the northern end of the current Lower North Gate Street. This was the main entrance to the city from the north and east. Here they were met by 'all the clergie' dressed in their copes and having with them crosses, carpets and cushions. In a wonderful and touching insight, it is easy to visualise what happened next: 'And his Grace and the Quene bothe being on horseback lovingly there kissed the crosse, and then rode forthe, every man after the seid maner throwght the towne bryngyng His Grace into the Abbey throwght Seynt Edwardes Lane [now College Street].'

Once into the abbey precinct, Henry and Anne were greeted by the 'Abbot [Parker] and his bretheren' in the porch of the abbey; all were sumptuously attired in their rich ceremonial copes, once more having carpets and cushions at the ready. This time they were clearly needed, for Anne and Henry dismounted and 'both kneeled down and kissed the crosse with greate reveraunce, and then went up to the highe alter, and so from thens [there] to there [their] lodgynges'.

The Abbot's Lodgings at Gloucester

Sadly, where those lodgings were is not specified. However, as we shall see, the royal couple set off hunting on subsequent days from the abbey yard. This is highly suggestive of the fact that they lodged in the abbot's lodgings, close to the cathedral and on its northern side, fronting on to modern-day Pitt Street. A report on the abbey wall (the only part of the abbot's lodgings to survive) by C. M. Heighway in 2006 summarises that

> the principal buildings, including the great hall, were towards the west ... Attached to the high end of the hall were the great chamber, chapel, private chambers, and a long gallery or 'walking house' which linked the hall and associated buildings to the late-medieval eastern ranges. The medieval bishop's palace was accessed from the south, from the western court of the abbey, through a gateway which still stands.

The *Victoria County History* (see British History Online) suggests that these earlier 'eastern ranges' contained the abbot's privy lodgings. It would be here, in the grandest apartments of the palace, that we would expect to find the king and queen most sumptuously lodged for the duration of their stay in Gloucester.

Today, only the northern wall of the Long Gallery, with its fine oriel window, remains of the palace, a building which burnt down and then was demolished in the mid-nineteenth century. King School now stands in its place. However, you can view the wall from both its exterior and interior façade from Pitt Street and from the publicly accessible precincts of the school, respectively. In the latter location an information board attached to the wall tells a little more of its history.

Six days in the Gloucestershire Countryside

The account makes it clear that the king and queen arrived on Saturday 31 July and departed on 7 August. The *Corporation Records of Gloucester* have preserved the movements of the king and queen for three of those days: Monday 2, Tuesday 3 and the day of their departure from Gloucester itself, Sunday 7 August.

Monday 2 August: Painswick

> Item, the Monday the second day of His Graces commyng to Gloucester, abowte X [10] of the clocke, His Grace and the Quene both being rydyng toward Paynswicke to hunting, the Maire [Mayor] with certen of his brethene mett His Grace in the Abbey Churche yarde, and presented hym there with ten fatte oxen ... for whiche His Grace gave unto them loving thankes.

The city of Gloucester lies in a broad, shallow valley and is surrounded on almost every side by gentle rolling hills. Nowhere is the countryside more beguiling than to the south of the city around the village of Painswick, known today as the Queen of the Cotswolds on account of its inestimable charms. The lush green pastures and leafy woodland surrounding the village set a charming green mantle about the yellow Cotswold stone used to craft its ancient houses. It is truly one of the most beautiful parts of the English countryside, and indeed also very wealthy in the sixteenth century, on account of the prosperous wool trade.

Even today, it is easy to imagine Anne as part of the royal hunting party wending its way through leafy woodland tracks toward the ancient site of Painswick Beacon, a place that gives truly magnificent views over Gloucester and its environs. One wonders if Anne and Henry made their way to the summit on horseback in order to drink in England's 'green and pleasant land'. Alternatively, they might have stopped just short of the Beacon at nearby Prinknash Abbey, directly en route from the centre of the city. Prinknash was one of the Abbot of Gloucester's country residences. Today it remains as a picture-perfect Cotswold-stone mansion, nestled into the north-facing side of a hill that also looks out toward Gloucester, a perfect place to take refreshment and enjoy similarly spectacular views away to the north. Prinknash Abbey now stands as a working Benedictine monastery. The current abbot reports that there are indeed rumours of such a royal visit, although no extant evidence seems to survive to confirm or refute this. Given its location and ownership by Abbot Francis, it is not hard to imagine that some substance lies behind the rumours.

In the *Letters and Papers of Henry VIII*, we hear of Sir John Dudley (the future Duke of Northumberland and father-in-law to Lady Jane Grey) writing to the well-informed Lord Lisle on 8 August after the visit. In this missive, he states that Anne and Henry had 'recently' paid a visit to the village of Painswick, some 6 miles south of Gloucester. Here the king had spoken with Sir John about a business matter concerning Lord Lisle. It seems that the royal couple probably rested at The Lodge, a property co-owned by Lord Lisle and Sir John at the time. It is clear that The Lodge was the major medieval house in the village in the early sixteenth century. Later, during the Civil War, the Court House would take pre-eminence. The former building is recorded as having a Great Hall arranged around a courtyard; today only two wings survive, the west and north ranges.

A Cotteswold Manor Being the History of Painswick by Welbore St Claire Baddeley, written at the turn of the twentieth century, also states that 'in July [Henry VIII] visited Painswick and Miserden with Anne Boleyn, while hunting during a visit to Gloucester'.

He goes on to say that a portion of nearby Longridge, a ridge of wooded land lying across the valley from Painswick village and within sight of Painswick Lodge, was long known thereafter as The Queen's Wood, and a parcel of land there was called Queen's Acre after Anne's fleeting presence during that brief stay in the summer of 1535. You can still walk through these woods today on account of many public footpaths that pass through it.

It must have been a full and bounteous day for Anne and the king, for as the *Corporation of Gloucester Records* tell us,

> And the same day in the darke evening they came from Panyswicke, and at Ailesgate [East Gate] mett them certen persons to the noumbre of xv. [15] with torches light, and browght there Graces into the Abbey, for whiche they gave hartie thankes, and the Quenes grace gave them in reward iiii. [4] angelleth nobles at that tyme.

As it was summer, it would have been light until nine o'clock at night. Anne and Henry had probably been away from Gloucester for around twelve hours. In understanding this, we get a glimpse of Anne's physical stamina, not to mention a wonderful image of numerous torches flickering, casting gentle, willowy shadows across Anne's face, and illuminating darkened alleyways as the hunting party picked their way through the narrow medieval streets of Gloucester after dark.

Tuesday 3 August: Coberley and Miserden

Perhaps enchanted by this little corner of England as much as the authors were, Henry and Anne decided to head out from Gloucester the following day in a similar south-westerly direction. This time hunting would be centred around the village of Coberley and the park at Miserden. The *Corporation Records* list

> Item, the Tewsday the thride day of His graces commying, he and the Quenes Grace also being rydyng toward Coberley, the seid Maire and his bretherne mett the Quene in the Abbey Chruche yarde, and ther presented hir with a purse of gold ... for whiche Hir Grace gave like loving thankes.

Coberley lies about 9 miles to the west of Gloucester, quite a fair ride if the royal party made it all the way to the village. However, it is quite possible that they broke the journey by stopping off at Brockworth Court, which lies almost halfway between Gloucester and Coberley, just off the only main 'road' in the area – the Roman Ermin Street.

At the time, Brockworth Court was owned by Lanthony Priory, the house itself the prior's private country lodging. There has long been a legend passed down that Anne Boleyn stayed/slept at Brockworth while Henry lodged with Katharine of Aragon at nearby Prinknash Abbey during the days before Katharine's expulsion from court. However, our suspicion is that a fragment of truth has become corrupted over time. *The History of Prinknash Park* by W. Bazeley states emphatically that Henry VIII visited Gloucester 'once and once only' – in 1535, when Anne Boleyn was queen. This has also been confirmed by a search of the *Letters and Papers of Henry VIII*, the *Privy Purse Expenses* and by the local pre-eminent historian for Gloucester, Phil Moss. Given that Brockworth lies directly en route to a documented location, combined with the existence of rumours of a visit, we believe that it is quite possible that these rumours in fact refer to a visit on 3 August 1535, much as are documented for the royal visits to Prinknash Abbey and Painswick Lodge the previous day.

Indeed there is further compelling evidence for this. In the first-floor solar, wall paintings contemporary to the early sixteenth century show a Tudor rose next to the religious monogram 'IHC'. Investigation of these paintings by Perry & Lithgow Partnership has revealed that beneath the letters is Katharine of Aragon's pomegranate. Clearly, this was painted over at some point, despite the fact that throughout its history the owners of the house retained its Catholic tradition and, at the time, one assumes their alliance to the deposed queen. It is not hard to imagine the prior being informed of Anne's imminent arrival a few days before the royal visit, as would be customary, and how he might have issued orders for Katharine's badge to be covered up in all haste!

It is possible that the royal party also called in at Coberley Hall in the village of Coberley. This lay some 6–7 miles to the west of Brockworth. The hall already had a pedigree for royal visits, including Henry VII and his consort Elizabeth of York, and afforded the perfect place for refreshment and rest, and indeed to build alliances with local gentry.

The king is then mentioned hunting 3 miles or so to the south at Misarden Park. Anne is not specifically named at this point in the records, although there is no reason to suppose that she wasn't with him. In visiting Miserden, the royal couple would have been guests of Sir William Kingston, who unbelievably just nine months later would serve as Anne's gaoler in his role as Constable of the Tower of London. That most hardy of soldiers would die at Painswick four years later after taking receipt of The Lodge following Cromwell's downfall in 1540 (Cromwell had briefly owned the property after wresting it off Lord Lisle and Sir John Dudley).

Returning again after dark, we hear no more details of the stay until the day of departure. Four days remain unaccounted for, although there is a hint that one of the other locations was another of Abbot Parker's country residences. In the margin of the 'geists' for the 1535 progress, we see the following note: 'The [Vin]yerd, the [Abbo]ttes place.' This possibly refers to the abbot's principal country seat, lying just 2 miles west of Gloucester across the River Severn. Although we will describe this property here, there is a note of caution to be added to this long-held interpretation. During our research, we found that the abbot's lodgings at Gloucester Abbey lay directly adjacent to an area of the abbey precinct known as The Vineyard, on account of the vines grown there. It strikes us that it is just possible that these notes in the margin of the 'geists' are referring to this latter Vineyard and not the Vineyard at Over.

The Vineyard at Over

The Vineyard was probably originally built by Abbot de Staunton in around 1337. It was subsequently enlarged, including the addition of an abbot's chamber, and moated in the late thirteenth century. There is no extant plan or sketch of the manor house. However, archaeological earthworks and remains of the original moat show that the west side was about 78 metres long and 12 metres wide; the north side 80 metres long and 9 metres wide and the southern side 67 metres long and 7 metres wide, giving an enclosure measuring about 60 metres north to south and 71 metres east to west.

In around the year 1540, Leland described the Vineyard as 'a goodly house on a hillet', and it was certainly situated in a prominent position, as the following description of the site also attests: '[Abbot] Staunton was the first who made a residence for the Abbats at the pleasant Vineyard, that from its gentle knoll overlooking the Severn to the eastward, commanded the city and Abbey, backed by the distant hills.'

After the Dissolution of the Monasteries, the Vineyard became the official country residence of the bishops of Gloucester. Then during the Civil War, this glorious manor house became embroiled in the siege of the city, which took place in 1643. It was burnt to the ground on 10 August of the same year, and afterwards plundered and robbed for its stone. Nothing remains to be seen above ground today.

Sunday 7 August

On the day of departure, Anne gathered alongside the king and court outside the abbey in the abbey yard. The same regal procession that had welcomed the royal party escorted them out from Gloucester through the city's Southgate (sited where the current Southgate Street intersects with Parliament Street) until they came to 'Quoddesley Green' (now Quedgeley Green), a small village lying 3 miles south of the city centre.

The land is low-lying and was long surrounded by meadows and pastures. A number of small brooks, including the Qued, converged on the village of around fifty inhabitants, all of whom must surely have come out of the houses, agog at the vibrant spectacle of monarchy that they would no doubt witness only once in their lifetime. There is a tradition that Anne Boleyn stayed in Little Thatch, a modest-sized, timber-framed building that still stands today in the village, and which now serves as a hotel and restaurant. Perhaps she took refreshment there, but it does not seem likely that she stayed there, for it is clear that by the same evening, they were lodged at Leonard Stanley.

As before, we hear, 'Alle the townes men sate on horseback in a raunge gevyng His Grace the right hand. And there did the Kyng take the Maire by the hande and so departed. And so both the Kynges Grace and the Quene passid by the seid townes men and gave them alle thankes.'

Visitor Information

On account of the detailed records of the royal visit to Gloucester, in many ways, the city is a little gem for following in the footsteps of Anne Boleyn. Several sites are specifically mentioned as being visited by the king and queen, several of which still survive in various states of preservation. Sadly, due to the rise of nearby Cheltenham as a spa town in the eighteenth century, Gloucester has subsequently diminished in importance and wealth. Today, it is a rather frustrating mix of ugly modernism next door to some of the most beautiful medieval delights you could hope to see anywhere.

Perhaps the best way to approach this tour is to download, or send off for, a map of the city centre (http://www.thecityofgloucester.co.uk) in advance of your visit, and use this as your guide in conjunction with this book. Head for the junction of Northgate Street and St John's Lane to find yourself at the site of the medieval Northgate, the first landmark on Anne's journey through the medieval town. Walk up Northgate Street towards the Cross (crossroads), then turn right into Westgate Street. This street is wide today, but in Anne's time would have been divided into two narrow lanes with shops, churches and market buildings down the centre.

104. East Barsham Manor, 1937. Very little is known about the Boleyn house at Blickling in Norfolk; however, it's believed that it was a decorated manor house in the style of East Barsham, pictured here.

105. Engraving of Hever Castle by Thomas Dugdale, c. 1845. This nineteenth-century engraving shows the castle and its immediate environs prior to the Astors' extensive remodelling programme, which transformed the rustic surroundings of the castle into the manicured gardens that we see today. It is evocative of the earlier simplicity with which Anne would have been more familiar during her time spent at the family home.

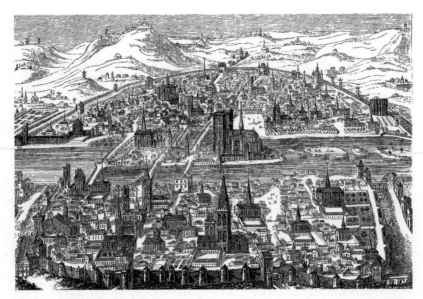

106. Engraving of Paris from 1607. This image shows the medieval city much as Anne would have known it, surrounded by the city walls. The top of the map is the north of the city, the bottom the south; west lies to the left and, therefore, the east to the right. The construction of the Enceinte Philippe Auguste was begun in 1190 and is clearly visible in this picture. One can clearly see the Île de la Cité in the centre of the Seine, which bisects Paris, Notre-Dame (toward the east) and Sainte Chapelle, part of the old Palais Royale (toward the west) of the island. The Île de la Cité, in turn, is connected to the right and left banks via bridges crowded with buildings. To the east of Paris is the bulky tower of La Bastille.

107. Le Palais des Tournelles, Paris. This building was so called because of the many small towers that adorned it. The Rue St-Antoine, which still exists today, runs along the right of the picture toward La Bastille in the background. It was here that Anne may have arrived in time to witness the celebrations of Mary Tudor's wedding to Louis XII, and she was almost certainly present when the king died at the palace on 1 January 1515.

108. Basilica of St-Denis, Paris by Félix Benoist. *Paris dans Sa Splendeur*, no. 94, 1861. Here we see the basilica from the north-east showing the apse and septentrional frontage of the abbey church.

34

109. A reconstruction of the Porte St-Denis. A magnificent medieval gateway that led directly from the heart of central Paris northwards toward the Abbey of St Denis.

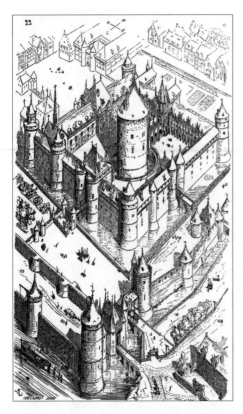

110. Reconstruction of the original, medieval palace of La Louvre, Paris. This was a splendid Gothic building whose central *grosse tour* was constructed by King Philippe Auguste in the twelfth century. In its time, the fortress was a huge and magnificent royal palace. It stood on the site of the current Musée Louvre, the later Renaissance palace that was commenced by Francis I in 1528, replacing its predecessor. The original building had long been abandoned as a royal residence by Anne's time but its outline would have dominated western Paris, easily visible from the Seine. Anne must have passed it on several occasions en route from central Paris to the Palais de St-Germain-en-Laye.

111. Engraving of the Château d'Amboise from the sixteenth century by Jacques Androuet du Cerceau. This is how the château would have appeared to Anne during her time at the French Court. A: *Grand-Salle*; B: Louis XII wing; C: St Hubert Chapel; D: Saint-Florentin Church; E: Logia of the Seven Virtues; F: Porte des Lions. The Château d'Amboise fell out of favour and into a gradual state of decay after it was all but abandoned as a royal residence following the untimely death of Henri II in 1559. It is now preserved and cared for by the Fondation Saint-Louis.

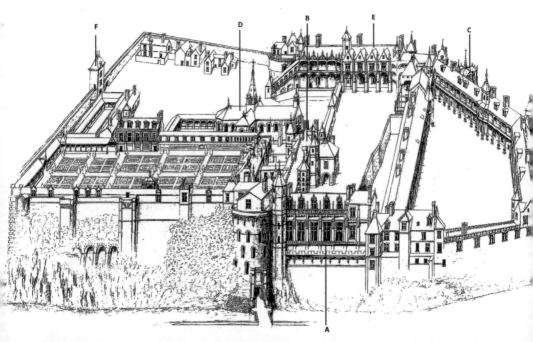

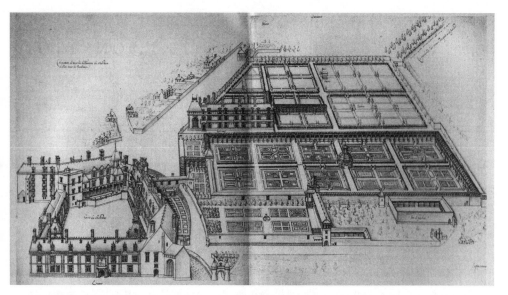

112. *The Château de Blois and Its Gardens* by Jacques Androuet du Cerceau, *c.* 1575. This sixteenth-century drawing shows the Château de Blois as Anne would have known it during her time growing up at the French court. We see the château arranged around a central *cour d'honneur*; the wing closest to us is the Louis XII wing, the original chapel forming part of the east wing (on the left). In the south is a wing that was demolished and later replaced by the Charles d'Orléans wing; the Francis I wing completes the irregular quadrangle to the west (the right-hand wing in this picture). The main château accessed the extensive gardens and leisure complex via the Galerie des Cerfs (Gallery of Stags), visible in this picture. We can well imagine Anne strolling in these gardens in attendance on Queen Claude or with other young maids of honour, such as her sister, Mary Boleyn.

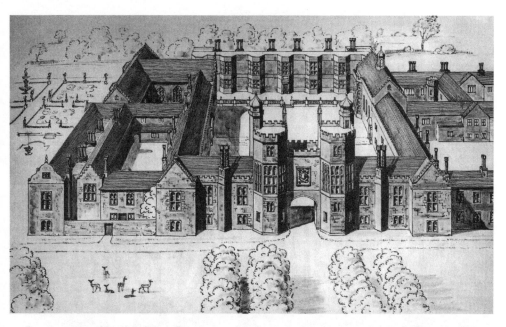

113. Reconstruction of Beaulieu Palace, Essex, as it may have appeared in the sixteenth century. The arms of Henry VIII can be seen adorning the grand gatehouse. The northern range, built by the Earl of Susex in around 1575, with its numerous chimneystacks probably housed the royal apartments. The Great Hall occupied part of the east range with the kitchens and associated offices to the east, and the entrance to the chapel stood opposite the hall in the west range. The palace was surrounded by large expanses of parkland, formal gardens, orchards and fishponds.

Above: 114. A view of the south-west of Richmond Palace, Surrey, as built by Henry VII, published in 1765. It stood on the south bank of the River Thames, on a site formerly occupied by the Palace of Sheen, constructed by Henry V and largely destroyed by fire in December 1497. Within its walls, the first and last monarchs of the Tudor dynasty took their final breaths.

Below: 115. *Windsor Castle* by Wenceslaus Hollar, unknown date (artist lived from 1607 to 1677). This engraving by Hollar shows Windsor Castle as Anne would have known it. Externally its form remains largely unchanged to this day, although the entrance to the upper ward on the south side has been changed and the courtyards, which were part of the royal apartments, were filled in to create additional rooms by later monarchs.

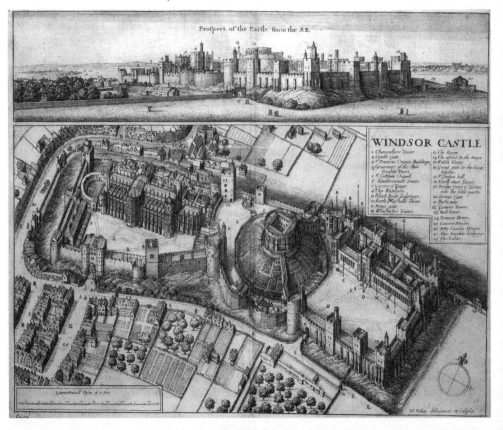

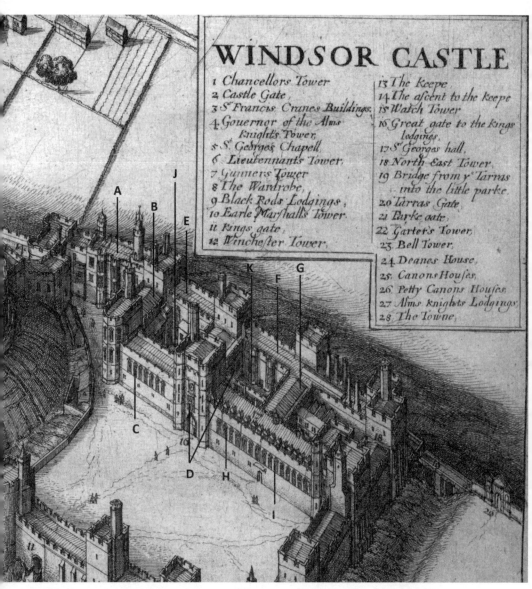

WINDSOR CASTLE

1 Chancellors Tower
2 Castle Gate
3 S.t Francis Cranes Buildings.
4 Gouernor of the Alms
   Knights Tower.
5 S.t Georges Chapell
6 Lieutennants Tower.
7 Gunners Tower
8 The Wardrobe,
9 Black Rods Lodgings,
10 Earle Marshalls Tower.
11 Kings gate.
12 Winchester Tower.

13 The Keepe,
14 The ascent to the keepe
15 Watch Tower
16 Great gate to the kings
   lodgings,
17 S.t Georges hall.
18 North-East Tower
19 Bridge from y.e Tarras
   into the little parke.
20 Tarras Gate,
21 Parke gate.
22 Garter's Tower,
23 Bell Tower,
24 Deanes House,
25 Canons Houses,
26 Petty Canons Houses
27 Alms knights Lodgings,
28 The Towne,

116. Detail of royal apartments at Windsor Castle, adapted from an engraving by Wenceslaus Hollar, unknown date (artist lived from 1607 to 1677). A: The Henry VII wing (Henry's library and other 'secret rooms'); B: Anne's bed and privy chamber; C: Anne's presence chamber; D: the queen's watching chamber; E: Henry's privy chambers; F: Henry's presence chamber (where Anne was ennobled as Marquess of Pembroke); G: the great watching chamber; H: the chapel; I: the Great Hall; J: brick court; K: inner court (now the Waterloo Chamber).

414.—Woodstock, as it appeared before 1714.

117. Woodstock Palace, Oxfordshire, as it appeared before 1714. The remains of Woodstock Palace as they appeared before being completely dismantled in the early eighteenth century. By the time of Henry VIII's ascension to the throne, Woodstock had been a favoured royal retreat for hundreds of years and one visited by most English monarchs, including Anne Boleyn. Woodstock was one of only a handful of royal residences that could house the entire court and so featured regularly on Henry VIII's summer and winter itineraries.

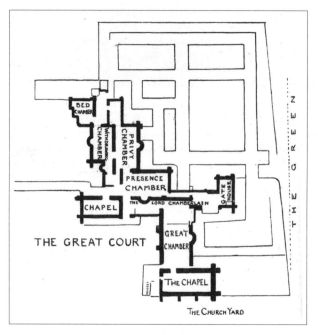

118. The floor plan of the Palace of Havering, Havering-atte-Bower. The palace that Anne inherited dated largely from the major building works of the thirteenth century. The layout was irregular, containing a Great Chamber (Great Hall), a presence chamber, royal apartments (privy chamber, withdrawing chamber, closet, and bedchamber), two chapels and various outbuildings. The royal apartments had views over the palace courtyard to the west and the gardens to the east.

119. Reconstruction of Havering Palace as it would have appeared in 1578. To the left of the picture is the public chapel, sited roughly where the current parish church is located. The building running perpendicular to it is the Great Hall, which leads on into the privy apartments overlooking the gardens in the foreground of the picture. Although Anne owned Havering, as far as we know, she visited only once briefly in October 1531.

120. Place House, St Stephens (Hackington), Canterbury. In the early part of the sixteenth century, Place House was the out-of-town residence of the archdeacons of Canterbury. It is traditionally believed that it was given to Sir Christopher Hales, Henry VIII's attorney general, after the Dissolution of the Monasteries. However, a letter to Thomas Cromwell, from 1532, clearly indicates that Sir Christopher is looking to take up a residence of some significance in St Stephen's, one controversial enough to require Cromwell's support. The old archbishop, William Warham, had died just weeks earlier in this property. Was this the house he was about to acquire?

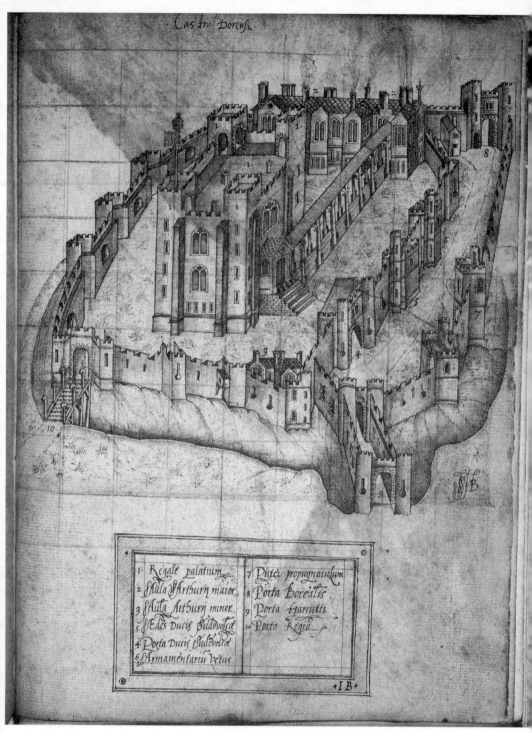

8

7

10

1 Regale palatium	7 Putei propugnaculum
2 Schola d'Arthurij maior	8 Porta Borealis
3 d'Aula Arthurij minor	9 Porta Harcurii
5 d'Edes Ducis Sudovolciæ	10 Porta Regia
4 Porta Ducis Sudovolciæ	
6 d'Armamentariū Vetus	

·I B·

121. *Dover Castle* by John Bereblock. Dated to the 1700s until recently, it is now thought that this engraving actually dates from the sixteenth century, making it relatively contemporary to Anne's time in Dover. The engraving shows clearly Henry II's massive central keep, or great tower, connected by a pentice (gallery) on ground-floor level to Arthur's Hall and the king's lodgings to the north (the top of the picture). We can see the splendour of these apartments with their many chimneys and large first-floor windows. Experts on the Tudor history of Dover Castle believe that, if the couple did lodge in the castle, they were likely to have stayed in this part of the building.

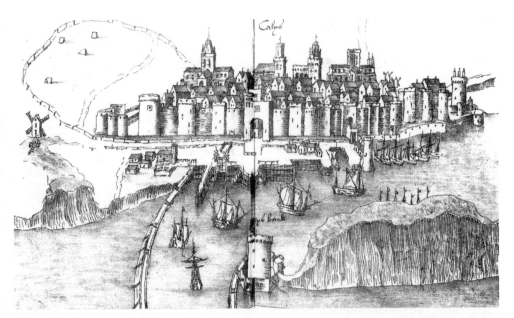

122. View of Calais in the time of Henry VIII in *Chronicle of Calais in the Reigns of Henry VII and Henry VIII*, John Gough Nichols (Ed.). In this contemporary drawing of sixteenth-century Calais, the port is clearly visible, defended by the Rysbank Fort whose remains are still extant at the entrance to Calais's harbour. The fortifications of the town are also clearly visible, with the main Lantern Gate positioned centrally. Through this gateway, Anne and Henry made their ceremonial entry into the town, accompanied by a great procession of powerful merchants and nobles. On the skyline we can see (from left to right), the church of St Mary (still standing today), the Town Hall, the Staple Hall and on the far right St Nicolas's Church.

123. Hôtel de Guise, Calais, *c.* 1925. Prior to the widespread destruction of Calais by devastating bombing in the Second World War, the main gateway to the Staple Inn, in the south of the town, was still standing, although it had clearly lost some of its former glory. It was considered one of the most splendid lodgings in Tudor Calais. It was here that, in 1532, Francis I was lodged during his stay in the town, and here that Anne and her six ladies famously danced at a masque given in the French king's honour. Today the northern end of the Rue Marie Tudor marks the spot of this now lost building.

124. Site of the Scaffold on Tower Hill, *c.* 1900. This photograph shows the site of the scaffold on Tower Hill, as it appeared before 1901. George Boleyn, Henry Norris, Francis Weston, William Brereton and Mark Smeaton were executed on, or near, this spot on 17 May 1536.

125. Engraving of Old St Paul's Cathedral. Two pageants were held in Anne's honour in the environs of St Paul's Cathedral during her coronation procession; one by St Paul's Gate, the other in the churchyard in front of the cathedral. Anne was reminded that through her unborn child 'there shall be a golden world unto the people', and three elaborately dressed women waited below an empty throne, the central figure holding aloft the cheerful message, 'come my love, thou shalt be crowned'.

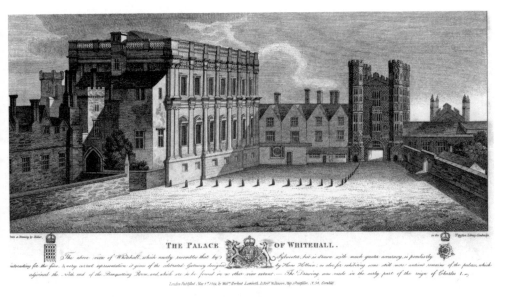

126. *The Palace of Whitehall and King Street, Westminster.* This engraving is from a seventeenth-century drawing by Wenceslaus Hollar. We are looking southward down the wide thoroughfare that was King Street. The beautifully executed Holbein Gate, where Anne and Henry were reputedly married, is shown in glorious detail. Beyond the gateway to the right are the four turrets of one of the tennis courts at Whitehall. The buildings to the left of the Holbein Gate made up part of the king's privy gallery, while the seventeenth-century banqueting house replaced an earlier version. On the far left is the original Tudor gatehouse marking the main entrance to the palace complex. Anne would have passed down King Street after her ceremonial entry into the City from the Tower of London prior to her Coronation on 1 June 1533.

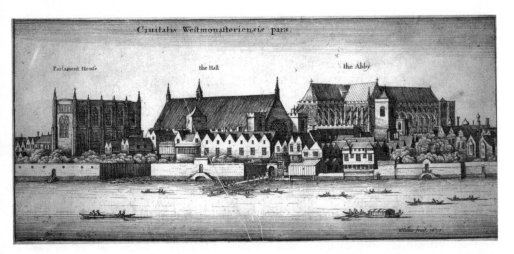

127. *The City of Westminster from the River* by Wenceslaus Hollar (1647). Although executed over 100 years after Anne's death, this engraving shows the City of Westminster as Anne would have known it. In the foreground are the king's steps, used to access Westminster from the river. In the background to the right is the Collegiate Church of St Peter in Westminster (Westminster Abbey), the steeply pitched roof of Westminster Hall is in the centre of the picture and the old St. Stephen's Chapel, part of the original Palace of Westminster, is to the left.

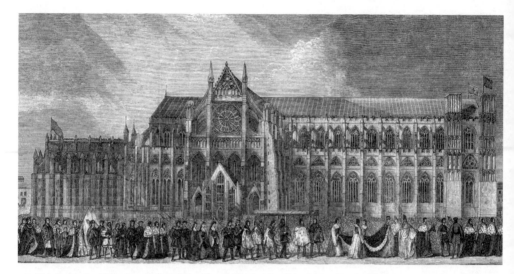

128. *The Coronation Procession of Anne Boleyn* (originally from a drawing by David Roberts in the Tyrrell Collection 1872–8). Here we see Anne in a nineteenth-century engraving walking in procession toward the great west doors of Westminster Abbey for her Coronation on Whit Sunday, 1 June 1533. A figure representative of Charles Brandon, Duke of Suffolk, walks directly in front of Anne, holding before him the crown of St Edward the Confessor. On either side of her are the bishops of London and Winchester. Anne wears her ceremonial robes including a purple velvet gown furred with ermine, set against a kirtle fashioned from cloth of gold. However, this later representation is missing the canopy of cloth of gold held above her head, carried by the four wardens of the Cinque Ports.

129. *Westminster Hall* by Wenceslaus Hollar (unknown date; author lived 1607–77). This engraving gives us a fabulously detailed view of the Outer or Old Palace Yard, part of the medieval Palace of Westminster. Access was either from the river via the king's steps, or through the gateway seen at the far right-hand corner of the yard. This great gate joined with the bottom of King Street, which ran past Whitehall Palace, and it also linked through to the area surrounding Westminster Abbey. Anne would have passed under this gateway coming from the City before her Coronation on 31 May 1533, and when she walked in procession to and from the abbey the following day. Westminster Hall can be seen on the left of the picture with its pitched roof, flanked by two square towers. It was here that Anne was received with great pomp after her ceremonial entry from the City of London, and where she presided over her coronation banquet the following day, Whit Sunday, 1 June.

130. The Coronation Chair. This was made on the orders of King Edward I to house the Stone of Scone. St Edward's Chair, or the coronation chair, as it has colloquially become known, has been used at every coronation since the early fourteenth century, with the exceptions of Queens Mary I and II. As such, it is a rare example of a piece of furniture that we know Anne would have used during her lifetime.

A VIEW OF St JAMES'S PALACE and WESTMINSTER ABBEY.
From the Village of Charing.

Above: 131. A view of St James's Palace and Westminster Abbey from the village of Charing. This engraving shows the palace's once-rural location, surrounded by open fields. The lofty roofs of Westminster Abbey and Hall lie due south on higher ground. We can see an uninterrupted view over Westminster and St James's Park and it is clear that, in its time, St James's Palace was indeed a stately residence, a country seat that dominated the surrounding landscape.

Below: 132. Guildford Manor House, Guildford. Guildford Manor House, Guildford, Surrey. An artist's impression of how the royal manor house, or hunting lodge, may have looked during the fifteenth and sixteenth centuries. The manor incorporated the following rooms: a hall, four chambers, a chapel, the king's and queen's dining chambers, privy chambers and bedchambers, and a separate kitchen.

133. *The South East View of Ewelme Palace, Oxfordshire, c. 1727.* This drawing is a copy of an engraving made by Samuel and Nathaniel Buck, showing the south-east view of the surviving range of Ewelme Palace, as it appeared before its partial demolition.

134. Gloucester from the west, by Kip, *c.* 1725. Henry and Anne stayed in Gloucester as guests of Abbot Parker for seven days from 31 July to 7 August 1535. Although drawn some 200 years later, this image shows Gloucester prior to the Industrial Revolution and therefore largely as Anne would have known it. Note that the city lies in the heart of the Severn Valley, surrounded by gentle rolling hills, covered in lush countryside. Here we are looking toward Gloucester from the west, with the cathedral on the left of the picture. Here Anne lodged with Henry, most probably in the abbot's lodgings.

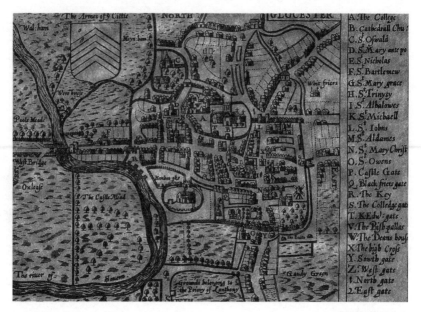

Legend (right side of map):

A. The College
B. Cathedrall Chu[rch]
C. S. Ofwald
D. S. Mary ante po[rt]
E. S. Nicholas
F. S. Bartlemew
G. S. Mary grace
H. S. Trinyty
I. S. Alhalowes
K. S. Michaell
L. S. Iohns
M. S. Aldames
N. S. Mary Chrift
O. S. Owens
P. Caftle Gate
Q. Black friers gate
R. The Key
S. The Colledge gate
T. K.Edw: gate
V. The Bifh-pallas
W. The Deans houf[e]
X. The high Crofs
Y. Sowth gate
Z. Weft gate
1. North gate
2. Eaft gate

135. Map of the town of Gloucester. On their formal entry into the town on 31 July 1535, Anne and Henry passed by White Friars, shown in the upper right-hand corner; through North Gate (1); along Northgate Street to the High Cross (X); westwards, past the church of St Mary's Grace (G); before turning northwards through St Edward's Gate (T) and finally reaching the abbey (B).

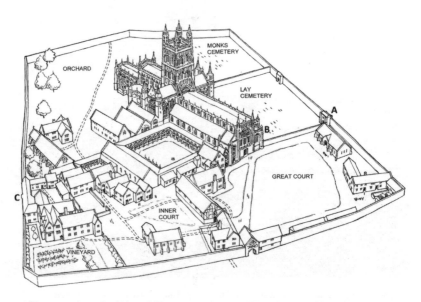

136. This image shows the Abbey of Gloucester as Anne would have known it. From the *Corporation of Gloucester Records* we know that they entered through St Edward's Gate (A); were officially welcomed by Abbot Parker at the South Porch (B, just out of view, on the far side of the abbey church) and most probably lodged at the abbot's lodgings by the vineyard (C).

137. *The South East View of Berkeley Castle in the County of Gloucestershire,* Samuel and Nathaniel Buck, 1732. At the time of Anne's visit, Berkeley Castle was in Crown hands. The couple probably lodged in the main privy apartments, shown here in the foreground of the picture. Where the south-facing wing (left) joins the east-facing wing (right), was the chapel (now the morning room). This was accessed up a flight of stairs via the Great Hall in the east wing and led on into the private apartments in the south. The earlier medieval keep is in the centre background, as is the parish church of St Mary (background left).

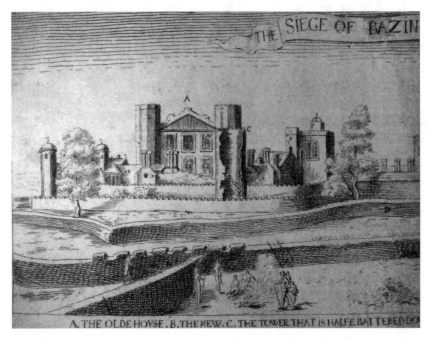

138. The Ruins of Basing House. Detail from a seventeenth century etching showing 'The Olde House' in ruins following the siege of Basing House. The view is from the south and shows the remains of the house that would have been known to Anne during her visit as part of the 1535 progress. Even in ruins, we can see the grandeur of the sixteenth century house, which in its time was compared with Hampton Court.

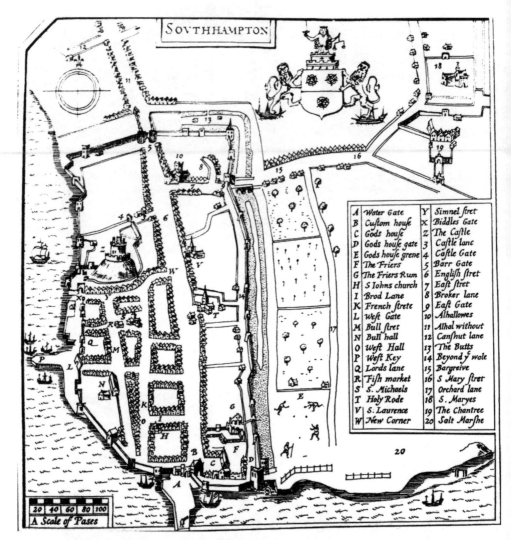

139. Map of Tudor Southampton, taken from John Speed's map of the Isle of Wight, 1611. This image shows the medieval town of Southampton as Anne would have known it. Bargate (5) is the main entrance from the north, through which Anne and Henry must have passed on their way from Winchester. This leads into the broad, main street, known as English Street (6), which leads to Castle Street (3). The castle, where Anne and Henry are thought to have stayed, is clearly visible. Tudor House was located on Bull Street (M), almost opposite St Michael's church (S).

Eventually turn right into College Street, originally St Edward's Lane, leading to the remains of St Edward's Gate at the entrance to the cathedral precinct. Once inside the precinct you are in the old abbey yard. The main south porch where Anne and Henry dismounted their horses, kneeled upon cushions and kissed the cross is directly in front of you. It is rare indeed to be able to pinpoint Anne to such a specific location. So, pause a while and imagine the ceremony in all its reverential splendour. From here, head into the cathedral. Follow in Anne's footsteps to the high altar, but do also take your time to enjoy the beauty of the old abbey church and its many treasures, including the chantry tomb of Bishop Parker (who played host to the royal couple during their stay in Gloucester), which can be found next to the tomb of Edward II. Also do not miss the cloisters, which are some of the best preserved medieval cloisters to be found anywhere in the country.

Here you have a chance to take a break at the cathedral's café, or enjoy a packed lunch in the peaceful setting of the cloister gardens.

Before you leave the vicinity of the cathedral, wander through the precincts under medieval gateways toward the north-west corner and the site of the modern-day King School. Here, fronting on to Pitt Street, is the abbey wall, the only remaining vestige of the abbot's lodgings, where Anne and Henry once enjoyed Abbot Parker's hospitality.

Finally, make your way back out onto Westgate Street up towards the Cross (crossroads) and on into Eastgate Street. Just adjacent to the heinous modern-day Eastgate shopping centre, the turret of part of the old medieval East Gate is visible underground on your right. Now is the time to allow the twenty-first century to melt away and instead conjure up in your mind torch-bearers greeting the royal party as they arrived back in the town from a hard day's hunting in the countryside surrounding Gloucester.

Visiting Gloucester's Environs

All the following locations are within easy reach of each other if you have a car, and are situated in stunning locations to the east, south-east and south of Gloucester, among some of the most picturesque countryside in England. It would be well worth booking into a local bed and breakfast and using that as your base to explore Gloucester and the other locations included here in this entry.

Prinknash Abbey (pronounced *Pinnash*) has a café and small bookshop, selling light refreshments, monastic gifts and books. It is well signposted from the road. The building is currently in use as a working monastery, so is inaccessible to the general public, but can be seen at a distance from a drive that runs down to a modern-day church and the café/shop. The views over Gloucester from this point are also worth stopping to enjoy. Alternatively, carry on along the road into Painswick until you see signs for Painswick Beacon pointing to the right. There is ample parking and it is a great area for exercising dogs. Take a stroll up to the old hill fort, which is now part of Painswick Golf Club, and enjoy the stunning view. Note the landscape is hilly and requires at least some level of physical fitness. Finally, if you are an adult male, you are welcome to stay for periods of retreat at Prinknash as part of the abbey's Benedictine rule of hospitality. Please visit the abbey website for further details: http://www.prinknashabbey.org/Index.htm.

Postcode for Prinknash Abbey: GL4 8EX.

The Lodge at Painswick is in private hands and is therefore not open to the public. However, you can view it from the road. There are two roads signposted on the left as you descend into Painswick from the north. Take the second exit, just before the village. About a mile or two along the road, you will find the house opposite a lane which is a no through road. The Lodge is set back along a tree-lined drive, identifiable by the house name Painswick Lodge, helpfully displayed at the entrance to the drive.

Postcode for the Lodge at Painswick: GL6 6UB.

Do remember to visit the picturesque village church of St Mary in nearby Painswick to see the tomb commemorating the last resting place of Sir William Kingston, Anne's gaoler, who died in Painswick in 1540. This tomb was desecrated during the Civil War, effigies (probably of Sir William and Lady Kingston) were removed, along with the brass plaques, whose outline can still be seen on the wall behind the figures that now adorn the tomb.

If you wish to follow in Anne's footsteps of Tuesday 3 August 1535, then head toward Brockworth Court, lying to the west of Gloucester. The manor is a little gem and not to be missed. It is Grade I listed, and dendrochronology has dated some of the timbers of the building back to the fifteenth century. Although the original house has been remodelled over the centuries, for example with the loss of the Great Hall, many medieval and Tudor architectural delights are preserved.

The owners, Tim and Bridget Wiltshire, bought the house in 1997, when it was in some state of disrepair. They have lovingly poured themselves into restoring the building and preserving its wonderful history for future generations to enjoy. The house is privately owned and not generally opened to the public. However, if you wish to visit, you can do so by contacting Tim Wiltshire on timwiltshire@hotmail.co.uk.

Postcode for Brockworth Court: GL3 4QU.

Afterwards, continue your journey to the tiny and almost forgotten hamlet of Coberley, a few miles south of Cheltenham. Once upon a time, a thriving village known to kings and princes served Coberley Hall, which had been built by Roger de Berkeley II in the twelfth century. The hall was lost in the eighteenth century, but part of the gatehouse, outer courtyard surrounded by vestiges of the service buildings, church and crenellated walls survive to hint at its more illustrious past.

You need to head a quarter of a mile east out of the village to find the site of the hall and its adjacent church. There is a signpost to Coberley Church showing the gated access. Only pedestrian access is possible through the private grounds of Coberley Court and dogs are not welcome. Notice the solid buttresses on the outer walls and grand gateway, now much-remodelled, which once led into an inner courtyard. Through the gate you will get a sense of this arrangement; a central courtyard is now laid to lawn, but an array of stone outbuildings leaves the visitor with the impression that this area was once a hive of activity.

Carry on forward passing through the gate into the churchyard of St Giles. The church has Norman origins, but sadly was much remodelled during the Victorian era. However, as you walk along the path you will see rather impressive, battlemented walls on your left and ahead of you. These walls are a sure sign of the magnificent building that once stood in a now-empty field to the south of the church. A blocked-up doorway hewn into the wall would have once been used by the family of the house to access the church from its south side, while villagers would enter from the west.

It is unlikely that you will stay too long in Coberley, so perhaps plan to spend most of your time in the area enjoying the delights of Miserden village and Misarden Park (yes, the spelling is different), lying roughly 3 miles to the south.

Postcode for St Giles church, Coberley: GL53 9RA.

Miserden village is a wonderful place to linger for a while. Buried deep in the Cotswold countryside it is less overrun than some of the other larger, better-known villages and towns in the region. On a lovely sunny day, as it was when the authors visited, there can be few more beautiful places to be in England. A profusion of blossom and early summer flowers set against emerald green lawns and azure blue skies made it easy to see why Sir William Kingston chose Miserden as one of his country residences. Although the Tudor house is gone, replaced by a later Jacobean building of still considerable charm, the steep wooded valleys and open fields must have made perfect hunting terrain to be enjoyed by the king and his consort.

If you enjoy walking, do make sure you walk the well-marked paths that take you through the park, some with stunning views of the house. It is a great place to sit by the lake or enjoy a picnic if the weather is fine. Although do not worry; there is also a fine pub (very popular) in the village, called the Carpenter's Arms, where you can take refreshment should you so wish! Although the house in Misarden Park is not open to the public, its renowned gardens are. You can visit them on Tuesdays, Wednesdays and Thursdays from April to end of September from 10.00 a.m. to 4.30 p.m.

For further information on opening times, group visits and entry charges, please contact the Miserden Estate Office via their website at http://www.misardenpark.co.uk. Telephone number: +44 (0)1285 821303.

Postcode for Misarden Park: GL6 7JA

The Vineyard at Over

There is nothing to see of the old manor house above ground today. Although apparently the site of the moat remains well marked in earthworks that are clearly visible to the naked eye, when the authors visited it was impossible to gain access. The best we could do was view the back of the site from a renovated waterway, accessed from the adjacent Wharf House Restaurant. On account of this, it is difficult to recommend visiting this site, but we include it here for completeness.

Postcode for Over: GL2 8BY.

Leonard Stanley, Gloucestershire

How our seid Soveraign Lorde and Kyng and the Quene also, departed from Gloucester the VIIth of August, then next folowyng at after none [noon], and that nygth laye at Leonard Stanley, and on the morowe thens towards Barkeley.

Corporation of Gloucester Records

The *Corporation of Gloucester Records* clearly state that Henry and Anne broke their journey to Berkeley Castle by lodging for one afternoon and night, on 7 August, at the small village of Leonard Stanley, 10 miles or so directly south of Gloucester. Even in 1640, only eight houses 'of two to six bays' and five houses 'of two to four spaces' were mentioned in the village. It is most likely that this location was chosen as an overnight lodging on account of a small Benedictine cell affiliated to the Abbey of St Peter at Gloucester that was located in the village. *Victoria County History* (British History Online) states that

> In 1535 the clear yearly value of the cell was £106 17s. Its possessions included rents in the village of Stanley St. Leonard, in Slimbridge, Stinchcombe, Easton Grey and elsewhere, the manor of Lorwing, the rectories of Cam, Arlingham, Coaley, Stanley St. Leonard and other tithes and pensions. At that time there were only three monks at the priory.

The village of Leonard Stanley is situated in a broad valley and is a typical, small English village, with streets converging upon the parish church and local pub, both situated next to what was probably once a small village green. The Street, which still exists today, was once the medieval high street, along which a few timber-framed and stone-built houses were clustered. At the end of the street was the priory of Stanley St Leonard, which had been founded in or around 1131 by the powerful Roger de Berkeley II (see also Coberley in the entry for Gloucester). The church, with its oversized tower, immediately hints that there is more to the building's history than might meet the eye. Indeed, it was this church that once served both the parish and the monastic cell of the priory.

It is most likely that the royal couple lodged at the priory or in the adjacent house belonging to it, which stood to the west of the priory site, but which has long since disappeared. This property was noted to be in existence in both 1287 and 1486, and seems to have been of some significance, as there were indications of a moat visible as late as 1967. This former house became the manor house in 1738, and was noted to have had nineteen hearths in 1672.

At the time of the visit, the priory consisted of a priory church; a small, eleventh-century single-celled chapel; a pond; a tithe barn (all still evident); cloisters and a number of conventual buildings. However, as the latter buildings have been levelled, the exact layout of the priory in its heyday is not known.

What is known is that the single-celled Saxon chapel, which is thought to predate the later priory church of St Swithun, was initially the main place of worship for both monks and villagers. Once the priory was expanded, with the addition of the later church, it served as a guest and private chapel for the prior. Local legend says that it was there that Prior John Rodley received his sovereign lord and lady upon their arrival; no doubt a Mass was heard, as would be customary. It is an incredible survivor, which has long since been used as a barn and currently stands in a precarious state of repair, although thankfully the owners of Priory Farm have a grant from English Heritage to repair the worst of the decay.

After their reception, Henry and Anne would have been escorted to their lodgings. Most often the king and queen would occupy the residence of the abbot or prior, although in this instance, it is also unclear as to where Prior Rodley maintained his household. Could it have been in the nearby house that would later become the manor?

Anne left the priory with Henry the following morning. The wheels of Cromwell's drive to dissolve the monasteries were turning, and would see the prior appear before the chancellor and council of the Court of Augmentations on 16 June 1536, upon pain of a fine of 500 marks. On 11 June 1538, Henry VIII sent an imperative request to the abbot and convent of Gloucester to recall the monks from Stanley St Leonard and the lease of the priory was granted to Sir William Kingston. The foundation was dissolved in 1538, after which the site became a farm, and the buildings were converted for use as farm buildings.

Visitor Information

Thankfully for us, there are a number of survivors from the time of Anne's visit; buildings that have endured, to one extent or another, the weathering of time. The best-preserved of these is the priory church. A wonderful Norman font stands immediately outside the entrance and inside additional, original Norman stonework remains, including doorways and windows in the nave and some wonderful embellishments on a number of stone pillars.

Most of the conventual buildings to the south of the church have been destroyed but a vault beneath the north end of Priory Farm may have formed a portion of the vanished part. On the south side of the church, you can still see the doorway that led into the small cloister, while the course of stone along the outer wall of the nave and south transept, called the weather-moulding, shows where the cloister roof would have met the church. Corbels (projecting stones) on the outer wall of the south transept would have supported the roof timbers of this same structure. The medieval tithe barn with its decorated gable window still remains, lying to the south of the pond.

The real gem for us is the ruined Saxon chapel, lying immediately south-west of the church. Today, this looks more like a small barn than a church, through its use as such over countless generations. However, if local legend is correct, in this small space Anne was received alongside her husband, no doubt with hearty words of thanks for the prior's hospitality.

During our visit, we were similarly received by the current owners of Priory Farm, Jo and David Pullin, who happen to run holiday cottages on-site. Over the large kitchen table, we poured over all the surveys of the buildings and surrounding land done by county archaeologists. We were interested in locating the site of the lost manor house, as we suspected that this is where Anne and Henry would have been lodged for the night. To our delight, the paperwork confirmed that in the adjacent field directly to the west of the site, on the far side of the pond, there was evidence of a moat and a pre-existing house. We dutifully tramped out over a wet field to stand on the spot, although sadly today it is difficult to even make out the earthworks of a moat.

Leonard Stanley is a location almost lost to all but a handful of local people. However, visiting is worth the effort, as enough remains to conjure up how the priory might have looked during Anne's fleeting visit. If you are intending to visit the site, which, with the exception of the parish church, lies on private land belonging to Priory Farm, do call ahead out of politeness. Jo and David, the landowners, are rightly very proud of the history and are keen to share it, but they request that you prearrange any visit by calling + 44 (0)1453 298 767 or emailing davidpullin@tiscali.co.uk.

If you are planning to visit a number of locations in the area, why not think of lodging at Leonard Stanley, just as Anne did. The website for the Priory Farm Cottages is http://www.prioryfarmholidays.com/index.html. Other locations within the vicinity are Gloucester (and its environs), Berkeley and Thornbury Castle.

Postcode for Leonard Stanley: GL10 3NP.

Berkeley Castle, Gloucestershire

Mark the year and mark the night,
When Severn shall re-echo with affright,
The shrieks of death through Berkeley's roof that ring,
Shrieks of an agonizing king.

> Gray's Bard referring to the murder of Edward II at Berkeley Castle

After resting at the priory of Leonard Stanley, we can imagine the royal party beginning to snake its way across the English countryside, Henry and Anne riding along amid a patchwork of golden fields, crops ripened by the late summer sun, while the sound of nature's symphony filled the air as skylarks warbled above them on the wing.

On 8 August, Anne and Henry rode into the cool shadows cast by Berkeley Castle's gatehouse and took up residence in a medieval fortress that Leland would later rather disparagingly label in his itinerary as 'no great thinge'. It was the first and last time that Henry and Anne would visit Berkeley, but clearly they were determined to enjoy its pleasant charms, as provision had been made in the 'geists' for them to stay there for the entire week. On 9 August there is confirmation that the royal party are lodged at Berkeley on account of the opening line of the following letter, written by Thomas Thacker to Cromwell: 'This Wednesday, 11 Aug., I received your letter dated Berkley Herons, the 9th.'

Cromwell was clearly keeping up a stream of letters for, in a second letter dated 18 August, Sir William Fitzwilliam made a reply to a letter also received from Master Secretary saying, 'I received at Dover your kind letter, dated Barkley Herons, the 11th.' Note: 'Barkley Herons' is probably a corruption of Berkeley Harness, which is the ancient name for the estate.

Thomas Cromwell was obviously still close to the king's side and from the profusion of letters recorded in *Letters and Papers* that continue through the first half of the progress, we can see the Master Secretary busily overseeing the 'visitations' already being made to a number of monastic houses. Yet, perhaps this stay at Berkeley was even sweeter for Cromwell, for at the time he was the castle's constable, receiving income from its lands; a position he was to retain until his execution in 1540.

A Brief History

Berkeley Castle had fallen into Crown hands back in 1492 as a result of a bargain struck between William, Viscount Berkeley, and Henry VII. Viscount Berkeley received a marquessate and title of Earl Marshal of England, while Henry VII would inherit Berkeley Castle upon the marquess's death. Thus, when Anne and Henry visited, the castle belonged to the king.

In appearance Berkeley did not dominate the local town as did some of the mightier Norman fortresses, such as Ludlow or Dover. Instead, the less political Berkeleys had focused on residential development within a pre-existing buttressed curtilage. In fact, the castle is well screened by the church and trees, such that its full glory can only be appreciated from the south, across the marshy meadows of the diminutive Avon River.

The Privy Apartments at Berkeley Castle

Berkeley Castle sits perched on a plateau that overlooks fields stretching away below it. Built on a typical Norman motte and bailey design in the eleventh, twelfth and fourteenth centuries, it is also highly distinctive, constructed from local pink, grey and yellow Severn sandstone, with its roofs mainly fashioned in Cotswold stone, slate or lead. It has been described as being in an 'original and good state of preservation' and one of the 'supreme residential survivals of the fourteenth century', retaining most of its original features down to doors, arrow slits and windows and even iron catches. The interiors remained largely unaltered from the sixteenth century until the 1920s, when the 8th Earl of Berkeley modernised and extensively altered the internal decor, installing many artefacts from elsewhere.

However, distinctive as it might be, the castle is also austere in its presence. Perhaps it cannot shake off the legacy of royal murder referred to in the quote above, an event for which the castle is probably best known in English history, when Edward II most likely suffered an ignominious end at the hands of his captors within the walls of the Norman keep.

On account of its exceptional state of preservation, the rooms used by Henry and Anne still survive in the 'great suite' that fronts the south-west façade of the building, although David Smith, chief archivist at Berkeley, adds a note of caution:

> The layout of the main apartments of the castle, as they were in the time of the visit, is still visible, i.e. the Great Hall, the chapel (now the Morning Room) and large parts of the keep, some of which are now in the private wing. But the interiors have been altered in the intervening centuries, and hardly any of the furniture dates from before about 1660.

However, in Emery's *Greater Medieval Houses of England and Wales, Volume III* a description is given of how the privy apartments would have been accessed from Edward III's Great Hall, allowing us to imagine more clearly the layout of the rooms which would have greeted Anne upon her stay at Berkeley:

> Access from the hall dais to the residential range is by a 1925 replacement Berkeley arch. It opened into a stair bay, presumably rectangular to balance the entry porch, but rebuilt in 1637 when the present stair was inserted ... In its early form, the stair would have risen to a rectangular ante-chamber above the ground-floor lobby, possibly with a ribbed ceiling. This was the prelude to the three first-floor family apartments, the chapel at the angle, and the great or outer chamber followed by the inner chamber filling the remainder of the courtyard range.

Today, we also leave the Great Hall from the high end, passing up the later staircase, as described in the quote above. At the top of the stair, we reach a lobby with the entrance to the chapel on your left. This was not the original entrance; that would have been at the other end of the chapel – it was swapped round by the 8th Earl of Berkeley in the early twentieth century.

What is of note here is the sumptuous wall decoration. The authors have heard two versions of a story about its origins, both of interest to us. The first is that the wall hangings were made for Anne and Henry's bedroom, but somehow found their way to Berkeley. Did the royal couple leave them behind here after their visit? The other is that they once adorned the royal apartments in Henry's temporary palace at the Field of Cloth of Gold. Whichever version is true, they are clearly of exceptionally high status, fit for a king, and have been dated to be around 500 years old.

Next, head into the fourteenth-century private chapel; this has been described as 'one of the most gloriously preserved in England'. Sadly, the 8th earl converted the chapel to a morning room by reversing the entry to the opposite end of the chamber, inserting a fifteenth-century French doorway, fireplace and overmantel, and removing the outstanding private pew to the adjacent room. However, its character is still recognisable with is generous proportions, 39 feet by 23 feet, with an apse located at its east end. The braces and ribs retain early painted decoration with an inscription added by John Trevisa, chaplain of the castle between 1379 and 1402. This is certainly something Anne would have read for herself. Emery states that 'the text is that of a thirteenth-century Anglo-French manuscript of the Apocalypse, the only surviving example of such an extended medieval Bible translation on a ceiling in France or England'.

However, we have to admit that we found it difficult to make out this inscription ourselves, the paintwork is so faded.

Beyond the chapel, we access the two delightful privy apartment rooms, which are fourteenth-century in their rectangular shaping. Intercommunication between the two rooms was by the charming open-sided turret lobby spanning the courtyard end of the partition wall (now containing a statue of the Madonna and Child), with a garderobe located in the opposite corner. These rooms are wonderfully warm and welcoming. It is easy to imagine the king and queen whiling away the hours at Berkeley in the evenings, playing cards or dice. In our minds' eyes, we might see Anne reading one of her many devotional texts in front of the window, facing out across the fields below.

In accordance with the usual layout of other royal residences, it is highly likely that the first room functioned as a privy/dining chamber, with the second as a bedroom. Make sure you take note of the wooden gallery that was once the privy gallery in the chapel. Undoubtedly, Anne would have attended Mass on a regular basis during her stay at the castle, looking down on the body of the church from this elevated position.

Events at Berkeley

Although the archives for the Berkeley family are extensive, very few records remain from the sixty-year period when the castle was in Crown hands. Thus, frustratingly, we have no record of what came to pass during the six or so days that Anne and Henry stayed there. No doubt they were hawking in the glorious countryside of southern

Gloucestershire, while evenings were filled with gambling, conversation, music and dance.

Sir William Paulet's household accounts confirm that on Saturday 14 August the court moved on to the beautiful and historic castle of Thornbury.

Visitor Information
For opening times and other visitor information, please visit the Berkeley Castle website at http://www.berkeley-castle.com/visit.php. Telephone number: + 44 (0) 1453 810332.
   Postcode for Berkeley Castle: GL13 9BQ.

Thornbury Castle, Gloucestershire

> The house or Castle of Thornbury aforesaid, is standing, and being within two miles of the river Seaverne which runeth on the north thereof, and is bounded and adjoyned unto the Church-yard of the Parish Church of Thornbury aforesaid on the south part; the Park there, called New Park on the North and East part; and one small parcel of ground called the Petties, on the West part.
>
> Extract from a survey of Thornbury made in the reign of James I

Thornbury Castle, on the edge of the Cotswolds in South Gloucestershire, is the only Tudor castle to be opened as a luxury hotel and as such offers guests the unique opportunity of staying in rooms where royalty and nobility sought shelter and hospitality hundreds of years ago.

A Brief History of Thornbury
In July 1510 Edward Stafford, 3rd Duke of Buckingham, obtained a licence to crenellate his large double-courtyard mansion built on the site of an earlier manor house at Thornbury. The licence also allowed him to enclose a park of 1,000 acres, extended in 1517 by a further 500.

   He was the eldest son of Henry Stafford, 2nd Duke of Buckingham, and Katherine Woodville and was, through his mother, a nephew of King Edward IV and, on his father's side, descended from the Plantagenet Prince Thomas of Woodstock, son of Edward III. After his father's death, his mother, Katherine, married Jasper Tudor, King Henry VII's uncle, and they resided together at Thornbury where Jasper died in 1495.

Buckingham's Unfinished Palace
Thornbury was to be one of the most magnificent building projects of the time, comparable only with Thomas Wolsey's Hampton Court Palace and inspired by contemporary royal palaces like Richmond. It intended to serve not as a fortress, but rather as a majestic and comfortable family home, although it could certainly have been defended if necessary.

   Unfortunately, only part of the duke's grand plans for his new house were realised before his distant cousin, King Henry VIII, ordered his execution for alleged treason in 1521. Following the duke's demise, King Henry VIII confiscated the castle and stayed with Anne at Thornbury from 14 August 1535 until their departure for Acton Court on 22 August.

On arrival, the royal party would have entered the spacious base court covering almost 2½ acres through an imposing gatehouse in the south, protected by a portcullis and flanking towers, with the great stable likely occupying the remainder of this range. Directly ahead would have stood the remains of Buckingham's north gate and the partially completed north lodgings and to the left, the west lodgings, both originally intended to house servants and men-at-arms, but all now lying abandoned.

Their attention would have no doubt been drawn to the unfinished yet still impressive west front of the castle. Only the south-western tower and adjacent turret were completed as per the original plan, the remaining buildings only rising to two storeys, rather than the intended four. Had Buckingham's design been realised, the west front would have consisted of a central gatehouse four storeys high, flanked by two four-storey towers and two intermediate turrets.

Passing through the gatehouse, decorated with Buckingham's coat of arms, into the smaller inner court constructed of fine ashlar, Henry may have noted the scrolled inscription above the gateway: 'Thys Gate was begon in the yere of owre Lorde Gode MCCCCCXI (1511) the ii yere of the reyne of Kynge Henri the viii by me Edw. Duc. of Bukkyngah' Erlle of Herforde Stafforde ande Northampto': Dorene savant.'

The Duke's motto, 'Dorene savant', means 'from now on, henceforth or hereafter' and was interpreted by some as signifying his ambition for the throne.

Opposite the inner gateway stood the east range dominated by the Great Hall, behind which stood a chapel and a range of lodgings probably erected by Jasper Tudor. The chapel consisted of an outer chapel where the household could stand to hear the services, and at a higher level were two rooms, each containing a fireplace, where the duke and duchess once sat to hear the Mass. These buildings were part of the old manor house but had been retained and incorporated into Buckingham's new building.

On the ground floor of the double-storey north range were the larders, bakehouse, boiling house, the great kitchen and privy kitchen with lodgings above, and to the south were the main apartments. This range originally housed Buckingham's own lavish suite on the upper floor, and on the ground floor those of his wife, Eleanor Percy, Duchess of Buckingham, whose nephew, Henry Percy, 6th Earl of Northumberland, was at one time romantically linked to Anne. The stacked lodgings consisted of three large chambers in the main body of the range and a bedchamber in the south-west tower; the duke's on the first floor and the duchess's directly below.

It was in these apartments that Anne and Henry stayed during their visit. The rooms were lit by magnificent and complex oriel windows, those on the first floor more intricate than the ones below. The grand suite overlooked the privy gardens described by Henry's commissioners as being surrounded on three sides by a 'goodly gallery'; accessible from the rooms at either end of the duke's suite, it consisted of a loggia on the ground floor and a gallery built of timber and covered with slate at first-floor level: 'Conveying above and beneath from the principal lodgings both to the Chapel and Parish Church, the outer part of the said gallery being of stone embattled and the inner part of timber covered with slate.'

An extension from the south side of the gallery led from the castle to a pew by the north chancel window of the adjacent parish church (St Mary's church) where there was found 'a fair room with a chimney and a window into the said church, where the duke sometimes used to hear service'.

To the east of the privy garden was another garden described by Henry's commissioners as 'a goodly gardeyn to walke ynne'. There was also an orchard set out with covered alleys and planted with hazel and whitethorn, a bush said to have been a favourite of Buckingham's:

> Beside the same privie gardeyn is a large and goodly orchard full of younge grafftes well loden wt frute, many rooses, and other pleasures and many goodly alies [alleys] to walke ynne oppenly; and rounde aboute the same orcharde is covered on a good height, other goodly alies with roosting places covered … From out of the said orcharde ar diver posterns in sundry places, at plasur to goe and entre into a goodly parke newly made, called the New Parke, having in the same no great plenty of wood, but many heggsrowes of thorne and great Elmes. The same Parke conteynneth nigh upon iii myles about, and in the same be vii^c (700) der [deer] or more … Nigh to the said Newe Parke there is another parke called Marlwood, noething being between them but the bredth of an high waie.

In the early sixteenth century, Thornbury had been called upon to accommodate a household of up to 500 personnel, and so no doubt Henry and Anne were comfortable during their stay. The original plan was to remain at Thornbury for a week before moving to Bristol, but an outbreak of plague prevented the royal party from visiting the town, and so instead a delegation of townsmen came from Bristol on 20 August to pay their respects and presented Henry with ten 'fatte oxen' and forty 'sheepe towardes his moost honorable household'. To 'the right excellent Quene Anne' they gave a parcel-gilt cup with cover, containing 100 'marks of gold'. Anne responded by 'promising to demand or have none other gift' other than being able to return to Bristol in the future.

Visiting Thornbury Today

Today, Thornbury Castle offers guests the rare opportunity of sleeping in the very room where Henry VIII laid down his head. The Duke's Bedchamber is reached via the original circular stone staircase that both Anne and Henry used during their stay. It is wonderfully atmospheric, spacious, tastefully furnished and boasts a beautifully carved Tudor fireplace and four-poster bed. The chamber overlooks the privy garden and is a perfect blend of history and the modern conveniences that you would expect to find at a luxury hotel. The experience is all the more enhanced by welcoming touches like the decanter of sherry you'll find on arrival.

Aside from the grand Duke's Bedchamber, there are another twenty-six rooms to choose from, including some that now occupy the site of Buckingham's former chambers.

The rooms where Anne would have spent much of her time, once the apartments of the Duchess of Buckingham, today serve as the library and lounge and the octagonal bedchamber where Anne slept during her stay is now the restaurant, all areas that you are free to access as a guest of the hotel.

You may also wander, at your leisure, in the breathtaking grounds of the castle for the duration of your stay, so take your time exploring the ruins of the partially completed outer court. Although the south range has long since disappeared, the remains of the north and west lodgings offer tantalising glimpses of what might have been – notice the fireplaces and the arrow-loop windows on the outer walls.

The inner court is much as Anne would have known it except that the east range, where the Great Hall once stood, and all the buildings beyond it are now vanished. The building on your right, as you enter the court, is the inner face of the southern range, where Henry and Anne were lodged. Take note of the fine oriel window and impressive double chimney of brick constructed in 1514 that together with the similar example on the other side of the range are described as 'unequalled in England'.

The opposite face of this range is breathtaking, with its intricate oriel windows that once flooded Anne and Henry's rooms with light. This was the only building in the castle to be fitted with such spacious windows. Elsewhere, the lower rooms were lit by unglazed arrow loops, examples of which can still be seen in the ruined western range of the outer court.

As you traverse the well-trodden garden paths, note the remains of the embattled walls of the gallery where Anne once walked and lose yourself in the ancient yew-hedged garden, said to be the oldest Tudor garden in England. Staying at Thornbury is like hurtling into the past without compromising on the comforts of today. The castle is a gift to guests who can appreciate the treasures it encompasses.

Authors' Favourites

Staying overnight at Thornbury is an unparalleled experience. The sheer elegance of the castle and its grounds, and the sumptuous interiors coupled with the five-star conveniences and premium service, gives us an insight into Henry and Anne's luxurious way of life. It enables us to live a little regally, however briefly.

Don't miss the many copies of famous drawings and paintings of notable Tudor personalities that line the castle's walls, in particular a modern painting of Anne commissioned by the previous owner that depicts her in a stunning crimson gown with her famous 'B' necklace adorning her delicate neck.

The gardens are enchanting and particularly atmospheric at dusk, when the past seems to descend with the first hint of night. The library and lounge are also serene and relaxing spaces, made all the more appealing by the knowledge that, within those walls, Anne once sat and chatted with her ladies.

And finally, be sure to sample the delicious cuisine on offer at the restaurant; mouth-watering delicacies now served in a room where a queen once lay down to sleep.

Visitor Information

To book a room at Thornbury Castle, telephone + 44 (0) 1454 281182, email info@thornburycastle.co.uk or visit http://www.thornburycastle.co.uk/.

Non-guests are welcome to dine at the restaurant; however, it's strongly recommended that you book ahead to avoid disappointment.

Postcode for Thornbury Castle: BS35 1HH.

Acton Court, Gloucestershire

Acton mannor place standithe about a quartar of a myle from the village and paroche churche in a playne grounde on a redde sandy soyle. Ther is a goodly howse and 2 parks by the howse, one of redd dere, an othar of fallow.

John Leland

In the dying days of summer, Anne and Henry, followed by a long train of courtiers, departed Thornbury Castle and journeyed for 7 miles across the Gloucestershire countryside, to Acton Court, the home of Nicholas Poyntz, on the outskirts of the village of Iron Acton.

Despite his grandfather having been vice-chamberlain to Katharine of Aragon, twenty-five-year-old Poyntz favoured reform and so was honoured with a two-day royal visit originally scheduled for the weekend of 21–2 August, but in actuality taking place on 23 and 24 August.

The house that greeted Anne was constructed from local pennant sandstone, covered in off-white render, and was a mix of the old and the new. It was not a traditional quadrangle courtyard house (although it would become more like one in the future), as there were only three distinct wings arranged quite tightly at oblique angles.

The East Wing at Acton Court: A Unique Tudor Survivor

Poyntz, eager to impress and clearly unfazed by the brevity of the visit, had spent the previous nine months and a great deal of money adding a magnificent new east wing to the existing moated house. The rectangular, two-storeyed addition, built on the site of the medieval kitchens, measured 32.4 x 8.7 metres and contained three grand state apartments at first-floor level (presence chamber, privy chamber, and bedchamber) each containing a fireplace and an adjacent garderobe (en suite) and decorated in the latest Renaissance style.

The first of the three chambers was hung with expensive tapestries, decorated with vibrant painted friezes and lit by an enormous rectangular window. Henry's throne and cloth of estate stood directly opposite the entrance and no one but the king was permitted to stand or sit beneath it. As the presence chamber was the setting for all major court ceremonials, it's almost certain that within its walls Poyntz was knighted, as a reward for his extravagant hospitality. Henry and Anne may also have chosen to dine publicly here, as ushers and waiters bustled to and fro, or they may have preferred instead to dine more privately in the chamber next door.

The privy chamber was guarded by the king's gentlemen ushers and was only accessible to the dedicated staff whose job it was to attend Henry around the clock, or to those that the king specifically invited. According to the Eltham Ordinance of 1526 (a set of rules designed to regulate the functioning of the king's privy chamber), there were six gentlemen, two ushers, four grooms, a barber and a page all under the direction of the Groom of the Stool, who since 1526 had been Sir Henry Norris.

In this central room, Anne no doubt admired the exceptional painted frieze on the south wall, which was almost certainly painted by a French or Italian artist. It was comparable to contemporary friezes found in the palaces of the Loire Valley where Anne spent several years in service to Queen Claude, and similar in style and quality to decorative work seen at Whitehall Palace. Robert Bell described the frieze in his article *The Renaissance Comes to Gloucestershire*:

> The frieze is divided into three panels by balusters and capped by a trompe l'oeil cornice. The panels contain three different schemes of grotesque ornament executed in grey, white and ochre with touches of red and green on a black background. The centerpiece is a roundel, containing a female bust with braided hair in profile … At the time, this type of design was known as 'antique work'.

The mastermind behind the original design may have been Hans Holbein, as the quality and inclusion of some of his favourite motifs, including pendant jewellery and dolphins, indicates. Holbein's portrait drawing of Nicholas Poyntz dates from 1535 and may have been made to commemorate the success of the royal visit, making Holbein's connection to the frieze more plausible. The remaining wall was panelled and painted in yellow ochre, a popular colour for internal walls and woodwork in Tudor palaces.

The final room in the series served as Henry's bedchamber and only Sir Henry Norris was permitted access. As in the south room, it was lit by a vast window and overlooked the formal gardens, which were surrounded by a gallery and accessible directly from the house. The walls were panelled and adorned with a painted frieze. The ceiling, like in the king's privy chamber at Greenwich Palace, was painted with false ribs and may have had gilded rosettes or another motif at the intersections. Poyntz wanted his guests to feel at home and spared no expense when it came to the interiors, even commissioning sets of Spanish and Italian ceramic plates and fine Venetian glass vessels to ensure that the rooms were not only magnificent but also well equipped.

A covered gallery led from Henry's bedchamber to the chapel and additional lodgings and chambers, presumably used to accommodate other members of Anne and Henry's entourage. From this wing, the royal couple could also enjoy the gardens by means of a covered gallery that spanned the moat. Henry, a voracious hunter, would have made the most of the sport on offer in Acton's two deer parks.

In the sumptuous new wing we can imagine Anne, clad in rich velvets and splendid silks, sipping wine from a fine Venetian glass, listening to the court musicians and dancing with her ladies. But once the revelries came to an end, where did the queen retire to?

Unfortunately, the arrangement of the rooms directly below those occupied by the king is unknown, as all clues to its original appearance and function were swept away when Poyntz had the ground floor completely remodelled some years after the royal visit. So it is uncertain as to whether or not, like at Thornbury, Anne had use of a suite of rooms directly below the king's. It is hard to imagine her being housed elsewhere, especially after Poyntz went to such extremes to please the royal couple and to demonstrate his unyielding loyalty.

It has, however, been suggested that the ground floor may have consisted of a single reception area, in which case Anne would then have stayed in the great chamber, located in the south range and connected to the new wing by a pentice.

The south wing had been rebuilt in the fifteenth century and refurbished by Sir Robert Poyntz, Nicholas's grandfather who in 1479 married Margaret Woodville – an illegitimate daughter of Anthony Woodville, Earl Rivers – whose sister was Edward IV's queen.

Sir Robert had installed new sculptured fireplaces, glazed floor tiles and an impressive oriel window that projected out over the moat, possibly in anticipation of the house's first royal guest, Henry VII, who visited Acton Court on 23 May 1486, and these rooms may have accommodated Anne and her ladies during their fleeting visit.

Visiting Acton Court Today

Acton Court survived until the seventeenth century at which time it was sold and several of the ranges demolished. The remaining buildings were converted into a farmhouse and used as such until 1984. Fortunately for us, the range still standing is the east range, that together with half of a north wing, built in the 1550s, forms the L-shaped house that welcomes visitors today.

From the moment you step foot on the grounds of Acton Court, it is clear you have arrived somewhere very special. The raw beauty of the house is formidable; it has not been smothered by layers of Georgian and Victorian alterations, like so many other properties, and so is free to speak to us of its Tudor past.

On the ground floor there are many Tudor gems worth looking out for, like a section of softwood panelling originally from one of the upper-floor rooms, plaster-impressed motifs depicting Tudor roses, ancient floor tiles and even Tudor graffiti hurriedly scratched into a windowsill and dated 1589.

But the climax of any visit is the first floor; Poyntz's superb state apartments, although now devoid of their two enormous windows and most of their internal decoration, still retain their ability to impress. Although Acton Court was never a Tudor palace, the apartments built by Poyntz were equal in quality and magnificence to those found in places like Hampton Court. As you walk from one room to the next, you get a real sense of their function, the progression from the public to the private. There is also something very satisfying about being able to walk in Anne's steps without being interrupted or rerouted by a Victorian wall!

The most spectacular survivor of Poyntz's Renaissance decoration is the frieze on the south wall of the central room. The symmetrical black and white design, with its beautiful gold and metalwork and touches of red and green, is breathtaking and hints at the room's opulent past. As you stand there admiring its intricacies, remember that it was likely designed by Hans Holbein and undoubtedly seen by Henry and Anne.

During Acton Court's restoration, what was left of the panelling was gathered and put in the north room. It is also possible to see some of the original floorboards, distinguishable from the more modern ones by their greater width, and Henry's garderobe, uncovered during conservation work in 1994 and today hidden behind a door. The second blocked doorway once opened onto a spiral staircase that led to the garden.

The surviving segment of Poyntz's Long Gallery, in the north range, built in around 1550, is home to a painted freeze of elegant biblical text and moralising verses in Latin and a splendid classical mantelpiece.

Acton Court remains an outstanding monument to the extraordinary lengths that one courtier went to in order to impress his king and queen. The house, as far as possible, has been left in its original state. The absence of furniture, portraits or collections of antiques, adds to the mystery and magic of a building frozen in time.

Visitor Information
We recommend combining a trip to Acton Court with a visit to Bristol City Museum, where artefacts found during archaeological excavations at Acton are displayed in the Curiosity Gallery and the front hall balcony. These include examples of expensive Venetian glass, Spanish ceramics and a polyhedral sundial attributed to the royal horologist, Nicholas Kratzer.

Acton Court opens to the public on selected days during summer, please check their website for dates (www.actoncourt.com) or telephone + 44 (0) 1454 228224. Full access to the house and grounds is with a professional guide only, tour times available on the website. The house also regularly hosts Tudor-themed special events so be sure to check their site for full details.

Postcode for Acton Court: BS37 9TL.

Little Sodbury Manor, Gloucestershire

[Little Sodbury Manor] is charmingly situated on the south-western slope of the Cotswolds, and enjoys a magnificent prospect over the richly-wooded vale of the Severn, to the distant hills of Wales.

Robert Demaus, 1871

On 25 August 1535, Henry and Anne made the short 6-mile journey from Acton Court, the home of Nicholas Poyntz, to Little Sodbury, which belonged to Poyntz's aunt and uncle, Sir John and Lady Anne Walshe.

William Tyndale, Anne Boleyn and a Manor at the Heart of the English Reformation
The Walshes, like their nephew, were among those that favoured reform and so too were bestowed the honour of a royal visit. In the early 1520s they had employed William Tyndale, who later translated the Bible into English, probably as a tutor for their sons. Tradition has him beginning his translation of the Bible in one of the bedrooms; difficult to confirm, however, as his first version of the New Testament was not completed until 1526, several years after leaving Little Sodbury. What is certain is that while in the employ of the Walshes, he met with and debated matters of religion with churchmen from the neighbouring monastic houses and also took to preaching in the local villages, the latter landing him in trouble with the authorities.

Tyndale went on to write other important controversial works that would attract Anne's attention, notably the *Obediance of a Christian Man*, published in 1528 while he was in exile on the Continent. Anne acquired a copy shortly after its publication and marked passages to show Henry. Tyndale set out to prove that 'all men without exception are under the temporal sword, whatsoever names they give themselves' and demonstrate that 'the king is in the person of God and his law in God's law'. In other words, Henry's subjects were required by God to obey him and if they did not, they were not only disobeying their prince, they were disobeying God. It goes without saying that Tyndale's message struck a chord with Henry and he is said to have declared, 'This book is for me and all kings to read.'

But then Tyndale made a decision that would eventually prove fatal for him. In 1530, he decided to write *The Practyse of Prelates*, which opposed Henry VIII's planned divorce on the grounds that it was unscriptural, and he even dared to speak approvingly of Katharine of Aragon. Henry was enraged and demanded his apprehension and extradition.

Nevertheless, over the next few years, Anne and Cromwell made discreet efforts to smooth things over. Anne even owned a copy of the banned revised edition of Tyndale's *New Testament*, which is still extant and today housed in the British Library in London. The fine craftsmanship suggests it was a presentation copy – printed on vellum, with gilded edges and full colour woodcuts.

When news that Tyndale had been arrested in Antwerp and imprisoned in Vilvoorde, near Brussels, reached the court, Cromwell was unsure of how to proceed and noted in his 'Remembrances', which have been dated to August 1535, 'To know the King's pleasure for Tyndalle, and whether I shall write or not.'

It's likely that Anne played a major part in the discussions that eventually led to Henry allowing Cromwell to intercede on Tyndale's behalf. Perhaps some of the talks even took place while Anne and Henry were lodged at Little Sodbury, Tyndale's former place of residence. Little did Anne know that she would end up facing the executioner months before the man whom she was trying to save.

Nonetheless, their efforts were in vain, Cromwell's letters were not enough to rescue Tyndale from the flames; in around October 1536 he was executed by strangulation and then burned at the stake.

What do we know then, of the house where Anne stayed in late August 1535? It had been largely built in the mid-fifteenth century, incorporating parts of an earlier timber-framed house and remodelled by Sir John Walshe in around 1510–20.

Its present approach is from the north and leads into a wing remodelled in 1703; however, in Anne's day the entrance was via a gateway at the south end of the upper terrace, for which only the foundations survive buried beneath a grassy patch.

Like all grand houses of the time, it contained several wings, a Great Hall, a solar, kitchens, services and offices, in this case arranged rather unorthodoxly as a result of its steep siting below the crest of the hills.

Visitor Information

Today, Little Sodbury Manor stands in the quaint village of Little Sodbury in South Gloucestershire, overlooking the Vale of Berkeley, and is the home of Lord and Lady Killearn, who do not open it to the general public.

It is a patchwork of various building periods built around the magnificent mid-fifteenth century Great Hall and two-storeyed porch. The sixteenth-century south range built by Sir John Walshe, with its beautiful oriel window, from where Anne is said to have watched the entertainments on the terrace below, survives.

The house is today privately owned and so not accessible to the public. However, the previous owner permitted the occasional tour and so who's to say that Little Sodbury may not one day reopen its ancient doors? Let's hope so!

Postcode for Little Sodbury Manor: BS37 6QA.

Bromham House, Wiltshire

> For whether she [Anne] rested at her palace or accompanied the king his majesty in his progress she would at all times express her care, her thought, her mindful remembrance of the poor and indigent people.
>
> William Latimer

As the end of August 1535 approached, the royal party travelled the 12 miles from Little Sodbury to Bromham House, the home of another supporter of reform and a long-time favourite of Henry VIII, Anne Boleyn's Vice-Chamberlain, Sir Edward Baynton.

Baynton inherited the manor of Bromham after his father's death in 1516 and set about enlarging and embellishing the house, according to John Leland, using stone from the nearby Devizes Castle.

By the time of Anne and Henry's visit, the house was reputed to have been almost as large as the Palace of Whitehall, decorated with stone carvings and very richly furnished. It is in this impressive residence that Baynton entertained his sovereigns and the court for a week in 1535. We know from William Paulet's household accounts that the royal party arrived on Friday 27 August, staying until 3 September before moving to Wolfhall.

While lodged at Baynton's house, Anne received a letter from Hugh Latimer, the future Bishop of Worcester, concerning one of his parishioners who had recently lost most of his cattle 'almoste to his utter undoing'. Anne interviewed the man's wife at Bromham and gave her a purse of gold with twenty pounds in it towards 'your present relief' assuring the lady that 'if this will not redress your lack, repair to me another time, and I will consider better of you'.

This is not an isolated occurrence; Anne was committed to helping the poor and needy, and issued an order to her chaplains to this effect, as was later recounted by William Latimer in his *Chronicle*:

> My pleasure is: that you all take especial regard in the choice of such poor people as shall be found most needy; not vagrant and lazy beggars, who in every place besides are relieved abundantly, but poor needy and impotent house holders over charged with children, not having any sustenance, comfort or relief otherwise; and to such I command mine alms liberally. [Spelling modernised]

Apart from distributing alms, Anne and her ladies also sewed clothes and sheets for the poor that were taken on progress and handed out at each of the locations visited.

Save for the above insight into Anne's altruism, the sources are silent and virtually nothing is known of the once-grand mansion that accommodated the court, as it was burnt down by Royalist troops on 5 May 1645. No drawings or paintings of it are known to exist.

The Tudor gatehouse was all that escaped destruction; it was subsequently dismantled, moved and re-erected at the top of Bowden Hill as the entrance to another Baynton family residence called Spye Park House, built in the mid-seventeenth century by Sir Edward Baynton's grandson using materials salvaged from the ruins of Bromham House. But sadly, this too was destroyed by fire on 8 August 1974 and afterwards demolished.

Incredibly, for the second time, the stone gatehouse was untouched by the flames and still stands today, the last vestige of not one, but two great Baynton family homes.

Visitor Information

Spye Park is not opened to the public but the gatehouse – Spye Arch Lodge, which once served Bromham House – is visible from the road. However, it is not so easy to find! From the A342 (Devizes Road) opposite the George Inn, take the road signposted to Bowden Hill and Lacock. About half a mile to a mile down the road you will suddenly come across the gatehouse on your left. There is space enough to pull over in the car and admire its unmistakable Tudor heritage. Beneath the splendid oriel window can be seen the arms of Henry VIII flanked by fine carved panels, and the arch spandrels are decorated with the arms of Sir Edward Baynton and his first wife, Elizabeth Sulliard.

Apart from the gatehouse, which stands in its new position, nothing else remains of Bromham House, which once stood close to the present Bromham House Farm, a modern red brick building standing on the east of Devizes Road.

Note that if you are in the area and love your Tudor heritage, you should not miss the fabulous Lacock Abbey, which can be found another couple of miles or so further along the road, although this has no known connection with Anne.

Postcode for Spye Arch Lodge: SN15 2PR.

Wolfhall, Wiltshire

The Manor of Wulfhall, as appears from an old Survey, consisted at that time of about 1270 acres … About the house, which is said to have been timber-framed, there were several gardens, 'the Great paled garden', 'My Old lady's garden' and 'My Young Lady's garden'. There was a Long Gallery, a Little court, a Broad chamber: and a Chapel.

J. E. Jackson, 1875

In early September 1535, Henry VIII and Anne Boleyn left Sir Edward Baynton's house at Bromham and rode east to Wolfhall on the outskirts of Savernake Forest, the home of Sir John Seymour, whose eldest daughter Jane would become – in less than nine months – Henry's third wife.

The royal party had originally planned to stay at Wolfhall near Marlborough from Thursday 2 September until Tuesday 7 September; however, they arrived a day late, on 3 September, as recorded in the household accounts.

On 7 September, several important documents relating to the appointment of three new reformist bishops – Edward Fox, Hugh Latimer and John Hilsey – were signed at Wolfhall in preparation for their consecration at Winchester on 19 September.

The visit lasted until at least 10 September, the date recorded in a letter from Cromwell to Eustace Chapuys:

Expressing the King's satisfaction at reading the letters of the Emperor and Granvelle relating to the storming of Tunis. The King could not have been better pleased if the victory had been his own, and he warmly congratulates the Emperor upon it. As to Chapuys' request, at the end of his letters, to be allowed to visit the Lady Mary, desires him to wait till Cromwell's return, when he hopes to give him satisfaction in this and other things at a personal interview. Wolfall, 10 Sept.

Wolfhall: the Scene of une Nouvelle Amour?

Henry was clearly enjoying the Seymour hospitality and in October even contemplated staying with Sir John's eldest son, Edward, at his house in Elvetham, although in the end he decided to stay at Bramshill House instead.

It is not known whether Jane Seymour was present during Anne and Henry's stay and only myth and legend suggest that this is where she first caught the king's wandering eye. In early October, the bishop of Tarbes, the French ambassador, did inform Francis I that Henry's affection for Anne 'is less than it has been, and diminishes day by day, because he has new amours'. However, this is contradicted by the correspondence of Sir Richard Graynfeld (2 October), John Bishop of Exeter (6 October) and Sir Anthony Wyndesore (9 October) that all describe Anne and Henry as 'merry' and in 'good health'.

The earliest mention of Jane Seymour by name is in a letter written by Chapuys dated 10 February 1536 where he informs Charles V that Henry is paying special attention 'to a lady of the Court, named Mistress Semel' and on 18 March refers to the relationship as *une nouvelle amour*.

It's likely, then, that the visit to Wolfhall in 1535 was not, as hindsight might lead some to believe, a pivotal moment in Henry and Jane's relationship.

Rediscovering the Lost Hall

The house that Anne stayed in has long since disappeared, and even its location is uncertain, but the most likely site is south of the present-day Wolfhall Farmhouse and about where Wolfhall Manor stands today. The house is largely eighteenth-century but incorporates fragments of an earlier building.

In the sixteenth century, Wolfhall was a large courtyard house with a chapel and Long Gallery, surrounded by three picturesque gardens. A visitor to the area in 1672, John Aubrey, noted that the house was timber-framed and that a great part of the house had already been demolished.

He reported that the king's wedding to Jane Seymour had taken place in 'a very long barne' on the site; the barn that Aubrey refers to was almost certainly a thatched barn that was still standing in the 1870s, albeit in a dilapidated state, but which had largely collapsed by the 1920s. Writing in 1875, the Reverend J. E. Jackson recorded that at that time 'there are still to be seen, against some of the beams and walls, nails or hooks to which were attached the tapestry and hanging used to smarten it up for the dancers at Queen Jane's wedding'.

Of course, Henry and Jane weren't married at Wolfhall, but rather in the queen's closet at Whitehall. It is unknown whether the said barn was even standing in 1536. However, an item recorded in Edward Seymour's account book for 1539 indicates that a barn existed and that it was indeed used for royal visits: 'Paid to Cornish the paynter for dyvers colours by him bought, for makyng certeyn frets & antiques on canves for my lord's Barn and house at Wulf Haull agenst the King's coming thether 9th Aug.'

A later entry suggests that the Earl of Hertford moved into the barn while Henry VIII occupied the main house. So it is conceivable that the said barn existed during Anne and Henry's visit in 1535 and there may be some truth to the story of a celebration having taken place there to mark Henry and Jane's wedding in 1536, although it was certainly not the site of the royal nuptials.

Visitor Information

The authors started their adventure at the church of St Mary in Great Bedwyn. Park the car with the churchyard on your left (this means you are pointing in the right direction to head on toward Wolfhall after your visit). Although (as you will shortly see) nothing remains of the house that Anne visited, stained glass showing Jane's phoenix badge, the Tudor rose and Prince of Wales feathers, originally installed at Wolfhall, were moved to St Mary's church after the destruction of the house and remain there until this day. The church also contains Sir John Seymour's impressive tomb and a number of other memorials to the Seymour family. Being passionate about Anne's story as we are, it was strange indeed to stand in front of the effigy of Jane's father, a man who surely played a very willing part in orchestrating Anne's fall from grace. St Mary's is a charming and very typical English country church that abides in stillness as it has done for countless generations. We left in a reflective mood, and admit to approaching the site of Wolfhall with a mixture of intrigue and trepidation.

Once back in the car, drive ahead (if you parked with the church on your left), down Church Street, which soon becomes Crofton Road. Follow the winding country lanes alongside the river and canal, keeping your eyes open for a sign pointing to Wolfhall. You may seem to be snaking your way along for some time before a sharp bend in the road to the right on the crest of a hill brings you between farm buildings, with a rather rundown red brick farmhouse on the left and cowsheds on the right. A sign saying 'Wolfhall Farm' tells you that you have arrived in the right location.

Park the car up on the lane opposite the cowsheds. Walk ahead some 10–20 metres. A track runs away into the distance in front to you, while another sign at the bend in the road announces you are at Wolfhall Farm. In front of you is a valley; nestled deep within it is a fine red brick house, supporting lofty chimneys that look a little too grand for its humble, arable surroundings. It is believed that possibly some remnants of the original Wolfhall are built into the current structure, although there is nothing to suggest that these chimneys were part of the original building.

Visiting a site now shrouded in myth, where so many believe Henry's attentions first seriously alighted upon Anne's lady-in-waiting, cannot fail to pull at the heartstrings. We ourselves have always been a little sceptical of that myth. So it was surprising that the site turned out to be one of those lost locations that still has the power to evoke emotion. Despite ourselves, we couldn't shake off the feeling that a long time ago something of significance occurred here, so far away from the bustle of London in this sleepy little valley. We came away with many ghostly voices keeping us company, and found ourselves haunted for some time by the place that refuses to pass into obscurity.

Great Bedwyn is opened to visitors on most days from between 9.00 a.m. and 4.30 p.m. The actual site of Wolfhall is not accessible, but it can be viewed from the road at any reasonable hour.

Postcode for Wolfhall: SN8 3DP.

Thruxton, Hampshire

Tuesday, 7 Sept., Whofall to Thrukstone, there till Thursday, 12 m.

Letters and Papers of Henry VIII

In September 1535, Henry VIII and Anne Boleyn, accompanied by Thomas Cromwell, stayed at Thomas Lisle's house in Thruxton, where he'd commenced his career in the household of his distant cousin, Sir John Lisle. Thomas inherited Thruxton manor in 1524 through his marriage to Sir John's niece and heir, Mary Kingston.

During Henry VIII's reign, the Lisles were among the leading members of the landed gentry in Hampshire. By 1535, Thomas held various offices at court, including esquire of the body – a personal attendant on the king – and so was well placed to host a royal visit.

Almost nothing is known of the house where Anne and Henry stayed. Sir John Lisle's will makes mention of a house but gives no further details. The remains of a moated enclosure, believed to be the site of the Lisle residence, were shown to the north of the churchyard in the 1872 edition of the Ordnance Survey. Disappointingly, nothing remains of the original residence, with the exception of a few stone windows and door surrounds visible in the gardens of the largely eighteenth-century, privately owned Thruxton manor house, built near the site of its Tudor predecessor. However, it is not known for certain whether these are in fact the last vestiges of the once-grand Lisle family home.

From the beginning of the fifteenth century, Thruxton appears to be the Lisle family's principal place of burial. Part of the village church of St Peter and St Paul's dates from the thirteenth century and houses a number of Lisle tombs and monuments, including the remains of a chapel with a tomb chest, built between 1524 and 1527 for Sir John and Mary Lisle who both died in 1524. The church also houses a rare Elizabethan wooden effigy of a lady believed to be Lady Elizabeth Philpot.

Visitor Information

Thruxton is a charming, sleepy village with a quintessential English green and a clear brook that babbles its way through the centre of the settlement. If you wish to visit the site of the Lisle manor house, make your way to the church (parking is plentiful in the village). The later, and still extant, Thruxton Manor sits atop a modest ridge next to the village church of St Peter and St Paul. On the other side of the church, next to the road, is an open field with visible earthworks, the site of the house once visited by a king and his lady. There is little else to see, sadly, so make your way into the church, which is opened every afternoon in the six months or so from Easter Day until Harvest (however, it would still be worth calling ahead to arrange for one of the church wardens to open the church for you, as it is sometimes locked: + 44 (0) 1264 772788 or Christine Barrett on + 44 (0) 1264 772904). Here, you can view the tombs and wooden effigy described above. If you are lucky the church warden will meet you and give you a personal guided tour, as happened to us quite by chance!

The village of Thruxton lies within an easy drive of Salisbury and Clarendon, should you wish to include this spot with other locations in this book.

Postcode for St Peter and St Paul, Thruxton: SP11 8NL.

Hurstbourne Priors, Hampshire

a fayre old house and large park with many ewe [yew] trees.

Royalist officer writing about the medieval manor at Hurstbourne,
just prior to the Battle of Newbury in the seventeenth century

In September, probably around 11th or 12th, Henry arrived with Anne and the court at the manor of Hurstbourne Priors. The ancient manor house had origins dating back to the eighth century when it was first owned by the monks of Abingdon, but it later fell into royal hands, including those of the Saxon king, Alfred the Great. Eventually ownership reverted to the monks of Winchester, and specifically the Priory of St Swithun; this was still the case when the royal party swept into Hurstbourne Park in the early autumn of 1535.

The manor house that Anne would have known was actually built over the River Bourne with an enclosed deer park lying to the north-west of the building; the Domesday Book had recorded five mills on the site. Sadly, absolutely nothing seems to be known about the appearance or layout of the medieval building. All that we have is a sixteenth-century map of Hampshire by Saxton, drawn in 1575. The map shows the manor of 'Hursborn' situated adjacent to the river, the imparked area of land reserved for hunting, located to the north-west as described above.

However, it does not seem likely that the king and queen enjoyed the delights of hunting in the enclosed park, for their stay was fleeting. If the couple kept to schedule, and we have no evidence to the contrary, then they lodged at Hurstbourne Priors for just one night, before heading the 13 miles or so south to the city of Winchester.

Interestingly, shortly after the visit we see an entry in the *Letters and Papers of Henry VIII* that details a grant made by Henry Brook, prior of the convent of St Swithun's Monastery to 'Thomas Cromwell, the King's secretary and Gregory Cromwell, his son and heir apparent of an annuity of 10*l* (*pounds*) out of the manors of Hurseborne and Crundall, Hants. From their Chapterhouse, 25 Sep anno etc.'

Had the king and Cromwell made their displeasure regarding corruption in religious houses clear? Did the prior understand the danger looming on the distant horizon? Was this a rather meagre attempt to bribe Cromwell and gain Master Secretary's favour? If it was, it was to no avail, for in 1539 the Priory of St Swithun was dissolved and the manor and park granted to Edward Seymour, Duke of Somerset, who held the manor until his execution on Tower Hill in 1552.

Visitor Information

The medieval manor at Hurstbourne has been replaced twice since Anne visited the property, with the current mansion dating from 1891 to 1894. The estate is presently home to the earls of Portsmouth. As such, no part of the park is accessible to the public, nor are there any vestiges of an earlier gatehouse to be seen. Because of its complete inaccessibility, the authors cannot recommend visiting the site. However, we include it here for completeness.

Postcode for Hurstbourne Park, Whitchurch: RG28 7RN.

Winchester, Hampshire

The King and the Queen is merry and hawks daily, and likes Winchester and that quarter, and praises it much.

Sir Richard Graynfeld, 2 October 1535

Set amid majestic rolling countryside and ancient woodlands, the capital of Anglo-Saxon England has long been associated with kings and queens. For Anne and Henry, approaching the city gates of Winchester after an overnight stay at Hurstbourne Priors, it would have felt like coming home, as aromas of wood fires, baking bread and roasting game scented the golden dusk of an early autumn evening.

As backdrop to the culmination of the progress, the ancient city staged a ceremony that David Starkey has deemed 'one of the most extraordinary scenes of the Reformation', the public consecration of three newly appointed reforming bishops – Edward Fox, Hugh Latimer and John Hilsey – at Winchester Cathedral on 19 September 1535. Thomas Cranmer, Archbishop of Canterbury, performed the ceremony in the presence of the king and Anne. She had worked tirelessly to solicit their appointments and was almost certainly by her husband's side to lend her support.

Although we cannot be certain where the court was lodged during their stay, as no records survive, it's likely to have been at the bishop's palace of Wolvesey, positioned next to the cathedral, as Winchester Castle had long since ceased to be used as a royal residence after an extensive fire destroyed the royal apartments in 1302. By the sixteenth century, it had declined in importance.

The intended plan was to stay at Winchester for four or five days, as specified in the original 'geists', before moving the 7 miles to Bishop's Waltham; however, the royal couple were so delighted with the sport on offer in the area, particularly the hawking, that they extended their stay to at least two weeks, moving to Bishop's Waltham for a short visit around 18 or 19 September (although it's possible that the court was split between Winchester and Waltham, as we know that Henry and Anne were present at the consecration on Sunday 19 September) before returning to Winchester on Saturday 25.

Not long after the royal party had arrived, Jean de Dinteville, a French diplomat, was granted an audience with the king and queen. On 15 September he wrote to Marguerite de Navarre, sister to King Francis I and wife of King Henry II of Navarre: 'Madame, the first time I saw the king and queen of England, I made your recommendations to them, and they were glad to hear of your recovered health. The Queen said that her greatest wish, next to having a son, is to see you again.'

Anne's strong expression of affection appears to be evidence of a close friendship between her and Marguerite. The two women certainly knew each other from Anne's time in service to Queen Claude, Marguerite's sister-in-law. However, the true nature of Marguerite's feelings towards Anne and the extent of their 'friendship' is the subject of debate and remains somewhat of a mystery. What the evidence does seem to suggest is that Anne viewed Marguerite as a role model and that overall Marguerite was pleasant in return.

While at Winchester, Henry and Anne received word that Catherine Willoughby, Duchess of Suffolk, had given birth to a son, Henry Brandon. He would die tragically during an epidemic of the sweating sickness in 1551, just shy of his sixteenth birthday and within an hour of the death of his younger brother from the same disease. While news of his birth was joyous, it must have left Anne and Henry hoping that they too would soon be blessed with the son they so desperately longed for.

Yet there were other matters occupying Henry's thoughts, as reported by Chapuys in a letter to Charles V on 25 September:

> The King having arrived at Winchester, where he is at present, caused an inventory to be made of the treasures of the church, from which he took certain fine rich unicorns' horns (licornes), and a large silver cross adorned with rich jewels. He has also taken from the Bishop certain mills, to give them to the community in order to gain favour. Cromwell, wherever the King goes, goes round about visiting the abbeys, making inventories of their goods and revenues, instructing them fully in [the tenets of] this new sect, turning out of the abbeys monks and nuns who made their profession before they were 25, and leaving the rest free to go out or to remain. It is true they are not expressly told to go out, but it is clearly given them to understand that they had better do, it, for they are going to make a reformation of them so severe and strange that in the end they will all go; which is the object the King is aiming at, in order to have better occasion to seize the property without causing the people to murmur.

Since joining the progress at Winchcombe, Cromwell had not ventured too far from the king's side, but he is not the only familiar name that we find accompanying Henry and Anne at Winchester. The correspondences of the Duke of Norfolk, Anne's uncle, reveal that he too intended to join the progress. On 24 September he wrote to Cromwell to ask him to 'speak to some of the harbingers for room for 24 horses in my company, and beg my servant to make my chamber ready against my coming [to Winchester]'. Charles Brandon, too, had left his wife and newborn son to join the progress, where we find him on 25 September.

Wolvesey Palace

The complete plan of the buildings where Anne and Henry probably stayed is not known for certain, but we do know that Wolvesey was a luxurious palace, largely constructed in the twelfth century by the powerful Bishop Henry of Blois, brother of King Stephen and the grandson of William the Conqueror. It was extended and refurbished over the centuries by its subsequent owners. The original approach to the palace was through a gate in the city wall, which led to an outer courtyard containing stables and barns. The palace buildings were arranged around an inner courtyard and included a Great Hall, chapel, domestic buildings and kitchens, a tower and a gatehouse, surrounded on three sides by a moat.

It is possible that the royal guests were accommodated in rooms in the west range, as this was used throughout its life as the principal residence and private apartments of the Bishop of Winchester, who at the time of Anne's visit was Stephen Gardiner. These lodgings would certainly have been grand enough to house royalty and, in Anne's own words, recorded by Sir William Kingston in a letter to Thomas Cromwell penned from the Tower of London during Anne's imprisonment, we hear that these lodgings were stacked, Anne's apartments being above the king's: 'But he [Mark Smeaton] was never in my chamber but at Winchester, and there I sent for him to play the virginals, for there my lodging was above the king's.'

From the early fourteenth century, the palace was used primarily for state occasions rather than as a permanent residence. In 1554, a feast was held in the east hall to celebrate Queen Mary's marriage to Philip II of Spain, which took place in Winchester Cathedral on 25 July 1554.

Today, all that remain of the palace that Anne would have known are ruins and a fifteenth-century chapel incorporated into a baroque palace built for Bishop George Morley in the seventeenth century on the site of the original one. This building is presently the private residence of the Bishop of Winchester. However, the ruins are in the care of English Heritage and are opened to the public. Look out for the graphic panels that tell the history of the palace and illustrate what the medieval buildings may have looked like.

Winchester Cathedral

Winchester Cathedral, where Anne witnessed the consecration of three new bishops, still stands as a glorious testament to the city's illustrious royal connections, its power and wealth. It is home to many treasures, including exquisite fourteenth-century oak choir stalls; seven chantry chapels, added between the fourteenth and sixteenth centuries; medieval floor tiles and wall paintings; over a thousand beautifully carved roof bosses and a sixteenth-century chair, said to have been used by Queen Mary during her wedding ceremony, now housed in The Triforium Gallery.

The nave is breathtaking and a perfect place to stop and imagine Anne walking regally and triumphantly beneath the fine vaulted ceiling towards the high altar, to witness the consecration of 'her' bishops. The queen's gaze perhaps fell on the painted statues adorning the ornately carved stone screen soaring up behind the high altar, now replaced with modern statues as the originals were destroyed during the Reformation. Luckily, there are a few unique survivals on display in the aforementioned gallery.

Apart from the cathedral and ruins of Wolvesey Palace, now known as Wolvesey Castle, the authors also highly recommend a visit to the only surviving part of Winchester Castle – its Great Hall. It is home to King Arthur's round table, made in the thirteenth century and painted during the reign of Henry VIII. But perhaps more importantly, the hall was built at the same time as the now-lost Great Hall at the Tower of London, where Anne feasted before her Coronation, and where the queen and her brother were tried on 15 May 1536. This extant hall gives visitors an insight into what the Great Hall at the Tower may have looked and felt like. Find a quiet spot and try to picture the special stands that were erected to cater for up to 2,000 spectators. Imagine each of the twenty-six peers delivering their verdict, one by one – 'Guilty, guilty, guilty ...' – their judgments reverberating around the room. Think about the Duke of Norfolk, who cried as he condemned his niece to 'be burned here within the Tower of London, on the Green, else to have thy head smitten off, as the king's pleasure shall be further known of the same' and Anne's composed response echoing throughout:

> I do not say that I have always borne towards the king the humility which I owed him, considering his kindness and the great honour he showed me and the great respect he always paid me; I admit, too, that often I have taken it into my head to be jealous of him ... But may God be my witness if I have done him any other wrong.

That such was her destiny would have been unimaginable to Anne, as she enjoyed the hospitality in Winchester. Today, visitors will also be captivated by the city's rich history, the myriad of historic buildings and the raw beauty of the landscape. In this city of kings, queens and bishops, the past finds its voice, eloquently speaking of days gone by.

Visitor Information

With so much to see in Winchester, we recommend that before you visit you download a Winchester Explorer Map from www.visitwinchester.co.uk, which includes a city map, opening times and admission prices, and a suggested circular walking trail around the town covering all the locations associated with Anne and many more. Among the many additional locations is The Westgate Museum, which houses an interesting collection of artefacts, including a Tudor ceiling from Winchester College, and The City Museum, home to a number of fascinating exhibitions about Winchester's intriguing past.

Bishop's Waltham, Hampshire

> Here the Bishop of Winchester had a right, ample, and goodly manor place, moted about, and a praty brooke running hard by it.
>
> John Leland, *Leland's Itinerary*

An entry in *Letters and Papers* dated 27 September states that 'on the 26th the King removed from Waltham to Winchester'. It seems that at some point, probably after the consecration of the three bishops at Winchester, Henry and Anne joined the wider court at Bishop's Waltham, before returning to Winchester again prior to the court's removal southwards to Southampton (although, as noted in the previous entry, perhaps Henry and Anne broke off their stay at Bishop's Waltham to return to Winchester to attend the service).

The summer must have been falling away, with the first hints of autumn creeping over the landscape when Henry and Anne arrived at Waltham, a moated building sitting in the middle of the Forest of Bere and lying north of an enclosed hunting park, which covered about 1,000 acres.

In the sixteenth century, Bishop's Waltham Palace was a substantial property, owned since the twelfth century by the bishops of Winchester. According to Camden who saw it standing, it was a 'stately seat' capable of lodging the entire itinerant court.

Having been created Bishop of Winchester in 1532, the formidable Stephen Gardiner was its owner at the time of the progress and must have had the job of formally entertaining his royal guests while they lodged in Winchester and Waltham. Like Sir William Paulet, who we will meet at Basing House, Gardiner was another Tudor survivor. Despite vacillating and finally backing the wrong horse in the question of the King's Great Matter, Gardiner had changed his step in the nick of time, just managing to retain the king's favour, although it is said that Henry never quite trusted the bishop as he once had.

The Palace Buildings

The buildings themselves had been constructed around a central courtyard, with the four sides nearly fronting the four cardinal points of the compass. This courtyard was divided into a larger northern courtyard enclosing a range of two-storey courtier lodgings fashioned from brick and timber, a bakehouse, brewery and kitchen. There was also a southern courtyard, where the state and privy apartments of the palace were located around a cloister, adjacent to the chapel.

In the early to mid-fifteenth century Cardinal Beaufort, then bishop of Winchester, had added a an extra storey to the bishop's privy apartments in the fine West Tower, along with a new chapel, the lodging range, and gatehouse, while the *Winchester Pipe Rolls* reveal continuous spending on maintenance and rebuilding, suggesting that the palace on which Anne laid eyes that autumn was a fine residence indeed.

The Visit of September 1535

There are no specific records of this visit, so we do not know for sure where the king and queen were lodged, or what took place while they were at Waltham. However, we can safely assume that Henry stayed with Anne in the finest rooms in the palace, those located in the West Tower. The room on the first floor had direct access from the Great Hall, whose ruins today hint at its long-lost splendour and scale. This was most likely in use as the principle privy chamber of the palace. Above this was the 'high chamber', or bedroom, with its own private latrine in the thickness of the walls. This room would normally have been occupied by the bishop, but again one assumes that this would have been the king's bedroom for the duration of his stay at Waltham. On the third floor was yet another grand room with its own fireplace and five windows. Could this have been Anne's privy lodging, a fine room just a few turns of a stone staircase away from the king's?

Archaeological finds, household accounts and other documents have left behind traces of the palace's sumptuous interiors. Everywhere Anne would have seen high-quality stonework, glazed windows with painted glass, floors laid with coloured tiles, her privy chambers probably clad in wooden panelling, with the walls painted with frescoes and hung with expensive tapestries.

As you peer into what remains of the ruined West Tower, perhaps it is not so hard to look skyward and imagine the rooms warmed by their glowing fires, a queen attended by her ladies as she looked out of one of those now-empty, ragged windows across the moat to the forest beyond.

The Decline of Bishop's Waltham

The end of Bishop's Waltham Palace came during the Civil War. The building was defended by Royalists, and when it was captured by Parliamentarian forces it was destroyed, leaving the ruins to be gradually dismantled and the valuable brick- and stonework to be taken away and used as building material elsewhere.

Visitor Information

It is easy to see why Henry and Anne were so charmed with the countryside around Winchester. We arrived when summer was bursting forth in a profusion of blossom, the hedges adorned with wildflowers and the fields a patchwork of vibrant lemon yellow from flowering rapeseed. The palace itself lies in substantial ruins, but there is enough to aid the imagination in recreating the place that Anne once visited. Particularly poignant were the broken fireplaces in the West Tower. Clearly, they had once heated rooms of considerable splendour.

Do try and visit on a weekend when the museum is open, if only to see a surviving courtier's room on the first floor. Although virtually bare, it is a rare chance to see the size of the room where you could expect to be lodged if you were a gentleman at court.

It is worth mentioning that you will not find any refreshments or toilets on site. There are, however, a couple of picnic tables looking out over the ruins. On a perfect sunny day, as it was when we visited, it is an extremely pleasant place to take a break and perhaps enjoy your own packed lunch, while you gaze upon what is left of the splendid ruins. However, the good news is that the palace is but a stone's throw from the charming little town of Bishop's Waltham, whose origins long predate the existence of the palace. You can easily walk to the high street and you will find enough tea rooms and restaurants there to satisfy your physical needs!

Bishop's Waltham Palace is owned and maintained by English Heritage. For visitor information and opening times, please visit: http://www.english-heritage.org.uk/daysout/properties/bishops-waltham-palace/prices-and-opening-times. Telephone number: + 44 (0) 2392 378291.

Note that this property is closed during the winter period and reopens toward the end of March. There is a small car park on site, and entrance is free of charge.

Postcode for Bishop's Waltham Palace: SO32 1DH.

Southampton, Hampshire

The town is handsome, and for its size has houses as fair as those in London.
Contemporary sixteenth-century account of Southampton from a visitor to the town

The town of Southampton lies just under 13 miles due south of Winchester, the ancient capital of Wessex. In Anne's time, it was just one day's ride from the aforementioned city, where the couple had spent around two weeks. Sadly, due to loss of certain key records pertaining to Southampton from this period, virtually nothing of absolute certainty is known of Henry and Anne's visit in October 1535. Certainly, a visit to the town had not been devised in the original 'geists' and Southampton marked the first divergence of the royal itinerary after the king and court left Winchester around 30 September. The original plan had been to head eastwards, marking the beginning of the return journey to Windsor. However, instead the king headed south to Southampton. One cannot help but wonder what inspired this turn of events? Other than the fact that it appears that Henry and Anne were thoroughly enjoying their time hunting and hawking together, the only possible other reason hinted at was the opportunity for Henry to inspect his navy at Portsmouth, although this does not explain the subsequent diversion to Salisbury.

Up until the sixteenth century, Southampton was a key trading port, importing wines from France, luxuries like spices, perfumes and silk from the Continent, as well as cargoes of alum and woad that were used in dying wool, the town's main export.

It had first been a Roman, then a hugely prosperous Saxon, settlement. After the conquest of England by the Normans, the city continued to flourish, and in the late thirteenth century the city walls were constructed in stone, entirely surrounding the settlement. Bargate, which still stands today, formed the most northerly entry point into the town. John Speed's map of the Isle of Wight from 1611 includes a town plan of the medieval city of Southampton. Here we see the wide, main thoroughfare of English Street almost bisecting the citadel. In the north-west quadrant of the town, the motte and bailey castle is clearly visible, while toward the centre ground is the tall spire of St Michael's church. The church stood on one side of St Michael's Square, directly opposite one of Southampton's most important Tudor houses, whose history and links to Anne Boleyn we shall come to shortly.

Since its inception, the town had always been a vibrant place of trade, full of skilled tradesmen and well-to-do merchants who flourished on account of its importance as England's third-largest port. Indeed, in 1530 the high street in Southampton was described as 'one of the fairest in all England for timber buildings', and in 1541 a visitor said Southampton had 'many fair merchants houses'. If the small handful of Tudor houses that still stand today are representative of the sixteenth-century town, it is easy to see why the Tudor visitor was left with this striking impression.

But by the time Anne visited Southampton with Henry in 1535, the town was already in decline. In 1533, just two years before the royal visit, the townsfolk complained that trade was diminishing, and by 1535 Cromwell was being asked to clear Southampton's debts in return for the people of town repairing the city walls. By the end of the century, those very same walls were said to be overgrown with 'elders, yew and such other weeds' while some houses, it was said, were 'greatly decayed and likely to fall down'.

Southampton and the Visit of 1535

The first we hear of the impending visit to the city is in a letter from James Hawkysworthe to Lord Lisle on 27 September, where he reports, 'On the 26th the King removed from Waltham to Winchester. On Tuesday next he comes to [South]Hampton, after which he goes to Portsmouth. It is not known whether he will come to the castle, but there is provision made with us.'

This gives us a tantalising suggestion that the castle was being prepared for the visit – as might be expected. Yet was this where the king and queen actually lodged? As local historian and expert on Southampton's Tudor history, Cheryl Butler, explains,

> The castle in Southampton was owned directly by the king, and he had a constable who had responsibility for it on a day to day basis. So it is the most likely place for them to have stayed. It is where Henry had lodged previously when visiting the town and where Anne's daughter, Elizabeth would also later stay.

However, we should also include the local tradition that states that Anne and Henry lodged in another building, which still stands today in all its Tudor glory on modern-day Bugle Street, now The Tudor House Museum. This was the house that had stood on one side of what used to be St Michael's Square, opposite the eponymously named church. It is clear that the building had a generous garden behind the property, a garden which backed onto the city wall and faced out toward the sea.

This striking-looking timber-framed building is magnificent indeed. Its sheer scale as a town house speaks of the wealth and influence of its sixteenth-century owner, Sir Richard Lyster (1480–1553), who had married the heiress of the property, Isabel Dawtrey, in 1528.

They were among Southampton's most pre-eminent citizens, enjoying considerable wealth and power. What is more, Sir Richard was well known to the king. His position as a judge and the Lord Chief Justice of England had placed him in an instrumental position to assist the king in obtaining his divorce from Katharine of Aragon in 1533. Within days, he was riding behind the new queen in her coronation procession.

By the time Henry and Anne arrived at Southampton, Sir Richard must have come to the city fresh from his involvement in the trial of Sir Thomas More. Given his obvious support for the Boleyn match, it is not hard to see why Sir Richard might have been so honoured.

A Walk through Southampton by Henry Englefield, published in 1805 when many of Southampton's medieval and Tudor buildings remained intact, provides us with wonderful descriptions of both of these places, that of the castle being particularly precious, since almost all of this building has long since been demolished.

Of the Tudor House we hear that

> there remains in one of the great windows some curious and very old painted glass. Many of the panes have each a bird performing different offices and functions of human life, as soldiers, handicrafts, musicians, &c. On the ground- floor behind the house is a large room, now quite modern, but which tradition says was a chapel. As it stands north and south, it was more probably a great hall.

It seems that the principal entrance to Southampton Castle was directly off English Street, now High Street, via Castle Lane. The same guidebook states,

> The area of the Castle was of a form approaching to a semicircle, or rather a horse shoe, of which the town wall to the sea formed the diameter. The keep stood on a very high artificial mount in the southern part of the area, and probably, as was generally the case, in the line of the wall. A small modern round tower has been built of the materials of the ancient one, which must have been large, as well as 'fair,' to use the words of Leland.

The household accounts of Sir William Paulet state that on Thursday 30 September, the king and queen removed from Winchester to Southampton. Henry and Anne were certainly in Southampton on 3 and 4 October, when on consecutive days the king issued commendations to two different ambassadors, clearly headed on embassy on behalf of the English king to both the Scottish and Palatine courts. Both of these letters were signed and dated from Southampton. Shortly after, as we shall see in the next entry (Portsmouth and Portchester), Henry and Anne left Southampton to sail along the south coast towards Portsmouth, there to inspect the king's navy. It is possible that the king and queen lodged once more at Southampton for a night en route to Salisbury, where they arrived on 9 October.

The Riddle of Cromwell and the 1535 Progress

Before we move on to look at what there is to see in the modern-day town, there is one more curiosity that has arisen in the research that seems worthy of note. It is widely stated that Master Secretary Cromwell, who had accompanied the king and court from Winchcombe, left the royal couple to return to London after the progress had departed from Winchester. However, two pieces of evidence seem to contradict this. Firstly, there is a letter dated 14 October in which a Roger Neckham, a monk from Worcester, acknowledges the receipt of Cromwell's letters, dated 3 October from Southampton; the very same day we know that Henry issued commendation for one of his ambassadors. We also have records for the city of Southampton, which detail entertainments associated with the king's visit. One particular entry states, '3 porpoises sent to the Duke of Richmond and Master Cromwell 22s and 2s 6d.'

Thus, far from returning to London from Winchester, it seems Master Cromwell travelled with the royal party at least as far as Southampton.

Visitor Information

Bargate still stands today, although sadly it is clear that its glory days are past. An ice rink blaring out loud music was abutting directly against it when the authors were there over the Christmas period, leaving this incredible, medieval monument looking sadly forlorn. However, it is undoubtedly the gate via which Anne and Henry entered the town from Winchester. Pass underneath its central arch in their footsteps, and imagine the wide thoroughfare of Tudor English Street stretching away from you into the distance, lined on each side by comely timber residences of the wealthy merchant class of the town. This does take some imagination though, as sadly all remnants are lost to the modern-day, concrete homogeneity of a busy shopping centre.

However, continue down High Street, bearing right to head toward Bugle Street. Here you will find two wonderful medieval survivors, the Tudor House Museum and St Michael's church. Do visit both and immerse yourself in Southampton's Tudor past, enjoying the current gardens of the Tudor House Museum, gardens that once graced Sir Richard's family home. Perhaps within its rooms you can imagine Henry's Lord Chief Justice playing gracious host to the king and queen. Before you leave, go across the road to St Michael's church. There, cocooned from the ravages of time, is the tomb of Sir Richard himself, lying silently in stone.

Bargate can be viewed at all times throughout the year. For visitor information relating to the Tudor House Museum and garden, please visit http://www.tudorhouseandgarden. com/. Telephone number: + 44 (0) 23 8083 4242.

Southampton Tourist Guides Association offer Blue Badge guided walks on Saturdays and Sundays throughout the year, starting from the Bargate at 11 a.m. Call + 44 (0) 23 8057 1858 (9 a.m. – 5 p.m. only) to book special paid-for tours for groups of eight or more people.

Portchester Castle, Hampshire

This day se'nnight the King will be at the Harry, Grace à Dieu, at night at the castle of Porchester.

An extract from a letter sent from Richard Towris to Lord Lisle

Three letters, which are recorded in the *Letters and Papers of Henry VIII*, speak of the king's visit to Portsmouth and nearby Portchester in late September/early October 1535. The first is a letter penned by James Hawksworth to Lord Lisle on 27 September. It states, 'On the 26th the King removed from Waltham to Winchester. On Tuesday next he comes to [South]Hampton, after which he goes to Portsmouth.'

In another letter dated 2 October, which was sent to the same Lord Lisle by Sir Richard Graynfeld, we hear in a postscript to the main letter: 'P.S. – It is said the King intends going on Monday to Porchester in your ship.'

Given the date of the letter, the Monday referred to must be 4 October. As we have seen, (see entry on Southampton), the king was in Southampton on 3 and 4 October, providing commendations to two of his ambassadors. We might then assume that, having arrived in Southampton about 30 September, Henry and Anne stayed in the city for around four days, before sailing onto Portsmouth and Portchester on 4 October, probably to inspect the king's navy. A gentleman called Richard Towris confirmed this, as he recorded the events of the day in a letter set out in the opening quote. However, there is a discrepancy, for this letter is dated 28 September. All the other evidence points to a slightly later arrival date in Southampton, as previously documented. However, the dating of this letter aside, the events unfolding concur with the other extant records.

The Lodgings at Portchester Castle

Portchester had originally been built by the Romans in around AD 280 as part of a string of defensive forts stretching around the south-east coast from Branchester in Norfolk, ending at Portchester in Hampshire. For the next 600–700 years, the Saxons occupied the site after the Romans had left England's shores. Eventually, sometime after the invasion of England in 1066, the inner bailey of the Norman castle was finally constructed, although initially in a much simpler form than we see today.

Then from the 1160s onwards, Portchester Castle became an important medieval royal residence. This was no doubt partly on account of the nearby Forest of Bere, which made for fine hunting ground, and also because the natural harbour at Portsmouth afforded a convenient point of embarkation for travel to the Continent.

However, by the sixteenth century the castle's glory days were fading fast. The keep, which had once housed fine medieval rooms, was by Anne's time used mainly for storage. Only Richard II's once-grand residential apartments, which had been built during the king's reorganisation of the castle between 1396 and 1399, would have been suitable as lodgings for the royal couple. Archivists from English Heritage suggest therefore that Anne probably stayed alongside the king in the king's lodgings. These lodgings comprised a Great Hall, a privy chamber, a bedchamber and an exchequer. The eroded remains of the once-handsome porch leading up to the Great Hall and the finely moulded, towering windows, which gave light into it and the king's privy chamber, tell of stately apartments that once occupied the south-west corner of the inner bailey, adjacent to the keep.

We do not know exactly how long Henry and Anne remained at the castle. It is unlikely to have been long for, relatively speaking, the lodgings were cramped and outdated. What is more, the next we hear of the royal couple is of their arrival in Salisbury on 9 October. The distance of nearly 40 miles would require three–four days' travelling. Therefore, we believe that it is most likely that Henry and Anne left Portchester the following day, perhaps lodging once more at Southampton before moving north-west overland toward Salisbury in Wiltshire.

Authors' Favourites

Portchester Castle occupies a magnificent site on the edge of the Solent, across the harbour from the city of Portsmouth. The smell of sea salt fills the air, and as Anne and Henry rode into the castle precinct it must have seemed a long way away from the bustle and dirt of Tudor London.

The castle perimeter is defined by the nearly 2,000-year-old Roman walls that embrace both the Norman castle and the remains of a twelfth-century Augustinian priory, which now serves as a very active parish church.

Once within the inner bailey, head for the south-west corner and explore the haunting remains of Richard II's once-lavish apartments. These apartments would have occupied the first floor, so as you wander through the shell of what remains of the Great Hall, the south-west chamber (probably a bedchamber) and the so-called Great Chamber (or privy chamber), look up and imagine Anne and Henry playing cards or dice, or perhaps dining in front of the roaring fireplace, whose ragged remains are still visible in the wall today.

Visitor Information

Portchester Castle is managed by English Heritage. Opening times do vary according to the season, so please visit their website for visitor information at http://www.english-heritage.org.uk/daysout/properties/portchester-castle/. Telephone number: + 44 (0) 2392 378291.

Postcode for Portchester Castle: PO16 9QW.

Church House, Salisbury, Wiltshire

> His Grace has been in Hampshire from about the 10th Sept., and intends to be till 19th Oct., except four days that he lieth in Salisbury.
>
> Sir Anthony Wyndesore to Lord Lisle, 9 October 1535

Henry VIII is known to have visited Salisbury on three occasions. In 1511 and 1514, he was accompanied by the then queen, Katharine of Aragon. He would return twenty-one years later for the final time, on this occasion with Anne Boleyn by his side. As contemporary records are silent after the couple's visit to Portsmouth and Portchester, we do not know exactly where the royal party went, or were lodged, between 5 and 9 October. As the authors have postulated in the entry for Portchester Castle, given the distances involved it seems likely that they made their way from Portchester directly toward Salisbury, and probably via Southampton, heading along the main Southampton–Bristol road, arriving on Friday 8 or Saturday 9 October.

Wiltshire Community History describes how, in an assembly held on 27 September 1535, it was agreed that if the King's Grace and the Queen do come to the city, then, Mr Mayor, and his brethren who shall have been mayors, were to receive them in scarlet gowns; and the forty-eight [i.e. members of the city council], and other honest men, in violet colour, after their best manner, to the honour of the city, on horseback. And that the mayor and commonalty shall give to the Queen's Grace a purse of gold, amounting to £20.3s.4d to be levied on the goods of the chamber, and to be delivered by the mayor. Also that all the torches and torchets, of all occupations within the city, be viewed and numbered by the mayor, at his discretion; so that if the King's grace do come late to this city, that then the said torches and torchets be in readiness to light, with convenient bearers, to give them due attendance, then to convey the King's Grace to his lodging, to the honour of the city.

It is splendid to imagine all the officials of the city bedecked in their finery, and perhaps even greeting the royal party by torchlight as they wound their way through the city's medieval streets, much as we know they did in Gloucester (see Gloucester and Environs entry).

Records show that Anne did indeed receive the purse of £20 3s 4d and the then Precentor, Thomas Benett, offered the royal guests the use of his house, Leadenhall in the Close, a building which still stands today close to Salisbury Cathedral and Museum. In the end, the king and queen were the guests of John Tuchet, 8th Baron Audley, for the duration of their two-day stay. We know this on account of a letter dated 10 October, written from Lord Audley to Cromwell in which he prays that the king and queen 'were satisfied with their poor lodging in his house'. That being so, it would seem that Anne and Henry stayed in the present-day Church House, on the south side of Crane Street, and in the oldest part – the western range – which faces onto the River Avon. Fortunately for us, this splendid Tudor house still stands today and forms offices for the Diocese of Salisbury, to which we shall turn in a moment.

Interestingly, though, before we do so there is another snippet of information associated with the events of the very same day. Clearly, the business of state and those of domestic concerns were never far away from the king and Anne. In a tantalising and fascinating insight into the life of the young Princess Elizabeth, we read that it was while at Salisbury that Henry decided that his two-year-old daughter was old enough to be weaned:

> The King having considered the letter to Cromwell from Lady Brian and other of the Princess's officers, has determined that she shall be weaned with all diligence, and that Langley shall be put in readiness. Sends letters to them, and one from the Queen to Lady Brian, Salisbury 9th Oct.

So we know that at least part of that day was taken with concerns about the welfare of Anne's beloved daughter. Did Henry and Anne discuss such matters in the house on Crane Street? Of course, we cannot know, but is a charming insight into the everyday conversation of the two concerned parents.

Church House, Crane Street

This is a little gem of a find, well-known to local historians but largely lost to those from a wider audience who wish to follow in the footsteps of Anne Boleyn. The current day Church House comprises a group of buildings laid out around a courtyard. The north range, which fronts onto Crane Street, is part of the oldest of these, dating from the construction of the house in 1455. At this time, the owner was a William Lightfoot and the building was known as *le faucon*, or 'the Falcon'. Quite apt when we think of the famous guest who lodged there some eighty years later!

The interior of the building sadly has been much altered over the years. However, the outside certainly retains a good deal of its medieval charm with a well-proportioned four-centred arch, old oak doors and a very elegant stone-built hall, which perhaps now serves as one of the most grand photocopying and storage rooms in the country! Viewing Church House from across the river, you can see its magnificent bow window facing west. This window once lighted the main solar, and was almost certainly part of the house that lodged Henry and Anne during their stay. As we shall come to see shortly, both this room and the Great Hall can still be accessed today.

Why Did Henry and Anne Visit Salisbury?

The four-day diversion of the royal party from Hampshire into the heart of Wiltshire is a little perplexing. Following the visit to Salisbury, Henry and Anne did not continue in a westerly direction, which would have taken them back toward Bristol, as they had originally intended. It seems that after lodging at nearby Clarendon for two days, the court headed back eastwards, eventually realigning with the original 'geists' at Easthampstead, close to Windsor. So why did Henry and Anne make the diversion?

Other than plans for the reception of the king and queen, there are no records of any notable ceremonies in Salisbury coinciding with the visit, such as occurred in Winchester. However, given what we know about the Tudor royal progress and the typical reception of the king and queen whenever they entered a major town or city (see Gloucester and Environs entry), it is unthinkable that the royal couple did not pay a visit to the cathedral, or give thanks at the high altar.

It is also clear that the couple spent time hunting and hawking in the surrounding countryside, hence accounting for their short sojourn to what had been one of the finest medieval deer parks in England – the Royal Park of Clarendon (see the entry on The Palace and Park of Clarendon). It might also be possible that Anne wished to visit nearby Wilton Abbey. In 1528, she had battled head-on with Cardinal Wolsey in order to promote Eleanor, the sister of her brother-in-law William Carey, to the position of abbess. In the end both Wolsey and Anne lost out when both ladies' reputations were found to be sullied. However, we also know that in the same year of 1535, Anne visited the Abbey of Syon. Perhaps reformation was on her mind, or maybe she just wished to take the opportunity to visit Eleanor, her kinswoman? Again, such thoughts are merely postulation and sadly, so long as the records remain silent, we shall probably never know the real motivation for Henry and Anne's brief return to the West Country.

Visitor Information

Church House can be viewed from Crane Street at any time. Since 1881 it has been owned by the Salisbury Diocese and today functions as part of their offices. A small number of the rooms inside Church House can be accessed by the public by appointment. Happily for us, this includes the old Great Hall and solar. To ensure the rooms are not being used for meetings, and therefore to avoid disappointment, the authors recommend contacting the reception in advance and enquiring about a suitable time to make your visit.

Church House is in the centre of Salisbury within easy walking distance of the cathedral, so very accessible if you are visiting the city. Please enter under the main gateway, turn right and present yourself at the main reception. We found the staff there wonderfully helpful, delightfully proud – and interested – in their royal connections.

Today, the Great Hall is used as a library and photocopying room. Although it has been altered and the interiors much remodelled over the years, it remains a charming example of a Great Hall befitting a medieval town house of a wealthy merchant or gentleman. Upstairs, which has again been extensive remodelled and its interiors adapted to office life, you can view the room that most likely provided one of the lodging rooms for the royal couple. Today it functions as a meeting room, containing modern office furniture. However, once again, the energy of the place sings of a nobler past, and it is possible to see glimpses of its earlier grandeur.

Salisbury Cathedral is close-by and, as it is both a wonderful historic monument and must have witnessed a visit from Anne during her stay in the city, we heartily recommend a visit.

Almost directly opposite the great west doors of the cathedral is Salisbury City Museum, where refreshments and toilets are available. If you are intending to combine your visit to Salisbury with the Old Palace of Clarendon, now might be a good time to buy the small booklet called *Clarendon: Landscape, Palace and Mansion* by Tom Beaumont James (see also entry on The Palace and Park of Clarendon).

Finally, if you also wish to take a guided tour of Salisbury and its Tudor delights in general, then you can book a guided walk through Salisbury City Guides via the following email address: info@salisburycityguides.co.uk or by telephoning +44 (0) 7873 212941.

Postcode for Church House, Salisbury: SP1 2QB.

The Palace and Park of Clarendon, Wiltshire

It is in the forest too that 'King's chambers' are, and their chief delights. For they come there, laying aside their cares now and then, to hunt, as a rest and recreation. It is there that they can put from them the anxious turmoil native to a court, and take a little breath in the free air of nature.

Richard Fitz Nigel, *Dialogus de Scaccario*

A Royal Visit

Thus, the scene was set for Anne and Henry's arrival at Clarendon, probably around 10 October 1535. We know from *Letters and Papers* that the king and queen were to travel to both Salisbury and Clarendon, and that the king had been in Hampshire since 10 September, 'except four days that he lieth in Salisbury (and Clarendon), and returneth to Hampshire again'. As we have already discussed in the entries for Portchester and Salisbury, it seems that the royal couple arrived in the latter town on 8 or 9 October. They had certainly left by 10 October. The most probable likelihood is that, according to plan, Henry and Anne moved the short distance to the nearby Park and Palace of Clarendon, where they stayed until around 12 October.

The Long-Lost Palace of Clarendon

The ruined remains of one of medieval England's finest palaces clings doggedly to the picturesque Wiltshire landscape, reminding us that it was once cherished by its royal owners as a place of pleasure and relaxation. For, rather tellingly, this twelfth-century palace was never embattled or fortified. Instead it stood in glorious isolation, just 2 miles or so outside of the city of Salisbury, close to the main Southampton–Bristol road and surrounded by the Forest of Clarendon, one of the richest hunting parks in the kingdom.

In its heyday, Clarendon was the most westerly palace in England; here medieval kings could run their territories away from disease-ridden London, yet enjoy privacy in a controlled and well-managed landscape. The king and queen and their family and guests had bountiful access to two of the sports most beloved of the medieval nobility: hunting and hawking, both of which took place in open countryside or woodlands, using hounds, hawks or eagles.

But more than this, the palace seemed almost to be woven into the fabric of its surroundings, as if it were a part of nature herself. Embraced by woodland and nestled in the heart of a deeply rural landscape, the man-made palace could easily touch the mysteries of the natural world, the stillness of the night outwith its walls disturbed only by the rustling of leaves or the screech of the owl as she went about her midnight hunt, the muted pools of light emanating from the Romanesque buildings unable to diminish the brilliance of the stars above.

Tom Beaumont James, author of the authoritative book on Clarendon, *Clarendon: Landscape of Kings*, stresses the point that the palace and its landscape are inextricably linked, and captures the essence of this when he says, 'We think of the palace's remoteness, its isolation, of its proximity to nature, of the relevance of that juxtaposition in a religious context and of the literary qualities of the forest as a place of conversion', that to go there was 'kind of [an] eremitic retreat, a withdrawal into the forest'.

It is as if its rise to glory and subsequent decay, its romantic isolation and connectedness to the landscape, present the Palace of Clarendon as almost mythical, an otherworldly Camelot, a seat of power and a palace of pleasure.

It is also clear that, for medieval royalty, Clarendon was a family dwelling, in which royal princes and princesses were brought up next to their parents at court. Thus, perhaps as young princes grew to be kings, the happy memories of a childhood spent in such an idyllic location drew them back to Clarendon in adult life. It was this that was probably responsible for maintaining Clarendon as a favoured royal abode until the fifteenth century.

However, when the Yorkist and Tudor monarchs came to the throne in the latter part of the century, supplanting their Plantagenet and Lancastrian forefathers, there were no such emotional ties in place. Thus Clarendon began its inevitable decline and was already falling into decay by the early sixteenth century when Henry and Anne made their visit to this ancient palace of kings.

Approaching the Palace

The old Palace of Clarendon was set in a vast park that covered 4,292 acres; this was called the outer park and at its peak was the largest in all England. Located at its centre was a smaller, inner park, which was defined by an area of around 26 hectares. This area was marked out by a ditch and bank, upon which a wall was probably built. The cluster of buildings that made up the palace complex itself lay within the south-west quadrant of the inner park, and was accessed by one of six gates from virtually every point of the compass.

When Henry and Anne arrived at the palace directly from Salisbury, they would have approached it through a holloway that runs parallel to the current Chalk Road, entering the inner park through the western Slaygate. Ahead of them, the imposing outline of the Old Palace would have been clearly visible situated, as Tom Beaumont James states, 'high up, isolated and set against a sylvan backdrop which contrasted with the open downland landscape to the north'.

Although all the evidence suggests that Anne stayed with Henry in Clarendon, it is not clear exactly where they would have lodged. Clarendon Palace in its time had been at the vanguard of taste and fashion. Yet, when Anne visited, it was nearly 500 years old and had been sadly neglected for nearly a century. No Office of the Works had existed at Clarendon for three decades. So, it is possible that on account of the decline in the state of the palace buildings, the king, queen and court lodged in tents in the park, or in the nearby Queen's Lodge, which is clearly shown on John Speed's map of 1611. Indeed, this was what Anne's daughter, Elizabeth, was to do when she visited Clarendon in 1574. By then the palace was described as a simple hunting lodge and noted to be in an extremely poor state of repair.

Certainly the couple would have hunted in the park. But all too soon the retreat into the mythical landscape of Clarendon was over. After just over three months, Henry and Anne finally headed back to London and the momentous events of the coming year, 1536, lay just around the corner.

Visitor Information

The ruins of the old Palace of Clarendon are open all year round. However, take heed, there are no roads that take you up to the site. Perhaps one of the best ways to plan your day is to follow in the authors' footsteps. Start at the Salisbury and South Wiltshire Museum, close to Salisbury Cathedral in Salisbury City Centre (note: you might also want to visit Church House in Crane Street, where Henry and Anne stayed while lodging in the city. See also the entry on Church House, Salisbury). Here you can take refreshments and buy the small booklet called *Clarendon: Landscape, Palace and Mansion* by Tom Beaumont James. Instructions for reaching the site are on page 24. We cheated and drove to Queen Manor Road and parked up in a lay-by, thus cutting down the length of the walk considerably. Do note, though, that to reach the ruins of the old palace, even from Queen Manor Road, it is a twenty to thirty-minute walk across the countryside, the last stage being up a quite considerable incline, the old holloway mentioned above.

When the authors visited, a number of rather curious llamas were kept grazing the site. They are clearly not much used to company. On the day we were there in February, with a freezing wind blowing, no one else was in sight and they quickly came over to investigate. Although a little intimidating, they seemed friendly enough, followed us around for a while, then promptly lost interest and continued grazing.

Clarendon is a haunting ruin, perched high on a ridge of land; only ragged remains give any hint at this long deserted site, once occupied by the might of medieval kings.

Ghosts will surely keep you company as you read the noticeboards placed around the site, describing what was once one of the most opulent and historic palaces in medieval England.

Occasionally, the Salisbury and South Wiltshire Museum organises public guided walks to the site of Clarendon Palace (please contact the museum using the following contact details for any up-and-coming events).

The telephone number for Salisbury and South Wiltshire Museum is + 44 (o) 1722 332151, and email: museum@salisburymuseum.org.uk. Alternatively, a private guided walk can be booked through Salisbury City Guides, website: http://www.salisburycityguides.co.uk/. Telephone number: +44 (o) 7873 212941 and email: info@salisburycityguides.co.uk.

Postcode for the Old Palace of Clarendon: SP5 3EW.

The Vyne, Hampshire

> The King and Queen came to my poor house on Friday the 15th of this month, and continued there till Tuesday.
>
> William, Lord Sandys, to Thomas Cromwell, written from The Vyne, 22 October

On Friday October 15 1535, Henry VIII and Anne Boleyn arrived at The Vyne, the home of William, Lord Sandys, one of Henry's leading courtiers and Lord Chamberlain of the Royal Household. This was not Anne's first visit to the house, as she had been by Henry's side when the court spent at least two days there in August 1531; however, it was her first sojourn as queen.

As stated in the 'Introduction' to 'The 1535 Progress', it is possible that Anne conceived for the final time at The Vyne. There is a suggestion that this child was the much-longed-for son Henry and Anne had so desperately wanted. Had he lived, he would have become heir to the Tudor throne and almost certainly saved his mother and uncle from the horrors of the scaffold.

But on this crisp autumnal day, the future would only have yawned brightly for Anne as she returned to The Vyne, trotting on horseback through medieval parks and formal gardens as the royal retinue approached the grand moated house. Described by Leland in around 1542 as 'one of the Principale Houses in all Hamptonshire', in its heyday The Vyne possibly even rivalled Hampton Court Palace in size. It was rebuilt primarily of brick on the site of a medieval house with much of the work carried out between 1524 and 1526, and consisted of multiple ranges that made up a series of courtyards. In this palatial house, surrounded by acres of lush greenery, Sandys entertained his monarchs and the court for four days.

Anne and Henry were provided with their own suites of rooms on the first floor, which were connected by a gallery and may have been arranged around a courtyard. A full inventory of The Vyne taken after Lord Sandys' death in February 1541, describes the contents of some sixty rooms, including 'the king's chamber', 'the Quenys grete chamber', 'the Quenys lying Chamber' and 'quenes pallet Chamber'. Interestingly, the queen's rooms appear to have been more richly furnished than the king's and as there exists no evidence of any subsequent visits by Henry VIII, it can be safely assumed that these rooms were appointed for Henry and Anne's visit. They were presumably occupied later on by Sandys and his wife, Margery, as the inventory records no other rooms for them in the house. We should, though, be mindful of the fact that the rooms were recorded as they were found more than five years after the royal visit, and so some of the contents may well have changed. Nonetheless, it paints a vivid picture of the level of luxury to which Anne and Henry were accustomed.

The queen's Great Chamber was a riot of colour and texture, dominated by a bed of green and crimson velvet, dressed in a valance fringed with silk and a gold and red satin quilt. There were also eight fine tapestries, a black velvet chair, four red and yellow satin curtains, a large pair of andirons (metal stands for holding logs in a fireplace) and a gilded 'loking glass'. In her 'lying Chamber' were found, among other items, five tapestries, a bed of cloth of gold and russet velvet with a matching valance fringed with silk and gold, a quilt of russet and yellow satin, two curtains and a medium-sized pair of andirons. The king's chamber had five small hangings, a pair of andirons, a green velvet bed and matching valance fringed with silk and gold. To the modern eye, such interiors might have appeared garish but to the Tudor observer, this was the height of opulence.

The queen's lodgings were followed by 'a great dining chamber', which served as the 'chief ceremonial room' during the visit. There, Anne and Henry spent time with their hosts and courtiers, eating, drinking and, as described in a letter by Francis Bryan to Thomas Cromwell on the day of their departure, being 'mery'. The walls were decorated with panelled or painted plaster and lined with a set of nine magnificent hangings, the floor covered with the most expensive Turkish carpet in the house. The furniture included one chair of black velvet, trimmed and garnished with gold, a large table, a pair of trestles and a cupboard. In addition, cushions of varying sizes appear in large quantities with more than forty recorded! Some were made of crimson velvet, others of red and blue damask and a dozen cushions described as 'very sore worn' depicting roses and pomegranates – a device adopted by Katharine of Aragon – perhaps these were stored by the hosts during Anne's visit...

Moving further east through additional first-floor chambers, Anne would have arrived at the closets for Lord and Lady Sandys, 'over' and 'next' to the chapel respectively. Both closets were furnished with 'hangings of great flowers with my lord's arms in the garter' and were used to hear Mass privately, while the rest of the household stood in the body of the chapel below. Outside those found in royal palaces, it was one of the most lavish private chapels of its time, richly appointed with embroidered altar cloths, hangings and vestments for a priest, a deacon and a sub-deacon.

In the base court there were many other rooms relatively comfortably furnished, presumably used to accommodate members of the court. Also recorded in the inventory are stables and kitchens, rooms for the schoolmaster, yeomen and cooks and an armoury where there was kept 'a pavilion conteyning iii chambers and a hall new with all their appurtenances'. Such pavilions were used for ceremonial or military purposes, as seen at the Field of Cloth of Gold. However, they were probably also erected to supplement a house's permanent accommodation and may have been used to house some of Anne and Henry's entourage during their stay.

As was the fate of so many grand Tudor houses, The Vyne was drastically reduced in size, altered and modernised by subsequent owners, thereby much of Lord Sandys' house lies today buried beneath the lawns north of the present house. Of the sixty or so rooms included in the 1541 inventory, only a few survive.

Among the most extraordinary is a richly decorated first-floor oak gallery, almost certainly part of the gallery recorded in the inventory as connecting Anne and Henry's rooms and one of only a handful of long galleries surviving from the early sixteenth century. At the time of Anne's visit, it was sparsely furnished and, unlike the majority of the other rooms in the house, contained no hangings. The showpiece was the exquisite floor-to-ceiling linenfold panelling installed between 1518 and 1526, which still lines the walls today. Sandys had the coat of arms of many of his contemporaries carved into the panelling creating a 'Who's Who' of early sixteenth-century Tudor England. Keen eyes will notice, among other devices, the pomegranate and castle of Katharine of Aragon, the TW initials and cardinal's hat for Thomas Wolsey and Sandys' own coat of arms and insignia, including a ragged cross, the initials WS, a winged half-goat and his badge of a rose merging with a sun. The panelling was painted in the early nineteenth century and some years later the bay window in the south end of the gallery was added. Before leaving, take note of the carving of the royal arms supported by cherubs above the east door, as it is believed to mark the entrance to Henry's suite of rooms.

Next, you come to a space presently occupied by the Gallery Bedroom and South Bedroom. If you could travel back in time to 15 October 1535, you would find yourself standing in Henry's lodgings, where gentlemen of his privy chamber, like Sir Francis Bryan who we know was present on this occasion, kept the king company, dressed and undressed him and performed a variety of other tasks. Sadly nothing remains of the rooms where Anne once held court, although we can get an idea of the panelling that would have lined the walls in her chambers by visiting the Dining Parlour on the ground floor.

Although not original to the room, the linenfold panelling is Tudor. The room is also home to a number of paintings of interest, including a beautiful portrait of Chrysogona Baker, Lady Dacre, aged six, and a portrait of Charles Brandon after Hans Holbein. Mary Neville, Lady Dacre and Henry VIII can also be found among the sea of faces.

The final remarkable survival of Sandys' Tudor mansion is the magnificent chapel. Although the ante-chapel is today a separate room, in the sixteenth century it formed part of the chapel itself. Most of the interior decoration is of a later date. However, there are a few important exceptions: the beautifully carved choir stalls are Tudor and largely unaltered, as is the stained glass in the east window, which is among the finest examples of painted glass of the Renaissance period in England. On the top row is depicted the Passion of Christ and on the bottom row, left to right, Queen Katharine of Aragon kneeling with St Catherine; Henry VIII, shown at about thirty years of age with his name saint, St Henry of Bavaria; and finally, Queen Margaret of Scotland, Henry's sister, with St Margaret of Antioch. The glass was originally commissioned by Sandys for the Chapel of the Holy Ghost in Basingstoke, where he and Margery were later buried. They were probably moved to The Vyne during the Civil War. At the time of Anne's visit, the window was probably glazed with some form of heraldic glass.

The exquisite chapel tiles were imported from Antwerp in the early sixteenth century but only moved to their present position in the nineteenth century. They are glazed in four different colours – lemon yellow, cobalt blue, orange and bright green – a luxury only available to the wealthiest in Tudor times, and are striking to behold. Similar tiles were ordered for Hampton Court Palace and The More, Cardinal Wolsey's manor house in Hertfordshire in the 1520s and '30s. It remains unclear, however, whether Anne saw them during her visit, as they are only first recorded in the chapel in the eighteenth century.

The surviving interior features of Lord Sandys' Tudor house are a potent reminder of a time when The Vyne was one of the greatest houses in Hampshire and Queen Anne Boleyn, possibly in the first bloom of pregnancy, still hopeful of living up to her motto – The Most Happy.

Visitor Information

The Vyne is managed by the National Trust. For more information on how to reach The Vyne and its opening hours, which are seasonal, visit the National Trust website at http://www.nationaltrust.org.uk/vyne, or telephone + 44 (0) 1256 883858.

Postcode for The Vyne: RG24 9HL.

Basing House, Hampshire

> The greatest of any subjects' houses in England, yea larger than most ... of the king's palaces.
>
> Fuller

On Tuesday 19 October 1535, Anne and Henry wound their way from Sherbourne St John towards the small town of Old Basing. The journey was short, probably of just two–three hours' duration, the court travelling for only 5 miles in a south-easterly direction until arriving at their destination: Basing House, the principal seat of Sir William Paulet, Comptroller of the King's Household.

The Lost House at Basing

Approaching along the main road from the north, Basing House must have been an impressive sight; even more so because this major Tudor building, which ultimately rivalled Hampton Court in both its scale and opulence, had been undergoing renovations for four years, since Sir William was granted a licence to crenellate in 1531. Because of the ultimate loss of almost all the records pertaining to the house, it is difficult to pinpoint dates for the construction of its various parts. There is, therefore, some debate about what Anne and Henry may or may not have seen when they came to Basing in 1535. It does seem unlikely, though, that the New House was in existence at the time of the royal visit. However, it is less clear whether the Great Gatehouse had already been constructed, as remains of an earlier structure have been found underneath a later replacement.

Yet, within a short time, Basing was being considered one of the finest residences in the country; it would come to contain some 360 rooms, with some parts of the building rising to five storeys in height, while in area it covered 14½ acres. *The Civil War Siege Diary*, which was written in 1644, contains the following description of the house, before it was destroyed in the famous two-year siege:

Basing Castle, the seat and mansion of the Marquis of Winchester, stands on a rising ground, having its form circular, encompassed with a brick rampart lined with earth, and a very deep trench, but dry. The lofty Gatehouse with four turrets looking northwards, on the right whereof without the compass of the ditch, a goodly building containing two faire courts … the south side of the Castle hath a park, and toward Basing town, a little wood, the place seated and built as if for Royalty, having a proper motto, Aymez Loyatte (Love Loyalty).

The description illustrates the rather unusual layout of Basing House; the Old House replacing the keep of the previous motte-and-bailey castle. This was located within a ring of earthworks and walls, which were used for defence. The second building referred to was the so-called New House; this stood outside the aforementioned protective ring. As it post-dated the visit by the king and queen, we shall not be concerned further with this latter phase of development, except to say that the two houses were linked by a bridge which spanned the defences, and it was this connection that was eventually to lead to Basing House's destruction during the English Civil War.

As a result of the famous siege of Basing House, and a fire which ultimately destroyed the building in 1645, very little, except the outer defensive earthworks of the Old House and some of the foundations of the buildings that once existed within it, can still be seen. Nevertheless, as you wind your way up the modern-day grassy bank that leads you from the remains of the outer gatehouse to the foot of the once-great, towering entrance, you might imagine the royal party being greeted by Sir William, that wily statesman of incomparable flexibility, who would come to serve every single Tudor monarch with assiduous loyalty.

Sir William Paulet – A 'Very Gentleman'

It is worth spending a moment reflecting upon the character of Sir William, whose life story was surely remarkable in its time. Born in around 1483/5, William Paulet began his meteoric rise at court at almost the same time as Anne. He was knighted in 1525 and appeared in the Privy Council the following year. By May 1532, he had succeeded the pro-Aragonese courtier, Sir Henry Guildford, as Comptroller of the Household and later that year he was with the king and Anne at Calais.

Paulet was at the centre of the historic events unfolding at the English court. Although often tasked with executing the king's will in a variety of politically sensitive missions, such as reducing the household of Katharine of Aragon in 1533 and joining the Earl of Wiltshire in his mission to persuade Princess Mary to renounce her title in 1534, he seems to have garnered few enemies. We have an insight into why this might have been from Anne herself. After being arrested at Greenwich and conveyed to the Tower in May 1536, Anne complained of her rough handling by members of the King's Privy Council, with the exception of Mr Controller, who she described as a 'very gentleman'.

Sir William himself has left behind his own thoughts on the secret of his longevity in royal favour; toward the end of his life, when asked by friends why he felt he had been able to survive the great religious and political upheaval following in the wake of each successive Tudor monarch, he replied that it was on account of being 'a willow and not an oak'.

The Royal Visit to Basing House

In 1601, Anne's daughter Elizabeth arrived at Basing House during one of her summer progresses. During this visit there are records of a dining and retiring room for the queen's use in the Great Gatehouse. Sadly, however, virtually all the documents relating to Basing House, including a possible diary of the first Marquess of Winchester, were lost with the destruction of the house in 1645. Therefore, next to nothing is known of how individual rooms were laid out for the 1535 visit, nor where the king and queen were lodged. Perhaps it was in the Great Gatehouse, perhaps in the old state apartments inside the defensive earthworks? I am afraid we will probably never know.

However, there is a wonderful vignette of information that has survived the passage of time. It seems that Sir William Paulet's grandson, George, must have seen the marquess's diary, for in documents that still survive, he reports reading his grandfather's account of Henry and Anne's stay. In the margin, Sir William notes that the impromptu two-day visit cost him in the region of £6,000. Clearly he was at his wits' end, despairing that he would ever recoup the cost. No wonder the future marquess refers to his 'poor house' in a letter written to Cromwell just three days before the visit!

Finally, before you explore this pleasant spot and the traces of a long-lost house, it is interesting to remember the context of the visit and what was happening to Anne and Henry's relationship at around this time. On the day of the royal couple's arrival at Basing, the king is described as being 'merry', and perhaps he had good reason. As we mentioned in the 'Introduction' to 'The 1535 Progress', it is possible that Basing House was one of the handful of locations from the latter part of the progress where Anne's longed-for, but fated, son was finally conceived; an intriguing thought!

Authors' Favourites

Basing House is split between two sites. The main visitor centre and adjoining barn are located on one side of the road that runs through the centre of Old Basing, and the remains of the house and gardens through a Tudor gateway on the other. The imprint of the old house is clearly visible in the earthworks, ditches and building remains, which do not rise above the level of the ground. There is plenty of open green space for children to run around or to enjoy a picnic. Don't forget to pop in and see the giant Lego model of the recreated house, or to visit the old barn, which has been definitively dated to 1535 by dendrochronology. You might also want to visit the parish church of St Mary in Old Basing. There, in the south chapel, you can see the stone monument to Sir William, built by the marquess during his own lifetime.

Visitor Information

Basing House is not open during the winter season. Therefore, for up-to-date information on opening times and prices, please visit the Basing House website at http://www3.hants. gov.uk/basing-house/basing-info.htm. Telephone number: +44 (0) 845 603 5635. Please also note that at the time of publication, Basing House was holding an annual Tudor Day in September each year.

Postcode for Basing House: RG24 7HB.

Bramshill House, Hampshire

> In the northern extremity of Hampshire, amid scenery of great beauty, in a noble park
> clothed with heather and bracken, Bramshill possesses a charm that is all its own.
>
> Revd Ditchfield, The Memorials of Hampshire

It seems that Henry and Anne were never meant to go to Bramshill House. Even as
late as 16 October, Sir William Paulet and Sir William Fitzwilliam were both writing
independently from The Vyne to tell Cromwell that the 'geists' had changed due to plague
around Alton and Farnham, but on neither occasion was Bramshill mentioned. Instead, the
royal party were due to head to Elvetham after a two- or three-day stay at Basing House.

The first we hear of this turn in events is in another letter to Master Secretary, penned
on 19 October by Sir Francis Bryan, when the royal household were still lodged at The
Vyne.

There is no record of why the king took such a sudden change of heart. Elvetham was
however another Seymour property, owned this time by Sir Edward, who was beginning to
rise in the king's favour. It is mischievous and highly speculative to think that Anne might
for some reason have had her fill of the Seymours at Wolfhall and have, by fair means or
foul, steered Henry quite literally in another direction. A conclusion of this sort is even more
tempting to draw when we realise that the owners of Bramshill at the time of the visit appear
to have been Lord and Lady Daubeney. Lady Daubeney was, in fact, Katherine Howard,
Anne's aunt on her mother's side. Indeed, she would be the chief mourner at Elizabeth
Boleyn's funeral in 1538, suggesting there was some closeness in this connection.

Katherine was twenty-seven years old at the time of her niece's visit, and had married
Henry Daubeney in 1532. Interestingly, Kate Emerson's *Tudor Women* gives us a fascinating
insight into the state of the Daubeney marriage at, or around, the time of the visit:

> [Lord] Daubeney was reportedly in poor health by 1534 and trying to get rid of his wife.
> They were already living apart. He may have thought he could get an annulment and
> marry again in the hope of a son to inherit or they may simply have been incompatible.
> In any case, in 1535, he offered her all her own lands and £100/year. In the winter of 1535/6,
> however, she wrote to Lord Cromwell that her only income came from Queen Anne,
> her niece. She also claimed that efforts had been made to discredit her with the queen.
> Daubeney, meanwhile, was pleading financial hardship. By March 1536, the queen's father,
> the earl of Wiltshire, had loaned him £400. It is not clear if Queen Anne's generosity
> extended to having her aunt at court.

As the couple were 'living apart', perhaps Lady Daubeney may not have been at Bramshill,
or perhaps they were merely estranged and living separately under one roof. At the last
minute, maybe Anne persuaded Henry to visit the Hampshire home of the Daubeneys,
so that together they might act as peacemakers and help resolve this difficult marital
stalemate, for it seems that Anne was well disposed toward her aunt Katherine, supporting
her financially, as Kate Emerson clearly indicates above. Although there may well have been
any other number of more mundane reasons for the visit that have now been lost to the

sands of time, the authors rather enjoy thinking that the application of Anne's persuasive guiles resulted in the change of itinerary, and that this was not only aimed at assisting her mother's younger sister, but cleverly engineered to avoid any further temptation being placed maliciously in the way of her philandering husband.

The History of Bramshill

On Thursday 21 October, Anne arrived with Henry at Bramshill House, whose history stretched back to before the Norman conquest of England. Today a truly magnificent Jacobean mansion stands on the site of a much earlier property.

After William the Conqueror quashed the native Anglo-Saxon people by brute force, he gave the manor of Bramshill to Hugh de Port, a favoured courtier who became possessed of many fair lands in the county and in whose family the estate continued for nine generations. Later in the fourteenth century, a certain Sir Thomas Foxley, Constable of Windsor Castle, obtained a licence from King Edward III to enclose 2,500 acres at Bramshill in order to form the park. He built or enlarged the house. In *The Memorials of Hampshire* the author, Reverend Ditchfield, states that elements of the earlier mansion erected by him still existed and were worked up in the present house, notably part of the cellars, the vaulting of which bears a striking similarity to that at Windsor Castle. He also goes on to say that the old house, as we might expect, was built around a courtyard, and that some of the old hall remained in the later Jacobean structure, though 'shorn of some of its length as the dais is too narrow'. No extant contemporary plans or drawings of the original house have been located that might further illustrate its appearance, although Helen Hills wrote a thesis on the architectural history of Bramshill as part of her MA at the University of London in 1984 (currently held at the Courtauld Institute of Art in London). As part of this, she sketched out a likely floor plan of the medieval house. This described an inner courtyard of 100 feet by 80 feet, accessed from the north-east via a gateway and surrounded by 'three or four ranges'. She also points out that the north-west front of the current building, with its distinct pointed gables, is probably of this period. A booklet containing this map is available free of charge when you visit the house.

Even today the parkland, which is Grade 1 listed, is breathtaking. A description of Bramshill's surroundings sweeps us up in the delicate and peaceful beauty that must have greeted the royal party:

> [Bramshill] is solitary, stately, unprofaned, and the broad balustraded terraces, the quaint gardens, and the venerable oaks and yews whose branches overshadow the walks, all conjure up visions of a bygone age, and speak of the growth of centuries of regular and peaceful existene ... but its chief charm lies in its own intrinsic beauties and the natural features of its picturesque surroundings.

The king and Anne lodged at Bramshill overnight. The following day, they set out on the penultimate leg of their journey, heading 10 miles in a north-easterly direction toward Easthampstead in Berkshire. Finally the county of Hampshire, where Anne had spent the best part of a month enjoying an Indian summer in her relationship with Henry, was left behind her forever.

Authors' Favourites

Getting your bearings in Bramshill House is a little difficult, as it has been significantly remodelled since the sixteenth century. Despite this, and the fact that it is now a working police training college, a good deal of the Jacobean interiors survive to charm the senses – particularly the ceilings, fireplaces and areas in which the original wooden panelling remains intact.

Although a library today, the Jacobean Long Gallery is a particularly splendid sight. It could well be that on the same spot a Tudor gallery once stood in its place. However, what is certain is that if you look out of the window into the garden, you will see a gravel path that once formed the pre-Jacobean main entrance to the house. The drive headed directly out, toward Windsor Castle. Along here we can imagine Anne and Henry sweeping into the inner courtyard. Underneath the gallery, on the ground floor, you will see what remains of that entrance, a huge arched gateway that led through into the courtyard, directly opposite the Great Hall.

Visitor Information

At the time of writing this book, Bramshill Hall was owned by the National Policing Improvement Agency but had recently gone up for sale. Its future, therefore, is uncertain.

It is not generally open to the public except on the annual Heritage Open Day, usually held during the second weekend in September. Entrance is free and there is no need to book in advance. Alternatively, if you are part of a special interest group and would like to arrange a visit, private tours can be arranged for groups of ten to thirty by contacting Jane George, Site Performance Manager on + 44 1256 692556 or via email at jane.george@college. pnn.police.uk. Cost per head is £10, comprising a one-hour tour of the house followed by tea, coffee and biscuits. Tours are conducted on weekday evenings between the hours of 6 p.m. and 9 p.m.

Postcode for Bramshill House: RG24 7HB.

Easthampstead, Berkshire

> The King's Grace is 'mery;' he and the Queen remove from the Vyne to Mr. Comptroller's to-day, and on Thursday to Bramsell House, on Friday to Esthamsted, and on Tuesday to Windsor.
>
> Sir Francis Bryan to Thomas Cromwell on 19 October 1535

October was drawing to a close and the landscape must have been a palette of Mother Nature's earthy hues, the forest canopy surrounding Easthampstead ablaze with vibrant reds and yellows, oranges and browns.

Henry and Anne had left Windsor Castle in the height of a summer noted for its rain and poor harvest. However, by the time they approached the final stop on their extended, sixteen-week progress, summer had no doubt given way to the chill of the encroaching winter, and we can visualise the royal party arriving on horseback, wrapped up in warm velvets, damasks and fur.

Quite fittingly, Easthampstead (Yethamstead) literally means 'gate homestead' and reflected the fact that the manor and park stood on the south-western edge of Windsor Forest. Since the Middle Ages, the park, which was surrounded by palings, had been reserved for royal hunting and at its heart was a medieval hunting lodge, built by Edward III in the mid-fourteenth century. Subsequently, it was widely used by him and his descendants with Richard II, Henry VI and Richard III all issuing decrees from Easthampstead.

Easthampstead also witnessed a particularly significant event in Tudor history. For it was from the royal hunting lodge at Easthampstead that Henry VII rode out to meet the fifteen-year-old Katharine of Aragon upon her arrival from Spain. It was also within the lodge itself that a young and gallant Prince Henry first laid eyes on his future first wife when they danced together at a banquet, no doubt to celebrate the safe arrival of the princess and the forthcoming nuptials between her and the then Prince of Wales. Indeed, Arthur and Katharine were subsequently married just weeks later on 14 November 1501.

Then, thirty years later, in the same summer that Katharine was banished from court, privy purse expenses place Henry and Anne at Easthampstead on or around 8–12 August 1531, before they moved north toward Woodstock on progress. Their final visit would be this one, in the autumn of 1535.

The Royal Hunting Lodge

The lodge within the park was more than a mere hunting lodge. After the Crown acquired it from John of Droxford, Bishop of Bath and Wells, in the fourteenth century, the house was converted to a royal abode. John Norden's map of 1607 shows a substantial structure on a square site, surrounded by a moat. Two gabled buildings ran parallel to each other forming, along with a building at the rear, a long, narrow courtyard. Clearly, there were separate lodgings for the king and queen as, during the period 1534–5, there are records of the king's glazier repairing windows in both sets of royal apartments, the queen's closet, as well as Master Norris's chamber and the Marquess of Exeter's lodgings. At various other times, there were references to a Great Hall, great chapel, kitchen and a spicery.

Henry is recorded as having visited Easthampstead 'frequently' and the maintenance of the house was the responsibility of the staff at nearby Windsor Castle, all overseen by the keeper of the lodge and park, William Sandys whose country seat, The Vyne (which Anne and Henry had so recently visited), was only 12 miles away. However, *The History of the King's Works* records that no major repairs were carried out to the royal lodge at Easthampstead during Henry's reign and that by 1548, a year after the king's death, the king's house at Easthampstead was 'so fare in decay as itt can nott contynew the next winter unlesse some reparations be done upon itt'.

From this quote, we can see that it seems that once more during the progress of 1535, Henry and Anne were calling upon another Crown property that had long since passed its halcyon days. Yet despite this the royal couple lodged at Easthampstead from Friday 22 October until Tuesday 26 October. The hunting and hawking in the 265 or so acres of parkland, stocked full of fallow deer, must have been fine indeed, keeping Henry and Anne away from court for a final five days.

One can only wonder how Anne felt as the itinerant court packed its bags for the final time and crossed the little drawbridge over the moat, heading deep into the heart of Windsor Forest and back towards its mighty castle.

It seems to us, peering through the looking glass of time, that this had been a period of carefree pastime and political triumph for Anne; reformist gentry had been very publicly honoured, three new reformist bishops occupied prominent new positions in the fledgling Church of England and, although she could not yet know it, Anne was once more pregnant. But it is also easy to feel that this was the last of Anne's carefree days. The storm was surely gathering on the horizon and Anne, her brother and the most loyal of her supporters were unknowingly riding away from Easthampstead and right into the eye of the tempest.

Easthampstead Today

Easthampstead was disparked in 1629 when Charles I granted the lodge and park to William Turnbull. Sadly, there is nothing left to see of the old house, whose foundations now lie buried beneath a golf course on the edge of a modern-day housing estate.

A nearby mansion, now called Easthampstead Park, is not on the site of the original building, although it lies close-by. It was built on the northern edge of the park in 1860 by the Marquess of Downshire. Today, the hall is owned by Bracknell Forest Council and is used as a wedding venue and conference centre.

Visitor Information

If you wish to visit the site of the long-lost manor, perhaps the best thing to do is to make your way towards Easthampstead Park Cemetery and Crematorium. The address is: South Road, Nine Mile Ride, Wokingham, RG40 3DW. You are now in the heart of the old royal park of Easthampstead. With the crematorium on your left, head down South Road until it turns sharply to the left, becoming West Road. At this point, turn right and park up next to a park. A housing estate will be visible in front of you and a children's play area on the green next to it. On the opposite side of the play area to the houses, a short distance down a track from where you have parked, is a drive to the left leading to Old Oak Farm (OS Ref. SU 84856695). This was the site of the original manor house. The farm is private property and cannot be visited.

Postcode for Old Oak Farm, Easthampstead: RG40 3DL.

Part 5
Boleyn Treasures

Queen Elizabeth's Locket-Ring (Trustees of Chequers)

The ring was removed from Elizabeth's finger after her death on 24 March 1603. It is made of mother-of-pearl, the band set with rubies and an 'E', containing six diamonds, set over a blue enamel 'R'. A stunning pearl is also clearly visible. What makes this ring so unique and moving is that its beautiful façade hides a secret – the head of the ring is hinged and within it lie two miniature enamel portraits, one of Elizabeth in around 1575 and one of an unnamed woman wearing a French hood and costume of Henry VIII's reign, almost certainly the queen's mother, Anne Boleyn.

The ring is housed at Chequers, the official country residence of the Prime Minister of the United Kingdom. It is not on public display.

Anne Boleyn's Portrait Medal (British Museum)

Anne Boleyn's portrait medal was made as a prototype in 1534 to commemorate the anticipated birth of a son. Sadly, Anne lost the baby at seven–eight months into the pregnancy, explaining why multiple copies of the medal were not commissioned. The medal is made of lead, is 38 mm in diameter and inscribed with Queen Anne's motto, The Moost Happi, Anno 1534 and A. R. for Anna Regina and is the only undisputed contemporary likeness of the queen. The prototype is today stored in the British Museum and not on permanent public display.

For information on how to reach the British Museum and its opening hours, visit http://www.britishmuseum.org.

Postcode for the British Museum: WC1B 3DG

Letter from Anne Boleyn to her father from Terveuren, Belgium, the Court of Archduchess Margaret of Austria (Parker Library, Corpus Christi College, Cambridge)

In the early summer of 1513, Anne Boleyn was sent to the court of the Archduchess Margaret of Austria in Mechelen, in modern-day Belgium, where she would take her place as one of eighteen *filles d'honneur*. Her first independent letter, written to her father in

French from La Vure (now Terveuren), survives and is housed in the Parker Library and contained in Parker MS 119, pp. 21–2.

It can sometimes be seen on display in the exhibition in The Wilkins Room. Public tours operate every Thursday afternoon (and need to be booked through the tourist office) and it is recommended that you email the library to check whether or not MS 119 will be on display the week you plan to visit.

For information on how to reach the Corpus Christi College visit http://www.corpus. cam.ac.uk.

Postcode for the Corpus Christi College, Cambridge: CB2 1RH

Letters from Anne Boleyn to Cardinal Wolsey and Stephen Gardiner (British Library and the National Archives)

Surviving letters written by Anne Boleyn to Wolsey and Gardiner are kept in the British Library and the National Archives respectively. The two letters reputedly from Anne to Wolsey are unsigned and slightly damaged. The originals are in the British Library under reference Cotton Vitellius B XII, fol. 4 and Cotton Otho C/X. Anne's letter to Stephen Gardiner of 4 April 1529 is housed in the National Archives: reference SP 1/53, fol. 150. These letters are not on permanent public display; anyone interested in seeing them should contact the British Library and/or the National Archives well in advance of their visit.

For information on how to reach the British Library and its opening hours, visit http://www. bl.uk/ and for the National Archives, London, visit http://www.nationalarchives.gov.uk.

Postcode for the British Library: NW1 2DB and for the National Archives, London: TW9 4DU

Anne Boleyn's Illuminated Book of Hours (British Library)

The illuminated Book of Hours is in two parts; the first dates from around 1500 and was made in Bruges, the second was made in England in the second quarter of the sixteenth century. At some point, the manuscript was in Anne's possession; below a miniature of *The Annunciation*, she wrote a couplet to Henry VIII:

> By daly prove you shalle me fynde,
> To be to you bothe loving and kynde.

To which Henry VIII responded, 'Si selon mon affection la suficnaire sera voz prieres ne scram yezs opic car je sus Henry Jamays [If you remember my love in your prayers as strongly as I adore you, I shall hardly be forgotten, for I am yours. Henry R. forever]'

This manuscript, which provides a rare glimpse into the private life of Henry VIII and Anne Boleyn, is housed in the British Library but is not on public display (Reference: King's MS 9, fol. 66v and f231v). You will require a reader pass to access most of the British Library's collection. However, please be aware that some collections require prior approval, illuminated manuscripts normally falling into this category. Please contact the British Library for details: http://www.bl.uk/.

Postcode for the British Library: NW1 2DB

New Testament Owned by Anne Boleyn (British Library)

Anne's personal copy of William Tyndale's 1534 edition of the New Testament is housed in the British Library but is not on public display. http://www.bl.uk/.

La Saincte Bible en Francoys Owned by Anne Boleyn (British Library)

Anne Boleyn's French bible, translated by Lefèvre d'Étaples, was made in Antwerp in 1534. The front and back covers are decorated with 'H' 'A' initials and Tudor roses. Today, it is in two volumes and housed in the British Library but not on permanent public display. http://www.bl.uk/.

The Pistellis and Gospelles Translated by George Boleyn for Anne (British Library)

George Boleyn, at the request of his sister Anne, translated two religious books for her, *The Pistellis and Gospelles* and *The Ecclesiaste*.

For over a century it was thought that George's father-in-law, Henry Parker, Lord Morley, had translated the texts but in 1998, as Eric Ives points out, James Carley read a damaged inscription and determined that the person responsible for the translation of *The Pistellis and Gospelles* was in fact George Boleyn. The inscription reads, 'Her moost lovyng and fryndely brother sendeth gretyng.' This is followed by George's dedication to Anne that demonstrates the close relationship that Anne and George shared. These are George's own words, although the spelling has been modernised:

> To the right honourable lady, the Lady Marchioness of Pembroke, her most loving and friendly brother sends greetings.
>
> Our friendly dealings, with so divers and sundry benefits, besides the perpetual bond of blood, have so often bound me, Madam, inwardly to love you, daily to praise you, and continually to serve you, that in every of them I must perforce become your debtor for want of power, but nothing of my good will. And were it not that by your experience your gentleness is daily proved, your meek fashion often times put in use, I might well despair in myself, studying to acquit your deserts towards me, or embolden myself with so poor a thing to present to you. But, knowing these perfectly to reign in you with more, I have been so bold to send unto you, not jewels or gold, whereof you have plenty, not pearl or rich stones, whereof you have enough, but a rude translation of a well-willer, a good matter meanly handled, most humbly desiring you with favour to weigh the weakness of my dull wit, and patiently to pardon where any fault is, always considering that by your commandment I have adventured to do this, without the which it had not been in me to have performed it. But that hath had power to make me pass at all times I shall be ready to obey, praying him on

whom the book treats to grant you many good years to his pleasure and shortly to increase in heart's ease with honour.

George clearly held Anne in great esteem.

The book is today housed in the British Library and is not on permanent public display. http://www.bl.uk/.

Anne Boleyn's Psalter (Private Collection)

The psalter was specially made for Anne in Paris or Rouen, sometime between 1529 and 1532, and is decorated with her arms and Henry VIII's monogram throughout.

The psalter is housed in a private collection of which the Wormsley Library has care. It is not on public display but can be seen if there is a good scholarly reason. http://www.wormsleycricket.co.uk/pages/thelibrary.html.

Henry VIII's Love Letters to Anne Boleyn (Vatican Library)

The seventeen love letters written by Henry VIII to Anne Boleyn during their courtship survive. The letters are written in Henry's own hand – ten in French and seven in English – and paint the English king as an ardent suitor. Unfortunately, Anne's responses have been lost or destroyed and so we can only speculate on the contents of her letters. Although they are undated, eminent historian, Eric Ives, was confident that some belonged to the summer and autumn of 1528, when Henry and Anne endured an extended separation; however, the ordering of the letters is still hotly debated.

Ironically, Henry VIII's love letters to Anne Boleyn ended up in the Vatican library, where they are presently housed but not displayed publicly. Individuals wishing to see the letters must meet the Vatican's strict admission criteria and be able to present a compelling case for why they require access to the original letters.

For information on how to reach the Vatican Library and its opening hours, visit: http://www.vaticanlibrary.va/home.php?pag=storia&ling=eng.

The Ecclesiaste (Duke of Northumberland, Alnwick Castle)

Perhaps the most splendid and beautifully preserved of the illuminated manuscripts produced for Anne is *The Ecclesiaste*; made sometime between 1533 and 1536, it provides a commentary on the Old Testament book of Ecclesiastes and is today housed within the archives of the Duke of Northumberland at Alnwick Castle.

The manuscript is not on public display within the castle. Access for academic research is by appointment only for those with a legitimate purpose and reason for study of the manuscript. A daily charge applies for access to the archives. For information on how to reach Alnwick Castle and its opening hours, visit http://www.alnwickcastle.com

Postcode for Alnwick Castle: NE66 1NQ.

Organ Screen (King's College, Cambridge)

Henry VIII was responsible for installing the magnificent organ screen in the chapel of King's College Cambridge early in Anne Boleyn's reign. The screen is decorated with the king's badges and ciphers but, more importantly for us, with Anne's falcon badge and the 'H' 'A' initials.

For admission prices and opening times, please visit http://www.kings.cam.ac.uk/
Postcode for King's College Chapel, Cambridge: CB2 1ST.

The Boleyn Cup (St John the Baptist's church, Cirencester)

The silver cup and cover, adorned with Anne's falcon badge, was made in 1535 for Anne Boleyn and a replica is on public display in St John the Baptist's church in Cirencester. It is not known for certain how the cup found its way to the church, as stories vary. One account has Anne gifting the cup to Richard Master, a leading sixteenth-century English physician, for looking after a young Elizabeth. Another story has the cup passing to Elizabeth I, who then gave it to her personal physician, Richard Master who in turn presented it to Cirencester church.

For opening times please visit http://www.cirenparish.co.uk/.
Postcode for St John the Baptist's hurch, Cirencester: GL7 2NX.

Valance Decorated with Honeysuckle and Acorns (Burrell Collection, Glasgow Museum)

Section of a valance from a bed hanging decorated with the 'HA' monogram and Anne and Henry's private motif, honeysuckle and acorns. Not on display but may be available to view by appointment.

For information on how to reach the Burrell Collection, Glasgow, and its opening hours, visit http://www.glasgowlife.org.uk/museums/our-museums/burrell-collection/Pages/home.aspx
Postcode for the Burrell Collection, Glasgow Museum: G43 1AT.

A Clock of Silver Gilt (The Royal Collection, Windsor Castle)

The partly sixteenth-century silver gilt clock is believed to have been a wedding gift from Henry VIII to Anne Boleyn. It is engraved with Anne and Henry's initials, intertwined in a lover's knot and inscribed with Anne Boleyn's motto, 'The Most Happye'. One of the weights is inscribed with the royal motto, 'Dieu et Mon Droit' ('God and my right').

The clock is in the Royal Collection at Windsor Castle and is not on public display. A replica of the clock, made in around 1900, can be seen in on the mantelpiece of the inner hall at Hever Castle.

Cast-Iron Firedogs (Knole House, Kent)

A pair of cast-iron firedogs (used to hold firewood in position), the tops of which bear the arms of Henry VIII, the initials HR and the falcon of Anne Boleyn, almost certainly royal property. These are on display in the Great Hall at Knole House.

For admission prices and opening times, please visit http://www.nationaltrust.org.uk/knole/.

Postcode for Knole House, Kent: TN15 0RP.

Portrait of Anne Boleyn by Unknown Artist (National Portrait Gallery, London)

Arguably Anne's most famous portrait, it is one of around 300 portraits of Tudor sitters on display at the National Portrait Gallery in London. The NPG holds the largest public collection of Tudor paintings in the world. For information on how to the National Portrait Gallery and its opening hours, visit http://www.npg.org.uk/.

Postcode for the National Portrait Gallery, London: WC2H 0HE.

List of Illustrations

29. The site of the Field of Cloth of Gold. (Author's collection)
30. Richmond Palace gatehouse, 2012. (Author's collection)
31. Henry VIII Gateway, Windsor Castle. (© Thomas Duesing, Wikimedia Commons)
32. New Hall School, Chelmsford. (© New Hall School, Chelmsford)
33. The royal arms of King Henry VIII. (© New Hall School, Chelmsford)
34. Carew Manor School. (© Katrina Simpson)
35. Bridewell Palace, *c.* 1660. (Author's collection)
36. Durham House, 1808. (Author's collection)
37. Sarah Morris at Waltham Abbey. (Author's collection)
38. Village of Grafton Regis. (Author's collection)
39. Notley Abbey. (Courtesy of Notley Abbey)
40. Notley Abbey reconstruction, as it would have appeared in the thirteenth century. (© Madeleine Smith)
41. Bisham Abbey. (Author's collection, courtesy of Sport England)
42. Reconstruction of Woking Palace. (© Lyn Smith)
43. Ashridge House *c.* 1761. (Courtesy of Ashridge Business School)
44. Katherine's Cross, Ampthill Park, 2013. (Author's Collection, by permission of Ampthill Town Council)
45. Hertford Castle gatehouse. (© Ana Barron, by permission of Hertford Town Council)
46. Lodge Farmhouse, Odiham. (© Edward Roberts)
47. Farnham Castle. (Author's collection)
48. Shurland Hall, Isle of Sheppey. (© The National Archives of the UK)
49. Stone Castle, Stone, Kent. (Author's collection)
50. Butchery Lane, Canterbury. (Author's collection)
51. Dover Castle. (Author's collection)
52. The *Hôtel de Ville* and lighthouse, Calais. (Author's collection)
53. Rope Walk, Sandwich, Kent. (Author's collection)
54. The Red Lion, Sittingbourne. (Author's collection)
55. Reconstruction of The More, Hertfordshire. (© 2011 Northwood Preparatory School and Michael Athanson)
56. Northwood Preparatory School aerial view. (© 2011 Northwood Preparatory School)
57. Greenwich Palace. (Author's collection)
58. Reconstruction of Greenwich Palace. (© Peter Kent)
59. The route of Anne Boleyn's walk to the scaffold. (© The Society of Antiquaries)
60. The route of Anne Boleyn's coronation procession. (Adapted from Wikimedia Commons)
61. Tower of London. (© Gemma Higgins)
62. Site of the Palace of Whitehall. (Author's collection)
63. Reconstruction of Westminster, *c.* 1530. (© English Heritage)
64. Site plan of the early gardens at Hatfield. (© Hatfield House, by courtesy of the Marquess of Salisbury/Hatfield House)

102. Reproduction of Anne Boleyn's portrait medal. (© Lucy Churchhill)

103. Easthampstead Lodge and Park (detail from contemporary map). (Courtesy of East Park Conference Centre)

104. East Barsham Manor. (© George Plunkett)

105. Hever Castle. (Author's collection)

106. Engraving of Paris from 1607. (Wikimedia Commons)

107. Le Palais des Tournelles. (Wikimedia Commons)

108. Basilica of St-Denis, Paris. (© Havang (nl) Wikimedia Commons)

109. Porte St-Denis. (Wikimedia Commons)

110. La Louvre, Paris. (Wikimedia Commons)

111. Château d'Amboise. (© Fondation Saint-Louis)

112. Château de Blois. (Author's collection)

113. Reconstruction of Beaulieu Palace. (© New Hall School, Chelmsford)

114. Richmond Palace, 1765. (© Jonathan Reeve JR945b20p788 15001550)

115. Windsor Castle. (Wikimedia Commons)

116. Detail of royal apartments at Windsor Castle. (Wikimedia Commons)

117. Woodstock Palace. (Author's collection).

118. Floor plan of Palace of Havering, Havering-atte-Bower. (Author's collection)

119. Reconstruction of Havering Palace. (© Derek Rowlands)

120. Place House, St Stephen's, Canterbury. (© Marten Rogers)

121. Dover Castle. (© The Royal College of Arms)

122. View of Calais. (Author's collection)

123. Hôtel de Guise, Calais. (Author's collection)

124. Site of the scaffold on Tower Hill. (Author's collection)

125. Engraving of old St Paul's Cathedral. (Wikimedia Commons)

126. Palace of Whitehall. (© Crown copyright: UK Government Art Collection)

127. The City of Westminster. (Wikimedia Commons, University of Toronto Wenceslaus Hollar Digital Collection)

128. Coronation procession of Anne Boleyn. (Author's collection)

129. Westminster Hall. (Wikimedia Commons, University of Toronto Wenceslaus Hollar Digital Collection)

130. Coronation chair. (Author's collection)

131. St James's Palace and Westminster Abbey. (© Crown copyright: UK Government Art Collection)

132. Guildford Manor House, Guildford. (© Helen Chapman Davies. Reproduced from *Guildford's Hidden History* and by kind permission of Boris Fijalkowski)

133. Reproduction of the engraving by S. & N. Buck of Ewelme, *c.* 1727 (Author's collection)

134. Gloucester, *c.* 1725. (Author's collection)

135. Map of the town of Gloucester. (Courtesy of www.oldmap.co.uk)

136. A reconstruction of Gloucester Abbey. (© Philip Moss)

137. Berkeley Castle. (Author's collection)

138. The ruins of Basing House. (© Alan Turton)

139. Map of Tudor Southampton. (Courtesy of Cheryl Butler)

Further Reading

Primary Sources

Brewer, J. S., ed., *Letters and Papers: Foreign and Domestic Henry VIII Volume 4* (1875).

Catley, S. R., ed., *The Acts and Monuments of John Foxe*, London: 1837.

Dowling, M., ed., *William Latymer's Chronickille of Anne Bulleyne*, London: Camden Society 1990.

Gairdner, J., ed., *Letters and Papers: Foreign and Domestic Henry VIII Volume 5* (1880).

Gairdner, J., ed., *Letters and Papers: Foreign and Domestic Henry VIII Volume 6* (1882).

Gairdner, J., ed., *Letters and Papers: Foreign and Domestic Henry VIII Volume 7* (1883).

Gairdner, J., ed., *Letters and Papers: Foreign and Domestic Henry VIII Volume 8* (1885).

Gairdner, J., ed., *Letters and Papers: Foreign and Domestic Henry VIII Volume 9* (1886).

Gairdner, J., ed., *Letters and Papers: Foreign and Domestic Henry VIII Volume 10* (1887).

Groos, G. W., ed., *The Diary of Baron Waldstein: A Traveller in Elizabethan England*, London: Thames and Hudson 1981.

Harding, D. P. and Sylvester, R. S., eds, *Two Early Tudor Lives: The Life and Death of Cardinal Wolsey by George Cavendish; The Life of Sir Thomas More by William Roper*, London: Yale University Press 1960.

Nicolas, N. H., *The Privy Purse Expenses of King Henry the Eighth, from November 1529, to December 1532: with introductory remarks and illustrative notes*, London: 1827.

Rawdon, B., ed., *Calendar of State Papers Relating to English Affairs in the Archives of Venice, Volume 4: 1527–1533*, London: 1871.

Russell, T., ed., *The Works of the English Reformers: William Tyndale and John Frith, Volume I*, London: 1831.

Smith, L. T., ed., *The Itinerary of John Leland in or about the Years 1535–1543*, London: G. Bell 1907.

Smith, L. T., ed., *The Maire of Bristowe is Kalendar*, London: Camden Society 1872.

Secondary Sources

[Anon.,] *The History of Basing House in Hampshire*, London: British Library 1858.

Arnold, P. and R. Savage, *Woking Palace: Henry VIII's Royal Palace*, The Friends of Woking Palace 2011.

Baddeley, W. St. C., *A Cotteswold Manor (Painswick)*, Gloucester: Kegan Paul, Trench, Trübner 1907.

Beaumont James, T. and C. Gerrard, *Clarendon: Landscape of Kings*, Macclesfield: Windgather Press 2007.

Bell Calton, R., *Annals and Legends of Calais*, London: John Russell Smith 1852.

Benton Fletcher, Major, *Royal Homes Near London*, London: John Lane The Bodley Head 1930.

Bertière, S., *Le Beau XVI Siècle*, Paris: Poche 1994.

Bordonove, G., *François I: Le Roi Chevalier*, Paris: Pygmalion 1987.

Bray, W., ed., *The Diary of John Evelyn*, New York & London: M. W. Dunne 1901.

Brook, R., *The Story of Eltham Palace*, London: George G. Harrop 1960.

Buckler, J. C., *An Historical and Descriptive Account of The Royal Palace at Eltham*, London: J. B. Nichols & Son 1828.

Casevecchie, J., *Paris Médiéval Légendes Bilingues Français-Anglais*, France: Hachette-Livre 2009.

Chapman Davies, H., *Guildford's Hidden History*, Stroud: Amberley 2010.

Clark, M., *Rochford Hall: The History of a Tudor House and Biographies of the Owners*, Great Britain: Allan Sutton Publishing 1990.

Clarke, H., S. Pearson, M. Mate and K. Parfitt, *Sandwich: A Study of the Town and Port From Its Origins to 1660*, Oxford: Oxbow Books 2010.

Cloulas, I., *Les Châteaux de la Loire au Temps de la Renaissance*, France: Pluriel 2010.

Colvin, H. M., *The History of The King's Works: Volume III 1485–1660 (Part I)*, London: Her Majesty's Stationery Office 1975.

Colvin, H. M., *The History of The King's Works: Volume IV 1485–1660 (Part II)*, London: Her Majesty's Stationery Office 1982.

Compton, P., *The Story of Bisham Abbey*, Bath: Thames Valley Press 1979.

Cox, M., *Abingdon Abbey: Its Buildings and History*, Oxford: Classic Press 1993.

Crepin-Leblond, T., *The Château de Blois*, Paris: Centre des Monuments Nationaux 2003.

Crowley, D. A., ed., *A History of the County of Wiltshire: Volume 16*, 1999.

Daly, A., *History of The Isle of Sheppey*, London: M. Arthur J. Cassell 1904.

de la Tour, D., *Château d'Amboise*, Paris: Connaissance des Arts 2004.

de Longh, J., *Margaret of Austria*, London: Jonathan Cape 1954.

des Cars, J., *La Véritable Histoire des Châteaux de la Loire*, France: Plon 2009.

Emery, A., *Greater Medieval Houses of England and Wales: 1300–1500 Volume III, Southern England*, Cambridge: Cambridge University Press 2006.

Englefield, H. C., *A Walk Through Southampton Including a Survey of Its Antiquities*, Southampton: Baker, 1801.

Fell, B. H., and K. R. MacKenzie, *The Houses of Parliament: A Guide to The Palace of Westminster*, London: Her Majesty's Stationery Office 1930.

Forsyth, N., *The History and Restoration of Pashley Manor*, Crowborough: Millennia Print.

Fritsch, J., and Saragoza, F., eds., *The Cluny Thermae and Mansion National Museum of the Middle Ages*, Nantes: Gulf Stream 2005.

Garvin, K., *The Great Tudors*, London: Nicholson & Watson 1935.

Gilbert, G., *Cathedral Cities of England*, London: William Heineman 1905.

Giry-Deloison, C., and S-A.Leterrier, *1520 Le Camp du Drap D'Or: La Recontre d'Henri VIII et de François I*, Paris: Somogy Editions d'Art 2012.

Goldsmid, E., ed., *The Maner of the Tryumphe of Caleys and Bulleyn and the Noble Tryumphaunt Coronacyon of Quene Anne, Wyfe Unto the Most Noble Kynge Henry VIII*, Edinburgh, 1884.

Goodall, J., *Portchester Castle*, London: English Heritage 2003.

Griffiths, E., 'The Boleyns at Blickling: 1450–1560', *Norfolk Archaeology* (2009).

Gringore, P., *Les Entrées Royales a Paris de Maris d'Angleterre (1514) et Claude de France (1517)*, Geneva: Droz 2005.

Hall, E., *Hall's Chronicle: The History of England During the Reign of Henry the Fourth and the Succeeding Monarchs, to the End of the Reign of Henry the Eighth*, London: Johnson etc., 1809.

Harper, C. G., *The Dover Road: Annals of an Ancient Turnpike*, London: C. Tinling, 1895.

Hastead, E., *The History and Topographical Survey of ... the County of Kent (4 Volumes)*, Canterbury: Simmons & Kirkby, 1778–9.

Hicks, C., *The King's Glass: A Story of Tudor Power and Secret Art*, London: Pimlico 2012.

Howard, M., *The Early Tudor Country House*, London: George Philip 1987.

Howard, M., and E. Wilson, *The Vyne: A Tudor House Revealed*, Great Britain: The National Trust 2003.

Ives, E., *The Life and Death of Anne Boleyn*, Oxford: Blackwell Publishing 2004.

Jacob, P. L., *Curiosités de l'Histoire du Vieux Paris*, Paris: Adolphe Delahays 1858.

Jeans, G. E., ed., *Memorials of Old Hampshire*, London: George Allen & Sons 1906.

Edward, J., ed., *The Antiquarian Repertory, Volume II*, London 1808.

Jenkins, J. M., and N. W. Simpson, *The Painted Glass of William, Lord Sayndys: 1470–1540*, London: J. M. Jenkins & N. W. Simpson.

Jennings, A., *Tudor and Stuart Gardens*, London: English Heritage 2005.

Kay, T., *The Story of the 'Grafton' Portrait of William Shakespeare 'Aetatis Suae 24, 1588' With an Account of the Sack and Destruction of the Manor House of Grafton Regis by the Parliamentary Forces on Christmas Eve, 1643*, London: S. W. Partridge, 1914.

Keay, A., *The Crown Jewels*, London: Thames & Hudson 2011.

Kingsford, C. L., *Chronicles of London*, London: Oxford: Clarendon Press 1905.

Lallart, J-Y., *L'Histoire du Château de Romorantin*

Lesueur, F., and Lesueur, P., *Le Château de Blois: Notice Historique et Archéologique*, Cressé: Editions des Régionalismes 2005.

Lipscomb, S., *A Visitor's Companion to Tudor England*, London: Ebury Press 2012.

Loades, D., *The Boleyns: The Rise & Fall of a Tudor Family*, Gloucestershire: Amberley Publishing 2012.

Martienssen, A., *Queen Katherine Parr*, London: Sphere Books 1975.

MacGregor, M., *The Story of France*, London: T. C. & E. C. Jack [Unknown date].

Mullally, E., *Guide de Paris au Moyen Age*, Paris: Biro & Cohen 2011.

Nichols, J. G., ed., *The Chronicle of Calais in The Reigns of Henry VII & Henry VIII to The Year 1540*, London: The Camden Society 1846.

Ogilvy, J. S., *A Pilgrimage in Surrey: Volume II*, London: George Routledge & Sons 1914.

Page, W., ed., *A History of the County of Gloucester: Volume 2*, 1907.

Page, W., ed., *A History of the County of Hertford: Volume 2*, 1908.

Page, W., ed., *A History of the County of Bedford: Volume 3*, 1912.

Pantin, W. A., 'Notley Abbey' in *Oxoniensia VI* (1941).

Priestley, J., *Eltham Palace*, Chichester: Phillimore 2008.

Richardson, A. E., and Donaldson Eberlein, H., *The English Inn Past and Present*, London: Benjamin Blom 1968.

Robinson, J. M., *Windsor Castle: The Official Illustrated History*, London: Royal Collection Enterprises 2001.

Russell, J. G., *The Field of The Cloth of Gold*, London: Routledge & Kegan Paul 1969.

Samman, N., 'The Progresses of Henry VIII: 1509–1529' in D. MacCulloch (ed.) *The Reign of Henry VIII: Politics, Policy and Piety*, Great Britain: Macmillan Press 1995.

Samman, N., *The Henrician Court During Cardinal Wolsey's Ascendancy: c. 1514–1529*, Ph.D. thesis, University of Wales 1988.

Scott, K., *St James's Palace: A History*, London: Scala 2010.

Smith, H., *A History of the Parish of Havering-Atte-Bower, Essex*, Colchester: Benham 1925.

Starkey, D., *Elizabeth: The Struggle for the Throne*, New York: Harper Collins Publisher 2001.

Starkey, D., *Six Wives: The Queens of Henry VIII*, New York: Harper Collins Publisher 2003.

Starkey, D., ed., *Henry VIII: A European Court in England*, United Kingdom: Collins & Brown 1991.

Stevenson, W. H., cal., *The Records of the Corporation of Gloucester (Historical Manuscripts Commission, 12th Report, Appendix Part IX)*, Gloucester, 1891.

Strong, R., *Coronation: A History of Kingship and The British Monarchy*, London: Harper Collins 2005.

Thurley, S., *The Royal Palaces of Tudor England*, London: Yale University Press 1993.

Thurley, S., *The Whitehall Palace Plan of 1670*, London: London Topographical Society 1998.

Thurley, S., *Whitehall Palace: Am Architectural History of the Royal Apartments 1240–1690*, London: Yale University Press 1999.

Thurley, S., *Hampton Court: A Social and Architectural History*, London: Yale University Press 2003.

Tremlett, G., *Catherine of Aragon: Henry's Spanish Queen*, London: Faber and Faber 2010.

Trowles, T., *Treasures of Westminster Abbey*, London: Scala 2008.

Turner, M., *Eltham Palace*, London: English Heritage 1999.

Walford, E., *Old and New London: A Narrative of Its History, Its People and Its Places: Westminster and The Western Suburbs: Volume III*, London: Cassell 1890.

Walford, E., *Greater London: A Narrative of Its History, Its People and Its Places*, London: Cassell 1894.

Walford, E., *Old and New London: A Narrative of Its History, Its People and Its Places: Westminster and The Western Suburbs: Volume IV*, London: Cassell 1897.

Wareham, J., *Three Palaces of The Bishops of Winchester: Wolvesey, Bishop's Waltham Palace, Farnham Castle Keep*, London: English Heritage 2000.

Weir, A., *The Six Wives of Henry VIII*, Vintage 2007.

Weir, A., *Henry VIII: King & Court*, London: Vintage 2008.
Weir, A., *The Lady in the Tower: The Fall of Anne Boleyn*, London: Jonathan Cape 2009.

Guidebooks

A Brief History of the Manor and Castle of Thornbury: With a Guide to the Grounds
Blickling Hall
Hampton Court Palace
Hever Castle & Gardens
Le Château de Chaumont, Paris: Centre des Monuments Nationaux 2003
Pashley Manor Gardens: Through the Seasons
The Lost Abbey of Abingdon
The Vyne
Tower of London

Author Contact Information

For further updates, author events and to contact the authors, visit either:

For Sarah Morris: www.letempsviendra.co.uk
For Natalie Grueninger: www.onthetudortrail.com or www.nataliegrueninger.com

Alternatively, you can leave messages for Sarah and Natalie on our Facebook Page: https://www.facebook.com/IntheFootstepsofAnneBoleyn.

We look forward to hearing about your adventures following in the footsteps of Anne Boleyn!

Tudor History from Amberley Publishing

   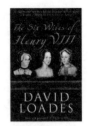

THE TUDORS
Richard Rex

'The best introduction to England's most important dynasty'
DAVID STARKEY
'Gripping and told with enviable narrative skill... a delight'
THES
'Vivid, entertaining and carrying its learning lightly'
EAMON DUFFY
'A lively overview' **THE GUARDIAN**

£9.99   978-1-4456-0700-9   256 pages PB 143 illus., 66 col

CATHERINE HOWARD
Lacey Baldwin Smith

'A brilliant, compelling account' **ALISON WEIR**
'A faultless book' **THE SPECTATOR**
'Lacey Baldwin Smith has so excellently caught the
atmosphere of the Tudor age' **THE OBSERVER**

£9.99   978-1-84868-521-5   256 pages PB 25 col illus

MARGARET OF YORK
Christine Weightman

'A pioneering biography of the Tudor dynasty's most
dangerous enemy'
PROFESSOR MICHAEL HICKS
'Christine Weightman brings Margaret alive once more'
THE YORKSHIRE POST
'A fascinating account of a remarkable woman'
THE BIRMINGHAM POST

£10.99   978-1-4456-0819-8   256 pages PB 51 illus

THE SIX WIVES OF HENRY VIII
David Loades

'Neither Starkey nor Weir has the assurance and command
of Loades' **SIMON HEFFER, LITERARY REVIEW**
'Incisive and profound. I warmly recommend this book'
ALISON WEIR

£9.99   978-1-4456-0049-9   256 pages PB 55 illus, 31 col

 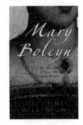  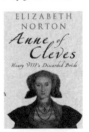

MARY ROSE
David Loades

£20.00 978-1-4456-0622-4
272 pages HB 17 col illus

MARY BOLEYN
Josephine Wilkinson

£9.99 978-1-84868-525-3
208 pages PB 22 illus, 10 col

JANE SEYMOUR
Elizabeth Norton

£9.99 978-1-84868-527-7
224 pages PB 53 illus, 26 col

HENRY VIII
Richard Rex

£9.99 978-1-84868-098-2
192 pages PB 81 illus, 48 col

THOMAS CROMWELL
Patrick Coby

£20.00 978-1-4456-0775-7
272 pages HB 30 illus (20 col)

ANNE BOLEYN THE YOUNG QUEEN TO BE
Josephine Wilkinson

£9.99 978-1-4456-0395-7
208 pages PB 34 illus (19 col)

ELIZABETH I
Richard Rex

£9.99 978-1-84868-423-2
192 pages PB 75 illus

ANNE OF CLEVES
Elizabeth Norton

£9.99 978-1-4456-0183-0
224 pages HB 54 illus, 27 col

Available from all good bookshops or to order direct
Please call **01453-847-800 www.amberleybooks.com**

More Tudor History from Amberley Publishing

HENRY VIII
David Loades

'David Loades Tudor biographies are both highly enjoyable and instructive, the perfect combination' *ANTONIA FRASER*

£12.99   978-1-4456-0704-7   512 pages HB 113 illus, 49 col

ANNE BOLEYN
Elizabeth Norton

'Meticulously researched and a great read' *THEANNEBOLEYNFILES.COM*

£9.99   978-1-84868-514-7   264 pages PB 47 illus, 26 col

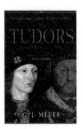

THE TUDORS VOL 1
G. J. Meyer

'His style is crisp and popular' *PROFESSOR DAVID LOADES*

£12.99   978-1-4456-0143-4   384 pages PB 72 illus, 54 col

THE TUDORS VOL 2
G. J. Meyer

'A sweeping history of the gloriously infamous Tudor era' *KIRKUS REVIEW*

£12.99   978-1-4456-0144-1   352 pages PB 53 illus, 15 col

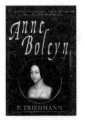

ANNE BOLEYN
P. Friedmann

'A compelling and lively biography... meticulously researched and supremely readable classic of Tudor biography' *DR RICHARD REX*

'The first scholarly biography' *THE FINANCIAL TIMES*

£20.00   978-1-84868-827-8   352 pages HB 47 illus, 20 col

MARY TUDOR
David Loades

£12.99   978-1-4456-0818-1   328 pages HB 59 illus, 10 col

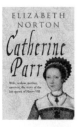

CATHERINE PARR
Elizabeth Norton

'Norton cuts an admirably clear path through tangled Tudor intrigues' *JENNY UGLOW*

'Wonderful... a joy to read' *HERSTORIA*

£9.99   978-1-4456-0383-4   312 pages HB 49 illus, 30 col

MARGARET BEAUFORT
Elizabeth Norton

£9.99   978-1-4456-0578-4   256 pages HB 70 illus, 40 col

IN BED WITH THE TUDORS
Amy Licence

£20.00 978-1-4456-0693-4
272 pages HB 30 illus, 20 col

THE BOLEYNS
David Loades

£10.99 978-1-4456-0958-4
312 pages HB 34 illus, 33 col

BESSIE BLOUNT
Elizabeth Norton

£25.00 978-1-84868-870-4
384 pages HB 77 illus, 75 col

ANNE BOLEYN
Norah Lofts

£18.99 978-1-4456-0619-4
208 pages HB 75 illus, 46 col

Available from all good bookshops or to order direct
Please call **01453-847-800 www.amberleybooks.com**